'This illuminating biography makes a significant contribution to Australian history, politics and culture.'

Emeritus Professor Konrad Kwiet,
Resident Historian at the Sydney Jewish Museum

'Few leaders are endowed with the vision and ability to transform their society. One such catalyst of change was Dr Fanny Reading, the Russian-born child of immigrants, community activist, courageous in the face of media bigotry, organisation builder, mentor. We are indebted to Anne Sarzin for making this biography available to a wide audience, providing readers with the opportunity to walk in the company of Dr Reading, trailblazer.'

Professor Andrew Markus,
Australian Centre for Jewish Civilisation, Monash University

'Sarzin's biography of Dr Reading is an extraordinary accomplishment that combines elements rarely brought together in a single work. The research is painstaking, exacting, and richly backed up by sources Sarzin has tracked down through audacity, tenacity and creativity. Yet the detail, far from inhibiting the story, serves as the foundation for a gripping portrayal of a larger-than-life figure worthy of admiration and even veneration. Reading's accomplishments – as musician and playwright, doctor and humanitarian, Jewish communal leader, Australian patriot and pioneering feminist – were truly extraordinary. Sarzin's book, a labour of love, is a precious gift – not only to a great woman whose legacy has justly been restored but especially to readers, who will emerge with a greater knowledge of critical chapters in Jewish and Australian history, and an appreciation for someone they can cherish as a role model and source of inspiration.'

Dr Daniel Polisar,
Executive Vice-President, Shalem College, Jerusalem

THE ANGEL OF KINGS CROSS

The Life and Times of Dr Fanny Reading

ANNE SARZIN

AʃP

© Anne Sarzin 2023

First published 2023 by
Australian Scholarly Publishing Pty Ltd
7 Lt Lothian St North
North Melbourne, Victoria 3051

tel: 61 3 93296963 / fax: 61 3 93295452
enquiry@scholarly.info / www.scholarly.com

ISBN: 978-1-922952-50-9

ALL RIGHTS RESERVED

Cover design: David Morgan
Cover image: Dr Fanny as a young woman. From the collection of Leigh and Lynne Reading.

Contents

Preface	vii
1. Introduction	1
2. Childhood and the voyage to a new land	11
3. Music and medicine	25
4. The National Council of Jewish Women – 1920s and 1930s	52
5. NCJW – The war years 1939–1945	113
6. An era of peace	173
7. Background issues to Dr Reading's defamation trial	204
8. The trial: *Dr Fanny Reading v. National Press Pty. Ltd.*	228
9. Conclusion	276
Appendix: Hyman Reading in court	293
Notes	295
Bibliography	337
Index	351
Acknowledgements	356

Preface

This biography traces the trajectory of Dr Fanny Reading's life. She was celebrated in her day but time has erased her from Australia's national consciousness. It seems right and timely to re-evaluate her role as a changemaker in the Jewish and general communities and as a former nationally significant figure in Australia, and as a community leader during the Second World War, who played a role in global events. The narrative of her life followed a familiar Jewish trajectory of persecution, flight, adaptation, education, renewal and achievement. Yet there was so much in her life that differentiated her from her contemporaries, including her drive to emancipate the women in her community from age-old societal expectations and constraints. All this and more drew me to her.

While playing a leading role in the Jewish community in Australia, she also belonged contextually to Australia and to the wider world, as events both at home and abroad shaped her life's mission and vision. Her life intersected with world affairs: the Russian pogroms of the late 19th century triggered the family's migration to Australia; and the Holocaust of the Second World War drove her to address problems encountered by refugees fleeing Nazi tyranny. Her belief system, ethics and philosophy – 'The Law of Loving Kindness' – underpinned her humanitarian program that included personally meeting migrants arriving on ships in Sydney Harbour and welcoming these refugees to Australian shores.

This biography explores background historic forces and events that shaped Dr Reading's thoughts, decisions and actions; and lays bare the bones of a life devoted to others. She was a relentless taskmaster, but there was nothing she asked of others that she was not prepared to do herself. In writing her story, I trawled through multiple disciplines: sociology, culture, religion, psychology, politics, feminist studies, education, history and the law, all of which contributed to my understanding of her multi-faceted life.

A core chapter on the 1949 defamation trial, *Dr Fanny Reading v. National Press Pty. Ltd.*, in which she was the plaintiff, presents for the first time a deconstruction of the court transcript of the trial. There is an in-depth exploration of the background issues to the trial, including the history of Youth Aliyah, which rescued Jewish children threatened with death during the Second World War, bringing them to safety in Palestine; and an analysis of Zionism and its proponents she encountered in 1925 when she travelled abroad, which provided the ideological background to evidence she gave in court almost three decades later.

Interviews with Dr Reading's surviving family, friends and colleagues provided original material that enhanced my understanding of who she was, what she set out to do, and how she achieved her goals. I have drawn on these rare oral histories that reveal much concerning her life and times. I am the first researcher to access her collection of musical scores, which is in private hands. This new material revealed the breadth of her musical knowledge, the depth of her passion for music, and highlights the promise of an artistic life abandoned for a career in medicine.

Dr Reading was a changemaker within the Jewish community and a progressive thought leader seeking societal transformation. She created an innovative socio-cultural organisation, the National Council of Jewish Women (NCJW), within which she mentored thousands of women as they journeyed from domesticity towards social activism. With her guidance, they became trailblazers for a new socio-political, cultural and educational dispensation that liberated them from many patriarchal constraints. She realised these goals with her unique blend of idealism and pragmatism. For these reasons, she deserves to step out of the shadows of history.

Chapter 1
Introduction

We have a great cause to work for, a cause dedicated to service for humanity.
– Dr Fanny Reading

Dr Fanny Reading (1884–1974) was a humanitarian with a big heart. She looked after the poor, the sick, the abused and the unemployed in the seedy suburb of Kings Cross, Sydney, where she lived and worked and where she was known as 'The Angel of Kings Cross'. She alleviated the suffering of women and children living there, 'Her practice, and even her little apartment, was a haven for the abused prostitutes, street kids, beaten wives and homeless dregs of humanity who haunted "The Cross …".'[1] She educated women on the prevention of venereal disease; and was active throughout her life in improving maternal and child health.

Dr Fanny (as she was called by all after her graduation in 1922 – and as she is referred to in this biography) was a leading figure in the Jewish and general communities in Australia across four decades of the 20th century. Her life of service in Australia and abroad was influenced by her Judaic heritage and its moral imperative *Tikkun Olam* – healing the world. Her humanitarianism was informed by compassion, tolerance, her creed of justice for all, and her dedication to social welfare and social justice causes.

Her story, however, is larger than that of a dedicated doctor and humanitarian. It is also the narrative of a child migrant fleeing persecution, finding sanctuary in Australia and creating a new life in country Victoria. The loneliness she experienced as a child refugee influenced her agenda as a leader in the Jewish and wider Australian communities.

Her recorded speeches and published articles speak to her work as a physician in Kings Cross and as an honorary medical officer in Sydney hospitals, her creation of a feminist model for her followers, and the enactment of her humanitarian agenda. Events in Russia, Australia, Europe, Palestine and post-1948 Israel impacted her identity, vision and mission. Antisemitism, childhood traumas, Judaism, Zionism, patriotism and humanitarianism shaped her responses to contemporary challenges. As Vice-President of the Australian branch of Youth Aliyah, she supported child survivors of the Holocaust who found refuge in Palestine. She also contributed to improving healthcare services for mothers and babies in Mandatory Palestine and, post-1948, in Israel.

A member of the Feminist Society in Sydney, she encouraged women to play a constructive role in society. In 1923 she established the Council of Jewish Women (CJW), which focused on 'Service to our religion, to our people and to the country in which we live'.[2] This evolved in 1929 into the National Council of Jewish Women (NCJW), dedicated to philanthropy, education, religion and social welfare. The CJW and the NCJW changed the destiny of thousands of Jewish women in Australia who, in turn, made a difference in the lives of ordinary Australians throughout the country. From the early 1920s to the late 1950s, she developed programs to emancipate Jewish women from their conservative backgrounds, enabling them to participate in policy development and social welfare work, and to take on leadership roles. She led philanthropic programs during the Second World War for the benefit of the Australian Imperial Force; and helped new arrivals fleeing Nazi persecution.

The NCJW in 1929 was 'A significant breakthrough for women in the communal structure ... after the First World War'.[3] Established two years before the creation of the National Council of Women of Australia in 1931, it was Australia's first national women's organisation with branches in every state of the country. Her feminist agenda transformed women from spectators to participants in public life. When she first outlined her program in 1923, it was revolutionary, given that 'women were for all practical purposes totally excluded from the Jewish community's power structure, both clerical and lay, and had no specific community-wide body to represent particular interests of Jewish women'.[4] Dr Fanny was 'a dreamer of great dreams with the courage to implement them even in the face of strong opposition'.[5] As National President of NCJW, she had a major impact on the Australian Jewish community, on Australians generally, on the wellbeing of migrants entering Australia, and on refugees in Palestine. While shaped by her times, she also shaped her times, leaving her mark on the history of the Jewish people in Australia and on Australian history.

In 1925 Dr Fanny and her brother, Dr Abraham Reading, established the Young Men's Hebrew Association, which 'strove to bridge the gap between the old and the new immigrants'.[6] Dr Fanny created organisational structures on a civic and national scale, within which she implemented social policies and programs. She motivated others to translate her ideas into actions for the wellbeing of Jews at home and abroad; and for improved social welfare measures for Australians. She urged her followers to engage with challenges facing Jewish people, Australia and the world. To this end, she connected with individuals, faiths and communities. She immersed herself in the big issues of the day, including the medical and educational fight against venereal disease, maternal and child welfare, the education of women and girls, the battle against antisemitism and racism, the welfare of migrants arriving in Australia, the plight of refugees abroad, Australia's war effort and prospects for world peace. She became a household name for her many achievements, 'With her boundless enthusiasm, energy and idealism she ... demonstrated what could be achieved with good leadership'.[7]

Dr Fanny operated across local and international platforms, addressing concerns in Australia, while networking with overseas stakeholders committed to agendas like hers. She represented both Jewish and gentile organisations in conferences abroad. In 1925, she attended the International Council of Women's Conference in Washington DC and was a member of the press corps at the 14th Zionist Congress held in Vienna, which strengthened her commitment to Zionism. Mindful of escalating antisemitism, she viewed Palestine as the salvation of oppressed Jewish masses in Europe. She visited Palestine for the first time in 1925 and saw the achievements of the early pioneers who 'drained swamps, paved roads, founded kibbutzim. They revitalized old cities, especially Jerusalem, and established new cities, most famously Tel Aviv.'[8] Her colleague Dora Abramovich said, 'After she visited Palestine she went to the United States ... and told them [the American NCJW] they had no soul if they didn't work also to help the Jews in Palestine'.[9] Dr Fanny returned to Australia with connections and plans for the benefit of her Council members.

Russian history shaped the world into which Fanny Rubinowich was born on 2 December 1884 in Karelitz[10] in the Minsk Governorate in today's Belarus – a part of the area known as the Pale of Settlement in Russia, within which Jews were confined. There, her family experienced poverty and persecution. The pogroms of the 1880s drove them to emigrate to Australia. A contemporary wrote, 'Harassed on every side, thwarted in every normal effort, pent up within narrow limits, all but dehumanized, the Russian Jew fell back upon the only thing that never failed him – his hereditary faith in God'.[11]

Searching for an escape, Russian Jews emigrated to the United States, England and South Africa, with a trickle of migrants settling in Australia. For Fanny's parents, Nathan Jacob Rubinowich and his wife, Esther Rose (née Levinson), it was a difficult decision and process. Nathan was born on 14 July 1861 in Grodno, Russia, and Esther on 9 August 1864 in Karelitz, so they were 23 and 20 respectively when Fanny was born. They were leaving family and friends to begin a perilous journey. Nathan left first, establishing himself in 1884 in the gold-mining environs of Ballarat, in country Victoria. Although he was a cabinet maker, in Australia he worked as a hawker and removalist, before setting up a general dealer business. He faced social disapproval, as 'Australian Jewry did not approve of Jewish hawkers, who tended to debase the entire community in the eyes of non-Jews'.[12]

In the intervening five years, Esther was solely responsible for supporting herself and Fanny in dangerous circumstances, including a sojourn in London. Esther followed Judaism's laws and taught these to her little daughter, known then by her Yiddish name 'Faiga' or the Hebrew 'Zipporah' (a bird). This Judaic heritage contributed to Fanny's sense of identity and lifelong adherence to Judaism and its ethics.

In 1889, mother and child sailed from Antwerp to Melbourne. Did they spend time at sea mourning those left behind – 'The work of mourning definitively separates the past from the present and makes way for the future'[13] – or did they embrace the art of forgetting. By interrogating these issues, a portrait emerges of the little girl, Fanny, poised on the cusp of a new life in a new world. In 1889, the family reunited in Melbourne.

This biography traces Fanny's childhood in Ballarat and environs; her life and career in Melbourne, where she studied music and medicine; and her medical career in Sydney. In Melbourne, she was acknowledged as an accomplished pianist and accompanist; and media reports commented on her pianistic brilliance. She supported herself teaching Hebrew and Jewish studies at the St Kilda Hebrew Congregation's Hebrew School and supplemented her income with music tuition in schools. In 1905, she enrolled at the University of Melbourne's Conservatorium and graduated in 1914 with a Diploma of Music, qualifying as a performer and teacher.

In 1916, profoundly affected by the outbreak of the First World War, Fanny enrolled in the University of Melbourne's Faculty of Medicine. She was influenced by the military participation of family and friends – her three brothers had enlisted in the Australian Imperial Force. She was caught up in family concerns for their safety and saddened by the injuries and deaths of friends and members of the Jewish community in Melbourne. She completed her medical studies in 1921 and graduated in 1922 with an MB BS, one of the University's early academically distinguished women graduates in medicine.

In March 1918, her father anglicised his surname 'on behalf of myself and my heirs and issue'. He admired an English Jew, Rufus Daniel Isaacs, the first Marquess of Reading, so chose the name 'Reading'.[14] This accounts for the anomaly that his daughter graduated in 1914 as Fanny Rubinowich and six years later as Fanny Reading. In 1922, she joined her brother's medical practice in the Sydney suburbs of Kogarah and Bondi Junction, and five years later established her own medical practice in her Kings Cross apartment.

In transitioning from music to medicine, Dr Fanny left behind the life of an artist and opted for science. Nonetheless, she used music as a tool to broaden the cultural horizons of Council's members and arranged concerts to promote refugee musicians. Medical practice, however, encapsulated her ideal of 'service above self'. She worked as a general practitioner, specialising in paediatric and maternal healthcare and anaesthetics. An honorary medical officer at several Sydney hospitals, she was dedicated to her patients' wellbeing. 'The moment that woman walks into my house I feel better,' a patient said.[15] In 1925, she undertook postgraduate medical studies in England, Ireland and Austria.

Dr Fanny played a significant role as a changemaker in Australian socio-cultural history. As a feminist, she imagined the new Jewish woman in Australia as a bulwark against religious assimilation and intermarriage. Her intention was 'to induce every Jewess to render communal service on behalf of her people and the Empire'.[16] In the 1930s, she campaigned against antisemitism and anti-Zionism. She liaised with Australian government representatives to secure a relaxation of stringent entry provisions. In 1928, when Australia introduced a strict immigration quota system, Dr Fanny was 'one of the few communal leaders to criticise this approach'.[17] She reproached those who welcomed the new legislation:

> Who are we to say that we are pleased that certain immigration restrictions will be placed on the admittance of our brethren into our country? That we are glad that our task will be made lighter while our brethren languish for freedom and the right to live.[18]

Dr Fanny interacted with people of every creed and profession, from feminists and doctors to politicians and artists. She seized opportunities to change perceptions and to speak up for Jewish people throughout the world. She envisaged a future for Jewish refugees in Australia. She never saw them as a burden or embarrassment, as many others did at that time. When they arrived crushed and needy, she reinforced their confidence, assured them they were welcome, identified their strengths and showed them what they could be. After meeting her, they walked taller and were more hopeful.

With NCJW's programs during the Second World War, Dr Fanny established benchmarks for women's participation in Australia's war effort; and developed organisational structures in Australia to meet the challenges of the Second World War. She never rejected appeals to her or to NCJW for services, funds or supplies for the military and the home front. Her fundraising won commendations from government and the military. NCJW led the Jewish community's efforts to construct and equip the Sir John Monash Recreation Hut at the Anzac Buffet in Hyde Park; and established and ran, with 300 Council volunteers, the Lord Mayor's Fund Kiosk in Martin Place. NCJW was concerned with the welfare of Jewish internees at internment camps at Hay and Orange in New South Wales, and at Tatura in Victoria, where 'their main enemies were boredom and bitterness'.[19] The internees – especially the religiously orthodox – felt neglected by the main Jewish organisations. Agonising over the destruction of their communities in their countries of origin,[20] they were grateful to be remembered by NCJW.

In the post-war years under Dr Fanny's direction, NCJW focused on refugees in Australia and abroad; 'an Immigrant Welfare Committee was formed to provide people to meet all the boats containing Jewish immigrants and to give the inevitable assistance they would require'.[21] Dr Fanny and NCJW were tireless in their efforts to welcome, feed, accommodate, and find employment for Jewish migrants arriving by ship in Sydney after the war. In Sydney, these migrants could attend their language classes, and in Fremantle, Perth's CJW was active in assisting Jewish refugees. Dr Fanny instilled in members her ideal 'of service and humanity towards our Jewish people; towards our local communities; and towards the wider community of Australia',[22] values to which NCJW's leaders pledge themselves to this day.

In 1949, Dr Fanny sued National Press for defamation on account of a libellous article published 31 May 1947 on the front page of *Smith's Weekly*. At that time, she was senior vice-president of Youth Aliyah in Australia, a global organisation that rescued Jewish children from Hitler's Europe and brought them to safety in Palestine. On 6 May 1947 in Sydney, Youth Aliyah held a meeting to raise funds for these children in Palestine. Grossly misrepresenting that meeting, *Smith's Weekly* headlined their article, 'Jews Raise Huge Funds to Fight the British – Heavy Levies on Hebrews in Australia'.[23] The newspaper's posters stated, 'Australian Jews Financing Terrorists in Palestine – Killing British Soldiers'.[24] The article provoked hysteria that 'also had an impact on the general public already opposed to Jewish refugee migration in Australia'.[25] The trial took place 26 to 28 April 1949 in the Supreme Court of New South Wales, in Sydney. Dr Fanny claimed £10,000 in damages to her reputation. She had the moral support of the Jewish community, including the Jewish Council, 'which was instrumental at every stage in bringing the suit to fruition'.[26] As Youth Aliyah's representative, she stood alone in the witness box, enduring three days of questioning that taxed her physically and mentally. Detailed textual analysis deconstructs the trial transcript – for the first time – in terms of Dr Fanny's persona, character, mental acuity and ideological convictions, delineating the meaning of words spoken by the protagonists in the courtroom. An evaluation of the judgement delivered by Justice

Leslie James Herron explores the implications and consequences of his view that Parliament address the absence of group-libel law in Australia.

Dr Fanny's world view and the *Zeitgeist* of the day illuminate fundamental issues at stake for her, the Australian Jewish community and Youth Aliyah. An exploration of community attitudes germane to the trial includes the debate over Zionism between the former Governor General of Australia, Sir Isaac Isaacs (1931 to 1936), and Julius Stone, Challis Professor of International Law and Jurisprudence at the University of Sydney (1942 to 1972). Her beliefs and allegiances recorded in that courtroom reveal her analytical ability and fortitude in withstanding the brutal barrage of questions. This was a woman capable of taking up cudgels against purveyors of antisemitism. Justice Herron, in his judgement, called her 'a woman of distinction'.[27] Despite losing the case because she was not personally identified in the article, the community believed she had won a moral victory. She emerged from this trial with an enhanced reputation, as a warrior for truth and justice.

This biography identifies Dr Fanny's strengths and contributions to the Jewish community in Australia, to the Australian nation, and to the welfare of people overseas. She responded to the suffering of others, whether victims of antisemitism and survivors of the Nazi genocide, or the disadvantaged residents of the Kings Cross area where she lived and worked. Born into a world of pogroms, a witness to the Holocaust, she understood the consequences of inhumane policies. Despite these traumas, she demonstrated a capacity for renewal, for herself and others. She was a catalyst who changed lives for the better. Where there was prejudice, she sowed understanding; where there was pain, she brought healing. In the early 1940s in Sydney, a contemporary with her at the docks to meet newcomers aboard the *Johan de Witt*, observed the effect of her warmth on others, 'Through all the anxiety and uncertainly, one felt an air of happiness, of spontaneous and heartfelt welcome'.[28]

This biography presents a portrait of a woman tethered to many worlds, while shaping her own. The social structures Dr Fanny established and the projects she initiated at home and abroad still serve as exemplars for future generations. Her humanitarian creed lives on and continues to motivate new generations. While today's challenges speak to different times, present members of NCJWA contribute to causes at home and abroad, as she did, highlighting her legacy that endures.

Chapter 2

Childhood and the voyage to a new land

Always in her mind was the memory of a child's loneliness on arriving in a strange country – a memory which crystallised into determination that one day she would do something to help new arrivals through friendship in its fullest meaning.
– Council Bulletin article on Dr Fanny

The Russia into which Fanny was born on 2 December 1884 was a place of poverty and pogroms. The family lived in Karelitz, a shtetl, a small town in the Minsk province in the north-west of the Pale of Settlement, the area within which Jews were confined. Three years before her birth, the situation for Jews deteriorated. On 1 March 1881, revolutionaries assassinated Russian tsar Alexander II, and his son Alexander III succeeded to the throne. Alexander III was a repressive tsar with an intense dislike of Jews and he reversed many concessions made by his father:

> Within six weeks of the assassination of his father ... a pogrom broke out in Elizavetgrad, in the southern province of Kherson. It was followed by others in Kiev and Odessa, where many of the rioters were displaced peasants. Soon, however, the unrest spread to the countryside. Of 259 pogroms, 219 took place in

villages, four in Jewish agricultural colonies, and only thirty-six in cities and small towns … It was certainly the worst outbreak of anti-Jewish violence in Europe since the Haydamak revolts in Polish Ukraine in the late 1760s.[1]

The Russian word 'pogrom' means 'massacre' or 'devastation' and it came to be commonly used 'to designate mob violence against Jews'.[2] These destabilising events fractured the world of Fanny's early childhood.

In Fanny's family, traumatic memories of experiencing pogroms were passed down from generation to generation, such as that recalled by her nephew, Dr Ian Burman,

> My maternal great-grandfather David (Dov Ber) Rubinowich, [Fanny's paternal grandfather] hid in a trench to avoid the troops of the Czar, to avoid being speared to death by the Cossacks during a pogrom. And my grandfather [Fanny's father, Nathan Jacob Rubinowich], when a baby, was hidden in an oven when the Cossacks came to kill the Jews.[3]

Fanny's family felt the Judeo-phobia raging through the Pale of Settlement. A contagion of fear afflicted the Jewish population. Although the destruction of property, assaults and murders took place mainly in the south-western areas of the Pale of Settlement, the Jewish population throughout the Pale felt threatened. It was known that the slightest argument or disagreement, provoked or not, in any public space such as a tavern or marketplace, could spark an outbreak of antisemitic violence.

The violence continued intermittently until March 1882, with outbreaks in Balta and Podolia. Conditions for the Jewish population deteriorated further when the Minister of Internal Affairs, Nikolai Ignatyev, proposed the harsh May Laws that Alexander III enacted on 3 May 1882. Historian Simon Dubnow termed these laws 'a legislative pogrom'.[4] Six months before Fanny's birth, the final pogrom of the 1880s took place in Nizhny Novgorod on 7 June 1884, when ten Jews were hacked to death with axes, the community's fear compounded by an accusation of ritual murder.

Given the upheavals Jews experienced routinely, and their powerlessness within the political and social landscape, Fanny's father Nathan Jacob Rubinowich and her mother Esther Rose (née Levinson) could not ensure the safety of their family or guarantee life's basic necessities. The pogroms generated an atmosphere of terror, exacerbating the prevailing insecurity. Rape was a particular feature of the 1881–1884 pogroms and the birth of a female child increased parental concern for the child's wellbeing. Rape, more than murder and looting, generated outrage abroad, yet was treated dismissively by local authorities and 'officials considered it a minor detail amidst the general pogrom violence'.[5]

For Nathan and Esther, as for their fellow townsfolk, life in Karelitz was harsh, subject to the restrictive conditions imposed on Jews residing within the Pale of Settlement. Nathan worked as a cabinet maker and struggled to earn sufficient for basic needs. The Karelitz Jewish community was poor and most earned their livelihood from small trades and crafts, such as peddling and leasing taverns and inns, depending on customers who were mostly farmers and who came to town on weekly market days and for annual fairs.[6]

While Nathan and Esther's everyday life in Karelitz was challenging, nonetheless they were embedded in the shtetl's religious and cultural life. Their traditionally observant community was literate and versed in orthodox Jewish scholarship. The Karelitz Yizkor (Memorial) Book recorded that the community had 'a high public-moral level and many well-known rabbis and illustrious scholars considered it a privilege to serve as rabbi or judge in the town.'[7]

The community instituted social welfare measures for the poor, such as the *Kupa Tzedaka*, a charity fund to support the needy, and *Hakhnasat Kala*, a bridal fund for poor girls; but there were no resources to further the dreams of would-be migrants planning lives in faraway lands where Jews could live without regulations that crippled existence in the Pale.

If Nathan and Esther wanted to give their unborn child the chance of a better life in another country, they understood they had to do it with their own resources, however meagre.

For Fanny's parents, as for others desperate to escape harsh conditions imposed on the Jewish population, there were four major options: Russification, Zionism, Socialism and Emigration. There were those who believed in the presumed benefits of a Russification policy for Jews, integrating and working towards their own acceptance within the secular world beyond the shtetls, an intellectual movement strongly influenced by the Jewish intellectual enlightenment, the *haskalah*, which flourished in Europe at that time. Others disparaged this belief as untenable, surmising that acceptance, at best, would be transitory until dominant powers needed scapegoats to divert attention from socio-economic and political failures. Instead, they advocated for commitment to the Zionist movement that proposed ending the 2000-year exile of the Jewish people with their return to their ancient homeland of Palestine, where groups of Russian Jews had already settled after an emigration wave known as the first *aliyah*, the Hebrew word denoting ascendancy, hence a 'going up' to the Holy Land. These early pioneers were dedicated to translating the Zionist dream into reality. There were also those who believed that the new socialist ideology surging through Russia represented the real future for Jews, firmly believing that Jews would find equality within a new egalitarian world order. Finally, an ever-increasing number put their faith in emigration to the United States of America and Great Britain, followed by smaller contingents heading for other parts of the world, including South Africa, with a trickle finding their way to Australia.

The family's migration

Fanny's birth marked the start of the family's emigration. In 1884, Nathan embarked for Melbourne, Australia, from where he planned to travel to the goldmining town of Ballarat in country Victoria, a train journey of about

100 km from Melbourne. In 1851, gold was discovered in Ballarat and the stories of 'great gold discoveries' lured adventurers from all parts of the world, including Nathan and his brother Wolf Rubinowich. Ballarat held many attractions for orthodox Jewish migrants, including a thriving Jewish community and an established synagogue and congregation. The consecration of Ballarat's first synagogue in Ballarat East took place on 12 November 1855;[8] and in 1856 the Ballarat Jewish Philanthropic Society was established to provide assistance for poor Jews, a welcome resource for indigent migrants settling in Ballarat.[9] The fine synagogue that still exists today, at the end of Barkley Street, was consecrated on 17 March 1861; and in 1886, Newman Friedel Spielvogel presented a *mikveh* (ritual bath) to the congregation, so that married women could observe Judaism's purity rituals. The congregation held Hebrew and religious classes after school hours on weekdays and on Sunday mornings.[10]

A member of the Ballarat Jewish community with journalistic flair, Nathan Spielvogel, contributed articles to a Hebrew journal, *HaMagid*, first published in 1856 in East Prussia near the Polish border. It is probable that issues circulated widely and news of Ballarat reached as far afield as Karelitz, where Nathan and Esther resided:

> Over the years, through Spielvogel's writings in *HaMagid*, Ballarat was given a rather unique place in the map of world Jewry and beyond ... Those items which Spielvogel contributed to the paper must have convinced many of its readers of the importance of the city in which he lived ... His voice reached out to the leaders and the learned of his people ... telling them of Jewish settlement in a new land some ten thousand miles away ... a message of hope in quarters and centres of European Jewry where it was so desperately needed ...[11]

At the Ballarat congregation's general meeting in 1894, a decade after Nathan's arrival in Ballarat and five years after the arrival of Fanny and her mother, it was noted, 'There was a large number of seat-holders rather than members of the congregation, the result of an influx of Russian Jews with little capital'.[12] They were not welcomed by a section of the community and were called 'foreigners' by those who themselves had arrived 30 years earlier as refugees, which confirms Fanny's sense of rejection on arriving in Ballarat: 'When we came to Ballarat – no one wanted to know us,' she said.[13] Nonetheless, newcomers like Nathan were industrious and successful; 'They began hawking fruit and other goods. By hard work and thrifty living nearly all of them managed, ultimately, to make good … In Ballarat they soon were found actively involved in Jewish community activities'.[14] Nathan's initial work as a hawker and general dealer funded the steamship tickets he needed to bring out his wife and daughter. Sometime after his family's arrival, he and Esther expanded their business activities and became hoteliers, running the Mafeking Hotel in Mount William in the Grampians.

Nathan's brother, Wolf Rubinowich and his wife Yetty (née Flacheur) also settled in Ballarat. Lynne Reading, Fanny's niece by marriage to her nephew Leigh Reading, stated that family records relating to Wolf Rubinowich (who later changed his name to Rubin) are scant, and it is not known whether the brothers established themselves in Ballarat at the same time, possibly travelling there together, or whether either Wolf or Nathan arrived there first. Their growing families would undoubtedly have provided mutual emotional warmth and possibly financial support in stressful times. Wolf and Yetty had seven children – Peggy, Joseph, Sarah, David who died aged 12 and was buried in Ballarat, Samuel, Rachael and Abraham. Nathan and Esther had six children – Fanny, Abraham, Hyman, Rachael, Lewis and baby Minnie who died aged 6 months and was also buried in Ballarat.

In 1884, however, with Nathan now 16,000 km away, Esther faced a lengthy separation and a distressing situation. Her challenges as the sole breadwinner for herself and Fanny would test her resourcefulness and courage. Although there is no evidence to pinpoint where Esther and Fanny lived in those intervening years, or how she supported herself and her child, there were several options available at that time. Many women remained with their families in the shtetl, living on funds remitted from abroad. In Ballarat, Jacob worked industriously as a peddler, hawking merchandise to miners in the environs and possibly sending funds to Esther. Alternatively, she could exploit the domestic, childcare or dressmaking skills she possessed to supplement her income.

The possibility that Esther worked for an aristocratic family in Russia emerged during an interview conducted with Warren Baffsky, the son of Fanny's close friends Leah and Harry Baffsky. The Baffsky's association with Dr Fanny was a close one, their circle including Warren's aunt by marriage, Roma Baffsky (née Lang), who worked for many years as Dr Fanny's medical receptionist and secretary in her Kings Cross practice and also at the Bondi Junction practice Dr Fanny shared with her brother, Dr Abraham Reading.[15] Dr Fanny attended Warren's barmitzvah (ritual passage from boyhood to manhood) and he forged a friendship with her. He visited her regularly. In her old age, he was a trusted confidante, seeing her every week at the Wolper Hospital in Woollahra, where she spent the last twelve years of her life. They would sit in her room or in the garden and she would tell him stories of her childhood. She said that sometime after Nathan's departure, Esther had worked for a noble family in Russia. Warren remembers Dr Fanny speaking appreciatively of this family's parting gift to Esther, a brass samovar embossed with gold medallions, which Esther cherished, later entrusting it to Fanny, who in turn gave it to Warren's parents when she moved into the Wolper Hospital.

He confirmed the story of Esther's employment with Russian aristocrats:

> Dr Fanny told me that in the late 1880s, when she was a little girl, her mother worked for a Russian royal family in some medical capacity, either as a midwife or nurse or nanny, as she had medical skills and was good with children. If she were only a domestic servant, this nobleman might not have helped her as he did. He advised her to hide with her child in the forests

nearby. 'Things will get dangerous for you, as they will for me,' he warned. They hid in the forest in a safe place; and from the forest they made their way out of Russia to London.[16]

Emigration from Russia was unlawful and obtaining a Russian passport involved the complicated bureaucracy in an expensive application process that could take up to six months. The majority of emigrants crossed the border illegally. Jewish and Lithuanian groups shared migratory networks and exit routes, the latter followed major railway and river transportation lines. Migrants from the Minsk and Vitebsk provinces – Karelitz was near Minsk in the Minsk Governorate – used two southern routes that started in Alytus and Grodno (where Nathan was born) and converged in the German town Eydtkuhnen, from where they could travel to Tilsit. The last stage of continental travel was by rail or steamer to the northern German ports of Hamburg and Bremen or the Dutch ports of Amsterdam and Rotterdam, while a minority, mainly from the Belarusian and Ukrainian provinces, left from the Latvian port Libau.[17] There were weekly steamers from Rotterdam, Libau, Hamburg and Bremen heading to the English ports of Hull, Grimsby and London.[18]

Several references support the idea that Esther and Fanny travelled to London and remained there for a lengthy period. It is possible the family travelled together to London, from where Jacob embarked alone for Australia. Jacob could protect them *en route* to London, a hazardous journey for an unaccompanied mother and child, with the added danger of highway robbers. Due to the prohibition on emigration from Russia, the family probably left under cover of darkness.

Other sources indicate that Esther and Fanny left Russia a year after Nathan Jacob's departure in 1884 and 'after some time in London' reunited in Ballarat.[19] If Esther travelled alone with Fanny to London, she chose to do so to prolong access to family in Karelitz, deferring the traumatic parting from parents, siblings and extended family and friends, especially knowing they might never see one another again. Fanny's contemporary, Mary Antin, who faced similar experiences at that time, described her departure from the shtetl Polotzk,

> The women wept over us, reminding us eloquently of the perils of the sea, of the bewilderment of a foreign land, of the torments of homesickness that awaited us. They bewailed my mother's lot, who had to tear herself away from blood relations to go among strangers; who had to face gendarmes, ticket agents, and sailors, unprotected by a masculine escort.[20]

Whether Esther and Fanny travelled to London with Nathan or remained for a while in Karelitz, they spent time in London before their embarkation for Australia five years later in 1889. The indigent Eastern European Jews fleeing pogroms in the 1880s encountered harsh conditions in London's East End. Arriving without resources or connections, Jewish refugees settled in London's East End, either in the Wentworth Street district of Spitalfields or in Whitechapel or in St George's, all overcrowded, dilapidated and unsanitary. English novelist Israel Zangwill described vividly the conditions in Spitalfields, 'Imprisoned in the area of a few narrow streets, unlovely and sombre, muddy and ill-smelling, immured in dreary houses and surrounded by mean and depressing sights and sounds …'.[21]

Zangwill's novel *The Children of the Ghetto* prompted questions among Victorian Londoners, concerning philanthropy, the acculturation of new immigrants, labour exploitation, housing, the politics of religion, and consumer culture.[22] Charitable organisations in London helped newly arrived migrants, but several imposed stringent conditions. Esther could seek help from the Jewish Board of Guardians of the Jewish Poor, but only residents in London for at least six months were eligible. There were the Board's Russo-Jewish committee and the Free Medical Missions, although the latter, as conversionist societies, were less appealing to orthodox Jews. The Four Per Cent Industrial Dwellings Co. Ltd., established in 1885 by Jewish philanthropists, relieved overcrowding in Church

Lane, Whitechapel, in the East End; and the Poor Jews' Temporary Centre provided a bed for the homeless, jobless and immigrants arriving straight from the docks, and guided them towards employment.

Esther needed skills to survive the 'indignities of poverty'.[23] Her efforts to find and fund lodgings and basic necessities were crucial to survival. Women in her position had few employment opportunities and there was competition for jobs that involved long hours and paid a pittance. She spoke only Yiddish and kept the sabbath, which ruled out a gentile workplace where instructions were given in English and employees worked on Saturdays.

Esther and Fanny probably found compatriots from Karelitz who extended a helping hand to newcomers, despite their own poverty:

> The 'greener', just arrived in London with scanty resources, will be sure to meet with hospitality from some 'landsmann' [compatriot]. If a poor family loses all its belongings in a fire, some kind friend will often make a collection amongst the neighbours to supply what has been lost. In times of sickness and death one sees most touching examples amongst the foreign Jews of unselfish help, of sacrifices freely given both of time and money.[24]

While Esther could manage their physical privations, she could not avoid gossip that intensified the insecurities of women without husbands, who were stigmatised as single mothers. Esther waited five years before reuniting with Nathan, years of disadvantage as an indigent single parent. In that time, with desertion common, how certain could one be of the loyalty of one's spouse and his commitment to the family unit? It was noted at the time, 'Wife-desertion is one of their common offences and gives rise to a difficult type of case with which the Jewish Board of Guardians has constantly to deal';[25] and 'emigration allowed some men to escape domestic difficulties, and the women they left behind were anxious that temporary separation did not turn into permanent desertion'.[26]

Esther's major focus was her child's wellbeing. Fanny and her mother were close throughout Esther's lifetime, a bond forged in Fanny's infancy. For Fanny's first five years, Esther created a safe space for her in challenging circumstances, giving her sustenance and security. Esther's religious creed and cultural background empowered and sustained her, enabling her to nurture Fanny in a caring and practical manner despite stress, financial hardship and difficulties encountered in Russia and England.

Esther's Jewish faith, precise and pragmatic, defined their lives. She structured their days according to customs seminal to a traditional Jewish life. Orthodox Jews, such as Esther and Nathan, aspired to keeping many of the positive *mitzvot*, biblical commandments or rules that governed interactions with family, friends, neighbours and society, and were a central part in Jewish identity. In Judaism, acts of kindness, *mitzvot*, defined the good and compassionate human being, the '*mensch*', a Yiddish word denoting someone who personifies the best moral traits of humanity. Judaism views life joyously rather than as a vale of tears. The sanctity of life transcends other considerations. There is a commitment to living and to ensuring the wellbeing of children, who represent the continuity of the Jewish people. No matter how dark the day or meagre one's resources, one says '*L'Chaim*' ('to life'). This reverence for life shaped Esther and Jacob's responses and actions.

As an observant Jewess, Esther accepted traditions and rituals central to Jewish life. She respected laws governing daily life that provided structure for herself and boundaries for Fanny. As a Jewish wife and mother, she perpetuated traditions upheld by generations of her family. Despite poverty and persecution, there were also joyous life events, sabbaths and festivals. The Jewish community in the shtetl knew how to celebrate life.

She was resourceful in surviving day-to-day, drawing support from her faith, traditions and compatriots in the East End. She never shirked hard work and did all she could to earn a livelihood in difficult circumstances to support herself and her child:

The shtetl valued hard work as well as diligence, self-control and sobriety. It prized learning, charity and devotion to family. Beyond the family, the shtetl placed a premium on mutual support. Tsedokeh (charity) was seen as a prime virtue. These intangibles accompanied the emigrants and would be of inestimable importance in re-establishing a communal life in the new country.[27]

As a child, Fanny experienced first-hand the suffering of her people. Did those memories fuel her sense of responsibility, her vigilance against racism and her lifelong agenda of humanitarian service to all? According to Freud, memories of traumatic events do not disappear but lurk in the subconscious, and surface in unguarded moments. Neither Esther nor Fanny recorded their memories or wrote them down, and there are no family diaries that document these events. Melbourne psychiatrist Dr Paul Valent, who studied the impact of trauma on child survivors of the Holocaust, states, 'because of their keen sense of political and social injustice … [they] are particularly aware of injustices to vulnerable groups, especially children, and they try to protect them in the social sphere'.[28]

Dr Fanny never acknowledged publicly her family's past suffering or insecurities. She was a pragmatic woman, who focused on meeting the needs of others. In 1929 in Adelaide, she said, 'We Jews have a double duty always to the country we live in and our own people. We can never forget our race. There is too much suffering in it. While there is a persecuted Jew in the world, we have work to do.'[29]

Sailing towards safe harbours

Esther Rose and Fanny left London and travelled to Antwerp, Belgium, where they embarked on 15 June 1889 on the SS *Nürnberg*, a Norddeutscher Lloyd passenger steamer, which lists Esther Rose Rabbinovitz [sic], age 26, and Fanny Rabbinovitz, age 3 [sic], as 'unassisted inward passengers' bound for Melbourne, Victoria.[30] The ship docked in Southampton, Genoa, Naples, Port Said, Suez, Aden, Colombo and Adelaide before arriving in Melbourne on 2 August 1889.

Esther and Fanny had been in a state of transition for five years. Aged 26, Esther had demonstrated strength, courage and optimism. Given the Jewish emphasis on nurturing the next generation, her focus on Fanny's wellbeing distracted her from memories of separation from family and friends, or nostalgia for home. The prospect of reuniting with Jacob and safety in a new country would ensure peace of mind.

Free at last from persecution and penury, released from tensions and insecurities, and stimulated by life at sea, Esther and Fanny entered this new phase, one that potentially fostered a more positive outlook. The impact of the voyage on Fanny could restore confidence and optimism in the child. While their ship hugged the coastline, they enjoyed the scenery. There were foreign ports with strange scents, sights and sounds. There was the drama of storms at sea when giant waves broke over the decks. Edith Gedge, who sailed on the *Sobraon* from London to Melbourne less than a year before Esther and Fanny's voyage, wrote in her journal, 'The seas was very high all day & a grand sight from the poop. I had never seen such waves before, it seemed as if they must break over.'[31]

There was the novelty of associating with fellow passengers. Dividing lines between first class and steerage passengers could exacerbate insecurities, as could differences in the way people of different religions were treated. The literature refers to hostility between Catholic and Protestant migrants, which leaves one wondering whether Esther encountered any religious prejudice that had plagued her life previously. On a positive note, the *Sydney Morning Herald* reported on 6 August 1889 that the Nurnberg's passengers had commended Captain H. Engelbart and the Purser, Mr O. Trott, 'They have received great thanks from the passengers for their kindness en route'.

When the ship sailed into Melbourne's Port Philip, first impressions were disappointing for new arrivals:

> We ... are making our way towards Williamstown ... A swampy-looking flat which manual labour has contributed to render in places habitable, and a wretched, muddy little river ... The buildings of the city are discernible in the distance, situated on higher ground, and far as the eye can reach from north to south, from east to west, are houses, townships, and villages extending in all directions.[32]

From Melbourne, the family made their way to Ballarat in country Victoria, where their new life in Australia began.

In 1925, Dr Fanny and her mother returned to Europe for the first time, visiting many of the ports they had glimpsed on their first voyage to Australia. By that time, Dr Fanny was a medical doctor and a leader in the Jewish and general communities. The roles of mother and child were reversed and Dr Fanny was the nurturer and protector. The path she travelled to arrive at that point in her life is the subject of the next chapter.

Chapter 3
Music and Medicine

I owe a debt of gratitude to Australia, the land of freedom and liberty which has given me everything.

– Dr Fanny Reading

Dr Fanny's decision to study medicine was not taken lightly. The death in infancy of Fanny's baby sister, Miriam, who died aged six months on 5 July 1898 in Ballarat – Fanny was thirteen years old at that time – potentially played a role. The decision to become a doctor was influenced mainly by reports of suffering and slaughter on the battlefields of the First World War. Her three brothers enlisted in the volunteer army for overseas war service – Hyman Samuel in 1915, Dr Abraham Stanley in 1916, and Lewis Judah in 1917. Their parents, Fanny and her sister Ray, who lived together in the family home, were extremely anxious about their safety. In this time of upheaval and anxiety, Fanny was determined to dedicate her abilities to the wellbeing of her fellow Australians.

Enrolling in Melbourne University's Faculty of Medicine was a pragmatic choice that defined the future direction of her professional life as a physician in private practice in Kogarah, Darlinghurst, Bondi Junction and Kings Cross; and as an honorary medical officer at several Sydney hospitals and institutions – the St George District Hospital in Kogarah, the Rachel Forster Hospital in Surry Hills and Redfern, Crown

Street Women's Hospital in Surry Hills, the Royal Hospital for Women in Paddington and the Dalwood Children's Homes in Seaforth.

One of Melbourne University's first female medical students, Dr Fanny specialised in childcare and maternal services, later fostering programs in these areas at home and abroad. In so doing, she diverged from the path she had chosen previously, working as a music teacher and performer. Both disciplines, music and medicine, the artistic and the scientific, shaped the person she became. Her studies in music in the earlier part of her life gave her a lifelong appreciation of classical music. Music added an aesthetic dimension to her life of service as a doctor. She did all that was in her power to assist musicians who migrated to Australia. In 1939, preoccupied with the fate of Jews fleeing Nazi tyranny in Europe, she told a Brisbane journalist, 'Many of the refugees from Europe ... possess exceptional musical talent, and to encourage them, cultural evenings are held each month, at which they perform, and often these performances lead to professional engagements'.[1]

Music in Ballarat and Melbourne

Fanny's musical ability was first nurtured during her school years in Ballarat. She was a pupil of the Bakery Hill Primary School at 34 Humffray Street, in the Bakery Hill precinct of Ballarat East, which was convenient as the family lived some distance away at number 129 Humffray Street. The opportunities for musical education at this public school were limited to 'vocal music' or 'class singing', and it is likely that Fanny's parents paid for private piano lessons. In 1897, aged 13, Fanny transferred to University College in Camp Street, Ballarat East, where, as in most private schools at that time, 'students learnt instruments such as the piano, violin and flute from visiting instrumental teachers'.[2] There she developed knowledge of music theory, polished her technical and interpretive abilities as a classical pianist, and performed piano solos in school concerts. She showed great promise, coming first in the piano solo under 14 years section in the competition held on 5 September 1898 in the Academy of Music, conducted under the auspices of the Royal South Street Society in Ballarat.[3] When the family moved to Melbourne, Fanny taught music on a sessional basis at Wesley college and the Methodist Ladies College, where several of her students won prizes.[4]

In Melbourne, the Rubinowich family encountered a vibrant Yiddish culture. In 1911, newly arrived migrants from Eastern Europe and Russia established a Jewish library in central Melbourne called Kadimah (Hebrew for 'forward'), and 'What began as a relatively modest pursuit started by a handful of cultural enthusiasts attracted 200 … to its first annual meeting in the following year'.[5] In this Yiddish milieu, Nathan and Esther felt at home,

> Eastern European Yiddishists found in the Kadimah an organisation that addressed their many needs … a secular oasis for the culturally starved immigrant … a part of der alter heym [the old home] … an institution that was relevant to their lives, that was for them and by them.[6]

In 1917, the Kadimah president was Samuel Wynn, who would testify in 1949 as a witness in the defamation court case *Dr Fanny Reading v. National Press Pty. Ltd.*

Although Fanny cherished and respected the Yiddish culture that represented her parents' world, her mother tongue and cultural background, her focus was on Melbourne's sophisticated musical scene. The University of Melbourne's Conservatorium of Music opened in 1894, with Professor G.W.L. Marshall-Hall in charge.[7] The city, however, upheld conservative musical values, 'The aim was to duplicate the English version of European musical life as soon and as handsomely as possible. Imitation, not invention, was the order of the day.'[8]

In 1905 aged 16, Fanny enrolled as a student in Melbourne University's Conservatorium of Music. Well known in both the Jewish and general communities, she acquired a reputation as a gifted pianist, accompanist, singer and music teacher, with a mastery of the conventional classical repertoire. She performed regularly at a monthly social organised by Rev. Jacob Danglow's Post-Biblical Class. The *Hebrew Standard* frequently commented on her performances and followed with keen interest her academic progress at the Conservatorium, noting, 'At the Ormond Exhibition in Music at the University, honors in History, Form and Analysis ... has been obtained by Miss Fanny Rubinovich of Carlton'.[9]

Melbourne's musical world attracted internationally famous musicians, many of whom Fanny encountered. As a Conservatorium student, it is likely she attended the ceremony on 26 November 1909 at which Dame Nellie Melba laid the foundation stone for a permanent conservatorium on the University's Parkville campus.[10] She probably attended Premier John Murray's official opening of the finished building on 16 April 1910.[11] By 1913, Fanny was the competent accompanist for singers and instrumentalists at concerts, the *Hebrew Standard* reporting: 'Miss F. Rubinovich acted as hon. pianist and accompanist during the whole evening, and gave every satisfaction in that capacity'.[12]

Melbourne society supported the University's Conservatorium and made efforts to improve facilities for music students. When Fanny first studied for the Diploma of Music, there were insufficient teaching rooms; several teachers, working to a roster, used the same room. The library was not properly organised, there was no dedicated rehearsal room and no cafeteria. What mattered, however, was the quality of tuition and student interaction with musicians and musicologists. Artists contributed to musical traditions throughout Victoria, for example, 'Madame Melba arranged a performance of opera ... £1000 was raised towards the building of the beautiful Melba Hall ... opened by the Governor-General, Lord Denman, on October 19th, 1913'.[13]

In 1914, Fanny's final year at the Conservatorium, Professor Marshall-Hall returned to take up his former position as Ormond Chair of Music. Through tuition and orchestral concerts, he shaped students' perception of what he believed constituted great music and performance. Fanny was exposed to his teaching techniques, 'music as it should be taught – as a natural and beautiful form of expressing human emotions and ideas'.[14]

In 1914, Fanny graduated with a Diploma in Music from the University's Conservatorium. Aside from an initial scholarship, she had supported herself, working to cover academic fees and associated costs. Undoubtedly, 'It must have taken enormous intelligence and perseverance for a migrant woman of non-English-speaking background to earn a living and get herself an education'.[15] She immersed herself in Melbourne's musical culture, hearing Australian musicians and overseas artists perform orchestral and operatic offerings. There were two major orchestras in Melbourne, the Alberto Zelman Memorial Orchestra and the University Symphony conducted by Marshall-Hall, the latter presenting concerts featuring orchestral works by Beethoven, Brahms, Mozart, Schumann and Schubert.[16] Fanny was familiar with the Alberto Zelman Memorial Orchestra, as she participated in Melbourne's annual Christmas production of Handel's oratorio, *Messiah*, which Zelman conducted to critical acclaim. Held in the iconic Royal Exhibition Building in Carlton, the performance attracted almost 6,000 music lovers, who filled the auditorium to hear principal singers such as tenor John McCormack, the Royal Melbourne Philharmonic Choir and the Victorian Festival Choir. Fanny's personal copy of the *Messiah* has pencilled notes indicating tempi, technique and interpretation, comments that point to her research and possibly Zelman's instructions at rehearsals.

Fanny pasted a music review headlined 'The Messiah: Philharmonic Society. A memorable occasion' in her copy of the *Messiah*, revealing her pride as a chorister in this celebrated annual performance:

> It has often been pointed out that it is impossible to do justice to Handel without adequate orchestral study and rehearsal, and Mr. Zelman has been wise enough to attend to this, with the

most happy result. The chorus, which included also the Victorian Festival Choir, was excellent ... The 'Hallelujah' and the final choruses were splendidly sung; so was 'Glory to God'.[17]

Fanny eventually abandoned music as a career but retained her love of music. It remained a part of who she was and the person she became. Throughout her life, she attended concerts whenever her schedule allowed and she valued this art form, to which she had dedicated years of study and practice. She invited musicians to her home in Sydney's Kings Cross, for Friday night dinner or Saturday lunch, and we know Yehudi Menuhin dined there one Friday evening.[18] One can presume she knew Menuhin's sister, Hepzibah, a gifted pianist who lived in Sydney from 1954 to 1957. While in Palestine in 1925, Dr Fanny and her mother attended a concert by violinist Jascha Heifitz and were enthralled by his virtuosity. Two years later, he toured Australia. While in Sydney, he gave Dr Fanny a signed photograph of himself,[19] inscribed 'To Dr Reading, Jascha Heifitz 1927', probably in appreciation of her 'at home' hospitality.[20] The photo records the concert given by Heifitz on 17 April 1926, on an improvised stage in the stone quarry used as an amphitheatre in the Valley of Harod in Palestine. Thousands packed the quarry, seated on stone boulders, to hear the violin maestro.[21] After establishing the CJW in 1923, Dr Fanny often asked migrant musicians to perform at Council meetings, which boosted their reputations, opened doors to engagements and provided entertainment for her members.

Dr Fanny mentors Sydney schoolgirl

In 1949, a musical bond between a 10-year-old schoolgirl and the then 65-year-old community leader enriched both their lives. Carole Singer (née Goodman), a promising pianist and Sydney student in primary school, started playing for Dr Fanny at NCJW' meetings, and for Dr Fanny alone, in her apartment in Kings Cross. Dr Fanny nurtured Carole's musical gifts and provided opportunities for her to perform:

Dr Fanny and I immediately just got on. I was only 10 and full of my own importance, I didn't really appreciate her attention. At meetings, I played Chopin, Mozart, Beethoven and Brahms. I'll never forget an AGM in Young Street, Dr Fanny announced 'we have little Carole Goodman here to play for us'. I knew she was formidable because of her standing in the community, and I knew how everyone looked up to her and were hugely respectful of her. But she didn't frighten me at all. I warmed to her because she had this lovely softness, and this connection, and she liked me and treated me so beautifully. She encouraged me to come and visit her, which I did.[22]

Singer recalls a large dark piano, laden with books and scores, dominated the cluttered interior of the apartment. Contrary to the Reading family's view that Dr Fanny never played the piano for them, Singer was convinced she played for her own pleasure:

> She must have played because the music [scores] she had is indicative of the highest diploma [standard]; and she played concerti, *Tchaikovsky Piano Concerto No 1,* which is very difficult … Someone who went so far would have needed an outlet. She would have had limitations because she didn't practise, but she would have played some Chopin. Don't forget she was living on her own, it would have been a source of comfort.[23]

A newspaper article confirmed that Dr Fanny continued to play the piano, although not as often as she would wish,

> Dr Reading graduated in medicine at the Melbourne University. She is honorary physician at the Rachel Forster Hospital for Women and the Langton clinic. She is also a brilliant musician, a pianist of remarkable talent, only, unfortunately, her profession and council duties prevent her from devoting much time to her music.[24]

Years later, in 1962, when Dr Fanny's health deteriorated – she had Parkinson's disease – she left her Kings Cross apartment and moved to the Wolper Hospital in Woollahra, where she stayed for the remaining 12 years of her life. Packing up, Dr Fanny contacted Carole and offered her a selection of her music books. 'I said I would love some of her music,' Singer stated, 'I must have gone with one of my parents to collect it in the Cross'.[25]

This trove of musical scores, cherished by Dr Fanny and now in Carole's care, reveals Dr Fanny's pianistic range and depth of musical knowledge. It charts her lifelong passion for music and the pieces she studied as a young girl. It confirms that she bought sheet music and scores in later years, which strengthens Carole's assertion that Dr Fanny never stopped playing the piano. Some of these works bear the signature 'Fanny Rubinowich', whereas other scores are inscribed with the name 'Fanny Reading', testifying to their acquisition post-1918, the year her father changed the family name from Rubinowich to Reading. Dr Fanny's copy of *The Jews in Egypt* was printed in 1926 and purchased at least 12 years after her graduation from the Conservatorium. She kept these scores for decades, only parting with them when she found the right recipient to whom she could entrust her music books. Her faith in Carole was justified, as she preserved this collection intact.

Newspaper reports confirm Dr Fanny performed in public and attest to the popularity of her performances. She would not have played before an audience had she lacked confidence in her technique and interpretation. On 4 February 1929 in Sydney, she gave a 'lecturette' on Jewish composers and pianists illustrated by songs, 'rendered with unusual proficiency by Miss Hilda Levy, accompanied by Dr. Fanny Reading herself'.[26] A report of a meeting on 2 May 1932 in Sydney stated that 'she delighted members with her artistic pianoforte solos'.[27]

Benno Moseiwitsch, one of the great pianists of his time, returned to Australia in 1932. Aged 42, he was at the height of his artistic powers, renowned for his poetic phrasing and technique. Dr Fanny hosted a reception for him and his wife during which she played the piano. Unless she was at concert pitch, she would not have performed before such a celebrated virtuoso.[28] Her passion for music sustained her throughout her life and never diminished in intensity. She hosted musicians and showcased their gifts. She shared with Council members her knowledge and her love of opera. On one occasion, 'After the business of the meeting, a wonderful treat was given in the form of a grand opera night by Dr Fanny Reading, who related the stories of Faust, Cavaliera Rusticana, and La Tosca ...'.[29]

She hosted a reception on 25 April 1933 in honour of a classical trio touring Australia – Jascha and Tossy Spivakovsky and Edmund Kurtz. The Spivakovsky brothers came from a dynasty of musicians, their father was a celebrated cantor in Berlin. Dr Fanny, aware of anxiety prevailing among the Jewish community in Germany in the 1930s, welcomed the trio warmly.[30] The Spivakovskys took up teaching positions at Melbourne University's Conservatorium of Music. As a Conservatorium graduate, Dr Fanny had contacts in Melbourne's music world. By 1933, she was influential across a spectrum of organisations nationally. It is likely she did whatever she could to ease their integration into Australia's musical, academic and community life.

Dr Fanny's reputation as an accomplished musician spread beyond the Jewish community. On 27 August 1933, a large audience gathered in the Sydney Council Rooms for a recital by Yiddish poet Melech Ravitsch, after which Dr Fanny accompanied the cellist David Sisserman. Together, they presented several items: *Prayer* (From Jewish Life) by Ernest Bloch, *Orientale*, by the Russian composer César Cui, and *Romance sans Paroles* by Karl Davidoff. A review described their performance as 'a musical treat'.[31]

First World War influences Dr Fanny's career choice

The impact of the First World War (1914–1918) determined Dr Fanny's transition from a career in music to one in medicine. The Jewish community in Melbourne was small and the war's casualties and death toll affected everyone. Thirteen per cent of the eligible male Jewish population in Australia enlisted – there was no conscription – compared to nine per cent of the total population. Fifteen per cent of Jewish soldiers died, so many families were bereaved.[32] As Vice-President of the Jewish Young People's Association (JYPA) in Melbourne, Fanny was affected by the death in 1917 of Sergeant F. M. Michaelis, who had served as JYPA President. Rev. Danglow of St Kilda Hebrew Congregation deplored his loss to the community.[33] In the Rubinowich family home in St Kilda, Fanny, her sister Rae and their parents, focused on the wellbeing of those fighting for king and country. Both Nathan and Esther were naturalised in 1897[34] and 1904[35] respectively and classified as British nationals of Russian origin. As patriotic Australians, they supported their sons' enlistment.

The enlistment of Fanny's three brothers in the Australian Imperial Force influenced her greatly. All three gave their address as 23 Charnwood Street, St Kilda, Victoria, the family home they shared with Fanny, sister Rae and their parents. The oldest of the three, and younger than Fanny by six years, was Abraham Stanley Solomon, who volunteered on 24 January 1916.[36] By then, he had graduated from the University of Melbourne with an MB ChB and had worked as a Medical Officer at Flinders Naval Base. Fanny's youngest brother, 21-year-old Lewis Judah, a medical student at Melbourne University, enlisted on 25 April 1917;[37] and 22-year-old Hyman Samuel, designated in army documentation as a mechanical engineer, enlisted on 20 April 1915.[38]

Hyman, the first brother to enlist, was declared fit for active service and appointed to the 6th Reinforcements for the 8th Australian Infantry

Battalion at Broadmeadows. Almost three years later, aged 24, he applied for service abroad. In his 'Attestation Paper of Persons enlisted for Service Abroad', completed on 24 January 1918 in Sydney, he expressed a preference to serve in either the Field Artillery or the Light Horse, and signed the following oath:

> I Hyman Samuel Rubinowich swear that I will well and truly serve our Sovereign Lord the King in the Australian Imperial Force from 24/1/18 until the end of the War, and a further period of four months thereafter unless sooner lawfully discharged, dismissed, or removed therefrom; and that I will resist His Majesty's enemies and cause His Majesty's peace to be kept and maintained; and that I will in all matters appertaining to my service, faithfully discharge my duty according to law. So Help Me God.[39]

When he applied to serve overseas, his military plans unravelled. On 30 January 1918, the Australian Military Forces Medical Board in Sydney found him 'unfit for active service' due to his 'history of rheumatic fever'. Fanny and the family had known that Hyman was sickly as a child, which exacerbated their fears for his welfare.

Fanny's youngest brother, Lewis Judah, served as a Private in the Army Medical Corps of the Australian Imperial Force from 25 April 1917 to 1919. Initially assigned to the Army Medical Corps at Broadmeadows General Hospital and hospitals in Bendigo and Seymour, he embarked on 15 December 1917 on His Majesty's Australian Transport *Nestor* bound for the Australian camp in Suez. A fortnight later, he boarded H.M.A.T. *Maple* for the camp in Alexandria. His nephew, psychiatrist Dr Ian Burman, said in a Sydney interview that the family believed 'Lew' was mentally affected by the war: 'There was some mention that he had been gassed, although he never showed problems with his chest to my knowledge, so probably he was not gassed. In DSM IV criteria I think he probably had a post-traumatic stress disorder'.[40] After the war,

Lewis discontinued his medical studies at the University of Melbourne.

When Abraham Solomon Stanley presented for a medical examination on 24 January 1916, Brigadier-General R.E. Williams endorsed the recommendation that he be appointed a captain and posted to AAMC squadron.

Both Abraham and Lewis studied medicine at different times and both led busy social lives. While family tradition asserts that Fanny studied medicine in order to encourage Abe's progress, documentation confirms it was Lewis whom Fanny supervised academically.[41] By the time Abraham enlisted in 1916 – Fanny's first year of medical studies – he was already a qualified medical doctor, with an MB ChB degree. When Lewis enlisted in 1917, however, he was still enrolled as a medical student at the University of Melbourne, where he and Fanny studied together.

Fanny believed she could make a more significant contribution to society through medicine rather than music. She had a serious attitude to duty in life: 'Service means the rent we pay for the space we occupy'.[42] In 1928, a Sydney paper noted: 'Dr Fanny's degrees and diplomas are not limited to medicine. She has a number of music diplomas, but during the war her thoughts turned to medicine'.[43] She enrolled as a medical student at Melbourne University in 1916, having complied with the entry prerequisites of Greek and Latin.[44] She thrived academically and, that year, won the University Medal. Numerous certificates confirmed her success in examinations in natural philosophy, chemistry, biology, anatomy, histology, botany, laboratory work, physiology, public health and therapeutics. In 1918, she completed three months' instruction in the preparation of medicines. She attended tutorial classes in surgery and medicine; in 1919 obtained a certificate in post-mortem demonstrations; and in 1920 a certificate for 'in patient surgical practice with junior dressership'. With a clinical assistantship at Melbourne Hospital, she completed out-patient medical practice. Additional certificates testified to her knowledge and proficiency in medical and surgical practice, diseases of children, diseases of the skin, mental diseases [sic] and venereal disease.[45]

In 2013, the Medical History Museum of the University of Melbourne published a commemorative book titled *Strength of Mind: 125 Years of Women in Medicine*, marking 126 years since the admission of women to the University's Medical Faculty. In the foreword, University Chancellor Elizabeth Alexander celebrated the contribution of women in the field of medicine, 'More than 50 individuals and events have been selected to illustrate the achievements, significant changes and diverse experiences of women in the medical profession'.[46]

Dr Fanny is not featured in this book, despite her achievements in medicine and across a broad range of humanitarian, educational and sociological endeavours. Nobody forwarded her name for inclusion, an omission that exposes her anonymity in the history of early women graduates of the University of Melbourne's Medical Faculty. Her story and achievements merited inclusion in this book. That she was overlooked in such a significant publication confirms the importance of shining a light on her career as a physician and as a transformative changemaker whose impact on others should be acknowledged beyond the confines of the Jewish community, where she is still remembered by a coterie of NCJWA members. Dr Fanny's medical career and socio-cultural agenda exemplify the ideals upheld by many of Melbourne Medical School's early women graduates. She was a competent physician, effecting improvements in maternal and child health, working in an honorary capacity in several Sydney hospitals and institutions associated with the healthcare of mothers and children and, at the same time, looking after her patients in private practice. She received the MBE in 1961 for social welfare services in New South Wales.[47] She was Life Governor of the Benevolent Society of New South Wales, the Crown Street Women's Hospital in Surry Hills, and the Dalwood Homes.[48] Dr Heather Sheard notes:

Although the gender of Victoria's early women doctors meant that their professional paths did not always lead in the direction they had hoped, they nevertheless explored and developed new professional authority and competencies. The joy they found in their work is patent in the extensive list of their achievements and their legacy – all is evidence of their strength of mind.[49]

'The Angel of Kings Cross'

Kings Cross was a Sydney suburb noted for its notoriety. Dr Fanny's decision to live and work there, in close proximity to pimps and prostitutes, in many ways defined the type of compassionate medicine she practised, where all were welcome to walk through her open door. After her graduation in 1922 with an MB BS from the University of Melbourne's Medical Faculty, she moved to Sydney and, at first, worked with her brother Dr Abraham Reading in the Sydney suburb of Kogarah and at hospitals in the area before moving to Darlinghurst. Finally, she settled in Kings Cross, where she opened a general practice in her apartment on the corner of Springfield Avenue and Darlinghurst Road, not far from an area known for obvious reasons as the Dirty Half Mile or Douche Can Alley. She also helped Dr 'Abe' in his practice at 253 Oxford Street, Bondi Junction, a more salubrious environment by comparison. She stayed in Kings Cross for the duration of her active medical career until she moved in 1962, due to sickness and old age, to the Wolper Hospital in Woollahra. Kings Cross was an economically depressed area, which reduced her earning capacity and, in conjunction with her honorary hospital work, made her reliant on revenue from her work in her brother's practice and on his unfailing generosity. According to family members, she gave her money away – including that given to her by her brother – to those in need and to charities. Her nephew Dr Ian Burman said 'Dr Abe' knew she did that but did not mind, 'He gave her money with one hand and she gave it away with the other'.[50]

When Dr Fanny began to practise in Sydney, it was a time of change in the medical profession in Australia. Prior to the 1920s, almost all doctors were general practitioners, who treated general medical and surgical complaints; and specialties were associated less with qualifications and more with experience. While considered a general practitioner, in 1925 she furthered her studies abroad in several medical disciplines. In October 1925, she enrolled at the Rotunda Hospital in Dublin, Ireland, and attended lectures in 'Clinical Instruction in Midwifery'. She studied in a number of clinics in Vienna; at the Great Ormond Street Hospital for Children, in London; and in the United States, where she also attended the Quinquennial Conference of the International Council of Women, which had as its theme child welfare.[51] Contemporaries viewed her as a specialist in maternal health, paediatrics, obstetrics, gynaecology and anaesthetics,

> Practitioners who described themselves as specialists or consultants did not possess formal post-graduate training, but usually had extensive experience in a particular area of medical practice. These consultants combined hospital work with general practice.[52]

Medicine aligned with Dr Fanny's principles of service to the community and her humanitarian ideals. She made a conscious choice to work in a deprived socio-economic milieu. Caring and empathic, she earned the respect and affection of those among whom she chose to live and work. She looked after maternity cases, delivered babies, treated patients in her practice and in their homes, cared for the sick in hospitals, and performed anaesthetics across several hospitals in the city and further afield.

Medicine conferred on Dr Fanny a social status in the community. Her achievement in winning community regard was greater than that of other women doctors, given that she surmounted what society perceived at that time as a social disadvantage, her family's migrant background. This compared unfavourably to that of her medical contemporaries from rural areas, most of whom commanded respect as the daughters of doctors, lawyers, teachers and clergymen,.[53]

> Of two other well-known rural-born women doctors, Constance D'Arcy was born in Mudgee, the daughter of a police sergeant (or perhaps a constable), and Fanny Reading (who, although born in Russia, was raised in Australia from the age of two) had a father who was described as a 'hawker' in Ballarat.[54]

Social or academic snobbery never troubled Dr Fanny, as her values were vastly different. She took pride in Jewish scholarship and education and revered learning. She was never influenced by social status. She appreciated the complexity of her parents' situation as migrants building a new life in Australia and surmounting innumerable difficulties. The regard in which she was held as a doctor is impressive when measured against her contemporaries' societal prejudice. Her disregard of monetary rewards, her modest practice arrangements and the working-class environment in Kings Cross contrasted with practice settings in suburban Sydney that attracted prosperous middleclass patients, as advocated by the *Medical Journal of Australia*,

> It is usual for the practitioner to set aside a portion of his house for his professional work. A separate entrance, a suitable waiting room for patients, and a consulting room with an ante-chamber adjoining for the examination of blood, urine and other excretions, are essential. A separate room for the performance of minor surgical operations will be found very convenient.[55]

By contrast, Dr Fanny's Kings Cross surgery was small, as was her whole apartment. Medically, she made a difference in the lives of local residents. Advances in scientific medicine enabled her to treat patients effectively and to reduce mortality in the community – insulin was introduced in 1921 to manage diabetes; pneumonia and streptococcal diseases could be controlled with sulphonamides discovered in 1935; and penicillin emerged as a wonder drug in 1941.⁵⁶ Kings Cross was a world away from the leafy suburbs of Sydney's North Shore,

> The 'Montmartre' of Sydney, people called it … Actually, it was fairly hideous; like all of urban Sydney being a dusty hodgepodge of low-built buildings … the upper halves flats and residential rooms and the lower halves shops, offices and cinemas. Between the two, cutting off the dirty stucco and dingy brickwork from the glaring neon signs, were the ubiquitous iron or concrete awnings.⁵⁷

Dr Fanny's nephew, her sister's son Dr Ian Burman, has vivid memories of her Kings Cross home, her surgery and her pressured lifestyle, as he stayed with her for two months when an 18-year-old medical student at Sydney University. He recalled that the apartment was 'right in the heart of Kings Cross', and that he slept on a mattress on the floor of the back verandah, while his older brother Lloyd occupied an adjacent bedroom. Dr Burman cast light on Dr Fanny's nature – recalling a younger woman whose sense of family duty was so strong that she forfeited the prospect of marriage to an American who might have taken her away from ageing and needy parents. She was dutiful, committed to family and community – an aunt who perpetuated her family's tradition of hospitality, and a doctor dedicated to her practice and civic activities. 'When I stayed there, I had more knowledge of what she did, she worked in the surgery morning and afternoon; and in the evenings she worked [on Council of Jewish Women projects] with her secretary Roma Lang'.⁵⁸

Dr Fanny worked extremely hard, never turning anyone away despite the hour, fatigue or a waiting room full of patients. Her patients belonged to a demographic characterised by poverty and disease. This was exactly why she had chosen medicine, to ameliorate in every way she could the lives of those needing her skills. Morris Ochert, a young student whom Dr Fanny befriended, asked her once: 'Must you live and work here, in the very centre of this unsavoury area of King's Cross?' She told him,

> 'Where else will I find such need, such human tragedies? No-one wants to know that, below its glossy exterior, there is so much heartbreak, suffering, sickness and degradation in The Cross. I *must* live and work here.' I can attest that her practice, and even her little apartment, was a haven for the abused prostitutes, street kids, beaten wives and homeless dregs of humanity who haunted 'The Cross' … She was highly regarded as a philanthropist and known as one who constantly sought to right the many wrongs of life. There was no limit to the compassion she constantly showed.[59]

Dr Fanny's reputation as the 'Angel of Kings Cross' was well entrenched. Morris always remembered an incident in Dr Fanny's apartment in King's Cross, when 'a badly injured young woman fell through the door':

> She had been badly beaten up by her lover who was also her pimp and she was terrified that he may have followed her. An even greater concern was for her baby whom she boarded with a neighbour nearby. Dr Fanny sent Ochert and one of the girls at the meeting to fetch the baby while she attended to the medical needs of the mother. She made up a crib for the baby and settled the mother in a makeshift bed. At midnight the meeting resumed and when it was finished at about 2 am she made omelettes and black coffee and drove the participants home. She told them that first thing in the morning she would drive the girl to have her jaw X-rayed and would then take mother and child to the Salvation Army shelter – after that it was back to the surgery where she had a full appointment book for the day.[60]

The 'Angel of Kings Cross' legend around Dr Fanny grew with similar stories related by patients, family, friends and strangers. When Dr Fanny's niece Jennifer Burman (née Reading) was hospitalised as a little girl, Dr Fanny moved a cot into the child's hospital room and slept there, monitoring her progress and reassuring her. 'My parents didn't do that for me, it was Aunt Fanny,' Jennifer recalled. Dr Fanny did the same for her nephew Leigh Reading when he had a tonsillectomy and was hospitalised at the Buenavista private hospital in Kings Cross.[61] Ray Ginsburg, a close associate of Dr Fanny's, described her as, 'The kindest person imaginable'. Dr Fanny looked after Ray's daughter, who suffered from asthma, and would not leave her until she recovered, usually in the early hours of the morning.[62]

Dr Fanny personified the family doctor of yesteryear. She was a woman of faith with a keen sense of gratitude for her health and strength that enabled her to treat her patients in The Cross and elsewhere. However, in 1936 aged 52, she fell gravely ill – all reports are in general terms and do not identify the condition – but, over several months, she recovered her health and returned to her practice. She stated:

> It is with a deep sense of gratitude and thankfulness to the Almighty that I have been spared ... [And] she quoted from the Psalms, 'Be strong and of good courage and walk humbly with me in the way of the Lord'.[63]

The Racial Hygiene Association

Dr Fanny was active in the area of family planning. She worked as an honorary medical officer at the Rachel Forster Hospital in Surry Hills, which enabled younger women doctors to gain vital medical experience, including training in its Venereal Disease Clinic, which treated patients in a family context. The clinic was renowned 'for the combination of treatment and counselling it offered ... an impressive number of unfortunate women'.[64]

In the 1920s, several women's organisations in Australia promoted sex education and family planning, mainly in an effort to stem the tide of venereal disease. Social activist Jessie Street proposed compulsory medical examination before marriage, which proved an unpopular view. That view received support, however, from the Racial Hygiene Association of New South Wales, a body promoting conservative views on human sexuality that aroused both opposition and support in the popular press. Concerned with enabling women to control their fertility, the Racial Hygiene Association attracted sufficient support to survive and, from 1934, ran a free clinic for contraceptive advice.

First known as the Racial Improvement Association, it was co-founded on 27 April 1926 by Lillie Goodisson and Ruby Rich (later Ruby Rich-Schalit), both members of the Women's Reform League. Ruby Rich and Dr Lindel Worrall were inaugural co-Presidents and Jessie Street the foundation Vice-President.[65] In 1927, the organisation changed its name to the Racial Hygiene Centre; and the following year the name changed again to the Racial Hygiene Association of New South Wales. Jessie was a close associate of three leading Jewish feminists: the barrister Nerida Goodman, Dr Fanny and Ruby Rich, the latter two involved actively in the Racial Hygiene Association.[66] In 1926, Ruby headed the Society's committee to educate women in sex matters and the prevention of venereal disease. At that time, like Dr Fanny, she was unmarried, but unlike Dr Fanny, she had no medical or nursing experience, so she had reservations about taking on this role: 'I thought it was a job for an older woman. But when I read the literature and realised that gonorrhoea could cause babies to be born blind or deaf, I was moved and agreed'.[67]

There was a darker ideology associated with the Racial Hygiene Association. While family planning was a core program of the Society's work, providing medical advice to women of all ages – the sphere that attracted Dr Fanny's participation – a number of its spokespersons, including Ruby, advocated for eugenicist ideals of racial stock.

The Memorandum and Articles of Association of the Racial Hygiene Association, published on 18 August 1932, stated that it was founded to 'collect provide and circulate accurate and enlightened information as to the prevalence of venereal diseases and as to the necessity for early treatment'.[68] It aimed to conduct throughout New South Wales a campaign 'for the prevention and eradication of venereal diseases and to encourage and assist the dissemination of a sound knowledge of the physiological laws of life in order to raise the standard both of health and conduct'. In 1933, the Association established Sydney's first birth control clinic. These aims and activities were in line with Dr Fanny's medical ethics and her work at the Rachel Forster Hospital's Venereal Disease Clinic, which rapidly developed into the largest of its type in Australia.[69] The Racial Hygiene Association was the precursor of the Family Planning Association.[70] Clearly, Dr Fanny valued the Association because it offered her a safe space within which to conduct family planning, to initiate birth control and to counsel and educate women and young girls, all valuable measures to stem the flood of venereal disease and to mitigate the effects of poverty.

The medical battle against venereal disease escalated during the Second World War, when Kings Cross became a centre for American servicemen on recreational leave, mainly from Brisbane where they were stationed under the command of General Douglas MacArthur, Supreme Commander of the Allied Powers. This 'invasion' had sexual, social and political consequences for Australia,

> National security regulations passed in 1942 empowered police to detain persons suspected of carrying venereal disease, and invariably many more women were targeted than men … Regulations banned the advertising of contraceptives, even as army authorities promoted prophylaxis among the troops. Schemes were devised to deny women access to alcohol and to promote healthy recreation and feminists joined church leaders in promoting early marriage.[71]

The Association's 1932 Memorandum[72] states: 'Groups of experts shall be formed to deal with the various sections of Hygiene such as Sex Education, Venereal Disease and Mental Hygiene'; and, 'The education of the community on eugenic lines'. The Association's General Secretary,

Lillie Goodisson, was committed to 'the selective breeding of future generations for the elimination of hereditary disease and defects'. She campaigned unsuccessfully for the 'segregation and sterilization of the mentally deficient and for the introduction of pre-marital health examinations'.[73] For the first five years, eugenics was at the forefront of the Association's agenda. Addressing the Racial Hygiene Association in 1933, clergyman Canon B.S. Hammond promoted sterilisation:

> In his opinion there were five classes from which the community might 'rightly' protect itself. They were: (1) The mentally diseased, who numbered about three times as many as 60 years ago; (2) mental defectives; (3) the mentally unstable; (4) those physically unfit, or those with transmissible diseases; and (5) sexual perverts. He added that sterilisation ... had no effect except to prevent parenthood. It was a protection of society, not a penalty on the individual.[74]

Less than a decade later in the name of eugenics, the Nazis murdered 'sub-humans' as a way of ensuring genetic dominance of a 'master Aryan' race. Viewed from a post-Holocaust perspective, it is puzzling that women actively involved with the Association failed to perceive its potential dangers. They failed to understand that their connection with the Association lent it credibility and, however unintentionally, seemingly endorsed the more extreme aspects championed by some of its spokespersons. The question has to be asked, how could Dr Fanny fail to see in those early years the potential trajectory of the Association's agenda, especially when its spokespersons advocated openly for eugenics. There was considerable support for its program and unqualified acquiescence from an educated elite:

> The surprisingly unanimous support given in Sydney by delegates to the [Racial Hygiene] Congress suggestion that sterilisation, voluntary or obligatory, should be the lot of low human types menacing the physical and mental standard of Australians ...

> the conviction ... that definite action is necessary if this nation is to attain the standard of excellence each one of us desires for it ... But there was not a word of dissent, a significant indication of the attitude of the experts towards the question of coping with the mentally sub-normal.[75]

It is unlikely that anyone in 1930s Australia could envisage the horrors Nazism would unleash in the years ahead. The very word 'racial' in the name of the organisation did not yet have the connotations for Australians that were implicit in Hitler's racist ideology and his Nazi propaganda. Words evolve over time and take on new meanings. The concept of 'racial' denoting a poison in the blood and therefore ineradicable except by death was an ideology remote from the sphere in which these women operated.

In September 1938, Ruby Rich led a deputation to the NSW government, voicing support for the principles of eugenics and calling for the establishment of segregation colonies for the 'Mentally Unfit'. Speaking on behalf of the Racial Hygiene Association, 'she argued that the unconstrained breeding of the "feebleminded" was causing a rapid increase in mental deficiency, undermining the racial fitness of Australia, and causing a rise in crime, poverty and sexual deviance'.[76] Although the Racial Hygiene Association is now remembered as a pioneer of birth control and the precursor of Family Planning Australia, 'in the interwar decades it was concerned primarily with fostering improvements in racial fitness. Following the principles of selective breeding, the RHA attempted to limit reproduction among the "unfit", encourage childbearing among the healthy, and curtail the spread of hereditary diseases'.[77]

Ruby Rich was an unashamed proponent of eugenics and she was not alone; however, that involvement with racial hygiene is less anomalous than it may appear initially:

> By tracing the pervasive influence of eugenics within medicine, psychiatry, social work and government policy, numerous

historians have demonstrated that support for eugenic ideas was widespread amongst Australian progressives from the late nineteenth until the mid-twentieth centuries.[78]

Was Dr Fanny tainted by association with these outspoken proponents of eugenics? Dr Fanny and Ruby enjoyed a close friendship. Both were accomplished pianists, Australian feminists and committed Zionists. Their shared interests brought them together and Ruby was an invited speaker at Council of Jewish Women functions. At Council gatherings, however, while she addressed issues of sexual health, there were no references to Dr Fanny speaking on eugenics. Perhaps this indicates the unspoken dividing line between them. As a doctor concerned with the health of women and children, Dr Fanny valued the safe places provided by the Association and the Rachel Forster Hospital, within which she could treat and advise women suffering the debilitating effects of syphilis and gonorrhoea, the two dominant venereal diseases at that time; and provide sex education to women and girls. Eugenics, however, in its pre-war manifestations in Australia would not have accorded with her medical values nor with her deeply observed Judaic value of honouring and preserving life, all life. There are no records of Dr Fanny's involvement in the eugenicist discourse at any time. She never put forward any suggestions or measures that discriminated against those with either intellectual or physical disabilities.

While the Racial Hygiene Association conducted pioneering work in birth control and sex education,[79] its promotion of eugenics influenced many prominent people,

> who carried this ideology into policy formulation in many of the health and education services which these experts helped to establish. Eugenists' efforts to improve national fitness encompassed maternal and child health, fighting VD and TB, and the provision of sex education and birth control.[80]

There is disagreement among scholars as to whether eugenics was central or peripheral to the mission of the Racial Hygiene Association in the interwar decades; and there is emphasis on its positive aspects as practised in New South Wales and Australia generally.

Few foresaw the extremist Nazi ideology that would propel the science of eugenics to its genocidal conclusion,

> In the post-Holocaust era, eugenics has acquired decidedly pejorative connotations, evoking images of sinister medical experiments and crude attempts at social engineering. Eugenics, it is often assumed, is conservative and reactionary, a xenophobic response to the degeneration anxieties which emerged in the wake of urban modernity.[81]

Eugenics was one of the pillars of Nazism. Ideologues manipulated eugenics to their own ends, reinforcing the concept of an Aryan master race and arbitrarily categorising others, especially the Jews, as 'sub-human'. The swift leap from theory to genocide demonstrated conclusively the dangers of eugenics and delegitimised this science. Dr Fanny learnt of the wholesale slaughter of Jewish populations perpetrated by the Nazis in the Second World War. She was devastated by reports of their annihilation and mourned those communities. Did the presence of some extremists within the ranks of the Association cause her to re-think her ongoing participation in the Association's activities, given her understanding of the slippery slope to madness that extremist views could trigger? It is salutary to remember that the Association's goals were not strictly eugenic:

> Marion Piddington [one of the Association's founders] was a eugenicist who supported mainline eugenic practices such as sterilization, the other founders were more interested in using 'eugenics' as an umbrella to advocate a wide variety of peripherally related issues like teaching sex education, eradicating venereal disease, and providing birth control.[82]

It is probable Dr Fanny continued to see the Association as an appropriate forum for her humanitarian agenda in sex education, venereal disease and birth control. As a doctor, medical ethics informed her actions. There are no records of Dr Fanny objecting publicly to the eugenics agenda of the Association, although she might well have done so in private conversations with Ruby Rich, Lillie Goodisson and other supporters of this ideology. Neither is there any record of her withdrawal from the Association.

There are several postscripts to the history of eugenics in Australia, including the forced removal of Aboriginal children – the 'stolen generations' – from their families that aimed at reshaping society into a homogenous 'white' race. These measures were justified on the basis of assimilationist policies and, by some, on the basis of eugenics.

In November 1943, Dr Fanny presented a paper at the Australian Woman's Charter Conference for Victory in War and Victory in Peace, held in Sydney, which she attended together with representatives of 91 women's organisations.[83] The conference developed the Australian Women's Charter of rights for women in the post-war world, a feminist manifesto,

> Their agenda was to formulate a charter for a new post-war social order for women that would secure their economic and political equality. Most of the guiding voices in this movement came from older women ... They believed that women's degradation stemmed from their social constitution as 'creatures of sex'. Prostitution they saw as paradigmatic of the female condition. Advancement for women, they believed, meant advancement beyond their condition as creatures of sex into the full citizenship of public life.[84]

Conference President Jessie Street highlighted the need for a publicity campaign to promote early treatment of venereal disease, and knowledge about the causes of venereal disease, such as promiscuous sex relations and ignorance about sex matters. She suggested,

> sufferers from venereal disease be under the supervision of officers of the Health Department, assisted by social workers and almoners, instead of the Police department; [and] the provision of adequate facilities for the free and secret treatment of venereal disease.[85]

At the conclusion of the conference, an event occurred that demonstrated Jessie Street's commitment to helping Jewish people who were, by then, the victims of an unprecedented and industrialised genocide powered by eugenicist ideology. The conference passed a special resolution urging immediate action 'to rescue the Jewish race from the systematic massacre being perpetrated by the Nazis in Europe ...'. Initiatives aimed at the safety and wellbeing of the Australian nation, in aid of Jewish children and adults fleeing persecution and death in Europe, and assisting refugees arriving in Australia, were part of Dr Fanny's work in the 1930s and 1940s and were conducted through the organisation she founded, the National Council of Jewish Women (NCJW), which is the subject of the next chapter.

Chapter 4

The National Council of Jewish Women – 1920s and 1930s

To embrace the problems, not only of our people, both here and abroad, but of common humanity.

– Dr Fanny, 1927

Few women rise from obscurity to national prominence in one decade, but that happened to Dr Fanny. In the 1920s, she expanded her social activism on a national scale, achieving this through her personal drive and compulsion to improve life in meaningful ways for her fellow citizens. In 1923 in Sydney, she created the Council of Jewish Women of New South Wales (CJW), which evolved in 1929 into Australia's first truly national women's organisation, the National Council of Jewish Women (NCJW). From this platform, she launched educational and social welfare initiatives to address issues in the Jewish community, Australia's changing needs, and global challenges. It didn't happen overnight; but her vision inspired others to support her social justice mission. Membership was open to all Jewish women, there was no discrimination and no snobbery. All were welcome, whether religious or secular, rich or poor, educated or uneducated. They represented the established Anglo Jewish community and recent migrants from Eastern Europe. She melded them all into a collective sisterhood and mentored their progression towards social activism. Motivated by her creed of 'service above self', they enacted her humanitarian agenda at home and abroad. She shepherded her members towards feminist goals and instilled in them a sense of social justice. From the beginning, there were two concepts that shaped their endeavours – Judaism's belief in 'Tikkun Olam', repairing the world; and Dr Fanny's personal creed, her 'Law of Loving Kindness'.

On Dr Fanny's arrival in Sydney in 1922, her professional and personal life changed radically. She moved to Kogarah, 14 kilometres south of Sydney, where she shared a house at 19 Belgrave St with her brother, Dr Abraham Reading. She joined his medical practice in Kogarah and Darlinghurst, and worked as an honorary medical officer at the St George District and Community Hospitals, and the Rachel Forster Hospital, She lived in Kogarah for five years, acquiring a reputation as a caring doctor and committed volunteer worker for social welfare projects. A press report described her as, 'Among the most prominent and enthusiastic workers';[1] and the Minister for Justice, Thomas Ley, paid tribute to the women volunteers who raised £800 for an ambulance presented to the St George Ambulance Brigade, mentioning in particular, Mrs H. Patrick (President), Mrs H. B. Primrose and Dr Fanny Reading (hon. secretaries).[2] In 1927, Dr Fanny moved to the heart of Kings Cross,[3] where she ran a general practice in her apartment in 'Claremont' at 33 Darlinghurst Rd, while also seeing patients at her brother's surgery in Oxford Street, Bondi Junction.

In June 1923 in Sydney, Dr Fanny met Bella Pevsner, an American representative of the Jewish National Fund (JNF), responsible for land acquisition and reclamation in Palestine. At the Fifth Zionist Congress in 1901 in Basel, Switzerland, Theodor Herzl pleaded for a national fund to build the foundations of a Jewish state and the JNF-KKL came into being with headquarters in Jerusalem. Pevsner told Dr Fanny about the National Council of Jewish Women in the United States – founded in 1893 by Hannah Solomon – dedicated to religion, philanthropy and education.[4] Pevsner encouraged Dr Fanny to create a similar body, urging her to make Zionism, the restoration of Palestine as a Jewish homeland, a central pillar of her organisation.

On 26 June 1923 in Sydney, Dr Fanny proposed a Council in Australia comparable to the American NCJW, an organisation that differed from fundraising charities with which women were traditionally associated. Her Council would be a trans-national body with a local, national and international agenda, 'where representative women from each State might ... deal with the serious problems of Jewry'.[5] After three subsequent meetings – on 8 July 1923, 15 July 1923 and 30 July 1923 – the Council of Jewish Women of New South Wales (CJW) finally came into being. Dr Fanny outlined what she had in mind, a voluntary organisation for women whose members would work for the greater good in a spirit of friendship.[6]

Dr Fanny defined their aims as educational, social, philanthropic, and the problems of world Jewry. She focused on expanding the intellectual horizons of members, with discussions and 'lecturettes', with topics ranging from 'The Status of Jewish Women of Ancient Israel', delivered by Rev. Leib Falk, to a lecture on four operas – *Carmen*, *La Boheme*, *Faust* and *Il Travatore*, given by Cecilia Goldberg, with arias performed by pupils of Louis Zucker and Signor Cacialli. Capacity audiences attended these advertised events, such as violinist Leo Cherniavsky's recital, popular with Sydney University music graduates. People from all walks of life attended, which enabled Dr Fanny to forge connections in the Jewish and general community to support Council initiatives. Her commitment to Zionism and resolve to aid the impoverished *Yishuv* (Jewish community in Palestine prior to 1948) was central to her agenda. From its inception, Council supported the Palestine Maternity and District Nursing Fund and the Palestine Infant Welfare Fund.[7]

The CJW came into being as amenities for the Jewish community burgeoned in Sydney. On Armistice Day, 11 November 1923, Sir John Monash opened the NSW Jewish War Memorial Building in Darlinghurst, comprising the Maccabean Hall with seating for 500 and adjacent rooms for social, literary, educational and communal purposes,[8] which served as venues for Council functions and dinners. On 4 August 1924 in the Maccabean Hall – before an audience of 200 members and a considerable number of well-wishers – Dr Fanny delivered her first annual report as CJW President,

> Your Council by its efforts in the Educational, Social and Philanthropic sphere of communal activities has provided the justification for its existence. It has brought together … the women and girls of our community, resulting in pleasure to themselves, benefit to the community, encouragement to the deserving, and assistance to the oppressed and needy of our brethren in foreign lands.[9]

She shared her vision for a national organisation united with Jewish women around the world, and expressed confidence 'in the much greater good they would do in the future', assuring the community that 'they were always eager and willing to help those in need'.[10]

When the men present endorsed the value of Dr Fanny's report, it signalled their goodwill and acceptance of her intention to emancipate members from the subservient position women occupied previously within the Australian Jewish community. When Aaron Blashki paid tribute to her leadership and Council's work 'for their suffering sisters in less fortunate lands'; and Sydney solicitor Percy Marks stated, 'they had kept in mind their brethren in other countries whose cry for help was more urgent than our own', they were acknowledging her innovative leadership, and the scope of Council's activities and reach internationally. With Dr Fanny's guidance, women became politically aware, tuned to contemporary events abroad affecting their co-religionists, which led them to devise ways to support them, when and where possible.

This emergence of a potent women's voice was doubly threatening to entrenched male leadership for several reasons. It occurred at a time when secular organisations were seeking leadership roles traditionally exercised by synagogues. Before 1920, 'there was neither an umbrella community body to provide a united Jewish voice in dealings with government nor a forum for debate among organisations serving the established community'.[11] A bastion of 'strong male opposition' voiced its hostility, 'to any possible interference by women in the running of the community. The Jewish woman's role was seen as wife and mother ... or as "ladies auxiliaries", assisting but subordinate to the male efforts.'[12]

Among reactionary opponents to women's leadership and emerging visibility within the Jewish community was Rabbi Francis Lyon Cohen, Chief Minister of the Great Synagogue. In 1923, he opposed the formation of the CJW. When Dr Fanny, a member of his congregation, suggested special Council Sabbaths at the Great Synagogue, he rejected the idea outright, as he was opposed to 'American innovations'.[13] A notable figure in Sydney whose sermons were published regularly on the front page of the *Hebrew Standard*, his views influenced his congregation and filtered through to the wider Jewish community. He was not alone in his fears that a change in women's communal status could endanger traditional observance,

> Other leaders feared that the movement [the CJW] would interfere with congregational activities and lead to the abandonment of such traditions as the segregation of the sexes in the synagogue ... The Council was also opposed because it was feared that its sectarian nature would foster anti-Semitism.[14]

Dr Fanny's defenders addressed these fears. Percy Marks championed Council's efforts, 'they should not dream of restricting their good work for fear of becoming conspicuous and thus engendering antisemitism'.[15] His comments were an acknowledgement of the opposition Dr Fanny encountered. Her Council was not universally approved by the Jewish community, there were dissenters with reservations. She recalled that at their first general meeting attended by 40 women at the Great Synagogue Chambers, 'opinions were voiced that a suggested body of

Jewish women might give rise to anti-Semitism, a feature practically absent in Australia ...'.[16] In her characteristic way, Dr Fanny defused these negative perceptions by focusing on positive outcomes,

> After being constantly in the communal limelight, your Council closed the first year of its existence with firm confidence that Australian and New South Wales Jewry remains as free from anti-Semitism as at any time in its existence.[17]

Despite these controversies dogging Council's early beginnings, the inaugural AGM's mood was congratulatory and praise of Dr Fanny fulsome. According to solicitor Sydney B. Glass, 'They had sown a harvest where before the ground was barren. They had proved they were loyal Jewesses – loyal to their King and their country – loyal to the cry of distress.'[18] Dr Fanny's report emphasised her reasons for creating the Council,

> It occurred to me ... that there existed in this city so much apathy and indifference regarding the affairs of our people, that there was room for a movement in which our women and girls could meet, discuss and attempt to solve our many problems. I realised ... the great and powerful influence for good, the Jewish women could yield, and felt that by appealing to the latter, we could overcome the apparent lack of responsibility, provided every Jewish woman and girl played her part.[19]

Dr Fanny did not allow opposition from the Great Synagogue or communal criticism to obstruct her initiatives in education, religion, culture, politics, philanthropy and social welfare. By 1929, when she convened the First Jewish Women's Conference of Australasia, there was recognition that Council provided a unique forum for Jewish women, 'who yet lacked a voice on the councils of the Jewish community at large'.[20] In 1929, when Council transformed into a national body, the National Council of Jewish Women (NCJW), it was already well respected throughout Australia. Dr Fanny, as President, had the necessary gravitas to access leaders at grassroots and governmental levels. It evolved swiftly into an organisation with its own identity, moral compass, agenda and spheres of influence. Dr Fanny subscribed to collaborative efforts across a broad spectrum of community projects, forging links with other organisations. She networked effectively to build these relationships, efforts sustained over many decades, as evidenced in her contribution towards the establishment of the New South Wales Jewish Board of Deputies in 1945, of which she was a valued founder member.

Assisting migrants to Australia

The biblical command to care for the stranger 'because you were strangers in the land of Egypt' was at the heart of Dr Fanny's agenda. Her 1924 report highlighted the formation of an immigration sub-committee to assist Jewish migrants to Australia, 'to meet them on their arrival and … advise them as to place of residence and extend to them the hand of friendship, so that they shall not feel strangers in a strange land'.[21]

Dr Fanny's family origins were mired in Russian antisemitism, so she understood persecution on a visceral level and empathised with communities abroad experiencing pogroms. She focused Council's efforts on ameliorating the worsening situation of Jews in European countries, including donations 'for the oppressed Jews in the Ukraine', and assisting the Jewish *Yishuv* by supporting the Palestine Maternity and District Nursing Fund, Infant Welfare Centres, and 'the women and girls in agricultural pursuits in Palestine'.[22]

Council enlarged its members' worldview beyond the parochial to encompass marginalised communities overseas. Members transformed into social activists, asserting themselves and raising their voices for the first time,

> The Council was the first Jewish women's organisation in Australia to combine an increasing feminist-inspired awareness

and promotion of the rights and status of Jewish women ... with the traditional idea that good and charitable works constituted for women the sole appropriate communal activity outside the home.[23]

Council established a reputation for good works nationally and internationally. In its first year alone, Dr Fanny and her 377 members implemented local initiatives in social, religious, educational and philanthropic spheres. Their efforts won the goodwill of many prominent Australians, who praised Council publicly. The Governor of New South Wales, Admiral Sir Dudley de Chair, was patron of the Council Fair held in 1925 in Sydney to raise funds for children in Palestine; and Sydney's Lord Mayor, Alderman David Gilpin, opened the Fair, where Dr Fanny spoke on Council's humanitarian mission. She described the 'sad and helpless condition of the little babes in Palestine', and Council's non-discriminatory work, stating that money raised supported children 'of all denominations in Palestine, be they Christian, Jew or Turk'.[24] Thomas Ley, NSW Minister for Justice in the cabinet of Premier Sir George Fuller, stated:

> I know that God will bless you in your wonderful work. I am a Gentile ... and when I see around me such glorious efforts to help the hungry and unhappy babes on the other side of the world, I feel that humanity owes a great debt to you Jewesses.[25]

Recognition followed from overseas organisations, such as the NCJW of America, the Bureau of Jewish Research, and the Women's International Zionist Organisation (WIZO), connections Dr Fanny consolidated in 1925, when she travelled abroad. Meeting leaders of national and international women's organisations reinforced her belief in what her own CJW could achieve. She left Australia on 26 March 1925 on board the *Tahiti*, sailing to San Francisco. In Washington DC, she attended the Sixth Quinquennial Conference of the International Council of Women, from 4 to 14 May 1925, as alternate delegate of the ten-person

Australian delegation. All National Council of Women (NCW) members were entitled to attend the conference as visitors, but only delegates or 'alternates', such as Dr Fanny, could vote or speak at meetings.[26] Alongside delegation leader Ruby Board, vice-president of the NCW NSW, she met fellow delegates from Western Australia, Tasmania, Queensland, South Australia and New South Wales.[27] Their organisation's Commonwealth patroness in Australia, Lady Rachel Forster, described these delegates as, 'remarkable for their fine public spirit and keen intelligent interest in public affairs ... unsurpassed, I believe, by any nation in the world'.[28] About 300 delegates from 43 countries attended the Conference, representing more than three million women.[29] The Conference agenda – aligned closely with Dr Fanny's mission for CJW – dealt with, 'matters pertaining to the health and happiness, moral and physical, of the nations, for the purpose of promoting co-operation in their efforts for the welfare of the family, the community, and the race ...'.[30]

CJW's collegial harmony fractures

Dr Fanny was never a ceremonial figurehead of her organisation. Her thoughts and feelings informed every aspect of Council. While travelling abroad in 1925, she could not monitor developments back home and, perhaps inevitably, fault lines erupted. This disunity highlighted the power of her intellect and personality in shaping cohesion and outcomes. A few weeks prior to her departure, Celia Symonds spoke of her own qualms in deputising for Dr Fanny, who encouraged Symonds 'to fill her shoes well' while she was away. She reinforced Celia's confidence by reiterating that Council had raised the status of Jewish women to a position not previously held. Before leaving, she wanted to ensure that all would run smoothly and spoke of her plans to visit Melbourne, Adelaide and Perth to organise Jewish women there.[31]

Without Dr Fanny's guidance, however, Council's course seemed imperilled. A schism threatened harmony between Council and community bodies, possibly among Council members as well. An article in the *Hebrew Standard* referred to criticism aimed at Council by unnamed sources. In a plea for goodwill, Celia tackled the hostility,

> The Council at all times welcomes criticism even though it is adverse, provided it comes from persons who follow its activities and wish to help by their criticism … but the Council has no time for the other kind who … mislead others and cause communal dissension.[32]

Council confronted the criticism and continued its work, which included endowing a bed in the Women's Hospital in Crown Street, Sydney, planning hospital beds elsewhere, welcoming immigrants and hosting them in members' homes. They raised funds to alleviate suffering, famine and epidemics in Ukraine, where 60% of the Jewish population lived in 'damp, congested hovels' and where 'The plight of thousands of orphan children who wandered about by day and settled on doorsteps at night in the cold and famine-stricken streets, was too awful to dwell upon'.[33] Importantly, Dr Fanny was re-elected President of Council *in absentia*.

Media interest in Dr Fanny

Dr Fanny proved newsworthy at home and abroad. While overseas, the media reported her activities and views. The London *Jewish Chronicle* featured her re-evaluation of Council's foundational values, now focused on youth and their future. She feared the perils facing adolescents, and growing rates of intermarriage and assimilation that threatened Jewish continuity. She stressed the need for a Judaic education,

> We are particularly interested in the problem of the adolescent girl, and we aim at continuing the education of Jewish girls after the age of fourteen in the knowledge of their race and religion. We seek also to stimulate among Jewish women a

greater interest in Jewish observances, both at home and in the synagogue ... which will assist them in the education of their children.[34]

Dr Fanny's first visit to Palestine opened her eyes to the reality of the Jewish dream. She witnessed Jews physically creating a viable Jewish homeland. The knowledge she gained influenced the scope of Council's medical and healthcare programs for mothers and children. Interviewed on board the *Esperance*, in February 1926 in Perth on her return to Australia, she spoke of Jewish idealism in Palestine,

Well educated people were to be found working on the roads, and in the marshes, helping to restore their country ... Dr. Reading instanced Tel Aviv, which four years ago had a population of 5,000, and to-day is a flourishing modern city with 40,000 inhabitants, mainly Jewish. Haifa ... was also expanding at a marvellous rate. Intense interest was being taken in agricultural development ... During the prior regime, Palestine was full of malaria, but the new arrivals combated this by planting thousands of eucalyptus trees and cleaning the town.[35]

Dr Fanny said that Jerusalem would always be revered by Christians, Jews and Moslems; and expressed faith in the harmonious interaction of Arabs and Jews. Her hopes sprang from Arab recognition of, 'the wonderful work they [the Jews] have done in introducing agriculture and establishing factories'. A power station to be erected near the Jordan River would supply current, clearly of benefit to all.[36]

Dr Fanny disembarked in Melbourne and travelled by train to Sydney, arriving on 4 March 1926 at Central Station to a warm welcome from Council members. A flurry of media interviews testified to her standing in the general community. The articles reflected her delight in being home, 'Give me Australia to work and live in and all the rest of the world in which to holiday,' she told the *Sun*, Sydney's afternoon paper. She said the 14th Zionist Congress in Vienna and her stay in

Palestine had inspired her. She had gained understanding of the situation and achievements in the Jewish homeland. She was impressed with its world-class hospitals Jews established, the pre-natal clinics and those devoted to child welfare. She gave her impressions of women's clinics in New York, Baltimore and Vienna; and her visits to children's hospitals in Berlin, London and Dublin.[37]

The *Sydney Morning Herald* recorded her impressions of the United States,

> I toured from the west to the east and found everywhere the same thorough methods in operation. Schemes for sight preservation, for a defence against possible tuberculosis, and other diseases, are in general operation. In the worst slums of New York, I saw supplies of pure food being given to poor children – all this to help build up their resistance against disease.[38]

Australian newspapers reflected a wider world for their readers, most of whom rarely travelled overseas. Dr Fanny's review of hospitals and institutions abroad enhanced her reputation in the general and Jewish communities. She mentioned that she studied at the Great Ormond Street Hospital in England; at the Rotunda Women's Hospital in Dublin; and at the Emperor and Empress Frederick Children's Hospital in Berlin, where she worked with the Hospital's renowned Medical Director, Professor Heinrich Finkelstein.

Even the suburban paper the *Propeller*, published in Hurstville, commented on her travels, describing Dr Fanny as 'a well-known resident of Kogarah'. Their article highlighted Council's welcome-home reception for Dr Fanny. The capacity attendance of 250, including her parents and brother, Dr Abraham Reading, reflected public interest. Vice-President of Council, Mrs John Marks, welcomed her home, 'She had been the founder of the Council and the inspiration of its good work in the past, and with the knowledge and experience gained abroad the work of the Council would be greater than ever'.[39]

There were no hints of disharmony in Council ranks in these press reports. Mrs Marks emphasised they had worked amicably together and were strong financially and numerically. Council's treasurer, Mrs Victor Cornfield, reviewed recent achievements, including a £100 donation to the Ukrainian Fund. When Dr Fanny rose to speak, the audience applauded before she uttered a single word, such was their regard for her. She did not disappoint her audience. Her address conveyed her emotions and motivated her members. She spoke of future Council programs, addressing issues dear to her. She reinforced pride in their organisation, as President she was well received because the CJW was respected – in America, England, Ireland and Palestine. The CJW, she said, was her first-born child and, while away, she acquired a second child – Palestine, the National Home.

Dr Fanny described her response to the ancient homeland of the Jewish people, conveying her elation at being on holy ground,

> They were making roads and were changing barren soil to Paradise ... The schools and the University and the revival of Hebrew were a wonder and surprise to her. It was a country in which the Jew is free – freer than anywhere else in the world and where no apology is needed for being a Jew or excuse for the practice of his religious rites and traditional customs.[40]

Hadassah's baby clinics inspired her and she hoped Council would undertake similar maternity projects. She intended to increase Council membership to 1000, so that she could enact 'the big ideas' she had after visiting various parts of the world.

Family letters from Palestine

Dr Fanny's letters from Palestine to her family reveal her shifting perspectives and vivid impressions in December 1925. They document experiences that seeded potential initiatives, and personalities with whom she connected in meaningful ways. In her first letter from Jerusalem, on Sunday 13 December 1925, she described their long journey from Cairo to Jerusalem, the ferry ride across the Suez Canal to East Kantara, thence to Lydda (Lod), where they changed trains and, three hours later, they beheld Jerusalem. She noted sights that included Samuel's tomb, the Mountains of Judea, 'an Arab boy with a flock of sheep [who] might have been David', and the Jewish settlements easily identifiable by their green trees. In Jerusalem, they stayed at the kosher Central Hotel run by the Amdursky family, just inside Jaffa Gate, within the walls of the Old City. Their first negative impressions – dirty streets, white sandy roads and 'crude methods of everything here', as well as the widespread incidence of conjunctivitis in the children – faded quickly. Dr Fanny wrote, 'This is a city the like of which there has been nothing in all our travels … the view of the city from any high point is beautiful. Taken as a whole it is a wonderful city and we are both enraptured with it.' On their first Sabbath eve in their hotel, Fanny and her mother enjoyed the traditional Friday night blessings and prayers. In a letter to family in Sydney and Melbourne, she described the Amdursky children's beautiful singing voices, 'a tiny girl has the sweetest of voices and a son has a magnificent tenor – they are most musical and it is a vocal treat, their benching [grace after the sabbath meal], well your mother just swallows it all in'. The next day they visited the Hadassah Infant Welfare Centre, where Dr Fanny admired their 'pre-maternity' work, 'I was amazed to see the thorough efficiency of their work'.

Seeing their Zionist dream translated into reality was an intensely emotional experience,

> We are most happy to be here, I can't express my feelings and mother's to you. It is as if you had lost something so dear to you and now had found it again. The atmosphere of purity, wholesomeness of the Jewish spirit pervades all things. At midnight a perfect peace hangs over the city – what a contrast to Cairo

with its night life, gaiety and laxity – here is all seriousness and the harmony of its diverse inhabitants to me is marvellous … Everything is of interest here, fancy having Jewish carriages, Jewish bus drivers, Jewish police (also Arabic and a few English officials) Jewish everything and Hebrew spoken by the children is a real live language.[41]

The primitive infrastructure and public services no longer troubled her. Two weeks later, with Jerusalem drenched in rain, she wrote, 'you ought to see the streets and pavements full of white mud but no one minds. They all look forward to the day not far distant when their streets will be clean like ours'.[42]

Every step Dr Fanny took brought history alive for her. In December, with Esther Rose, she visited Balfouriya, a moshav in northern Palestine named for Lord Arthur James Balfour, who signed the Balfour Declaration on 2 November 1917. Established in 1922 by 18 Jewish pioneers, Balfouriya was the first village founded in Palestine after the Balfour Declaration. Lord Balfour, who attended the opening of the Hebrew University on 1 April 1925 on Mount Scopus, visited Balfouriya a few days later, on 6 April 1925, and gave it his blessing, only eight months before Dr Fanny's visit there that year. Balfouriya was near Afula in the Jezreel Valley, which they also visited. Their tour included Ein Kerem, an ancient village south-west of Jerusalem; Ein Harod, a kibbutz founded in 1921; Tel Joseph (originally part of Ein Harod), where they slept one night in the barracks; Tiberius on Lake Galilee, where Esther Rose bathed in the hot springs, and where they visited the tomb of Rabbi Meir Baal-HaNess (Rabbi Meir the miracle worker); and Safed, the centre of mystical Judaism. They spent sabbath in Haifa and, from Mount Carmel, admired the port that Fanny predicted 'would be a great harbour'. They visited Migdal (Magdala in Aramaic, the ancient settlement where Mary Magdalene had lived) near the Sea of Galilee; and the old colony of Rosh Pina, the first supported by Baron Edmond de Rothschild, which in 1922 had a population of 468, of whom 460 were Jews. From there they travelled to Rehovot and on to Tel Aviv, which captivated Dr Fanny, who described it in glowing terms,

> Tel Aviv is a 100 percent Jewish city. It is such a peculiar sensation to see everything here built, made and traded by Jews. Only Jews parade the streets and it is a busy, noisy place. Yesterday Shabbos not a shop open, everyone going to shool [shul] or promenading the beautiful streets. On Friday night through every window one saw the Shabos candles.[43]

Dr Fanny met several dignitaries, including Russian-born Zionist leader and President of the Jewish National Fund, Menachem Ussishkin. She had met him four months previously, in August 1925 in Vienna at the Zionist Congress. Ussishkin played a role in the establishment of the Hebrew University and attended the University's opening by Lord Arthur Balfour. Ussishkin was a Labour Zionist, who advocated for the establishment of agricultural settlements, some of which Dr Fanny visited. It is likely she discussed with Ussishkin the future of these kibbutzim and moshavim and their role in the revival of the Jewish homeland, and what her Council could do for their social welfare and for the Jewish National Fund (JNF). The meeting would clarify the potential contributions of the Jewish diaspora to their work in Palestine, which focused mainly on the acquisition of land so crucial to agricultural initiatives.

In 1925, Dr Fanny believed the British Mandatory power would honour the Balfour Declaration and promote the development of a Jewish national home. She respected British institutions, and her family had demonstrated their loyalty to the British Empire during the First World War, when her three brothers enlisted to serve 'King and Country'. The (Acting) High Commissioner for Palestine in Lord Herbert Plumer's absence, Sir George Stewart Symes, who was also ending his term as Governor of the Palestine North District (1920–1925), invited Dr Fanny and her mother to their 'At Home'. While Symes' hospitality was a social highlight of her stay in Jerusalem, later an ideological chasm would divide her from the views of the Mandatory Administration Symes represented, especially when Britain reduced Jewish immigration to Palestine to a trickle in desperate times for Jewish people. Two years after their meeting, in November 1927, Symes told the League of Nations, 'in present circumstances, the Administration … realised the necessity for restriction on the number of Jews entering Palestine immediately'.[44]

Dr Fanny's meeting with the first Attorney-General of Mandatory Palestine, Norman Bentwich, was warm and cordial. He and his wife invited her and her mother to a luncheon at their Jerusalem home, an opportunity for an exchange of ideas in a private setting. This gathering was a success and Dr Fanny wrote, 'Very fine English people, would have seen more of them but they went last week for a trip to Mount Sinai'. Their friendship revived in September 1938, when Professor Bentwich sought support in Sydney for the Hebrew University of Jerusalem.

The 'orphans and baby home' in Jerusalem touched Dr Fanny profoundly. The head of the American Jewish JOINT distribution relief work in Palestine, Miss Berger, took Dr Fanny and her mother there. Afterwards, she invited them to her home, where they met 'interesting women', including Mrs Magnes, wife of the First Chancellor of the Hebrew University, Dr Judah Magnes. That same week, they visited a Hebrew kindergarten,

> So beautifully arranged and lovely children all speaking Hebrew – their ages from three to six, and even have an orchestra of 20 themselves conducted by each one in turn. You would have loved to have seen them. We gave some sweets to be distributed … and the thanks in Hebrew gave us so much pleasure.[45]

Dr Fanny had toured the country, met the chalutzim, the pioneers, and admired their progress. It had been an emotional journey for her, witnessing the partial fulfillment of the Zionist vision. As a pragmatist, however, she knew there were challenges ahead. Many influential people she met thought she should stay and work in Palestine and urged her to do so. Whether she could be tempted to throw in her lot with the *Yishuv* was a proposal made and discussed seriously at that time by her admirers in Palestine, who respected her reputation in medical and public spheres. If she had taken such a step, it would have had dire consequences for her Council in Australia, which already showed signs of stress in her absence. In December 1925 in Rehovot, Dr Fanny addressed 100 women in the home of her friend Rose Slutzkin,

> I was asked to tell them what I thought of their work and to tell them about the CJW, which I did. They all enjoyed what I said and many of them have tried to prevail on me to stay here and organise some unity between them. There are so many factions, cliques, institutions here that they need some sort of federation and they think such a leader and outside force as I would be, is needed here. But my home ties and dear ones are more to me and there is plenty to do in our part of the world and I told them I could do more for them in Australia perhaps.[46]

They returned briefly to Jerusalem and left there on 19 January 1926 to board the *Esperance Bay* two days later in Port Said, bound for 'home sweet home',[47] and scheduled to arrive on 17 February 1926 in Melbourne.

Family relationships

Dr Fanny's personal letters to her family during this extended period apart tell an intimate story and provide evidence of a close-knit and mutually supportive family. She and her mother were homesick and yearned to be with their family again in Melbourne and Sydney. They had left her father, Nathan, alone in the family home in Melbourne, with his daughter 'Ray' and her husband Benjamin as Nathan's sole support in his wife's lengthy absence. Dr Fanny's brothers 'Abe' (Abraham) and 'Lew' (Lewis) were in Sydney. Hyman, who spent some time with them in the USA, returned to Melbourne for a period of time. Dr Fanny's letters shuttled back and forth between the families in Melbourne and Sydney. In her letters, Dr Fanny addressed them collectively as 'Dear people'.

Dr Fanny's concern for the family was always uppermost on her mind, as evident in a letter she penned on 16 July 1925 from the Regent Palace Hotel in Piccadilly Circus. She was deeply invested in the health of every member of the family, assuming responsibility for their wellbeing. Both Fanny and her mother, she wrote, were 'delighted' to receive letters from home but distressed by news of her father's health issues. Her letter conveyed an explicit reproach to the family whom she thought failed to act in his best interests, her response sharpened by her realisation that, had she been there, she would have acted differently, 'he should have gone to Sydney where Abe could have looked after him … instead of Dad suffering at home'. She was relieved that Ray's baby boy 'is getting on better now'. She reassured the family that their mother was fully recovered from the flu contracted in the United States, 'She picked up so wonderfully on the boat and she is now very well too'. They were both 'glad to hear from Abe that he too is better and not so troubled with indigestion', adding somewhat tongue-in-cheek, 'Lew I imagine is always very well'.

Dr Fanny missed especially her brother Dr Abraham Reading, with whom she enjoyed a close personal and professional relationship. While spending one month in Dublin studying obstetrics and midwifery at the Rotunda Hospital, he was in her thoughts constantly. She wrote several lengthy letters to Abe, filled with medical news concerning new surgical instruments, advances in surgical procedures and different ways of treating complicated obstetrical cases. In passing, she mentioned she had not been sightseeing at all. Clearly, she had no time to explore the world around her in Ireland, either ideologically, historically or scenically. She was focused exclusively on the work in hand and wished that her brother could have benefited from the introduction to new surgical methodologies, which she promised to talk about on her return. In Ireland, professional work was her priority and she seized every opportunity to advance her qualifications. While letters from Dublin to her brother are medical in content, her terms of endearment reveal the strength of their sibling relationship. Writing from Dublin's Rotunda Hospital on 13 October 1925, she asks him to 'Apply for extension of leave of absence from Kog. [Kogarah] Hosp. [Hospital]. Please dear boy for me'.[48] Abe was ever present in her thoughts, especially when she watched an operation conducted by the brilliant surgeon Dr Solomon, who kept up a commentary and gave 'tips'. She wrote, 'I will endeavour to explain these to you. Wish you could have seen him at work – you could have learned a lot. A new edition of his book will be out next week and I'll bring it back home'. Dr Fanny ends her letter affectionately,

> Well, dear boy, I feel so selfish being away so long and I can assure you Mum and I are most anxious to get back and be with you all again – we are counting the weeks and hope to return as soon as ever we can. Our best love to you and all in Melb [Melbourne] … Yours ever, Fanny.[49]

Dr Fanny was indebted to her brother Abe for his financial support. On 16 July 1925, writing from London, she thanked him for money he had sent, 'our Bank … let me know that the money you cabled had arrived, for which you have our most heartfelt and grateful thanks. We do appreciate all you are doing for us and you can depend on us we will do our best to make it go as far as possible.'[50] She and her mother were frugal, despite the attractive goods available. From Venice, on 13 August 1925, she wrote that shops in St Mark's Square were so tempting, 'the beads that only Venice makes, the glassware, the lace, the shawls, leather goods etc. If only one had tons of money what beautiful things there are to buy'.[51] On a strict budget, Dr Fanny splurged on medical instruments bought for her 'dear boy' Abe. She reported on their 'cheap' accommodation and on unexpected expenses in Lucerne, 'On the continent, you have to pay for soap and baths – so you can't have a bath every day … Also the beer in Switzerland is wonderfully good, v.light [sic] and so cheap'.[52] On 18 September 1925, writing to both Abe and Lewis, it's clear that Lewis also contributed to their trip. She also reveals she hasn't curbed her one extravagance – buying Abe the latest medical instruments, this time in Vienna,

> Vienna cost us a great deal, we were there three weeks and five days, and money went there on Clinics and a Zeiss cystoscope, which I hope you will be pleased with. I couldn't resist buying these for you. I got some Wertheim and Weibl forceps for hysterectomy etc. and other uterine op instruments.[53]

The letter ends affectionately, 'Our best love to you both and our best wishes to you all for a happy and prosperous new year, Yours ever, Fanny'.

On 23 November 1925, writing from British Medical Association House, London, Dr Fanny penned a loving letter to her father, addressing him as 'My dear Dad'. They were so glad to hear he was well, 'Sorry you miss us so much, we miss you and will be glad to be back home again – we didn't imagine we would be away so long'. She told him that she had been busy in London attending hospitals and completing an anaesthetics course.[54] A letter written from Jerusalem on 28 December 1925 once again highlights warm family bonds. Abe remembered her 41st birthday on 2 December 1925 and sent a cable that, in turn, reminded her she had neglected to send 'best wishes to Lew, Abe and Hyam for their respective birthdays and this is somewhat late, all the same we wish you all very many happy returns of the day and trust you will all be spared to us for 120 years (as your mother would say)'.[55]

From Jerusalem, she wrote they would leave Palestine on either 19 or 20 January 1926 to board the *Esperance Bay* in Port Said on 21 January, bound for Melbourne. She emphasised their longing for a reunion with loved ones,

> We shall soon be with you again and you can have no idea how anxious we are to be with you all – as the time draws nearer we

are more and more homesick – don't know how the time has gone and we have been so long away. Keep well all you dear people, the best of all love from all of us to you all. Until we see you, Yours ever, Fanny.[56]

Centrality of youth in Council's future

Educating youth to play their part was central to Dr Fanny's vision for Council's future. Their participation was vital to ensure Council's leadership succession, to guarantee a viable and enduring organisation, and to create linkages between diaspora Jewry and the *Yishuv* in Palestine. She created age-appropriate sections and challenged youth to implement social justice programs. On 15 March 1926 in Sydney, ten days after her return, more than 200 young boys and girls held a welcome-home party in her honour,

> ... this gathering of young people compared most favourably with all the institutions and associations of Jewish young people that she had come into intimate contact [with] during her visit abroad. She had been proud to be able to tell others what a fine body of young people Australian Jewry possessed.[57]

Dr Fanny spoke about Junior Hadassah, an organisation with 5000 members in 106 centres in the United States that supported the Girls' Village for orphans in Palestine, where children worked domestically and in agriculture. She investigated the Inter-University Jewish Federation, in London, which contributed to the Hebrew Library in Jerusalem and raised funds for a student hostel at the Hebrew University. She spoke of Palestine's youth,

> ... these young pioneers were seriously shouldering the responsibilities of our people and were working wholeheartedly with mind and body to show the world that the Jew can once again be a tiller of the soil and produce from these tracts of country

which had lain idle for centuries, the richest of grain and cereals. Their enthusiasm for the Hebrew language was as great as their love for the Holy Land …[58]

Dr Fanny's new worldview focused mainly on young people, their recruitment and education. She was pleased a Jewish Boy Scout movement had started in Sydney and hoped a girl guide movement would follow. They should increase membership, reduce the annual subscription, and improve the choir, and dramatic and sewing circles. She suggested a first-aid class, a Hebrew conversational class and a Council Juniors section. The girls' sub-committee report mirrored her inclusive approach, 'it is desired in the interests of young Jewish womanhood of this State, that every girl lend her aid and co-operation in the work to be undertaken'.[59]

Dr Fanny encouraged youth and young women to participate in community affairs for the betterment of humanity. She noted overseas youth projects suitable for Australia. American Jewish women, through organisations such as the Young Women's Hebrew Associations and the Crippled Children's Organisation, supported the involvement of younger women. Younger married women 'realised their responsibilities and devoted much time to the work of these various organisations – many of them had most prominent positions and were excellent public speakers'.[60] In England, women and girls did excellent work among the poorer Jews in the East End of London. In particular, 'The youth of Palestine, especially the girls, were working on the land with an idealism that did not find its equal in the world. The conditions prevailing and the increasing immigration need our sympathy which should be practical'.[61]

New projects and initiatives

Stimulated and energised by her year abroad, Dr Fanny translated her 'big ideas' into realities. Eager to maintain links made with overseas organisations, she began the monthly *Council Bulletin*, filled with educational articles and reports, to be circulated at home and abroad. Her major priority remained the work of Council's Immigration Welfare Committee in Sydney, and the Welcome Association in Fremantle. However, she expanded Council's services for newcomers, establishing an employment bureau, 'to assist the immigrants who will surely come to these shores in the next few years'. Impressed with NCJW's Americanisation classes, 'where young and old "foreign Jews" were being taught English', she pioneered the concept in Sydney, under the aegis of Dora Abramovitch, who also edited the *Council Bulletin*.[62]

Dr Fanny encouraged members to liaise with organisations aligned with their own ideals – at the invitation of the New Settlers' League, Council's Immigration Committee hosted all immigrants arriving on the *Baradine*. The committee viewed it as an opportunity 'to educate newcomers to Australia in ideas of religious toleration. By showing what Jewish hospitality means … much good could be effected.'[63] Dr Fanny liaised with metropolitan and national organisations, nurturing her connection with the National Council of Women and friendships with leaders such as Jessie Street and the delegates with whom she had attended the International Quinquennial Conference in Washington. With 40 members in tow, on 29 April 1926 she attended National Council of Women's luncheon in honour of Lady Stonehaven.[64] She participated in their programs that mirrored her stand on socio-political issues. On 18 April 1929, for example, she participated in their discussions on 'sex prejudice' that denied competent career women positions they deserved; the nomination of women representatives on standing committees of the League of Nations and the International Labour Office; the increasing number of assaults on women and children; and the potential amendment of the Crimes Act.[65]

From the moment Dr Fanny returned to Australia in 1926, she emphasised the role of youth, education, philanthropy, Zionism and new services for immigrants,[66]

> The Immigrant Welfare section's work during the year has been a boon to Sydney Jewry. The Jewish Men's Hostel during the four months of its existence has provided nearly 15,000 beds. Assistance of all kinds in all problems is given to immigrants and they are made to feel welcome in the land of their adoption.[67]

Philanthropy abroad and at home was also her priority, Council paid £2,000 towards the Maternity Ward in the Misgav Ladach Hospital in Jerusalem; and donated a bed to the Crown Street Women's Hospital in Sydney.

Nothing was too big or too small to merit Dr Fanny's attention. Aside from organising Council in every state of the Commonwealth, Dr Fanny focused on the future construction of Council House; the development of her Big Sister mentoring movement; and the endowment of additional beds in the Misgav Ladach Hospital. She hoped 'that all their efforts in the years to come would be crowned with success for their work in the ranks of Judaism and humanity'.[68] Interviewed in Sydney, the reporter noted that she was most interested in the construction of a hostel for Jewish immigrants, 'Ground has been bought in Francis Street, and Dr. Reading is pushing ahead the work of raising funds that will make it possible to begin building operations'.[69] Sadly, there is no record of that dream being realised. While fundraising for major projects in Sydney, Dr Fanny supported Council activities in other States. On 16 April 1929 in Brisbane, she endorsed Council Juniors' '10,000 shillings appeal' to maintain a cot in the maternity ward of a hospital in Palestine, which 'would provide comfort for at least 50 mothers in that country'.[70]

First Jewish Women's Conference of Australasia

The Council emerged as a powerful conduit for social activism. With a substantial membership and multiple welfare programs, recognition of its importance in the social welfare arena came swiftly. Council's first national conference – held 17–25 May 1929 in Sydney – attracted 115 delegates, including representatives from Tasmania, Queensland and New Zealand. Council was ready to transition to national status, with the establishment of the National Council of Jewish Women of Australia (NCJWA),

> Such a united Jewish womanhood will work with a oneness of purpose to give service to themselves, their race, and humanity. It will be an inspiration and force in the lives of all Jewish women. It will bring to them a broader vision, a better understanding, and keener appreciation and knowledge of Jewish women's work … By such a united sisterhood working together, bigger things will be accomplished … The work of such an organisation will know no limitations, all manner of human service will come under its Programme.[71]

In Dr Fanny's presidential address, she focused on secular and religious education of Jewish women and girls, hygiene, child welfare, contact with Jewish women in the 'outback', the education of children and youth, the promotion of Hebrew and training of Hebrew teachers, representation on Jewish education boards, and combatting intermarriage. She highlighted social welfare, immigration, Council Houses in every state, and helping Jews in Eastern Europe and Palestine,

> Such problems concern all Jewish women and only by meeting in such conferences can the best results accrue. These conferences will arouse the Jewish consciousness in our women and girls, making those interested still more keen, and those not so interested will be awakened to a sense of their responsibilities. It is hoped that … the Council spirit of love, understanding and service, [will] be infused throughout the land.[72]

Dr Fanny was delighted that junior delegates ran their own proceedings. She urged boys and girls to continue their Judaic and Hebrew studies, as speaking Hebrew linked Jewish youth around the world.

Seizing opportunities to further her feminist goals, she suggested public-speaking classes for girls to promote their debating skills.[73]

At a National Council of Women luncheon, Dr Fanny reported with undisguised pride that the Jewish women's conference, the first of its kind to be held in Australia, had been most successful, 'and all States in Australia and New Zealand would now be linked up into one Council of Jewish women'.[74] Never one to rest on her laurels, less than four months later she travelled by train across the breadth of the Australian continent to Perth, eager to establish the first Council of Jewish Women in Western Australia. She arrived there, on 16 September 1929, to a warm welcome from a delegation at the station. Media interviews confirmed the international scope of her diplomatic efforts and her activism on behalf of persecuted Jews desperate to reach safer shores. She emphasised Council's aim of educating members, subsidising Jewish education and linking members to important civic and national movements. With rising antisemitism in Europe, she focused on her major priority,

> ... lending financial support to the cause of the brethren in Eastern Europe, and to the restoration of Palestine, meeting Jewish immigrants and advising them on their arrival, supplying information on all immigration problems, co-operating with the States of Australia, Europe and America in immigration problems and aiding Jewish men and women who had become stranded in returning to their relatives overseas.[75]

With a flourishing movement in the Eastern states, she envisioned a unified and truly national organisation. By banding together, 'it was possible to give assistance to Jewish women who had problems of their own which were not common to the rest of the community'.[76] Aside from helping immigrants, members visited the sick, endowed cots, aided the poor and helped to raise the standard of living for Jewish people. She also mentioned a scheme for £100 three-month-long tours to Palestine, so Jews could learn about their homeland.[77]

The *West Australian* reported that Dr Fanny would visit South Australia on her way home to start a Council there. After ten days in Perth forming a Council of Jewish Women, she boarded the train for the long journey home. Seven hours later and 550 kilometres further, on 5 September 1929, the train pulled into Kalgoorlie station, where representatives of the town's Jewish community had gathered on the station platform. Defying fatigue, she addressed them in the Railway Refreshment Rooms and, in that brief whistle stop, formed a Council for Kalgoorlie. She made a great impression on those present and, on behalf of the Kalgoorlie Hebrew Congregation, Mr I. Masel testified to Council's power working for the good of humanity. Dr Fanny outlined Council's two-pronged approach – the particular and the universal – firstly, addressing problems in the Jewish community and, secondly, enacting its humanitarian agenda for 'mankind in general'. She spoke softly and eloquently of the strength of Jewish women to combat antisemitism and alleviate suffering,

> The Council has set before its members the brightest and noblest of Jewish ideals and has proved quite practically that all these ideals can be carried out and used for the benefits of humanity. Only knowledge can break down the ignorance and prejudices of the ages, and Jewish women are equipping themselves with that knowledge of their own people, which alone can make possible a right pride of race and stem the tide of religious intolerance. The Council of Jewish Women is always glad to participate in any movement that is intended to benefit the community and mankind in general.[78]

As far as Adelaide was concerned, Dr Fanny was determined to bring South Australia within Council's ambit and said with dogged determination that she would not leave Adelaide until one was formed.[79] On 29 September 1929, in a motivational speech to energise potential members, she addressed the city's Jewish community. By now, her marketing and communication skills were finely honed and she condensed her agenda into targeted messages that emphasised individual contributions and collective efforts. Merging philosophy and pragmatism, she outlined her greater mission of ensuring the future of the Jewish people and the viability of Judaism,

> Service means the rent we pay for the space we occupy, and some of us do not pay our rent. We ask all our members to give personal service – labour and effort mean so much. More than just money, because they involve sacrifice. Our chief aim is to make Judaism a living force, we want to do away with the present apathy and indifference to Jewish ideals … We want to educate our young girls to knowledge and love for everything Jewish, and to this end we give lectures and arrange study classes for religious and secular subjects.[80]

Dr Fanny's campaign against assimilation and intermarriage – defined as 'acculturation to Australian ways and the disintegration of ethnic distinctiveness'[81] – was her response to challenging trends in the 1920s threatening the continuity of the Australian Jewish community. She planned clubs for young people where they could 'find more happiness among themselves'. Addressing international concerns, she shared her distress at witnessing the devastation of post-war conditions in Eastern Europe and the unhappy lives of many Jewish girls in Vienna and Berlin, who had no freedom or employment and faced 'the menace of the streets'.[82] Her phrase, 'the menace of the streets', implied rape or prostitution, possibly both. Her solution was a 'Big sister' movement, 'to bring girls out as children and give them a chance to grow up as daughters of Israel',[83] and, with her usual optimism, she hoped 30 young girls every year could start their lives anew in Australia. Big Sisters would guide and support Little Sisters from unhappy Eastern Europe.[84] Assisting their brethren in Eastern Europe and helping in the upbuilding of Palestine were Council's foundational objectives.

Dr Fanny spoke passionately of young Jews transforming the land in Palestine, which she witnessed in 1925,

> We have to show the world that Jews can go back to the land, and only the young people can do that. In Palestine we are going to raise ... a peasantry that is intellectual, and that brings all the wealth of science to bear on the problems of the land, and all the beauty of Jewish art to make the life splendid.[85]

Not one to rest on her laurels, on 9 December 1929, Dr Fanny inaugurated the Newcastle Council in New South Wales.[86] She could look back on 1929 as a year of progress and triumph. NCJW now comprised ten Councils and 1500 members in Sydney, Newcastle, Brisbane, South Brisbane, Melbourne, Ballarat, Geelong, Adelaide, Perth and Kalgoorlie; with five Junior Sections in various states and the innovative Sub-Juniors in Sydney for girls aged 9 to 16. She attended the first performance by Sydney Council Juniors' orchestra, comprising 14 instrumental players.[87] This little orchestra represented her dream – young people committed to social justice programs also sharing their passion for music in a social setting that fostered friendships.

By year's end, Dr Fanny's humanitarian agenda had won recognition throughout Australia, and articles published nationally testified to her philanthropic role in the Jewish and general communities,

> Dr. Reading ... is a woman of the highest endeavours and ideals. By her untiring zeal and devotion on behalf of humanity in general, she has won admiration of every Jewish community in Australia ... Her career has been one full of public-spirited acts, the result of wisdom and devotion. Her paramount ideals being philanthropy and education.[88]

National press coverage was consistently positive. The *Sydney Morning Herald* described NCJW as 'an organisation to unite all Jewish women and girls with the ties of love, goodwill, and sisterhood'.[89] In the preceding seven years, 'the highest ideals of sisterhood, co-operation and peace had been promoted'.[90] Dr Fanny spoke of a new era for womanhood, seeing NCJW as the conduit through which Jewish women could work for the benefit of mankind. She hinted at her lifelong re-imagining of the Jewish woman, a transformative process that mobilised women socially, politically and ideologically. She achieved this with religious and secular education; cultural initiatives; social activism; increased political awareness; networking with other faiths, ethnicities and organisations; feminist goals enabling members to fulfill socio-political roles in public affairs; creating organisational structures; and personal and intensive mentoring at all levels of the NCJW,

> The lofty ideals of such a national body will enrich the lives of Jewish womanhood, will banish misunderstanding, and will inculcate a greater expression of Jewish life, religion, and culture. By building up a superior character of fine Jewish womanhood, the council hoped to have a permanent influence for good in Australia. In addition to this, their status would be raised, and they would be able to participate in world conferences of women.[91]

Challenges of the 1930s

The challenges of the new decade would test Dr Fanny's resources and resilience. The Wall Street crash in 1929 in the United States led to the 'Great Depression', bringing about the collapse of the Australian economy. Unemployment peaked at 32 per cent in 1932, and it took almost a decade for Australia to recover.[92] The depression affected all Australian philanthropic institutions, including NCJW. However, according to the President of the Great Synagogue, John Goulston, 'whilst some were thinking of the depression, she [Dr Fanny] accomplished things by hard work'.[93]

Despite unprecedented difficulties, Council balanced its budget.

Council's Thrift Shop collected garments for the poor; assisted Montefiore Home and ran the Employment Bureau.[94] The Great Depression curtailed immigration and the British preference for British migrants remained; and only aliens with £500 landing money or close relatives in Australia to support them were granted government permission to enter the country.[95] The Government estimated the total of Jewish migrants to Australia in 1935 at less than 100.[96] In this restrictive immigration era, Dr Fanny never ceased representations to Government to secure a relaxation of stringent immigration requirements.

In August 1931, Dr Fanny took on the role of National President, relinquishing the position of Sydney Council's President that she held for eight years. When Council conferred Life Presidency on Dr Fanny, she responded that what she had done was only her duty and she would continue the work she loved 'for as many years as strength would be given her'.[97] Two months later, her successor Mrs Harris Cohen presented a formal portrait of Dr Fanny to her, and a roll-top writing desk, 'as an expression of love and admiration for her successful and tireless efforts for the benefit of Judaism and humanity. 1923–1931'.[98]

The portrait taken a few months before her 47th birthday reveals the self-assurance of a mature woman with a confident and unflinching gaze. There was no attempt at the simpering smiles of fashion portraiture of the day. It is the face of a woman who inspires confidence in others, with a serious expression befitting a leader of a national organisation. If one can discern shadows of fatigue under her eyes, it speaks to her arduous hours, her dedication to her medical profession by day and her work for the Council by night. This is clearly an individual who has shed girlish frills and frippery and has emerged as a woman of substance in the community.

At the presentation, Dr Fanny deflected praise from herself, maintaining that Council made her who she was. She urged members to make the most of opportunities and not hide their qualities. She emphasised the commonalities and not the differences of members. They were never asked to show their bank balances, as there were no distinctions between rich and poor.

While appealing for funds for furnishing Council Rooms and, ever the optimist, she hoped 'to even buy the building'.[99] Dr Fanny's focus on a permanent centre for the Jewish community, bringing them together synergistically for the greater good, was her lifelong aspiration. A year later in Melbourne, she lamented, '… our forefathers eighty years ago, when … land was cheap, did not establish a centre for Jews in the city'.[100] Her dream of vacating rented premises and moving to their own Council House in Sydney would be realised only in 1963 when the Fanny Reading Council House opened in Woollahra, where it continues to serve the NCJWA NSW.

Antisemitism threatens Jewish communities in Europe

1930 started happily for Dr Fanny, who played the piano at a Sydney concert, accompanying a gifted violinist.[101] It proved a deceptive start to the decade. In the years ahead, she confronted her worst nightmare – the resurgence of antisemitism that threatened Jewish safety and continuity throughout Europe, beginning in Germany and Austria. Hitler and his Nazi Party's accession to power in 1933 in Germany unleashed antisemitism; and militaristic Brownshirts persecuted Jewish communities. Hitler's antisemitic ideology and the Brownshirts' reign of terror spread rapidly, with countries around the world developing local versions of the Nazi 'shirt' movement. With conditions deteriorating for Jews in Europe, Council's philanthropic work increased, attempting (not always succeeding) to help those fleeing Nazi tyranny, sustaining the few arriving in Australia and providing humanitarian aid for refugees in Palestine. Council's program included immigrant welfare, meeting boats to assist Jewish passengers, supporting their stay in temporary hostels, running an employment and labour department, conducting educational classes, and establishing Council houses for immigrants and homeless boys and girls.[102]

Dr Fanny was preoccupied with Jewish survival but had no conception of the unimaginable genocidal horrors ahead. On 4 January 1932, addressing the Victorian Council in Melbourne, she surmised that, 'should the Hitler faction gain control of the Government … the Jews would certainly be expelled from the country'.[103] She added, 'We are trying to make a national Jewish womanhood of Australia, and then link up with other Jewish women of the world, to help those who are dear to us and are suffering in other lands'. The *Argus* reported,

> Dr Reading appealed for sympathy for those members of the race who were suffering desperate hardships in European countries, especially in Russia and Turkey, and also in Germany … The councils stood … for the survival of the ideals of Judaism and the removal of the evils and problems that beset the Jewish race at present.[104]

With the introduction of the Nuremberg Laws on 15 September 1935 in Germany, Dr Fanny's concern for co-religionists abroad intensified. These laws deprived Jews of citizenship, curtailed their civil rights and imposed a Jewish identity on people of partial Jewish extraction and Jewish converts to Christianity.[105] Discrimination progressed relentlessly, marginalising, disenfranchising, dispossessing, dehumanising and, finally, murdering the Jews. The plight of European Jewry featured prominently at the 2nd Jewish Women's Conference of Australasia in 1932 in Sydney – held eleven days before the opening of the city's Harbour Bridge on 19 March 1932 – which attracted delegates from around Australia and New Zealand. Given what we know now about the wholesale slaughter of the Holocaust, there was a certain unreality about Sir Daniel Levy's opening remarks that 'the days of Jewish persecution were not yet over',[106] and 'They are still feeling an undeserved antagonism'.[107] Mrs Edmond Gates from the National Council of Women declared, 'Hitler's invidious anti-Jewish plans would be met with the greatest opposition from the women of Germany'.[108] While history proved Gates wrong, her comments reveal that the National Council of Women at that time knew of the suffering of Jewish people and were prepared to speak up on their behalf.

Dr Fanny set the tone of conference, 'The best of all impressions to take back from this conference to your States, your cities, and your homes is, that the Council of Jewish Women stands, above all things, for the law of loving kindness,' she said.[109] Rabbi Kirsner's tribute to NCJW touched Dr Fanny so deeply that she 'was unable to reply for several minutes, so great was her emotion'.[110] At a conference luncheon attended by Lady Gwendoline Game, wife of NSW's Governor Sir Phillip Game, and the Lady Mayoress, Mrs S. Walder, Dr Fanny said Jewish women could be relied on to help any cause of benefit to mankind.[111] Lady Game validated this sentiment, 'Your race has a reputation for philanthropy, wit, and brains, and any movement in which you are engaged must be a progressive one'.[112] Dr Fanny's ecumenical approach was evident, with speakers of diverse faiths and beliefs, including Mrs A.H. Austin from the Young Women's Christian Association, who spoke on 'National Ideals', and Professor Francis Anderson from Sydney University, whose subject was 'The League of Nations'.

Dr Fanny's involvement in the movement for peace[113] focused on how the country's Jewish women could unite with their compatriots to 'make their voices heard', 'on such vital questions as the peace of the world and disarmament'.[114] Despite alluding to the 'movement for peace', there is no evidence linking her to the Women's International League for Peace and Freedom Australia (WILPF), which was active in Australia. Nonetheless, she kept her finger on the pulse of feminist-inspired movements in Australia and it was well known that, in 1931, the WILPF collected 117,740 signatures in Australia for a worldwide disarmament declaration initiated by WILPF International. General Sir John Monash, widely respected in the Jewish community, was among the signatories.[115]

In 1932, the Geneva Conference on Reduction and Limitation of Armaments failed WILPF expectations.[116]

These were stressful times but cultural events always diverted her. She gave a recital on 2 May 1932, which 'delighted members with her artistic pianoforte solos';[117] and played two months later at a reception for Benno Moiseiwitsch and his wife.[118] In 1932, Dr Fanny was 48 years old, in the prime of her life but also vulnerable to the toll her medical and Council work had on her health. Was the community sensitive to these pressures? Mrs Harris Cohen, who described her as 'a leader among women … along a road which will have no ending', showed some concern, 'I pray the Almighty to bless her with good health and fullness of years, that we and the community in general will benefit through her leadership'.[119]

The depression curtailed many NCJW' initiatives, and the future of Council's Jewish Men's Hostel in Sydney was uncertain. Opened by Aaron Blashki in 1928,[120] 'the Hostel has been doing good work in sheltering Jewish men who are unemployed', and fortunately a bequest kept it going.[121] At this time of financial hardship, Dr Fanny supported Jewish and gentile causes equitably, including funds raised at a 'Bush Nursing fete' held in September 1932 at Sydney's Government House,

> The objects of the fete are so urgent and vital, viz. the saving of human lives in far out Bush centres, by having a bush nurse stationed in these country districts, that we Jewish women feel that we should assist this very necessary movement in NSW by giving it our support.[122]

Towards the end of 1932, Dr Fanny travelled to Hobart, Tasmania, to create a branch of the NCJW. She spoke of NCJW's commitment to work with other organisations 'for the good of the community'.[123] While there, she also established a Young Men's Hebrew Association (YMHA), a comparable but smaller organisation. Dr Fanny and her brother, Dr Abraham Reading, were jointly responsible for establishing the YMHA in 1930 in Sydney. She urged members to assist the Jewish community in Hobart that had been isolated from Jewish interests, 'but now being a part of the NCJW and the YMHA. they would feel even so far south as Tasmania is, they could be an important and integral part of the Australian Jewish community'.[124]

Outreach and philanthropy

Travelling across vast tracts of the continent, Dr Fanny's outreach to remote parts of Australia represented a radically innovative approach. The outreach that existed in Australia was conducted mainly by Christian churches as part of missionary and conversion programs. Dr Fanny's outreach was aimed at her own community, embedding Jewish women within ethical structures of their ancient faith, while moving them towards personal growth and community development. As her outreach penetrated urban and country areas across the continent, radio broadcasts and newspaper articles told Australians about her work for Jewish women, Judaism, the Jewish homeland and the many causes her organisation supported in Australia. Her profile grew nationally and she earned respect as a woman who worked across ethnicities and faiths, supporting organisations that improved societal standards and structures. Recognition came from diverse sources. Already in 1933 there was acknowledgement in the wider community of her leadership and the impact on Australia of her philanthropic initiatives and her contributions to medicine. The Feminist Club invited to its reception on 30 March 1933 in Sydney 100 women who were the 'most distinguished and fully representative in their own field'.[125] The invitees in medicine were Dr Fanny Reading, Dr Constance d'Arcy, Dr Margaret Harper, Dr Lucy Gullett, Dr Grace Boelke, Dr Elma Sandford Morgan and Dr Kate Ardill-Brice. Two years later, in 1935, Dr Fanny received the King George V Jubilee Medal, in 1937 the King George V1 Coronation Medal and, in 1961, the Member of the Order of the British Empire (MBE) for social welfare services in New South Wales.[126]

Three weeks before the Feminist Club luncheon, Dr Fanny addressed congregants attending the CJW's annual Sabbath Service, a feminist tradition maintained by Councils to the present day. It is held the sabbath before Purim, the festival that honours the courage of the Jewish Queen Esther of Persia, who saved Persian Jews from genocide. After the service, Dr Fanny spoke of antisemitism threatening Jewish people throughout Europe. 'Would that an Esther would rise up today and save our people in Eastern Europe and Germany,' she said.[127] She believed that Jewish women were responsible for perpetuating Judaism, that a Jewish home should become a temple in the service of God, and that Jewish women should do all in their power to help those unjustly victimised,

> by establishing bonds of mutual love and sympathy with our sisters in far distant lands and by encouraging our Australian Jewish women to unite together in one big body, in order to be ready to protect our brethren when oppressed.[128]

She appealed for the preservation of Jewish 'distinctiveness', 'by upholding the customs and ceremonials of our creed and not casting them away'.[129] At Council's tenth anniversary celebrations in 1933, she reflected on their 'noble endeavour for the uplift of humanity generally';[130] and, in a national broadcast to women in eleven Australian cities, she recalled that the NCJW's 22 sections comprised approximately 2000 Jewish women united in one sisterhood for the higher interests of humanity,

> This organisation was established to give service (a) to our God, (b) to our race, (c) to the country in which we live. These aims are based on humanitarian principles and can be well illustrated by what we may call our motto 'Service to God and humanity'.[131]

She highlighted the role of religion in inspiring members to greater efforts and deeds on behalf of humanity, making the world a better place,

> We teach that religion lies in what we do each minute of the day … In education, we have given the Jewish women of Australia a newer outlook and a broader vision … We have discovered potential power amongst them … for unselfish service for the country in which they live. We have educated Jewish women to a better understanding of their duties as citizens …[132]

Dr Fanny spoke of NCJW's philanthropy, which included supporting cancer research, general welfare, and funds, food and clothes for the unemployed. A central pillar of NCJW's mission was their work on behalf of migrants to Australia,

> We are the friends of the immigrant … Immigrants without knowledge of the language, were met, on arrival, were housed, taught the language and customs, found employment and made worthy and respected Australian citizens. For this work alone the Hon. F. S. Boyce, Attorney General of N.S.W., speaking in 1929, called us 'Empire Builders' because of our interest in the new citizens of this mighty continent.[133]

Dr Fanny reviewed NCJW's achievements – the Hospital Committee's visits to hospitals, charitable institutions and asylums that brought 'comfort and cheer to the sick and weary'; the endowment of hospital beds in Melbourne, Perth and Sydney; and financial grants to kindergartens, bush nursing, blind institutes, the Salvation Army, orphanages, crippled children's funds, as well as materially assisting Jews in Europe and Palestine. She touched on her dream of a Council House of their own, and its potential impact on the community,

> Here the stranger and newcomer, the homeless and friendless man or woman, the student away from home will find a home in this city, a roof over their heads and food for their bodies … we shall be rendering a great service to those who for no fault of their own cannot help themselves.[134]

Visiting Melbourne in February 1934 to spend time with her ailing father, she was gratified to learn that Melbourne's CJW had secured a building in Collins Street, which opened on 14 April 1934 and, in her eyes, constituted a heritage for their children.[135] In her broadcast, she referred to another of her cherished goals, the establishment of a hospital and Jewish community centre in the old Montefiore Home in Sydney.[136]

Dr Fanny networked with diverse organisations, including the National Council of Women, the League of Nations, New Settlers' League, and Travellers' Aid Society.[137] She spoke of Council's willingness to work with them, and foreshadowed Council's engagement with the challenges of the next decade,

> I want the women leaders in Australia ... to know that their Jewish sisters of the National Council are ever ready to cooperate and assist worthy national and local causes, that in us they have an organised band of trained workers who are able and willing to render service ... I appeal to all our members ... to begin our second decade with renewed courage, perseverance and understanding.[138]

The playwright and director

Having mastered music and medicine, Dr Fanny for the first time tried her hand at drama. She wrote and directed a theatrical presentation that formed part of the larger British Empire Pageant in Sydney, which brought together 650 participants from all sectors of society. Her play, staged on 26, 27 and 28 September 1933 in the Sydney Town Hall in aid of the United Charities Fund, attracted attention. Her first and only foray into drama, the play, entitled 'Palestine: The Seventh Dominion', was a central feature of the pageant,

> This pageant within a pageant will begin with Isaiah, the Hebrew prophet, and will follow the epic of Jewish history throughout the ages, and particularly within the British Empire, ending with

the handing of the Charter of Palestine to the Jewish race. This unique episode ... is under the direction of Dr. Fanny Reading (president of the National Council of Jewish Women) and Mrs. Victor Cornfield (president of the Sydney section).[139]

The pageant comprised 14 sections, including 'The Seventh Dominion', 'arranged by Dr. Fanny Reading under the auspices of the National Council of Jewish Women'.[140] Several YMHA members were in the cast of biblical heroes and luminaries associated with Zionism and the Jewish homeland, characters such as Isaiah, Moses, Disraeli, Lord Rothschild, Theodor Herzl, Captain Trumpeldor, Chaim Weizmann, Lord Balfour and Queen Victoria,

> Miss Sylvia Hertzberg was the able chronicler who unfolded from a scroll, written by Dr. Fanny Reading, the history of our race, what they have suffered and what they have given to the world ... Amidst great applause the episode closed with the unfurling of the Union Jack to the stirring sound of the trumpet.[141]

Surprisingly, Dr Fanny excluded Ze'ev Jabotinsky from her play. When she attended the Zionist Congress in 1925 in Vienna, she heard both Chaim Weizmann and Jabotinsky deliver keynote addresses and was impressed with their oratorical substance and style. Was her omission of Jabotinsky a hint of her preference for the ideology expounded by Weizmann, and condemnation of that proposed by Jabotinsky? Both were political Zionists, but Weizmann believed that diplomacy with power brokers could achieve Zionism's objective of a return to the ancestral land of the Jews. Jabotinsky's militaristic stance – his proclaimed readiness to fight the Mandatory authority in order to achieve his Revisionist Party's aims – if incorporated in the pageant, could potentially have alienated a substantial number of the Jewish and general public, who were confirmed British loyalists. Dr Fanny clearly weighed up these competing claims and sought to portray Weizmann's moderate Zionism. He was a figure admired universally, esteemed by the British establishment. Her decision was well considered in the context of world events in 1933. Dr Fanny's views on Zionism, however, ripened with the decades. The views she held in the 1930s differed from those she expressed during her defamation trial in 1949, *Dr Fanny Reading v. National Press Pty. Ltd.*, when her responses were based on the new historical dispensation for the Jewish people at that time. They were diametrically different stages in her life and in the history of the Jewish people.

Josiah Wedgwood's The Seventh Dominion

The Seventh Dominion, the title of Dr Fanny's drama, was inspired by the book written by Colonel Josiah Wedgwood. Her appropriation of Wedgwood's title in its entirety was not an act of plagiarism but a validation of his political views on the future of the Jewish people and their ineradicable connection to their homeland Palestine – views that mirrored her own convictions. Dr Fanny enjoyed a close friendship in Sydney with Josiah Wedgwood's daughter, Camilla Hildegarde Wedgewood, anthropologist, educator and firm advocate of her father's views. She and Dr Fanny would have discussed his book, published in February 1928, five years before Dr Fanny wrote and directed her own play. It is likely that Camilla either lent or gave a copy to Dr Fanny sometime after Camilla's arrival in Australia in 1928 to take up an anthropology lectureship at Sydney University. She left in 1930 for the University of Cape Town; and returned to Sydney, in June 1935, as Principal of Women's College at Sydney University. A member of the Australian Student Christian Movement, the Australian Federation of University Women, and the Australian Institute of International Affairs, she was also associated with the Rachel Forster Hospital for Women and Children, where Dr Fanny worked as an honorary Medical Officer of Health.[142] Camilla's Fabian and Quaker social conscience led her to champion many causes dear to Dr Fanny's heart,

She pleaded the cause of Jewish and non-Aryan Christian victims of Nazi persecution before (Sir) John McEwen, minister for the interior. In close contact with her father, she raised money for refugee passages to Australia ... She publicly protested against the treatment of the internees in the *Dunera* and the refugees in the *Strouma* which sank in the Black Sea.[143]

Her father, Josiah Wedgwood, a member of the British House of Commons, visited Palestine in 1926. Appalled by antisemitism among British officials tasked with administering the Mandatory government, he wrote his book in protest against their obstruction of Jewish social and economic advancement, westernisation, and their constraints on immigration and Jewish land purchase in Palestine. Wedgwood noted that British officials who had served in Egypt before 1920 resented the Balfour Declaration; and British administrators saw the Jewish vision of a prosperous country teeming with factories as a vulgarisation of the Holy Land. He argued,

> ... since the British Commonwealth was already multinational – French Canadians and Dutch South Africans were loyal subjects of the Crown – admitting Jews into the Commonwealth would not be a radical policy move. Moreover, Britain would benefit from the arrangement. Palestine ... was the universal link to Africa and Asia: all air, land and sea routes crossed between Suez and Haifa ... Since the Jews of Palestine depended on British protection, Britain could rely on them. The two peoples also had a common foe: Mussolini and his expansionist tendencies.[144]

Wedgwood highlighted the benefits of an expanded Jewish presence, including imported agricultural methods, new markets in Jerusalem and Tel Aviv, the draining of malarial swamps, an increase in physicians and veterinarians, and new roads. He referred to two documents responsible for the British Mandate – the Balfour Declaration and the League of Nations Mandate for Palestine, the latter transforming 'the intent of the

Balfour Declaration into the reality of internationally accepted policy. Article II stated that: The Mandatary shall be responsible for placing the country under such political, administrative and economic conditions as will secure the establishment of the Jewish National Home ...'[145]

Wedgwood concluded, 'London ... ought to convert Palestine from a Mandate into a Crown Colony, encourage Jewish immigration for a generation, and then grant the colony independence as the Seventh Dominion within the British Commonwealth of Nations'.[146] Response to Wedgwood's book was mixed. In 1928, President of the World Zionist Organization, Chaim Weizmann 'did not feel that a Jewish state was politically, diplomatically, or even demographically possible'.[147] Jabotinsky, leader of the Revisionist Zionists, supported the idea of the Seventh Dominion; and the All-Palestine Zionist' Revisionist Conference in Jerusalem 'endorsed and welcomed' a formal resolution in support of creating Palestine as the Seventh Dominion within the British Commonwealth. On 24 January 1929, with Jabotinsky's support, Wedgwood inaugurated the Seventh Dominion (Palestine) League to promote Palestine as the national home of the Jewish people in cooperation with the British Administration in the hope that when independence came the inhabitants of Palestine would choose the status of a self-governing Dominion. The League hoped 'to further the friendship between the British and Jewish people, based on Justice, on common interests and common ideals'.[148]

In 1929, Dr Fanny's friend, Henrietta Szold, founder of the women's Zionist organisation Hadassah, saw the League as a repudiation of the Mandate, 'To Szold, the movement was premature and excited difficulties between Arabs and Jews and between Zionists and friendly non-Zionists'.[149] The violent 1929 Arab riots in Palestine ended Wedgwood's hopes of the Seventh Dominion. After the findings of the Shaw Commission, Lord Passfield (Sidney Webb) suspended new immigration and, in October 1930, released his report. Its conclusions were devastating for Zionists, 'In effect, it called for a cessation of Jewish immigration and land purchase. The Seventh Dominion idea collapsed under this prevailing atmosphere of distrust and mutual recrimination'.[150] Wedgwood stated,

> About two years ago I helped to found a Seventh Dominion League of Englishmen and Jews ... to develop a friendly Palestine and a sound prop to the Empire. We had fair success in the House of Commons and outside; but the business was not quite approved by the Zionist Organization. They thought that the Jews in Germany and America ... distrusted England and would suspect the cloven hoof of imperialism.[151]

The question arises as to whether, in 1933, Dr Fanny's title of her play endorsed Josiah Wedgwood's view that at the end of the British Mandate, Palestine should be granted a status similar to Australia, Canada, South Africa, Newfoundland, Irish Free Republic and New Zealand and become a Jewish state within the British Empire, the 'Seventh Dominion'. Eight years later, on 7 May 1941 in Newcastle, she answered that question, 'The hope that Palestine would become a Jewish country and be included in the British Commonwealth of Nations was already an ideal with much foundation'.[152] Her title for her play affirms unambiguously Wedgwood's political world view. She had a reverence for Zionism and its aim of restoring the national homeland, and she dedicated her organisation to the humanitarian needs of the *Yishuv*. She also affirmed her own loyalty to Britain and that of the NCJW. She told Lady Wakehurst, 'they were proud to be a part of the great British Commonwealth of Nations, which stood for the highest principles of humanity, truth, justice, freedom and liberty'.[153]

As news of rampant antisemitism in Europe reached Australia, Dr Fanny understood this threat was existential for the Jewish people. She focused on the role of women in the creation of the Jewish homeland, which represented the fulfillment of biblical prophecy concerning the return of the Jewish people to their ancient land. For her, Palestine offered safety for the persecuted Jewish masses in Europe. On 1 November 1933 in Sydney, she proposed a toast to Jewish women in Palestine,

> … when the history of the redemption of women is studied it is found that the women of Israel have done the greatest part. They work hard – not merely as idealists, but with practical enthusiasm … university girls gave up careers, to till the soil and work in fields. They worked in unison with the men. The Hadassah medical work staffed and run entirely by women in Palestine stood to their greatest credit. Orphanages and other institutions had been likewise established by women.[154]

Dr Fanny increased the tempo of work in response to the crises abroad. The *Sun* noted, 'Few women in Sydney have greater organising ability than Dr Fanny Reading'; and that she was working on the third Jewish Women's Conference to be held in Melbourne in November 1934. The article added, 'Dr. Reading has sent invitations to delegates in Canada, Palestine, England, South Africa, and the East, and she hopes that most of these countries will be able to send representatives'.[155]

Death of Nathan Jacob Reading

Dr Fanny's 'Dear Dad', Nathan Jacob Reading, died on 19 February 1934, aged 73, in Richmond, Victoria, and was buried in Caulfield South Cemetery in Melbourne. He was well regarded in the Melbourne community as a charitable and hospitable man. The door to his home was always open and the needy were never turned away. He had been sick for some time before his death and Dr Fanny was able to visit him. Deeply attached to her father, as her letters written in 1925 attest, she expressed concerns for his health and regretted that, in her absence, he suffered unnecessarily. 'My dear Dad' was the salutation with which she began letters to her father. In those letters, she told him that both she and her mother missed and loved him and were looking forward to their reunion with him. After his death, his widow Esther Rose left Melbourne for

Sydney, where she spent the remaining 12 years of her life living with Dr Fanny. Her mother now accompanied her to meetings and social functions. The new arrangement was apparent three months after their bereavement, when she accompanied Dr Fanny to a Council meeting. The bereavement affected Dr Fanny deeply and she reflected philosophically on what was truly important in life and in society,

> Dr Reading ... felt that in every phase of human activity, more tolerance should be shown, not only in Council's sphere but in our relations with all Jewish organisations and to those of non-Jewish origin also. Only in this way could happiness result.[156]

Three days later, she urged members to avoid pettiness, and reiterated her message of 'service, tolerance and goodwill',

> With these as their watch words, this band of wonderful women would become a great blessing to humanity in general. They would rise above the small and petty jealousies so often present in women's organisations and become better and superior types of Jewish womanhood.[157]

Later that year, she emphasised 'the giving of self' in services to others.[158] On 25 October 1934, accompanied by her mother, she travelled to Melbourne to finalise arrangements for NCJW's conference to be held 7–19 November 1934.[159]

Third Jewish Women's Conference of Australasia

The Third Jewish Women's Conference represented a triumph for Dr Fanny and underscored the achievements and prestige of NCJW. State Government and City Council representatives attended, and international delegates included South African parliamentarian Morris Alexander.

Melbourne's Lord Mayor, Sir Alexander George Wales, declared the Empire offered opportunities to the Jewish race and that Jews appreciated British policy, giving in return the very best of their race to England and her Dominions, 'Men who had held the highest positions in almost every walk of life had been Jews, showing loyalty and courage which, in itself, was proof of their gratitude'.[160]

Despite virulent antisemitism abroad, Dr Fanny never shrank from publicly identifying herself with the Jewish people and their destiny, positioning herself as spokeswoman for her disadvantaged sisters abroad. Participating in the National Council of Women's International Congress – held almost concurrently with her own in Melbourne – she spoke of challenges faced by Jewish women who migrated to Australia; and Council's efforts to assist them in adapting to new conditions in a strange land, as well as helping them to develop a civic conscience,

> We Jewish women realise as others have done, that a country or a nation will be as strong as its women, so in the countries in which we reside we try to make that country strong by supplementing the education of Jewish women, so that they may understand better the responsibilities and duties which they owe to that country.[161]

When Dr Fanny welcomed Lady Isaacs, wife of the Governor-General of Australia, at a reception in March 1935 in Sydney, she emphasised that the most valuable aspect of Council work was 'to bridge the gap between their own land and their new home for foreigners who came to Australia to settle'.[162]

Presenting to the gentile world the complex challenges of contemporary Jewish life in Australia was part of Dr Fanny's brief as an ambassador for her people. She articulated the loyalty of the Jewish community to Great Britain and, simultaneously, their own duty to Jews suffering in other lands. At a reception on 26 May 1935 in Sydney marking the King's Silver Jubilee year, she addressed 200 people, including the Lord

Mayor, Alderman A.L. Parker, and the Minister for Education D.H. Drummond. She described her speech as 'a mixture of joy and sorrow'. She emphasised the allegiance of Jews to the British throne, 'which granted them the liberty and tolerance of citizenship'. They also had to remember the duty due to their own race and to combine these two duties in work in the community in which they lived.[163] 'We feel gratitude to the British Empire. We have felt the tolerance that is accorded all of her citizens ... I must speak of our sadness, for the fate of Jews in far countries, and the lack of peace in the world'[164] In closing, she summed up her work ethic, stating simply that she preferred 'the hand that helps to the hand that claps'.[165]

The proliferation of splinter bodies in Jewish communal life and the wasteful duplication of efforts concerned Dr Fanny and she supported the formation of a body to unify and represent the Australian Jewish community. On 18 November 1935, she pleaded that the Jewish community should focus on the common good of Jewry,

> It was a duty of the Council to assist in creating a strong unity and a solid community representing Jewish life in its manifold features ... By more complete understanding a unified community would be able to promote Jewish life in its truest and best aspects.[166]

This culminated in her support for the New South Wales Jewish Board of Deputies created in 1945, which represented the NSW Jewish community 'With one voice'.

Dr Fanny's illness

For a woman very much in the public eye, there was a disconcerting gap in media coverage of Dr Fanny's activities from the end of November 1935 to the beginning of May 1936. It is clear from newspaper records that in September 1935, accompanied by her mother, she attended the

British Medical Association Conference in Melbourne and met Council representatives. On 18 November 1935, she participated in a meeting to promote peace and unity in Sydney Jewish organisations. Her absence from Council affairs begins at that point, indicating the start of an illness, certainly from early December 1935 to the beginning of May 1936. While there are no medical records identifying her illness, it was serious enough to distance her from all Council activities, as it spanned a period of escalating antisemitism abroad that otherwise would have prompted her to representations on behalf of her people. Instead, there was silence. There were expressions of regret at the illness of 'our National President, Dr Fanny Reading'.[167] More than five months after the onset of her illness and still far from well, on 4 May 1936 she gave 'an interesting and informative address on the ideals and aims to be striven for by ... young Jewish women'.[168] It was impossible for her to resist, at least, partial involvement with her Council, despite her frailty at that time.

After an absence of almost six months, on 1 June 1936 Dr Fanny documented important changes in Australian immigration procedures. The Federal Government began issuing landing permits to non-guaranteed migrants, provided they held £500, and were experts in certain industries, 'However, selection would be based upon "general assimilability", which meant that people of Northern European stock would be given preference and the possible establishment of "alien communities" avoided'.[169] The Minister of the Interior in Canberra informed NCJW that stringent immigration restrictions were relaxed and that entrance to Australia would be easier.[170] In previous years, she had longed for just such a development. 'It would now be imperative for the Council to continue immigration work,' she said,[171] and immediately requested that members donate £1/1/- or more to the German Relief Fund, irrespective of amounts given by their husbands.

Firmly at the helm of her organisation again, Dr Fanny immersed herself in a demanding schedule. She spoke at a memorial meeting for Dr Nahum Sokolow, who died on 17 May 1936 in England. Members stood in silence in tribute to a Zionist who had been with Herzl from the beginning. Sokolow's death revived memories of her attendance at the Fourteenth Zionist Congress in 1925 in Vienna, where she heard him speak.

Three weeks later, Ruby Rich, President of the Racial Hygiene Society addressed Council members on venereal disease and related topics. Dr Fanny and Ruby Rich shared several interests – Rich was a concert pianist, community leader and Dr Fanny's longstanding (non-medical) colleague. The Council constituted a valuable forum for Rich, who sought support among women's organisations for the Society's agenda. Although she entitled her talk 'Women's Problems', it was broader than an exposition on curbing venereal disease. She described the trafficking of women in various parts of the world and urged that women's organisations co-operate to help those involved. She spoke about world peace, with which both she and Dr Fanny were preoccupied; and said a committee was recently formed with the aim of sending a representative to the Peace Conference in Geneva.[172] Dr Fanny invited Rich to deliver a paper at the Fourth Jewish Women's Conference of Australasia later that year.[173] She spoke on how women could contribute to world peace through 'ardent pacifism', by supporting the League of Nations' Union, cultivation of international friendships linking mothers of the world, and studying world problems. The major issue, she said, was moral disarmament, 'Disarming the mind of war tendencies, banning war toys, and eliminating from school text-books all references likely to instil animosity to other nations ...'.[174]

Fourth Jewish Women's Conference of Australasia

Ominous signs of war were omnipresent when Dr Fanny presided at the opening of the Fourth Jewish Women's Conference of Australasia, on 10 November 1936 in Adelaide. The next day, Armistice Day, a crowd gathered at the city's war memorial to observe a two-minute silence. The *Advertiser* quoted Hitler, 'The movement [National Socialism] will never perish. It will lead Germany for ever'.[175] Dr Fanny revealed the depth of her pain at events threatening her people. At a mayoral reception in Adelaide's Town Hall, it was clear she was disturbed by the deteriorating situation abroad and the perilous position of Jews. She thanked Adelaide's Lord Mayor, Jonathan Cain, 'for … a reception without regard to race or creed', adding that their reception in Germany would have been very different.[176]

The official opening, attended by delegates from all Australian states and New Zealand, took place with much fanfare in the Adelaide Synagogue in Rundle Street. The *News,* noted, 'Dr Fanny Reading, who presided, was called "Dr Fanny" in a friendly fashion by everybody'.[177] Greetings came from Jewish women's organisations in Palestine, South Africa, England, the United States, New Zealand and all Australian States. On behalf of the Government, E. Anthoney MP, welcomed delegates and praised 'the ideals of the Women's Council – service to God, race, and the country in which its members lived …'.[178] Government and civic representatives at the opening added gravitas; and they conveyed their understanding of the crisis confronting the Jewish people, support that meant much to Dr Fanny. National Council of Women's Federal President, Adelaide Miethke, said conference contributed to understanding each other's problems, 'The sympathy of all women in Australia goes out to your race, a race which has contributed so much of art and culture to civilisation'.[179]

Addressing the twin themes of the devotion to Australia, and love of the Jewish homeland, Dr Fanny stated,

> Australia has no more loyal citizens than the Jew and while we have a duty to and love for the country and people from which we have sprung, it is an entirely separate devotion from that to the country of our habitation. I hope that what we shall achieve

at this conference will be of great service to humanity and to the Jewish race in general.[180]

At the conference dinner, the 'Jewish blue and white flag', adopted twelve years later as the flag of the State of Israel, was displayed between the Union Jack and the Australian flag,[181] possibly the first occasion that the flag of the Zionist movement flew alongside the Australian flag on Australian soil. Despite the demanding conference schedule and the plethora of papers, Dr Fanny managed to address a Sunday afternoon service at Maughan Church. Characteristically, she seized the opportunity to build bridges and to speak to the gentile community on 'Palestine of Today'. She believed conference achieved its purpose, 'We shall all go away from Adelaide better than when we came, and stimulated to greater effort,' she said.[182] The greatest value of conference, she said, was the gathering together of Jewish women, the social contacts, the friendships and the experience of 'a united sisterhood'. She spoke on the plight of Jewish people in Europe that was never far from her thoughts,

> By hearing papers read on modern problems, delegates learned more of the world they were living in, and had their outlook broadened by contact with women from different parts ... The conference was important at present to bring before their people and the general public the serious state of the Jewish people in Europe and the persecution they were suffering there. The final days of the conference ... would be devoted to drawing up a plan of action for the help of persecuted Jews.[183]

At a luncheon for delegates, the guest list spoke to the recognition and support of Council by women's organisations, including the National Council of Women, the Women's Non-Party Association, the Country Women's Association and the Housewives' Association. Gratified by evidence of Council's broad affiliations and seeing it as a conduit for united efforts, Dr Fanny issued a call to all present to work together for the common good and to prepare for the challenges ahead,

We are in sympathy with all work that is for the good of the community and welcome this opportunity of meeting leaders of many good movements. My message to you all is – Let us work together, for who knows what fate tomorrow will bring ...[184]

Social contacts with women leaders, in-depth conference papers and bonds forged with organisations were valuable. Nonetheless, sentiments of support could only partially assuage the anxiety she felt as the situation of Jewry abroad worsened daily. She remembered the small child who fled persecution in Russia, so her people's suffering was close to the bone. She drew on the unity of her organisation, on her faith and the comfort of Jewish prayers and traditions, themes she addressed in a 1937 broadcast on 'Guarding Great Traditions'.[185] As the situation in Europe deteriorated, the necessity of transferring Polish and German children to safety in Palestine was paramount; and she supported an appeal on behalf of children in Palestine by WIZO representative Ida Bension;[185] and attended a reception for her in Sydney.[186]

Throughout this demanding period, NCJW supported local charities. Dr Fanny and a large contingent of members visited Dalwood Children's Home for mothers and babies; and she undertook to collect £100 for the Home.[187] She served as Honorary Medical Officer of the Home for many years;[188] and was awarded Life Governorship of the Dalwood Home for 'splendid work on behalf of the Dalwood Home'.[189]

Visit to Newcastle: 'Service and sacrifice'

Throughout Dr Fanny's life, she led by example and promoted the values by which she lived. Ethics powered her deeds as a medical doctor and as NCJW President, and she shared her values with members. In August 1937, she visited Newcastle, a short car journey north of Sydney. It was easy to get there and, since its inauguration in 1929, she had maintained close contact with their Council. Her visits sprang from interest in their progress and she never missed their AGM. In addressing their members, she acknowledged that Jewish women were fond of the kitchen and loved to give their husbands and children good food, but she urged that this should not be a woman's entire world,

> It was an easy matter to give money when it meant only writing a cheque, but to give personal help with kindness was a far greater gift … By virtue, goodness and wisdom women could help a nation to great heights … The Council needed Jewish women to learn the meaning of service and sacrifice, and to know the past and future of their religion and their country.[190]

The phrase 'service and sacrifice' encapsulated Dr Fanny's core belief. She never spared herself and conducted her Council work in the evenings after seeing patients in her surgery and in hospitals. There were no boundaries between Council work and her medical career, and she was constantly 'on call' for both. In November 1937, she welcomed Lady Wakehurst to a gathering in Sydney and spoke on Council's service at home and abroad,

> We Jewish women formed this organisation 14 years ago, primarily to teach our young women to take up responsibilities and to be good citizens in the country in which they live We must also help our own people, who are being so persecuted in some parts of the world to-day.[191]

Dr Fanny's onerous duties tended to mask her deeply felt *joie de vivre*. She had a ready laugh, enjoyed her brother's (Dr Abe) earthy jokes and could sashay around a dance floor. At a CJW Juniors' dance at the end of 1937, she taught the young girls a 'Palestine folk dance, which many of us joined in and which will be a feature of all our coming dances'.[192] Her dance demonstration dispelled any notion that she was always sedate and staid.

At the last meeting of the year, on 29 December 1937, Council celebrated Chanukah, the festival of lights that dispelled darkness. Given the gloom that enshrouded Jewish people in Europe, this festival of miracles brought hope to celebrants. Rev. Fraeser of Ashfield, recently returned from Palestine, delivered an address that lifted their spirits,

> ... he expressed regret at the suffering that the Jews are bearing in both Palestine the seat of their good work and Germany. He expressed his assurance that the Jews would overcome all this ill feeling, the Jews, Rev. Fraeser exclaimed, 'Have stood at the gravestone of all nations who have persecuted Jewry'.[193]

The new year, 1938, started auspiciously when Dr Fanny created a new section, Sub-Juniors, for 60 children. It was also gratifying that international visitors attended Council meetings, with visitors from South Africa, Germany, Poland, China, England, New Zealand, and locally from Melbourne and Wentworth Falls.[194]

Fifth Jewish Women's Conference of Australasia March 1938

Two major themes – gratitude for the safety and prosperity of Australia as a British Dominion that ensured the wellbeing of its people; and sorrow at the situation of Jews in Europe – dominated the agenda of the Fifth Jewish Women's Conference of Australasia held 9–20 March 1938 in Sydney. Papers explored constructive options and policies, including women's responsibility in world affairs, Jewish contributions to civilisation, Australia's immigration policy, the role of social agencies in meeting the difficulties of refugees, and the position of Jews in Germany. There was also a panel discussion on 'Jewish people and the Future'.[195]

The breadth of Dr Fanny's connections with high-powered women was evident in the presenters from public, academic, professional and social spheres. They included Ruby Rich, Life-Vice-President of the Racial Hygiene Society, and the first Federal President of WIZO; WIZO activist Rose Mandelbaum; Dora Abramovitch, Council's National Secretary and Editor of *Council Bulletin*; Nerida Cohen BA LLB, the only woman barrister in New South Wales; Linda Littlejohn, President of the Women Voters' Association; and Camilla Wedgwood, Principal of Women's College at Sydney University, who addressed delegates on 'Our responsibilities to youth'.

The social program highlighted Council's prestige in the wider community. Premier of New South Wales, Bertram Stevens, provided a launch to take delegates around Sydney Harbour. There was a fund-raising garden party in the grounds of Ruth Fairfax's home, 'Elaine', in Double Bay. Guests at the Conference luncheon included the Governor's wife, Lady Wakehurst, and Lady Mayoress Mrs Norman Nock. At the mayoral reception for delegates, Dr Fanny spoke of her gratitude for present blessings and distress at the rising tide of Jew-hatred abroad,

> In Germany we would not be honoured guests, but we are proud to live in a country over which the British flag so gloriously flies … We would be happy to devote our interests only to the country in which we live and of which we are loyal citizens, but our people in other countries are oppressed, and we have to work for them.[196]

As State Premier Bertram Stevens could not attend the official opening of conference on 9 March 1938, Assistant Minister, J.H. Ryan MLC, welcomed delegates.[197] The press covered the ten-day conference and the *Hebrew Standard* featured Dr Fanny's presidential address on its front page, in which she paid tribute to early Australian pioneers,

> … it was with gratitude in our hearts that we fully appreciated what they had done in founding a country over which flies the British flag of freedom, liberty and justice. We gain inspiration and courage because we live in a dominion which is a part of the British Empire that makes its inhabitants happy and blessed. But because we are so happy and free, we must think of our oppressed race in non-democratic countries who are suffering because of racial discrimination.[198]

Dr Fanny emphasised service above self, envisaging a world devoid of prejudice and hatred,

> The chief theme of this Conference will be how best to serve our people and their future, as well as making the Jewish women of Australia alive to their responsibilities in the service of humanity. In our 15 years of existence we have given every human service and ... we shall build up a force that will shower love and peace upon its fellow men no matter what race, creed or colour.[199]

Mrs Edmond Gates, representing the National Council of Women of New South Wales – an organisation with 75 affiliated bodies, including the NCJW – told conference,

> ... women who wanted this world to be a fit place for their children to live, had to organise, in order to realise their ideals. The National Council was very proud of the Council of Jewish Women and felt sure that the injustices of the world today must die and the world be encircled by a Golden Chain of love.[200]

Despite Mrs Edmond's optimism, the situation for Jews in Europe over-shadowed conference deliberations, as the weekend brought bad news from abroad. Dr Fanny said, 'We are terribly troubled to think that half the Jews in the world will now have no home in Central Europe'.[201] In support of NCJW in a time of crisis, Lady Wakehurst told delegates, 'We are living in very troubled times, and I feel very deeply for your people in Austria and Poland and other countries where they have not a happy home'.[202]

Alarm bells were also ringing in Australia, as emboldened Nazi sympathisers gathered support. In May 1938, Sydney barrister, J. McClemens, addressed Council members on 'Respect for the Law', outlining the danger of setting aside laws, as Hitler did in 1933. He warned 'that New South Wales had allowed the organisation of the New Guard, which was an unofficial arm against a Government ruling by constitutional authority' and he pointed out its similarity to the Brownshirts, the Nazi Party's paramilitary.[203] The New Guard, founded in 1931 by a group of Sydney businessmen led by Colonel Eric Campbell, was a 'militaristic quasi-Fascist movement which soon claimed over 85,000 members'.[204] Despite Campbell's claim decades later that he deplored Nazi antisemitism, according to historian Hilary Rubinstein, he visited Hitler in 1933 and expressed admiration for the 'orderly, patriotic and determined' Nazi regime and voiced concern about what he perceived to be the Jews' stranglehold on Russia. The New Guard's publication, *Liberty*, disseminated antisemitic tropes such as Jewish control of the world's press. Notwithstanding the decline of the New Guard in 1932 and the strong British democratic tradition in Australia, the fact that an organisation in Australia could disseminate antisemitism caused unease in the Jewish community. It 'undoubtedly reinforced the cult of group invisibility foreshadowed in the 1890s …: "a minority is always wiser to be careful"'.[205] Rubinstein points out that there were several antisemitic organisations in interwar Australia, such as the Unity League, and the Guild of Watchmen of Australia, the latter publishing in 1933 the notorious antisemitic fabrication known as the *Protocols of the Elders of Zion*.[206] Dr Fanny responded to manifestations of Jew-hatred in ways she knew best. Firstly, her organisation was founded on good citizenship, being a responsible and helpful neighbour, delivering pragmatic humanitarian programs and a social justice agenda. This strategy was shaped by the Judaic ethics to which she subscribed, especially her belief in *Tikkun Olam*, repairing the world. Secondly, she networked extensively across organisations and communities, speaking about the deteriorating situation for Jews abroad and eliciting goodwill and support from community leaders and government representatives, obtaining generous press and radio coverage locally and nationally. When antisemitic smears in Australia threatened to bring the community into disrepute, she spoke up and, in one celebrated instance, took legal action as the plaintiff in a defamation case that rocked the country, *Dr Fanny Reading v. National Press Pty. Ltd.*

NCJW peace initiatives

Within Australia, NCJW accomplished a great deal in the areas of philanthropy, hospital visits, immigrant welfare, support for local charities, public health and social welfare generally. NCJW raised funds for institutions in Palestine, such as the Girls' Orphanage in Jerusalem; contributed towards the greening of Palestine; and supported the Ort-Oz Appeal, which funded education and skills training for young refugees fleeing oppression and settling in Palestine and other countries.[207] In September 1938, Council raised funds for a Polish Appeal, 'as the plight of our people is so desperate'[208] and, in October 1938, Council supported the General Refugees' Fund, 'the very deserving cause … which in the present crisis is more urgent than ever'.[209]

The ferment around events abroad lent urgency to CJW's peace initiatives. Dr Fanny's friend, Ruby Rich, promoted participation in Peace Week; and her play titled *Every Woman's Peace Play*, was staged in the city. Council members placed a wreath at the Cenotaph at the Peace Dedication Ceremony on 21 August 1938 in Sydney's Martin Place. Dr Fanny presided at a Special Peace Luncheon and introduced guest speaker Linda Littlejohn, President of the United Associations.[210]

The Editor of the *Sunday Sun*, F.E. Baume, was among more than 200 guests attending Council's 15th Anniversary Banquet on 29 November 1938, to mark Dr Fanny's establishment of the first CJW on 30 July 1923 in Sydney. It was time to celebrate this achievement and Dr Fanny and the National Junior President, Kae Israel, broadcast to the nation from the banquet venue. Dr Fanny was deeply moved by the celebrations,

> The Council was proud to know that they had gained the respect and esteem not only of the Jewish Community of Australia but of the non-Jewish also … A call had now come to the N.C.J.W. to mobilise its members for service to King and Country. The National President was happy that she had created such an

organisation which, everywhere in Australia, was and is a power and an influence for good in every branch of endeavour.[211]

Dr Fanny's phrase 'service to King and Country' foreshadowed NCJW priorities in 1939 that led to the suspension of their regular agenda and their dedication to war work. From 1939 to 1945, Dr Fanny emerged as a different leader, playing a significant role in Australia's war effort. Her response to Australia's participation in the Second World War and her attempts to aid co-religionists in Europe comprise the substance of the next chapter.

The family reunited in Ballarat in 1889, Nathan Jacob Rubinowich, his wife Esther Rose, and daughter Fanny.

Studio portrait of Esther Rose Rubinowich as a younger woman.

The Ballarat synagogue in Barkly Street, constructed in 1861, is the oldest on the mainland of Australia.

Nathan Jacob Rubinowich in Ballarat with his horse and buggy.

Nathan Jacob Rubinowich establishes his business in Ballarat in the 1890s.

The Rubinowich family in 1896 in Ballarat. Nathan Jacob, with his wife Esther Rose, holding baby Lewis Judah (Lew); front row, from left: Fanny, Hyman Samuel (Hymie), Rachael and Abraham Stanley (Abe).

Portrait of a young Fanny Rubinowich.

Dr Fanny as a young woman.

In 1914, Fanny Rubinowich graduated with a Diploma in Music from the University of Melbourne's Conservatorium of Music

Dr Fanny Reading's graduation in 1922 with MB BS, from Melbourne University's Faculty of Medicine.

Fanny Reading (seated, right), holding an infant, July 1920, with University of Melbourne lecturers and students.

Fanny Reading, seated second from left, with 5th-year medical students at Melbourne University in 1920.

University of Melbourne senior anatomy class in 1918, Fanny is seated fifth from right in front row.

Rush hour in King's Cross, 1938; printed (c. 1986). Max Dupain. National Gallery of Victoria, Melbourne

Above Family portrait in 1926 in Melbourne, standing from left, Hyman Reading, Dr Abraham Reading and Lewis Reading; seated from left, Rae Burman, Nathan Jacob Reading and his wife Esther Rose, and Dr Fanny Reading. Image courtesy of Leigh and Lynne Reading.

Left Dr Fanny's three brothers, from left, Hyman Reading, Lewis Reading and Dr Abraham Reading; from the family collection of Leigh and Lynne Reading.

Delegates attending the first conference of the Council of Jewish Women of New South Wales, held in 1929 in Sydney.

Conference delegates, in 1929, outside Newcastle Synagogue. On 9 December 1929, Dr Fanny Reading established the Council of Jewish Women in Newcastle.

CJW membership badge commemorating the inauguration of the Council of Jewish Women in Sydney in 1923 (right), and a badge marking the establishment in 1927 of the Council of Jewish Women of Victoria.

First Council of Jewish Women's rooms, 145 Castlereagh Street, Sydney.

Portrait of a mature Dr Fanny presented to her by the Council of Jewish Women in New South Wales in August 1931.

Percy J. Marks, Sydney solicitor and historian, was one of Dr Fanny Reading's staunchest supporters.

Dr Fanny presenting a cheque to Lady Wakehurst, wife of the NSW Governor.

The Reading family photographed, probably 1932, in Melbourne: standing from left, Benjamin Burman, Hyman Reading, Lewis Reading; seated from left, Rae Burman with baby Ian on her lap, Nathan Jacob Reading, Esther Rose Reading, Dr Fanny Reading. In front Lloyd Burman (left) and Alan Burman. Image courtesy of Dr Ian Burman

Welcoming Dr Reading and her mother on their arrival at the Adelaide Railway Station, on 5 November 1936, from left: Rev. L. Rubin-Zacks, First Minister of the Adelaide Hebrew Congregation; Esther Rose Reading; Dr Fanny Reading; Mrs Nat Solomon, President of the South Australian Council of Jewish Women; and Mrs J. Garcia, Council Secretary.

Dr Fanny Reading and her mother, Esther Rose Reading, photographed in Brisbane, *The Telegraph*.

Above Karl and Slawa Duldig with their daughter Eva, Compound 3D Tatura, 1941. Photo: Sister Burns, © Duldig Studio Melbourne.

Left Eva Duldig (front row, third from left). Tatura children, Compound 3D Tatura, 1941. Photo Sister Burns, © Duldig Studio Melbourne.

Fifth Jewish Women's Conference of Australasia held in March 1938 in Sydney. At a conference luncheon, Dr Fanny (second from right) seated between Lady Mayoress, Mrs Norman Nock (right) and Margaret Wakehurst, wife of the NSW Governor, Lord Wakehurst (left).

In 1947, Dr Fanny initiated plans for the Jewish Hospital in Wentworth Street, Point Piper, Sydney, NSW.

Portrait of Sir Leslie James Herron, distinguished Supreme Court judge and Chief Justice of New South Wales (1962–72), painted by Esme Bell. He was the presiding judge in the case *Dr Fanny Reading v. National Press Pty Ltd*. Image courtesy the Australian Golf Club.

Dr Fanny attends the Coronation Ball, Melbourne, 1952.

At Newcastle Section's celebration of NCJWA's 30th Jubilee in 1953. From left (seated) Ettie Simons, Dr Fanny Reading, Rebbetzin Jana Gottshall; (standing) from left, Vera Cohen and Elsie Goldring.

Dr Fanny receiving the MBE from Sir Eric Woodward in 1961 in Sydney.

Dr Fanny speaking to Alex Gottshall, at NCJW's Golden Jubilee Dinner in 1973, probably one of the last photographs of her. She died on 19 November 1974 in the Wolper Hospital, Sydney.

Chapter 5

NCJW – The war years 1939–1945

Women working together can achieve anything.
– Dr Fanny

The Second World War transformed Dr Fanny into an acknowledged leader of women on the home-front in Australia. With a national reputation for social welfare and social justice, she emerged as a formidable warrior for victory in war and a persuasive proponent for peace. She recognised the existential nature of the crisis, both at home and abroad. She understood the threat rising antisemitism and Nazi ideology posed to Jewish people and the world. With war declared, she immediately suspended all routine NCJW activities, articulated new policies and goals, initiated humanitarian programs at home, and united her members in their efforts to contribute to Australia's war needs.

The home-front became Dr Fanny's theatre of war, where she deployed her resources strategically. She served on every committee that enlisted women volunteers. From 1939 to 1945, the NCJW made a quarter-million garments for the troops, they raised £300,000 for Commonwealth War Loans and £18,000 for the Australian Comforts Fund, and they donated to the Red Cross, UNRRA, the Food for Britain Appeal and countless other causes. They knitted camouflage nets; they refurbished hospital wards, provided beds and medical equipment; they visited the injured and sick; and they ran refreshment centres and manned hospitality venues for serving the troops. It was a sustained effort to meet Australia's changing needs and goals. Undaunted by the gargantuan task, Dr Fanny encouraged her members to fulfill what she perceived as their obligations to Great Britain and Australia, the country they called home.

An acute observer of world events, already in 1938 Dr Fanny was profoundly concerned about the persecution of Jews in Germany and Austria. Her friend Jessie Street visited Vienna in August 1938, only a few months after Germany had annexed Austria on 13 March 1938. She noted the despair of the Jewish community,

> Their whole status was changed in one night. They are now dismissed without notice or compensation; their businesses are confiscated or closed; they are forbidden to employ or be employed by Aryans; their money and property is taken from them, they are driven out of their homes; they are arrested and imprisoned without any charge being brought against them … The witnessing of this application of every possible means of terrorising, humiliating, and insulting people who have been rendered helpless by the deprivation of all legal means of protection or redress, arouses in one a feeling of anger …[1]

Dr Fanny knew about the delegitimization and disenfranchisement of Jews under the German Reich, the terror attacks, arbitrary arrests and incarceration in concentration camps. Although antisemitic movements were active in Australia, attacks on Jewish communities were ideological, inspired by Nazi propaganda. From 1935, the Nazi regime fostered contacts with German minority groups in foreign countries, including Australia. However, only German citizens, not Australians of German descent, were permitted to join the Nationalsozialistische Deutsche Arbeiterpartei (NSDAP), the National Socialist Workers' Party. Australia's Minister for External Affairs, Sir Henry Gullett, admitted that 'certain

Nazi elements were undesirably active within the Commonwealth'.[2] Among homegrown Nazis by the late 1930s, conspiracy theorist Eric Butler was 'an established activist on behalf of antisemitic and extreme right-wing causes', who 'regularly unleashed anti-Jewish tirades in the *New Times*'.[3] The manifestations of antisemitism in Australia created unease in the Jewish community, 'The growth of indigenous anti-Semitic political groups such as the Australia First Movement, a new phenomenon in Australian political life, was very disturbing for Australian Jews'.[4]

For Dr Fanny, who resumed the Presidency of NCJW's Sydney section in 1936, it was a worrying time. In 1939, with prospects for peace fading, she readied NCJW for the challenges ahead, her watchwords of 'Service and Sacrifice' foreshadowing the organisation's wartime ethos. With new national priorities, NCJW focused on defence – the needs of Australian and Allied Forces – and the wellbeing of the country's population. She urged members to sign the National Service Register issued by the Commonwealth Government.

That year, Dr Fanny recalled NCJW's many achievements: the Hospital Committee made more than 2000 visits to hospitals and institutions; the *Council Bulletin* had appeared continuously for 14 years; and her two broadcasts from Sydney were heard throughout Australia. Council's philanthropy included contributions to the Dunningham Memorial Fund, Peace Week, the Bushfire Appeal, the Immigrant Welfare Fund, German Relief, the Happy Day Fund, and several health, maternal and childcare initiatives in Palestine. In a very real sense, she readied her own troops for action in Australia's hour of need. She encouraged her members and 'hoped that they would be granted the vision, understanding, courage, and determination, to help them carry out the work of the world today'.[5]

Prior to the outbreak of war, Dr Fanny toured Australia, speaking to NCJW members. In May 1939 in Melbourne, she endorsed Ida Bension's school-feeding scheme for children in Palestine, and their support for the Rothschild Hadassah University Hospital, Jerusalem.[6] Almost a month later, she addressed members in Adelaide. At their AGM, she told a heart-warming story of a Viennese family called Borer, who, eager to find relatives in Australia, sent a letter to an address with that name in the Melbourne telephone directory, requesting help in obtaining permits to emigrate. On arrival in Australia, they discovered they had written to an ant-borer extermination company, where the employees felt sympathetic enough to help them, providing guarantees for permits and preparing a home for them in Melbourne. 'We realise there is some hope for humanity when a case of this type is brought to notice,' Dr Fanny said.[7] While in Adelaide, she called on women's organisations to increase philanthropy to alleviate distress at home and overseas, noting that Council co-operated with any movement for public welfare. She emphasised that two-thirds of NCJW's funds raised were given to non-Jewish charities.[8]

NCJW's plans for Jewish refugees

Perturbed by dangers facing Jewish children in Europe, Dr Fanny told Adelaide's Council about Youth Aliyah, which brought children from Central Europe to Palestine at the cost of £100 per child; and that WIZO's representative, Ida Bension, would launch the forthcoming Youth Aliyah Appeal. Committed to the wellbeing of migrant Jewish children in Australia, Dr Fanny visited Kiotpo Farm, an agricultural training centre 35 miles from Adelaide, where eight Jewish boys were supported by the Australian Jewish Welfare Society.[9] Dr Fanny's detailed understanding of conditions on the ground was crucial to her decision-making, as it enabled her to modify Council's programs in response to local needs. This was also evident in Kalgoorlie, where she met the small pool of women workers who needed desperately to augment their numbers. Her solution was an invitation to 'the Jewish men to participate in local Jewish work … and refugee work',[10] an unusual step for the leader of a women's organisation that showed, should the need arise, she was not wedded to an all-female constituency. At a mayoral reception in her honour, she met representatives from all the women's organisations in the city with whom she could share her thoughts on their duties as Australian citizens.[11]

On this whirlwind tour of Australian cities, Dr Fanny spent ten days in Perth as the guest of Council President, Fanny Breckler. She discussed how Jewish women could co-operate for the benefit of the State, and held up as an example the way Sydney members supported local police clubs, which kept boys off the streets.[12] Unaware that within two months the Second World War would commence – Germany invaded Poland on 1 September 1939 – Dr Fanny spoke optimistically of NCJW's plans to bring to Australia every year 100 Jewish refugee girls, aged 14–16, from Central Europe, to be trained as domestic workers and educated in Australian ways. She outlined a resolution NCJW intended submitting to the Minister of State for the Interior, Senator Hattil Spencer Foll. She envisaged a scheme similar to the Barnardo plan, with girls staying in private homes that could be inspected,[13]

> There have been many requests from Europe and there are homes ready to take the girls … The fares will be paid by the employers or by the Jewish Welfare Society. We have ten sections in Australia which could easily assimilate 100 girls a year, and we also have people in Europe to select the girls.[14]

NCJW was especially concerned with the welfare of women refugees, many of whom had professions, such as nursing and dentistry, but were turning to domestic work in Australia. Children aged 12–16 'needed careful handling' and, by meeting Australian children, 'they would be educated in Australian ways and customs'.[15] She said NCJW was anxious 'to secure the absorption of refugees into the community and to that end arranged classes in English and other subjects'.[16] Dr Fanny told a reporter, 'other methods of assimilation include giving advice to the refugees in the matter of customs to be lost – such as kissing hands … and talking German in the streets'.[17] Moved by her description of the perils Jewish women and girls now faced abroad, Perth Council agreed to assist

100 German and Polish girls, all these projects sadly thwarted by the outbreak of war.

Dr Fanny was delighted with what Perth members achieved. The Breckler family established a scholarship in their mother's name. There were now two Council scholarships: the Fanny Reading and the Fanny Breckler scholarships awarded to Jewish boys and girls on the basis of financial need. She was impressed with Council's Sub Juniors, 'their earnestness to help their young co-religionists in Europe and Palestine and to maintain personal connections with them'.[18] With young members rising through NCJW ranks, she felt reassured that 'the work of the N.C.J.W. must remain permanently'.[19] Due to the outbreak of war, plans for the 6th National Conference in 1940 were cancelled and, instead, it was held in Sydney in 1943, when it focused on war work, the alleviation of the position of European Jewry, Palestine, and post-war reconstruction.[20]

Ever conscious of the needs of migrants, Dr Fanny praised Mrs N. Rosenwax, 'the guardian angel of refugees in Perth … who gives personal service to every refugee entering Australia in Fremantle'.[21] She also urged members to re-double their efforts for 'our people' in Palestine because of the tragedy unfolding in Jewish history,

> … to counteract that challenge to democracy and freedom by giving our loyalty to the Empire, that has protected the persecuted and given all liberty, Great Britain, and to retain our courage and strength in face of the crisis due to countries overrun with hatred and intolerance.[22]

In response to Dr Fanny's directives, leaders of women's organisations promised practical assistance in their States. She addressed gentile women's organisations on the same issue she canvassed with NCJW – duty to their country. In Perth, these organisations included the Women's Service Guild and the National Council of Women, whose President and conveners hosted her at a luncheon. At these non-Jewish gatherings, she pleaded for practical sympathy, fair play, and more tolerance in helping refugees assimilate and adapt to the customs and life of Australia,

> She pointed out to them the great asset the refugees themselves have, not only by creating employment for Australians, but for the loyalty to this country that they and their children would show, for they have no loyalties to those countries, who had driven them out. She appealed to the representatives of the bodies of women in each State, to help the Council in making the lot of the children coming here, who had suffered deep humiliation, a happier one, for they would later become the most desirable of Australian citizens.[23]

The Perth visit completed her country tour, which had started in May in Brisbane, followed by Melbourne, Adelaide and Kalgoorlie. Generous press coverage addressed NCJW's services to Australia and humanity. Her main aim was to unify Councils and women's organisations generally for the tasks ahead, in response to local defence problems in Australia and the perilous international situation of Jews, 'For this reason, Dr Reading thought it imperative to visit all the States to inculcate into the minds and hearts of Jewish and non-Jewish women, their duty to their country, their race and humanity in general'.[24] After four months of travelling the length of Australia, by August 1939 Dr Fanny, accompanied by her mother, returned to Sydney.

Dr Steinberg and the Freeland League

The plight of Jews subjected to Nazi persecution and the resulting Jewish refugee crisis were discussed at the Evian Conference in July 1938 in France. President Franklin Roosevelt stipulated to nations attending, including Australia, that no country would be required to admit more persons than allowed by their existing legislation. Australia's delegate, Colonel T.W. White, stated that Australia had always preferred British migration, 'It will no doubt be appreciated also that, as we have no real racial problem, we are not desirous of importing one by encouraging any scheme of large-scale foreign migration'.[25] According to Michael Blakeney, 'The Evian Conference had been doomed to failure by the assumption that the refugee crisis of 1938 could be solved within the confines of traditional attitudes toward immigration'.[26]

In Perth, in 1939, Dr Fanny had met for the first time Dr Isaac Steinberg, Secretary of the Freeland League for Jewish Territorial Colonization, on whose behalf he launched his one-man mission, in May 1939, to obtain the Australian Government's permission to settle a limited number of Jewish refugees in the Kimberley region of Western Australia. Many believed – including the pastoralist Durack family on whose leased land of seven million acres the projected Jewish colony would be sited – that this sparsely populated region would benefit from agricultural and pastoral development. The Freeland League scheme prompted antisemitic and philosemitic responses; and 'Many who objected to the scheme did so in the traditional language of antisemitism'.[27] Steinberg discounted the strength of antisemitism in Australia, as he received support from leading, as well as grassroots, Australians across the country, 'including trade union representatives, Church leaders, university men, and leading businessmen'.[28] He wrote, 'it was obvious from the start that the Jewish character of the proposed colonization was in no way a hindrance. Rather the reverse'.[29] He acknowledged the existence of antisemitism in Australia but differentiated it from the violent racism abroad, 'it possesses neither the passionate force nor the deep roots that it does in Europe'.[30] On 25 May 1939 in Perth, the Premier of the Labor Government of Western Australia, John Willcock, told Dr Steinberg, 'We have no prejudice against Jewish colonization'.[31]

During Dr Fanny's ten-day stay in Perth in 1939, she was struck by his passion for helping Jewish refugees. At this juncture in history, her principles aligned with his values. They were both dedicated to saving Jewish communities threatened with destruction and death in Europe. While both Dr Fanny and Dr Steinberg were driven by humanitarian zeal, they differed markedly. Dr Fanny, unlike Dr Steinberg, was a committed Zionist, who believed in the Jewish people's return to their ancient homeland. Her dream was to see the persecuted masses of Europe find sanctuary in Palestine. However, in 1939, Britain's Mandatory authority in Palestine virtually closed the doors to Jewish migration at a time when entry permits were needed desperately, thus thwarting the Zionist dream. Dr Fanny explored every avenue that promised some measure of relief and safety for Jewish refugees anxious to escape Hitler's Nazi regime. Given the constraints on Jewish migration to Palestine, her support of Dr Steinberg's Kimberley scheme that envisaged large-scale Jewish migration to Australia was therefore not a betrayal of her commitment to Zionism. Dr Steinberg's ideological position differed from Dr Fanny's. He was not Zionistic, although he admired the ability of Jews drawn from professional and urban backgrounds to adapt to agrarian life in Palestine, creating thriving agricultural settlements and developing an attachment to the land, 'which proved conclusively what the average Jew could achieve'.[32] He was a pragmatist, ready to explore the potential for large-scale settlements whether in the Kimberley or, alternatively, in Tasmania, an area where he travelled extensively with the help of Critchley Parker Jr, an idealistic Christian who devised an ambitious Jewish settlement scheme in Tasmania. Parker wrote, 'I am so glad that you think our trip in Tasmania will help the many oppressed people in Europe, a cause for which I shall always be happy to work'.[33]

Dr Fanny's initial meeting with Dr Steinberg had a sequel in Sydney, on 31 March 1940, when he addressed a capacity audience on the proposed settlement of refugees in the Kimberley region. Dr Fanny – seated on the platform with Rabbi Max Schenk and Julius Karpin – openly and publicly supported Steinberg's work. Dr Steinberg emphasised he had not come to Australia to ask for money, but to confront Jews of this continent with a problem that Jews in Europe had to grapple with since the advent of Nazism in 1933. Rabbi Leib Falk, who acted as chaplain to the Australian Military Forces and to Jewish internees in Australia during the war, appealed for support for Dr Steinberg's mission. While accused of a lack of sympathy for the internees, he had worked hard to secure their release.[34] He served as Assistant Minister of the Great Synagogue, where Dr Fanny was a member and where she attended services regularly, so she was familiar with his outspoken views. His sermons advocating a militant Zionism alienated many in his congregation. Rabbi Falk had served as chaplain from 1918 to 1921 to the First Judeans, the 38th, 39th and 40th Royal Fusiliers in Egypt and Palestine, Judean battalions formed following representations made to the British Government by Ze'ev Jabotinsky, aided by Chaim Weizmann. Rabbi Falk enjoyed a close friendship with Jabotinsky, shared his views, and was honorary president of the Sydney Revisionist movement.[35] Jabotinsky had opposed Theodor Herzl's plan to colonise Uganda, a proposal put forward by the British Government, shocked by the brutality of the Kishinev pogrom in 1903 in Bessarabia. At the Sixth Zionist Congress, the first following Herzl's death, 'a majority rejected Uganda and regarded Palestine once again as the sole end-goal of the movement'.[36] Despite Jabotinsky's opposition to the concept of Territorialism and Rabbi Falk's political loyalty to both Jabotinsky and his Revisionist Party, in this singular instance Rabbi Falk had the courage of his convictions to run counter to Revisionist' party line in support of Dr Steinberg and alongside Dr Fanny. Sydney Jewry was thus witnessing a novel spectacle, two committed Zionists – Dr Fanny and Rabbi Falk – supporting the Freeland League's settlement scheme in the Kimberley. Rabbi Schenk moved and Dr Fanny Reading seconded a resolution in support of Dr Steinberg's mission.[37]

Australian Zionists divided over the Kimberley Scheme

Steinberg understood but deplored the Australian Zionists' opposition to the Kimberley plan. They feared 'the idea of Jewish colonisation outside Palestine may be harmful in two ways: in relation to the world at large and within the ranks of the Jews themselves'.³⁸ He countered these fears by affirming that a strong Jewish community in Australia and a worldwide Jewish diaspora could support materially the Zionist vision of a Jewish homeland. 'There can be no Zionism in Australia without Jewish people in Australia,' he wrote.³⁹ He returned to his theme of preparing a home in Australia 'for a part of our homeless people', who would need security at the end of the war,

> This is the way Jews should feel in Canada, South Africa and Argentine. The same applies to Jews in Australia. Our reply to the Jewish catastrophe in Europe must also be the reconstruction of Jewish life in Australia ... A nation that does a big and generous thing for people in dire need will never regret it ... God will see to that.⁴⁰

Dr Fanny's unqualified support of the Kimberley Scheme put her at odds with many of her fellow Zionists in Australia, who adhered rigidly to party ideology. In early 1939 her humanitarian priority and that of the NCJW was saving Jewish lives during the period of Nazi persecution of Jews that preceded the annihilation of Jewish communities in the Holocaust. Dr Fanny was aware of the immigration barriers facing Jews desperate to escape Nazi brutality and widespread European antisemitism. As Chaim Weizmann noted, 'The world seemed to be divided into two parts – those places where Jews could not live and those where they could not enter'.⁴¹ Pragmatic in nature, more concerned with the value of human life than ideological exactitude, Dr Fanny endorsed the Kimberley Scheme for its potential to save Jewish lives when few, if any, alternative options were available.

Alan Crown has noted that early Australian Zionism was hampered by the territorialist movement in European Zionism. 'When the Seventh Zionist Congress in 1905 rejected all plans for settlement outside Palestine and when Israel Zangwill founded the Jewish Territorial Organization, a number of Australian Zionists, especially in New South Wales, espoused Zangwill's plan and split the Australian movement'.[42] In 1906, Dr Richard Arthur, President of the Immigration League of Australia, wrote to Zangwill advocating that a Jewish colony be established in the Northern Territory or Queensland. The scheme collapsed when Prime Minister Alfred Deakin opposed the idea. In 1920, Zangwill revived the scheme but the Premier of Western Australia, Sir Newton Moore, also rejected the proposal. Crown contends, 'the struggle of Australian Zionism between the Territorialists and their opponents, the antipathy of the Great Synagogue in Sydney and the hostility of the *Hebrew Standard* shattered Australian Zionism'.[43] Later, 'the fate of European Jewry and the wrath of the community inspired by the MacDonald White Paper of 1939, which further restricted Jewish immigration into Palestine, gave cohesion to most of the disparate elements of the community'.[44] With Dr Steinberg's arrival in Australia as emissary of the Freeland League for Jewish Territorial Colonization, 'the Zionist movement was … forced to divert some of its efforts to combat a resurgence of the Freeland League and the territorial movement'.[45]

Dr Steinberg's response to Jewish and Zionist opposition in Australia

Established on 26 July 1935, the Freeland League for Jewish Territorial Colonization – a revival of Zangwill's Jewish Territorial Organisation, which disbanded in 1925 – did not call for politically independent settlement, 'aiming instead for culturally distinct settlement flourishing within the political and economic framework of an established country, and for the settlers to become citizens of that host nation'.[46] The League had four criteria: a large area for economic expansion and the absorption of refugees; good climatic and soil conditions; a free and democratic host country; and, importantly, 'the area was to be sparsely populated to avoid any friction between the Jewish settlers and the established inhabitants …'.[47] In 1938, the League responded positively to a pamphlet, published on 6 January 1938, written by Australian journalist C.H. Chomley, who envisioned a settlement scheme in north-west Australia for Europe's persecuted Jews.

As one of the League's founders and its official emissary, Dr Steinberg spent three weeks inspecting part of the East Kimberley owned by lease-holders Connor, Doherty and Durack Ltd., who were prepared to sell to the League an area of 10,600 square miles (27,454 square kilometres) extending across the border between Western Australia and the Northern Territory.[48] Dr Steinberg toured the country, speaking to community leaders of all faiths. With the outbreak of the Second World War, stranded in Australia, he used his time to secure support for the Kimberley Scheme. In June 1943, he published a brochure, *Plain Words to Australian Jews* (translated from the Yiddish version published in 1939), in which he outlined the Kimberley plan, 'A place ... where Jewish colonists will work on a large scale, where they will develop agriculture and cattle raising, as well as industry and handicrafts, where they will engage in building houses and roads, bridges and ports'.[49]

Although the Western Australian Government applauded the scheme, as did advocates in the gentile and Jewish communities, he was disappointed by the negativity among sections of the Jewish and Zionist community, 'the most vehement critics were the local Jews ... Only a fraction of the Jews supported it. The established Anglo-Australian community, fearing that a sudden influx of migrants arriving *en masse* could unsettle the racial balance, were generally ... opposed to the scheme'.[50]

Dr Fanny was one of the few Zionists in Australia to support the scheme, which many believed undermined the Zionist dream of a national homeland in Palestine. Did her support of Dr Steinberg alienate her from mainstream Zionists in Australia? Her public endorsement of the Kimberley scheme did not affect in any way her friendship with Max Freilich, President of the NSW Zionist Council. Aside from Dr Fanny's open demonstration of support for Dr Steinberg at the Sydney meeting in 1940, she – together with 54 eminent citizens of the State – signed Dr Steinberg's published manifesto,

> If Australia is to lay claim to being a democratic and humane nation, she cannot neglect her duties towards the victims of oppression in Europe. To offer them ... a home in Australia would raise our moral status throughout the world ... We urge the citizens of Australia and the Commonwealth Government to give these people the right to work alongside us in the task of upbuilding this country.[51]

In Dr Steinberg's book, he makes special mention of 'Dr Fanny Reading and Mrs Jessie Street [who] spoke for the women of N.S.W'.[52]

Steinberg was disappointed that, after his four-year campaign, some members of the Jewish community still had doubts about his plan.[53] He ascribed their opposition to ignorance of the magnitude of the disaster in Europe and their failure to understand 'how great could be his own help for his tortured brethren'.[54] He stated prophetically, 'we now face the immediate danger of annihilation and of physical disappearance that threatens our people: to be destroyed, to be slain and to perish'.[55] He noted, on 17 December 1942,

> The German authorities are now carrying into effect Hitler's oft-repeated intentions to exterminate the Jewish people in Europe. From all occupied countries Jews are being transported in conditions of appalling horror and brutality to Eastern Europe. In Poland, which has been made the principal Nazi slaughter-house, the Ghettoes established by the German invader are being systematically emptied ... None of those taken away are ever heard of again. The able-bodied are slowly worked to death in labor camps. The infirm are left to die of exposure and starvation or are deliberately massacred in mass executions.[56]

Steinberg reproached those who thought that, by opposing the Kimberley plan, they were defending the interests of Australia. This touched on an issue central to the objections of assimilated Jews in Australia, their dread that an influx of Eastern European Jewish masses might provoke antisemitism; and he referred to the 'let-me-alone' Jews, the majority of the 30,000 Jews in Australia, who felt anxiety for their relatives but not for the Jewish people as a whole.

Defence of the Kimberley Scheme

While Dr Fanny's support for the Kimberley Scheme was not representative of the Jewish community as a whole, she was in good company among the Christian community, from whom Steinberg received stalwart support. Steinberg praised the Christian 'died [sic]-in-the-wool Australians' who supported the Kimberley plan. 'Besides,' he noted, 'not only material interests, but also purely humanitarian ideals move them to stretch out a helping hand to the persecuted'.[57] There were many in the Christian community in Australia who supported the Kimberley plan, including the Chancellor of the University of Western Australia, Walter Murdoch. In an article 'Our Opportunity: A Home for Refugees', he wrote that supporting the scheme enabled Australians to do their duty and to serve Australia's economic interests.[58] According to George Melville, an employee of the Pastoral Research Trust, who accompanied Dr Steinberg to East Kimberley,

> the proposed colony in the north would have in it nothing of nationalism, it would be a settlement of homeless human beings who seek a place on the earth on which to live at peace, who would be Jews by blood, but who would adopt the nationality of the land in which they found that place and give it loyalty and love.[59]

Editor Henry Boote in an article, 'Commendable Jewish Settlement Scheme', wrote that the scheme was non-political and loyal to Australia, 'Australian habits and customs are to be followed closely and the English language introduced right from the outset'.⁶⁰ He emphasised that the proposed scheme had been endorsed by the Australian Council of Trade Unions, Tasmania, South Australia, and the Western Australian Labor Government. 'It remains only for the Federal Government to give its permission for the launching of the scheme'.⁶¹ The Synod of the Anglican diocese of Perth supported the proposal, as did the primate of the Church of England in Australia, Sir Frank Gibson. In Melbourne, 46 leading citizens signed a public appeal, including historian Sir Ernest Scott and zoologist Georgina Sweet. Dr Daniel Mannix, Melbourne's Catholic archbishop, gave his support. In Sydney, 55 eminent citizens signed a public manifesto, including Lord Mayor Stanley Crick; the Chancellor of Sydney University, Sir Percival Rogers; Supreme Court Justice, Sir Thomas Bavin; and scholar Sir Mungo MacCallum.⁶²

In Sydney, a group of Steinberg's supporters started the 'Sydney Group of Friends of Jewish Settlement in the Kimberleys'. Among them was Jewish historian Solomon Stedman, who wrote a brochure entitled *A Jewish Settlement in Australia: On behalf of the Friends of a Jewish Settlement in Kimberley*. Acknowledging leading politicians' preference for British stock, he quoted British Colonial Secretary Malcolm McDonald, 'The British Government has made up its mind that the Commonwealth must, if it wants migrants in large numbers, seek them outside Britain'.⁶³ Stedman outlined the desperate situation of Jews under Nazi domination,

> Robbed of all their possessions and deprived of the means of earning a livelihood, the Jewish masses find themselves in a position so tragic and hopeless that, unless countries could be found to admit them, they must perish ... AUSTRALIA IS ONE OF THESE COUNTRIES. The Freeland League for Jewish Territorial Colonisation ... proposes to settle Jews in the Kimberley districts (W.A.) ... at its own expense and to develop the land at no cost to Australia ... Quite apart from any humanitarian considerations, it is a good business proposition.⁶⁴

Countering the objection that Jews should go to Palestine instead of Australia, he described the reality in 1940, 'Unfortunately the gates of Palestine were never opened sufficiently wide to admit even a fraction of the numbers that wished to go there. Now the gates are almost completely shut'.[65] Predicting the transformation Jewish migrants could effect in the Kimberley, he described how Jews returning to Palestine had transformed barren land, drained malarial swamps and built Tel Aviv 'on the hot sands of Palestine', which was 'a monument to Jewish labour'.

Stedman expressed views that Dr Fanny also espoused, 'The Jew, when he arrives in a new land, does not owe any allegiance to the country which expelled him ... The country of his adoption will become his country and the country of his children ... Was not Sir John Monash a good Australian?'.[66] He also answered critics of the Kimberley Scheme who predicted Jewish migrants would drift to the cities, 'Throughout the world, the trend of population is from the country to the city. In Palestine the reverse is taking place ... 90 per cent of those who settle on the soil become deeply and permanently attached to it'.[67] He paid tribute to the Government of Western Australia that approved the scheme; and the Australasian Council of Trades Union's resolution in support of the Kimberley settlement, a resolution confirmed by the Trades and Labor Councils of New South Wales, Victoria, South Australia and Tasmania. He concluded, 'By granting the necessary permission, the Commonwealth Government would reveal to the world its broadminded outlook and the humanitarian qualities of the people of this beautiful land'.[68]

Despite the best efforts of Steinberg, Stedman, Dr Fanny and supporters – Jewish and Christian – from all walks of life, in July 1944 Prime Minister John Curtin on behalf of the Australian Government rejected the Kimberley plan.

NCJW's response to Declaration of War

Australia entered the Second World War on 3 September 1939 shortly after Britain declared war when its ultimatum for Germany to withdraw from Poland expired. The Declaration of War instantly transformed NCJW's agenda. Ten days later, Sydney Section's Sewing and Knitting Group met in Council Rooms and that day completed 100 pairs of flannelette pyjamas, a humble beginning to their war effort that escalated to a quarter-million garments by the end of the war. On 19 September 1939 in Sydney, Council instituted Air Raid Precaution Classes in Council Rooms, followed by First Aid and Home Nursing classes. As NCJW President, Dr Fanny was elected to the General Committee of the Lord Mayor's Patriotic War Fund, the first of many civic and national appointments linked to the war effort. She became identified with every organisation ensuring the safety and welfare of the home population and providing resources for the Second Australian Imperial Force (Second AIF, the volunteers) in its fight, from 1939 to 1945, against Nazi Germany, Vichy France, Italy and Japan. Dr Fanny stated that Council members,

> ... have thrown themselves wholeheartedly and enthusiastically into the defence work of this country. It was decided that the members would offer their services through the Council in addition to the work they intended to do in their municipalities and thus render extra cooperation in the present trying times of war.[69]

In November 1939, Dr Fanny assured Lady Wakehurst, wife of the Governor of New South Wales, that Council members were committed to co-operating in emergency services,

> ... they were proud to be a part of the great British Commonwealth of Nations, which stood for the highest principles of humanity, truth, justice, freedom and liberty. The Jewish women wished to play their part in saving humanity and civilisation. Their

organisation endeavours to teach Jewish women what they owe to themselves, to the country in which they live and to their race.[70]

Lady Wakehurst acknowledged Council's loyalty to the British flag, 'I realise what wonderful citizens of the British Empire you are. More than ever in this crisis we must all stick together for the ideals we believe in'.[71] Council's donation to the Lord Mayor's Appeal Day represented the 'untiring efforts' of their stall-workers in Martin Place and Council button-sellers, 'who worked unceasingly for us in the city'.[72] On 20 December 1939, Council presented to Lady Nock, Chairman of the Women's Comforts' Branch of the Fund, 'several hundreds of garments … for the soldiers in camp'. Dr Fanny promised that 'the N.C.J.W. would assist her in the future in the big work of helping our country win the war'.[73] Lady Nock praised the 'magnificent contribution from the National Council of Jewish Women', and 'The wonderful array of Council sewing … would be an inspiration for others'.[74]

The War Emergency Board

Dr Fanny designated 'war work' NCJW's priority, followed by Palestine, Jewish education and local charities.[75] She created a War Emergency Board comprising 30 members, each of whom pledged to contact a further 20 women 'in an endeavour to carry this urgent work into as vast a channel as possible' and to raise funds 'for all war contingencies',[76]

> Realising the urgency of the present world situation and that of the British Empire in particular, the members of this Board have wasted no time in putting forward two very important projects to do their share in this crisis.[77]

Sydney's CJW obtained rent-free an Angus & Coote shop, which opened on 18 June 1940 as their 'Community War Chest Shop'.[78] Dr Fanny relied on financial and material contributions from diverse sources. In a prime position in Her Majesty's Arcade in Castlereagh Street, the shop contributed substantially to the Lord Mayor's Patriotic Appeal, with proceeds also donated to St Anne's military hospital in Waverley. Run by volunteers, they sold 'foodstuffs, fancy work and knitted goods'.[79] On 3 June 1940, at the AGM in Sydney, Dr Fanny issued a call to members 'to render immediate service to the British Empire in the present National crisis'. In view of the danger facing Great Britain, it was imperative 'to temporarily suspend the many projects and causes to which Council has given generous support, and that all future activities should be directed to the nation's effort to "Win the War"'. CJW pledged 'to give every ounce of strength and support it could muster from the Jewish Community for the salvation of our country and the salvation of Judaism'.[80]

News and press censorship

Many members were concerned for the safety and survival of relatives living under Hitler's rule. The Dutch capitulated to Germany on 14 May 1940, and three months later, on 20 August 1940 in Sydney, the President of the Joodsche Vrouwenraad (the Jewish Women's Council) in the Netherlands, Adolphine Schwimmer-Vigeveno, spoke to Council's Mosman committee and passed on news about their families in Amsterdam. She related the very sad experiences of their country and her gratitude to be 'in this free British land'.[81] Talks such as this, under the aegis of the NCJW, brought eye-witness accounts from abroad directly to the Sydney Jewish community. This was a valuable NCJW initiative in the context of strict press censorship enforced during the war in Australia to ensure military security, to prevent a deterioration in public morale or patriotism, to prevent obstruction of the war effort, and to protect the political interests of Government. Press censorship also forbade discussion of the Australia First Movement, a fascist antisemitic organisation. The constraints of press censorship were crippling for media companies, 'Many American correspondents and newspaper proprietors expressed their hostility to censorship and the manipulation of information by both

Canberra and [General] MacArthur's Headquarters in Melbourne [and later Brisbane], by withdrawing completely from Australia and expressing their displeasure from the U.S'.[82]

News filtered through by several means, including an article on 'the greatest massacre in the world's history', based on a report smuggled out of Poland. On 26 June 1942, the *Newcastle Morning Herald and Miners' Advocate* ran the news story headlined, 'Polish Jews slaughtered: Nazis exposed in smuggled report', a story London's *Daily Telegraph* sent via the wire service,

> a report smuggled from Poland to the Jewish representative on the Polish National Council says that more than 700,000 Polish Jews have been slaughtered by the Germans … The Germans are also reported to be carrying out a system of starvation, deaths from which are expected to be nearly as high as when their extermination began in Eastern Galicia last year. The procedure everywhere is similar – men and boys aged from 14 to 60 are assembled, usually in a public square or cemetery, where they are knifed, machine-gunned or killed by grenades, after digging their own graves.[83]

They read that deaths in Vilno and Koko (Lithuania) districts totalled 300,000, and at Rowne (Poland), 15,000 over three nights. In Chelmno (Poland) 5000 people from four towns were killed from November to March, and 35,000 from Lodz ghetto were killed in vans fitted as gas chambers, 'Into each of these 90 Jews were crowded at a time'. The article included death totals of 30,000 in Lvov (now Lviv in western Ukraine), 15,000 in Stanislawow, 9000 in Slonim, 5000 in Tarnopol, and 4000 in Brzezany. In March, 25,000 Jews were taken from Lublin in sealed wagons, 'and all trace of them was lost'. The article stated that 600,000 Jews were in the Warsaw ghetto, averaging 19 to a room and 'There was minimum aid to combat the ravages of typhus and other epidemics'.

This report published in June 1942 left Australians in no doubt that the Nazis were annihilating Jews throughout Europe. Dr Fanny, as head of the NCJW, received cables from abroad with the latest news, ahead of news disseminated in the wider community. The Jewish community looked for information to newspapers and Jewish publications, such as the *Hebrew Standard*, which enjoyed a wide readership. The *Jewish Weekly News* began publication in 1934, changing its name in 1935 to the *Australian Jewish News;* and in 1939, a Sydney edition, the *Sydney Jewish News*, appeared. Both papers were printed in Melbourne and had a wide circulation in both cities. Newman Rosenthal edited the weekly *Jewish Herald*.[84]

In 1944, Dutch migrants in Australia read,

> German authorities had issued a decree ordering the registration of all children under 15 years of age ... The Dutch people who have learned to their cost to read between the lines ... have every reason to suspect that the new decree is directed mainly at the comparatively large number of Jewish children who have been hidden these past years by courageous Dutch Christians.[85]

A month later, the *Hebrew Standard* reported 'grim eye-witness accounts of Nazi brutality towards the Jewish community of the Netherlands'. The article recounted events that had taken place two years previously, in 1942. For Dutch readers in Australia, it was painful to learn, 'the ghastly features of the deportation of thousands of Jews to Poland in sealed cattle trucks in which most of the travellers, owing to crowding and lack of food and water, succumbed, so that only a fraction reached Poland, the remainder having died or become insane'.[86]

The challenges facing Jewish women featured in Rabbi Falk's lectures delivered at NCJW meetings,

> We Jews in Australia, have a sacred duty in the larger vision for we must extend our activities ... The day of reckoning is coming and the women will have to shoulder the burden and

come to the fore for the defence of the Empire. Women have the strength to endure great suffering and sacrifices.[87]

Sir John Monash Recreation Hut

Dr Fanny was at the centre of the Jewish community's war efforts; on the lighter side, her activities included entertaining Jewish members of the fighting forces at Council's Springtime Ball, on 21 August 1940. At a luncheon eight days later. NCJW presented cheques totalling £448 to representatives of the Lord Mayor's Patriotic and War Fund, the Food for Babies' Fund and the Isabella Lazarus Children's Home, the latter offering Federal authorities its facilities for housing and caring for evacuated children. In response, Lady Wakehurst stated,

> I know that we are all together in spirit behind the great war effort of our Empire because we all know how little life is worth living under the Nazi regime, I am glad that you are not supporting only the Patriotic Fund, but also some of our civil good works which need so much help just now.[88]

Lord Mayor, Alderman Stanley Crick, who received a NCJW' cheque of £241 for the Lord Mayor's Patriotic and War Fund, acknowledged the patriotic efforts of the Jewish community, 'War had only just been declared when you started work within twenty-four hours. Your efforts are received with gratification at the Comforts' Depot'.[89]

In Melbourne, Dr Fanny convened a NCJW' inter-state conference 'to discuss war work of the Council, and the best way in which members can assist the Government in its war effort'.[90] Co-ordinating NCJW's war effort, Dr Fanny headed service initiatives that won acclaim from Government, the military and the Australian public. These included the erection of the Sir John Monash Recreation Hut, next to the Anzac Buffet in Hyde Park, supported by several Jewish community organisations in Sydney. The New South Wales Jewish Congregation Advisory Board and

Auxiliary's executive committee – comprising Dr Fanny Reading, Saul Symonds, Rabbi Dr Israel Porush and Rabbi Max Schenk – organised the project; and this committee was then constituted as the Council of the NSW Jewish Citizens' War Effort. This body co-ordinated activities for 'patriotic funds and to avoid unnecessary duplication of effort' and ensured 'every encouragement will be given to new workers to join existing groups doing war work'.[91] The Sir John Monash Recreation Hut for the free use of His Majesty's forces, was a major project with floor space equal to the main hall of Sydney Town Hall. Equipped with hot showers, it had rooms for reading, recreation and writing. The Governor, Lord Wakehurst, opened the Sir John Monash Recreation Hut and Anzac buffet on 19 September 1940, commenting that 'Jewish citizens of Sydney contributed £5000 towards the costs of the buildings';[92] and the Lord Mayor of Sydney, Alderman Stanley Crick's official invitation to the opening stated that these buildings were 'gifts of the Jewish Citizens of Sydney'.

The scale of NCJW's war work captured public imagination. NCJW supported and managed three major projects – the Martin Place Kiosk on the corner of Martin Place and Phillip Street in the city, which raised £100 per week; the Anzac Buffet Building in Hyde Park with the adjoining Sir John Monash Recreation Hut; and the War Chest Shop in Her Majesty's Arcade, which brought in an average of £20 per week, with Council volunteers serving 'al fresco' teas.[93] The *Sun* commented,

> Since the outbreak of war the Jewish women have given more than 3000 garments to the Lord Mayor's Fund, and every Monday between 60 and 80 women meet at the clubrooms ... to do knitting and machining. In addition they have equipped and furnished a ward containing 12 beds at St. Anne's Convalescent Home for Soldiers in Waverley.[94]

These initiatives boosted fundraising for a range of causes at home and abroad, including a donation to the London Air Victims Appeal.

On 8 October 1940, the Lord Mayor, Alderman Crick, opened Council's second War Chest Shop in Martin Place, which was followed by an Art Auction in aid of the Anzac Buffet Building.[95] Council's War Emergency Board decided all proceeds would fund the Anzac Buffet Building until the full sum had been raised.[96]

Troubled by the fate of Jewish youth in Europe, Dr Fanny focused on Youth Aliyah, the organisation responsible for Jewish children fleeing the terrors of Europe for Palestine. In December 1940, Council participated in a 'WIZO Aliyah Bazaar', which raised funds for their welfare and maintenance.[97]

International Women's Day

Despite the pressure of her medical duties and overseeing NCJW's multiple projects, both large and small, Dr Fanny hosted a fundraising party on 16 November 1940 in her home.[98] As National President, she delivered an address on 7 March 1941 in Sydney to mark International Women's Day, sharing the Feminist Society's platform with Jessie Street, President of the United Association of Women; Laura Gapp, President of the Women's Union Service; and Lucy Woodcock, President of the New Educational Fellowship. This occasion confirmed her solidarity with leaders of women's organisations and fostered strong connections. In the midst of war, these women leaders were looking ahead to the dawn of peace and national priority areas. With their menfolk fighting overseas, women had stepped up to fill positions they might be expected to relinquish, which they were reluctant to do,

> International Women's Day is important, because women's organisations must keep together during wartime. If they do not, when the war is finished, and the time comes for social reconstruction, women will not have the unity they will need to carry on their fight for recognition of women's rights in this new order.[99]

Dr Fanny and NCJW's war efforts won plaudits from a broad range of people. On 19 March 1941, Lady Wakehurst commended Council on the welcome they gave Jewish women refugees. She commented on the committee these newcomers formed to work at night in the 'restaurant kiosk' in Martin Place, contributing the proceeds to the Lord Mayor's Fund. Dr Fanny presented a cheque for £350 to Lady Wakehurst to equip and furnish a ward of 14 beds in the Lady Wakehurst Red Cross Home in Waverley. 'We have particular pleasure in marking this money for the home, which is called after Lady Wakehurst, who has always shown sympathy with Jewish women,' she said, adding that Council's Hospital Committee had offered 'to visit and provide comfort for the men who will occupy the beds in the ward'.[100]

Dr Fanny guided NCJW's war projects through the early months of 1941. Although a team effort, it was the team leader who encouraged members to achieve their goals, and who monitored their complex operations. Her report, delivered at Council's 18th AGM on 5 May 1941 in Sydney, gave an overview of projects and achievements. She documented Council's donations to a remarkable array of charities, causes and institutions, including the Red Cross, the Polish Appeal, the British Civilian Bomb Victims' Fund, the Rothschild Appeal for Jewish Bomb Victims, the Jewish Education Board, the Shanghai Appeal, local immigrant welfare, and the internees at Hay. She reviewed the work of the sewing and knitting group, who completed 5000 garments for the Lord Mayor's Comfort Fund. Zionist work resumed with donations to WIZO, the JNF, the Hebrew University and the Jewish Blind Institution. She commended Council's 770 members, the Hospital Visiting Committee, the Local Charities' Committee, the War Emergency Younger Set and the work among internees;[101] and spoke of future projects, such as their New War Effort Appeal to supply a mobile canteen for British air-raid victims. In appreciation of her work, Council presented a filing cabinet to Dr Fanny, an appropriate gift given the plethora of files and documents in her apartment.

As yet, ignorant of the enormity of Hitler's genocidal solution for 'the Jewish problem', Dr Fanny envisaged a redemptive Jewish destiny ahead, when she addressed Council's Newcastle Section on 7 May 1941: 'although the world was passing through dark days and the Jews, especially, were under heavy clouds, there was every hope that at the end of the conflict the Jewish problem would be solved'.[102]

Dr Fanny congratulated Newcastle Council on assisting Jewish appeals in Australia and abroad, and 'patriotic appeals' in Newcastle, 'they had endeavoured to put their shoulder to the many war efforts, and so were helping to maintain the prestige of Jewish women'.[103] A Newcastle journalist described Dr Fanny as 'one of the most capable women in public life today',

> Her broad vision and keen sense of duty have made it possible for her to understand the problems, not only of her own people, but of the world in general … Of special interest was the story of the work being done among the newcomers to this land. Refugees is a word we don't like using as a rule in this country. I am sure that the setting up of local committees in various suburbs by the National Council in Sydney has stopped many of these people from being lonely and isolated. Banded together with members of the Council to lead them, they are not only being given comradeship in a strange land, but also being shown the way to put their shoulder to the very big war effort being made by the Council.[104]

A month later in Melbourne, Dr Fanny presided at the AGM of the Victorian NCJW's War Emergency Board, attended by the Lady Mayoress, Mrs F. Beaurepaire; philanthropist and charity worker Lady Jacobena Anglis; and Lady Bruche. The Board's charity shop in the Midway Arcade raised £570 for 38 beds in the Kurneh Red Cross Convalescent Hospital in South Yarra, provided a transport truck to the Red Cross for use in Malaya, and sent £300 to the Lord Mayor's appeal for bomb victims. Dr Fanny outlined a scheme for raising £500 for a mobile canteen for bomb victims in England, which would supplement £300 already raised in Sydney.[105]

NCJW acquired a reputation for patriotism, hard work, generosity and commitment to worthy causes. On 21 August 1941, the Honorary Director of the Lord Mayor's Patriotic and War Fund in Sydney wrote to Dr Fanny,

> During the past eighteen months we have received very generous support from the National Council of Jewish Women in direct donations ... For all this we feel warmly grateful and, at the present moment, I think that a special expression of appreciation is due to you as President of the Council. We have fully realised the great organising ability and patriotic feeling which have been attended by the highly successful results to the benefit of all Australian Servicemen, and I warmly thank you and all members of your Association for their magnificent co-operation.[106]

On 31 August 1941 in Sydney, CJW hosted 67 members of the Palestine Jewish Military Police. For Dr Fanny, it was a special occasion in the history of Sydney Jewry, 'as these young men are representative of what the youth are doing for the prestige of Jewry all over the world'.[107] She never rejected an Australian or overseas appeal for help, including a cabled request from Chief Rabbi Dr Joseph Hertz of London, asking for funds for refugee rabbis, teachers, scholars and children 'freed from concentration camps with all its terrors' and presently in England. Dr Fanny asked NCJW sections throughout Australia to assist. At the same time, Sydney's CJW gave financial support to the Kindergarten Union's Home at Thirroul; and endowed two beds at the Isabella Lazarus Home.

Jewish internees in Hay and Tatura camps

In 1940, the British press was outspoken about the risk of harbouring enemy agents posing as victims of the Nazi regime. Consequently, 'After spending time in police stations or collecting points scattered throughout Britain, German- or Italian-born internees were sent to internment camps ... Many camps were located on the Isle of Man'.[108] On 8 July 1940, however, a group of 2500 men and boys, ranging in age from 16 to 66, boarded the *Dunera* bound for incarceration camps in Australia. As well as genuine refugees from Germany, Austria and Czechoslovakia, of whom approximately 80 per cent were Jews, there were also Nazi sympathisers among this contingent. On board, the British tormented the Jewish internees, who endured physical and mental cruelty at their hands. A court martial in May 1941 recorded the abuse of internees on the *Dunera*,

> This degree of official recognition of the injustice done to these men was hardly commensurate with what they had experienced. But by May 1941, everybody concerned – from Churchill down – recognised the story of indiscriminate civilian internment and deportation of German-and Italian-born refugees as a regrettable consequence of official panic in the darkest days of the war.[109]

In July 1940, German and Italian 'enemy aliens' resident in Singapore were told they were to be expelled. On 17 September 1940, the *Queen Mary* sailed from Singapore, with 295 internees on board, including 232 Jewish refugees and 63 Italian or German nationals. Their experience on board for the relatively short voyage to Australia was very different to the cruelty meted out to Jewish passengers on the *Dunera*. There were several families with children on board.[110] On arrival in Sydney on 25 September 1940, they travelled by train and bus to Internment Camp 3 at Tatura in northern Victoria. The Singapore internee families were housed in D compound and the single men in C. While children over the age of 12 were sent to the Larino Children's Home in Melbourne, run by the Australian Jewish Welfare Society, 25 younger children remained in the camp; and two internee kindergarten teachers set up a kindergarten for them.[111] Among these children was two-year-old Eva Duldig, whose Austrian parents, Karl and Slawa, were established artists. A Jewish couple, they fled to Singapore following the Anschluss, Germany's annexation of Austria in 1938. According to Melinda Mockridge, curator of the exhibition, 'Art behind the Wire: The Duldig Studio',[112] the internees appealed for release to Prime Minister Robert Menzies without success. 'The inappropriateness of children confined was also a consideration,' she states, adding that after release in 1942, 'the [Duldig] family were still considered enemy aliens and subject to strict parole conditions'.[113]

NCJW launched an appeal for toys for internee children at Tatura camp in Victoria.[114] The *Hebrew Standard* stated, 'Mrs Elsa Raymond of the Bellevue Hill Committee, who has interested herself in the welfare of internees in Tatura, especially the women and children, makes the appeal'.[115] Eva Duldig commented, 'I was too young to recall receiving any toys … I have not heard about this, though I did receive a doll from a friend in Singapore'.[116] In 1990, Eva visited the camp for the first time since leaving it in 1942. Revisiting the 'cradle of her memories', she stated, 'This was where I and my toddler mates … squabbled over the meagre toys at our disposal'.[117]

On 29 September 1941, only four days before NCJW launched their appeal for toys, the Jewish families in Camp 3, D compound, were subjected to National Socialist activities, such as Nazi taunts and 'Heil Hitler' salutes, by German families interned in the same compound, which resulted in a 'riot' that was quelled when the Australian Camp Command fired gunshots into the air. Although categorised officially as a 'disturbance', 'it involved people fighting each other with brooms, spades, pieces of wood and stones'.[118] Gerhard Seefeld, the leader of the Jewish families in D Compound, had complained previously to

Official Visitors that the presence and actions of German Nazis and Italian fascists in their family camp led to tensions. Nothing was done, as 'the Army countered with the fact that D compound was the only family compound available'.[119] Did any hint of this riot leak out to the Australian Jewish community at that time or were reports suppressed while the riot was investigated officially? Dr Fanny was dedicated to the wellbeing of mothers and children. Had she heard about this, it is likely she would, at the very least, have registered a protest, of which there is no record; or made representations to relevant authorities on behalf of minors exposed to these events in order to secure for them a more favourable outcome. Eva Duldig, who lives in Melbourne, was three at the time of the riot. She has only positive memories of her time in Compound D, which she viewed as an adventure. She had lots of playmates and was happy there, cared for by her parents, Slawa and Karl Duldig.[120] In 2020, survivors and descendants of the internees brought from Singapore to Australia on the *Queen Mary* organised an 80th anniversary webinar. None of the participants referred to the 'riot'. Clearly, adults had shielded their children from these events. Overall, however, the loss of freedom weighed heavily on Karl and Slawa Duldig and, in April 1942, Eva's father volunteered for the Eighth Australian Employment Company and was sent to Melbourne. Shortly thereafter, Eva and her mother were permitted to leave the camp, although they were kept under surveillance and had to report weekly to the police in Melbourne.

President of the Zionist Federation, Dr Leon Jona, visited Tatura and 'suggested that Australian Jewry might not be doing enough to assist Jewish internees there and this was certainly the view of some of the internees'.[121] Certainly, there was a lack of empathy in the attitude of Sydney representatives of the Australian Jewish Welfare Society. Newman Rosenthal stated in the *Australian Jewish Herald* in mid-1941, 'it was altogether undesirable that private people, however well-meaning, should start making collections for the internees'.[122] NCJW's support was, therefore, significant and a welcome departure from prejudicial and unsympathetic attitudes prevailing in the community. Despite this communal bias, NCJW maintained its ongoing connection with the internees, responding to their needs. Adult camp internees acknowledged with gratitude even relatively small gifts from NCJW. In July 1942, NCJW launched an independent appeal for warm clothes for men internees in the camp, including coats, underwear and boots, because 'They are badly in need of these garments as the winter is very severe'.[123] The internees expressed their gratitude to NCJW. An internee wrote to the Chairman of Council's Internees' Section, Mrs O. Angel, thanking them for cigarettes, 'your present was all the more appreciated, as it arrived for Channukah and helped to please quite a lot of our people'.[124]

NCJW's tributes and contributions

Towards the end of 1941, three eminent Zionist leaders died, whom Dr Fanny had known personally: Russian-born Jewish leader Menachem Ussishkin, head of the JNF; Louis Brandeis, Associate Justice on the American Supreme Court; and Bella Pevsner, JNF representative. Dr Fanny and Pevsner met for the first time in 1923 in Sydney, meeting again at the Zionist Congress in Vienna in 1925. During Pevsner's stay in Australia, she told Dr Fanny about the work of the American NCJW founded in 1893 by Hannah Solomon 'to unite in closer relation women interested in the work of Religion, Philanthropy and Education'. Inspired by Pevsner and already 'involved in fundraising for Jews in the Ukraine',[125] Dr Fanny started CJW in Sydney that year. With this close relationship between Pevsner and Dr Fanny, she delivered a eulogy at Council's general meeting on 3 November 1941.[126]

Commensurate with NCJW's work and sterling reputation, tributes testified to NCJW's contributions. Rear Admiral Muirhead-Gould, Commodore-in-Charge, Sydney, and chairman of the Sydney Royal Australian Naval Relief Fund, wrote to Dr Fanny on 9 January 1942,

> The Honorary Organising Secretary (Mr. A. A. Joel), has advised me of the personal and valuable help given by the members of the National Council of Jewish Women to the Royal Australian Naval Relief Fund 'Jack's Day N.S.W. Appeal,' on December 19th last. This practical sympathy has been very greatly appreciated; and on behalf of my Committee and of the personnel of Australia's Navy, I thank warmly all who helped and thereby contributed in no small measure to the success of the Appeal.[127]

The honorary administrator of the Lord Mayor's Comforts' Fund, Mr Docker, appealed to NCJW for additional support for the fighting forces. In response, Council increased production and their sewing circle handed 3203 garments to the Fund; and Council's Australia War Emergency Board contributed £104/9/1, proceeds from the Martin Place Kiosk during January 1942. His letter of thanks to Dr Fanny included an explicit request for ongoing support,

> I know the members of your Council are fully conscious of the vastly increased demand for comforts for all services and will do their utmost to assist us in the future provision of these, as they have in the past.[128]

In early 1942, demands on CJW and Dr Fanny increased, and media reports document their expanding range of initiatives. In February, Dr Fanny assisted Teachers' Federation staff in delivering first-aid classes in Sydney, modestly describing her own contribution as 'hints from the medical aspect'. Viewed as 'urgently necessary for all to have first aid knowledge in case of an emergency',[129] Council members obtained permits for these classes, and the local registration officer permitted newcomers to attend. Council's EZRA Sewing group, which assisted mothers and babies in Palestine, dispatched 150 baby garments to Palestine 'where warm clothing is so greatly needed'.[130] As part of defence work, Council conducted an Aluminium Drive, appealing to members to donate all 'unneeded aluminium for building of fighter planes'.[131]

1942 brought more disturbing news of the destruction of Jewish communities in Europe,

> Appalling and tragic though it is there are now no Jewish communities left in Europe because of Nazi rule, and European Jews after the war will have to again migrate, this time migration being to the English-speaking countries of the world. The seats of Jewish life will now have to be transferred and developed in the Jewish communities of Great Britain and America, and it behoves those who are at present in these countries, to keep the flame of Judaism ever alight.[132]

Dr Fanny wanted to encourage Jewish youth's participation in Council's work for refugees in Palestine. With this in mind, on 21 June 1942, she invited Council's Younger Set to her home in Kings Cross, where they met Dr Shlomo Lowy, who arrived in Australia in 1939 to establish a branch of the JNF. He confirmed 'the necessity of active work for Palestine on behalf of Jewish youth', and 12 members formed a JNF youth group, adopting tree-planting in Palestine as their first project.[133]

In the light of the devastating fate of Jews abroad, Dr Fanny focused consistently on Palestine as a sanctuary for survivors of Nazism. In March 1942, at a Sydney farewell for Dr Michael Traub, an emissary of the Jewish Agency and Keren Hayesod (fundraising arm of the Zionist movement), she pledged support for his humanitarian mission that aided Jews fleeing Europe for Palestine, assisted in their absorption and 'provided the newcomers with homes and jobs, and developed the economic, educational, and cultural framework of the Yishuv'.[134] Her support was vital, given the apathy he encountered among sections of the Jewish community,

> Our organisation was very happy to help him in his appeal as we had helped every appeal from Zionist headquarters over a period of twenty years. We ask Dr. Traub to take back a message to the people of Palestine – that our members are deeply conscious

of the responsibility we have towards Palestine and we shall continue supporting Zionist efforts, especially in these crucial times.[135]

The urgency of Dr Fanny's support for Zionist institutions assisting Jewish survivors was clear in July 1942, when the Australian Jewish community received cables reporting the German slaughter of 700,000 Jews in Poland and Lithuania, at that time 'the greatest massacre in the world's history'.[136]

Twenty years after the founding of Sydney's CJW in 1923, Dr Fanny announced that NCJW would mark their 20th anniversary with a £20,000 contribution to the Third Liberty Loan. The *Daily Telegraph* noted that Council members in NSW 'are engaged in many wartime activities, including the kiosk in Martin Place … and the proceeds given to the Australian Comforts Fund'.[137] The article stated that Council's birthday would be commemorated at an inter-state conference in July 1943 in Sydney.[138]

Battle against entrenched resistance to migration

The news from abroad in 1943 was deeply disturbing for Dr Fanny and the Jewish community in Australia. There were reports of the Warsaw Ghetto uprising that began on 19 April 1943, after German troops entered to deport the ghetto's remaining Jews to death camps. The Jews held the might of the German army at bay until 16 May 1943, when the Nazis reduced the ghetto to rubble. These reports accelerated Dr Fanny's campaign to find a refuge for Jews fleeing extermination at the hands of Nazis and their collaborators. As National President of the NCJW, she networked effectively and built diplomatic alliances with a broad range of organisations and, in so doing, she spoke out directly and fearlessly on behalf of Jewish people suffering under Nazi domination.

Dr Fanny's efforts to secure entry for Jews to Palestine and to Australia involved a long history of representations to the Australian Government,

> There was a decrease in Jewish immigration to Australia in 1928, when the Australian Government refused to set up a special quota for East European Jews as it had done for several other nationalities. Dr Fanny Reading was one of the few community leaders to criticise this decision – her attitude was contrary to the complacent Australian Jewish leadership of the time which opted mainly for preserving the status quo of restricted Jewish immigration.[139]

Dr Fanny was not intimidated by members of the Jewish community who supported immigration restrictions. The dominant voice in the Jewish community was that of the culturally assimilated Anglo-Jewish constituency, many of whom shared the Government view that Jews from Poland were poor and uneducated, would form clusters in city slums and be a burden to the Jewish community as a whole. In 1927, Rabbi Frances Lyon Cohen of Sydney's Great Synagogue wrote to the Government, 'We must guide and control our own immigration [or] we shall in the next generation find the present amicable relations between Jew and gentile undermined and our children painfully faced with all those present costly anxieties of American Jewry'.[140] Appalled by this lack of compassion among the Jewish community, their degree of self-interest and desire to preserve the status quo, Dr Fanny lashed out,

> Who are we to say that we are pleased that certain immigration restrictions will be placed on the admittance of our brethren into our country? That we are glad that our task will be made lighter while our brethren languish for freedom and the right to live?[141]

She rallied support from Jewish and gentile organisations that shared her concerns about the fate of the Jewish people and the welfare of Jewish refugees. At NCJW's birthday conference in Sydney, on 6 July 1943, she put forward a resolution on the refugee problem in Europe. The Principal of Women's College at the University of Sydney, Camilla Wedgwood, moved the resolution, which Dr Fanny planned to send to British Prime Minister, Winston Churchill, and President Franklin Delano Roosevelt of the United States,

> The undersigned express the deepest anxiety at the threat of murder by the Nazis of the surviving four million European Jews, including 600,000 children, and dismay at the negligible results of the Bermuda Conference, since delay involves annihilation. In the name of justice and mercy we ask that immediate measures of rescue and asylum be taken, including opening the door of the Jewish national home.[142]

1943 Australian Women's Conference

Amid reports of the slaughter of Jewish men, women and children, Dr Fanny addressed delegates to the Australian Women's Conference for Victory in War and Victory in Peace, held 19–22 November 1943 in Sydney. She described the plight of Jews in Europe as 'a challenge to the world for action in the name of humanity'.[143] She suggested that an Anglo-American agency should be created, with authority to act immediately and on a large scale to facilitate the immigration and rehabilitation of refugee Jews from Europe. She said, 'our minds were too blunt to realise that four million Jews in Europe had been cruelly done to death in most fiendish ways. That was a world catastrophe unprecedented in history'. She added, 'We have been asked to wait for impending victory, but, unless something is done speedily, there may not be a single Jew left in Europe to enjoy the benefits of victory'.[144]

Dr Fanny's audience represented diverse constituencies. Delegates representing 91 women's organisations heard Dr Fanny's plea, her words filtering through at grassroots and leadership levels. Jessie Street and her organising committee had invited 'not only the women's organisations but also factory workers, housewives, trade unions with women members and all political parties to send delegates to the Charter Conference'.[145] The emphasis was on eliminating 'social evils of poverty, disease and crime to achieve peace at home and to establish and maintain international peace'.[146] A document incorporating their 28 resolutions was distributed to Federal and State parliamentarians, municipal councillors, trade unionists and representatives of political and economic organisations. Street affirmed her commitment to helping Jewish people. She and the delegates recognised that Jews were victims of an unprecedented and industrialised genocide. Conference passed a special resolution urging immediate action 'to rescue the Jewish race from the systematic massacre being perpetrated by the Nazis in Europe',

> Realising that the Jewish people were the first victims of Hitler's barbarism; that already over 4,000,000 Jewish men, women and children have been massacred; and that the Jewish people alone have been selected by the Nazis for complete annihilation.
>
> We Australian women, in conference assembled, urge that in accordance with uprooted European Jewry's desperate need, relief and rehabilitation be provided, and equal status restored to them by the United Nations at the earliest moment possible.
>
> Further. We urge, in the name of justice and mercy, that those who can escape shall be provided with opportunity for migration and settlement in Palestine and elsewhere, and that the Australian Government be asked to approach the authorities concerned to further these purposes.[147]

It is difficult to evaluate the power of Dr Fanny's direct appeal to women delegates at the Charter Women's Conference. What is clear is Jessie Street's determination to intercede on behalf of the Jewish people. She was a humanitarian and proponent for peace. Dr Fanny's advocacy for oppressed Jews found in Street a vigorous campaigner. As President of the United Associations of Women, Street emerged in 1944 as an articulate friend of the Jewish people. She had support from the British Empire Union, the Christian Social Order Movement, the Australian United Nations Assembly, the World Jewish Congress, the New Education Fellowship, the State Labor Party and Communist Party of Australia, the Fellowship of Australian Writers and the Council for Women in War Work. With that support behind her, Street's United Associations of Women put forward to the Australian Government the following recommendations, among others:

1. In view of the process of extermination of the Jewish population of Europe, which is being carried out systematically by the Nazis, we urge the Commonwealth Government without further delay to resume the implementation of their undertaking made at the Evian Conference in 1938 to give asylum to 15,000 Jewish refugees, the implementation of which was interrupted by the war, and whereas 7,000 of this quota has already been admitted to Australia, we ask that immediate arrangements be made for the admission of the balance of 8,000 Jewish refugees so that they may escape slaughter.
2. In view of the great volume of transport which is now available, we urge Commonwealth Government to make representations to the British and United States Governments to make available the maximum shipping space possible.
3. In view of the proximity to Europe, we request the Commonwealth Government to make urgent representations to the British Government to open immediately the doors of Palestine to as many European Jewish refugees as are able to escape to that country.[148]

Nothing touched Dr Fanny as keenly as the fate of Jewish children in Europe. She redoubled efforts for Youth Aliyah that brought surviving Jewish children to Palestine. In 1943, she issued an urgent plea to support these children. She felt compelled to answer the children's 'call of anguish' in the best way she knew, motivating others to stand up and be counted in this crisis, and launching an appeal for financial aid. She used simple words – such as 'cry', 'pitiable', 'desperate', and 'anguish' – that mirrored her own pain,

> The cry of 1800 Jewish boys and girls from Europe has reached our shores to rescue them from their pitiable and desperate plight. I know that every member of the NCJW throughout Australia will answer this call of anguish and save them from the clutches of Hitler.
>
> The appeal of the Youth Aliyah goes forth now for each of us in Australia to do our utmost and save 500 of these children if possible. Children should have a life of happiness. Let us therefore, to the task of making them happy by sending them to Palestine. Eretz Israel is the only land of their hopes. They are waiting for us to help them. I beg of all, help us to bring them out before it is too late.[149]

1943 Sixth NCJWA Conference in Sydney: 'To bring happiness to this sorely tried world'

An impressive roll call of delegates –from Brisbane, South Brisbane, Melbourne, Ballarat, Kalgoorlie, Perth, Geelong, Adelaide and Newcastle – attended the Sixth National Council of Jewish Women of Australia Conference, which opened 4 July 1943 in Sydney, marking Council's 20th anniversary. With 900 members, it was widely acknowledged as a representative and positive force in the Jewish and general community. Major resolutions were framed around future war work, the alleviation of the plight of European Jewry, Palestine, and post-war reconstruction.[150] Australian dignitaries – including Lady Zara Gowrie, wife of the former Governor of New South Wales; and Abram Landa MLA, representing the Premier of New South Wales, William McKell[151] – highlighted Council's prestige and paid tribute to Dr Fanny's leadership. The Editor of *Council Bulletin*, Dora Abramovich, wrote,

> Dr Reading was the first to encourage the modest and humble to feel that they had within them the power to do great things both for their own community and the country in which they lived. The NCJW of Australia is strong because every member feels she is important. This feeling of equality in our organisation is due more than anything to the personality of our founder and President.[152]

Media reports reflected Dr Fanny's pride in the organisation first considered at a meeting on 8 July 1923 in Sydney,

> The reasons for the formation of the N.C.J.W. were the urgent need of a Jewish movement … where problems could be discussed, local and abroad, and the value of an organised body of Jewish women could work bringing young and old women together. In short, to render service for our people and the Empire. The Council had never intended to be a charity organisation giving individual relief. Its philanthropy rather was on a large scale, dealing with the welfare of people as a whole, and for the larger education of its members.[153]

This was a time for enumerating and acknowledging Council's many 'firsts'. Dr Fanny conveyed her depth of emotion at the success of innovative programs implemented over two decades. Council was the first organisation in Australia to organise women on a broad platform and to train girls as future leaders. It was the first national organisation in Australia with sections in every State; the first to form suburban sections, and to organise inter-state conferences from 1929 onwards. It was the first to arrange special educational programs, lectures and study groups for women and girls; to subsidise Jewish education boards; and to establish scholarships in Australia for Jewish boys and girls. It was the first

Jewish organisation to consecrate their work with an Annual Council Sabbath. It was the first to establish a monthly periodical, the *Council Bulletin*, which never missed a publication date in 18 years. Council was the first to begin immigration and refugee work by meeting the boats, welcoming newcomers, finding them homes and assisting them to adjust to their new country. Council was the first to establish under its aegis a Jewish Men's Hostel in Sydney, an Employment Bureau, and English classes. The Council's annual Queen Competition, begun in 1927, raised £1,135 that year. Finally, Dr Fanny mentioned that Council was the first to organise Zionist work among Jewish women and girls in Australia. This had been difficult in 1928 but, she added with bitter irony, in 1933 Hitler had made the task easier.[154] She added,

> ... practically every society and organisation which has sprung up since then [1923], has come from our organisation. The leaders and background have been provided by us. Therefore, after 20 years, the N.C.J.W. takes credit for so much the Jewish women have done in Australia.[155]

Reviewing their philanthropic achievements in Palestine, she recalled that Council maintained a district maternity nurse in 1923 in Palestine; donated towards the creation of a WIZO Infant Welfare Centre in 1924 in Tel Aviv; contributed through the EZRA Association towards the Maternity Hospital in Jerusalem; and donated to the JNF, Keren Hayesod, WIZO, Youth Aliyah, the Hebrew University and EZRA. Council supported appeals for Ukraine Ort-Oze, and Polish and Central Europe Appeals. For 20 years, members had visited patients in hospitals throughout Australia. Local philanthropy flourished, with Council endowing hospital beds and donating funds to hospitals, institutions and appeals for cancer research. Council established their own rooms in Brisbane, Sydney, Melbourne, Adelaide and Perth.[156]

In relation to war work, Dr Fanny recalled the magnitude of Council's sewing, knitting and netting (camouflage nets) for the

Australian Comforts Fund and Red Cross. She mentioned proceeds from the War Shops in Sydney and Melbourne, the Kiosk in Martin Place, and the financial and volunteering services for the Sir John Monash Recreation Hut in Hyde Park, Sydney. Council financed and handed over three canteens (mobile trucks) operating in London, Sydney and Palestine. Council established wards in convalescent soldiers' hospitals in Sydney and Melbourne; and supported Button Days, the Bomb Victims' Appeal (London), the Y.W.C.A., and Merchant Marine. In honour of Council's 20th birthday, Council contributed £20,000 to the 3rd Liberty War Loan. Dr Fanny also mentioned material and financial aid given to internees in Hay and Tatura.[157]

She thanked NCJW pioneers and members throughout Australia for devoted service, loyalty, perseverance and enthusiasm in their work for the benefit of humanity,

> The N.C.J.W. feels that after 20 years it has gained the confidence of Jewish and non-Jewish Committees in Australia and with true prophetic vision has carried out the objectives formed at its formation ... We stand to-day convinced of the righteousness of our cause and realise the great work confronting us in the future, but with God's help we shall go ahead in our noble endeavours to help to bring happiness to this sorely tried world.[158]

The conference highlighted her ability to build bridges of understanding with multiple constituencies. Representatives from 36 women's organisations – 30 gentile and six Jewish – attended the luncheon on 6 July 1943. They focused on their commonalities and the goals that united them. Camilla Wedgwood spoke on 'The Injustice to the Jew'; and moved the following resolution,

> The undersigned express their deepest anxiety at the threat by the Nazis to destroy the surviving four million European Jews including six hundred thousand children. We are dismayed at the negligible results of the Bermuda Refugee Conference since

delay involves their annihilation. In the name of Justice and Mercy we ask that immediate measures of rescue and asylum be taken including opening the door of the Jewish National Home.[159]

All 490 women present signed Wedgwood's resolution, which they submitted to their own organisations. This political resolution aligned with Dr Fanny's priorities. She devoted years to assisting young refugees fleeing persecution for new lives in Palestine. The White Paper of 1939, which restricted Jewish immigration to Palestine, blocked the path of those attempting to escape Nazi tyranny. Conference considered a resolution 'concerning the immediate abrogation of the White Paper of 1939 and that the gates of Palestine be opened for unrestricted immigration'.[160] Delegates resolved to ask Commonwealth authorities to increase immigration to Australia.

Four months later, on 19 November 1943 at the National Women's Conference in Sydney, Dr Fanny spoke on 'Racial Persecution'. This was an important platform from which to disseminate her views to 250 NSW delegates and 30 inter-state delegates, all connected to the political sphere. The conference was opened by Mary Evatt, wife of the Attorney General and Minister of External Affairs in the Curtin Government, Herbert Evatt.[161]

The New South Wales Jewish Board of Deputies

Dr Fanny was one of the community leaders who pioneered the formation of the NSW Jewish Board of Deputies. Her participation ensured that NCJW had voting rights from the beginning of the Board's existence. Three weeks after the NCJW's birthday conference, on 29 July 1943 in Sydney, Dr Fanny and 72 representatives of 19 organisations met to ratify the formation of a new democratically representative body of Jewry in the State, the New South Wales Jewish Board of Deputies, charged with overseeing matters affecting the welfare of the Jewish community. Dr Fanny, a member of the Public Relations Sub-Committee (PRC) of the Jewish Advisory Board set up in February 1942,[162] was also a member of the Provisional Committee set up in March 1943, to draft a constitution for the Board of Deputies. Max Freilich, who served on the Provisional Committee, noted that it was not until 1944 that the constitution was finalised.[163] Those present at the 29 July 1943 meeting passed the following resolution,

> That this convention of Jewish organisations and synagogal bodies recognises the principle of a unified Jewish community and a single controlling, directing and representing authority as fundamental to the welfare of New South Wales Jewry, and to this end endorses the establishment of a New South Wales Jewish Board of Deputies.[164]

The Board's formation changed the structure of the community, 'its creation emphasised the synagogues were no longer the only focal point of Jewish life, since, as a result of the secularisation of society, there were different ways in which members of the community identified as Jews'.[165]

Committee chairman, Harold Bloom, addressed problems confronting the Jewish community, views that coincided with Dr Fanny's,

> ... the most urgent, surely, is the salvation, resettlement and rehabilitation of our devastated European Brethren. Some of them may come to this country and we shall need all our wisdom to assimilate them happily into our communities, to heal their broken bodies and spirits, and to receive them as members of a family rather than as strangers ... This can only be attained if we can achieve a unity of purpose and of action as envisaged in the creation of a Board of Deputies. All the circumstances of the present time demand this of us. Our Brothers and Sisters and

their little children in their torture and in the dawning new hope demand it of us. We cannot do less …¹⁶⁶

Some criticised PRC's plans for a new communal organisation – the PRC responded to a letter by Lieutenant Sulman in the *Hebrew Standard* that cast 'unwarranted aspersions on the character and honour of the members of the Public Relations Committee of the New South Wales Jewish Advisory Board', among whom were communal luminaries such as Chairman Sydney Einfeld; Harold Bloom from the Great Synagogue; Gerald de Vahl Davis, Vice-President of Temple Emanuel; Rabbi L. A. Falk, Chaplain A.M.F.; Max Freilich, President of the Zionist State Council; Dr Fanny Reading, President of the NCJW; Abram Landa, MLA; and Saul Symonds, President of the Great Synagogue.¹⁶⁷ The PRC acted quickly to defuse this negativity, and there was consensus in the community that it was time to create a democratically representative body to oversee concerns of NSW Jewry in troubling times. Dr Fanny brought tolerance and understanding to the new organisation's debates, hallmarks of her *modus operandi*, traits that were of immense value in times of controversy. Although another string to her bow, regrettably it added to her workload, as she attended weekly meetings connected with Board matters, in addition to NCJW' commitments and her medical work.

Five weeks later, Eleanor Roosevelt, wife of the President of the United States, flew into Sydney on 7 September 1943, addressing the women of Sydney that afternoon in the Town Hall. The invitation was open to all Sydney women and 3000 packed the Hall and 12,000 listened outside to her address. There is no documentation confirming a meeting between Dr Fanny and Roosevelt. However, the National Council of Women and the United Associations of Women selected 200 representatives of women's organisations to meet her.¹⁶⁸ Given Dr Fanny's close connections with both organisations, it is unlikely her name was omitted.

Individual and collaborative war efforts

While NCJW's war work on the home-front was paramount, at the same time Council was fearful of the fate confronting Jewish communities abroad. At Council's meeting on 27 October 1943, Dr Fanny reported they had raised £6,253 in the past 15 months; and the shop in Melbourne's Midway Arcade had generated £987 for the Australian Comforts Fund. Rabbi Friedman stated that when peace came and homes would be needed for survivors, 'Palestine was of vital importance to the solution of this problem'.[169]

As a member of the NSW Jewish War Services Committee from its inception on 14 May 1942, Dr Fanny agreed they could establish their Jewish Information and Hospitality Bureau in Council's Kiosk in Martin Place, a popular centre for military personnel. The Bureau provided information about home hospitality, religious worship and entertainment, as well as a list of hosts and hostesses willing to entertain servicemen in their homes. The Bureau distributed chocolates and cigarettes to servicemen at High Holyday services; and wine and cakes after the Great Synagogue's Soldiers' Services.

As a member of the NSW Jewish War Services Committee, NCJW organised entertainment for the troops, in conjunction with Maccabi, the Young Men's Hebrew Association and Temple Emanuel, holding an open night weekly for servicemen. NCJW distributed information cards and copies of Australian Jewish weeklies, and sent magazines and books to country towns, such as Darwin, Cowra, Bathurst, Tamworth and Liverpool. For Passover, 354 invitations to home seders (Passover services) were sent to Australian soldiers and many stayed in private homes. This enterprise offered a home away from home for these servicemen,

> The Information and Hospitality Bureau's list of homes was largely called upon, and Mrs. J. B. Saulwick, the Hon. Secretary of the Bureau, and others, were kept busy arranging hospitality for both Australian and U.S. personnel. In all the foregoing

activities of entertainment, welfare and arrangements for religious services, etc., provision for U.S. personnel was always made.[170]

NCJW collaborated with the Jewish War Effort Circle of Melbourne, distributing Passover parcels to Jewish soldiers in the Australian Force, and providing equipment for football and cricket. In Sydney, members visited Jewish soldiers in the Yaralla Soldiers' Hospital in Concord West, distributing home-made cakes, books and fruit.[171]

All NCJW members contributed to fundraising – bazaars were held in private homes, and there were market days with stalls of groceries, jams, vegetables and flowers. Dr Fanny's sister-in-law, Esmé Reading (Dr Abraham Reading's wife), organised a dance. The Sewing Circle obtained lists of items needed for the Red Cross Store and members worked to fulfill these requirements, 'for the sick, wounded and convalescent members of the Forces, and for the relief of those who are Prisoners of War in enemy lands'.[172] In November 1944, NCJW members made more than 200 garments for 'European Relief' victims, which were sent for distribution to Lady Edith Muriel Anderson, widow of the former Governor of New South Wales, Sir David Anderson.[173]

The success of NCJW's sustained fundraising efforts was acknowledged nationally. In February 1944, in the Quota competition of the 4th Liberty Loan, NCJW came first in the number of subscribers and second in the amount subscribed, raising 'the splendid sum of £51,455'.[174] Australians believed they were investing in victory and ensuring the continued freedom of the country, and 'everyone had a responsibility to 'back the attack'.[175] In April 1945, NCJW still encouraged members and supporters to invest in the Third Victory Loan.[176]

NCJW's 21st AGM in August 1944

War funds for Australia's needs and money for rescuing and rehabilitating European Jews were uppermost on Dr Fanny's mind when she chaired the 21st AGM of National Council, on 8 August 1944 in Sydney. She announced with justifiable pride that members had raised the 'magnificent sum of £134,455' for the 3rd and 4th Liberty and 1st Victory Loans. Martin Place Kiosk had raised – since its inception seven years previously – £7,000 for the Lord Mayor's Comforts Fund.[177] Cheques for more than £3700 were handed to eleven charities. Newspapers praised NCJW's efforts on behalf of war causes,

> In four years and a half of war, the council has helped support the Anzac Buffet, built by Sydney's Jewish Community, the Lord Mayor's Patriotic and War Fund, Red Cross POW Fund, the Far West Children's Home, Sydney Day Nurseries' Association, the Deaf, Dumb and Blind Institution, and many other non-Jewish charities.[178]

CJW's Local Charities Committee reported that more than £800 had been distributed to the Montefiore and Isabella Lazarus Homes, the Crippled Children's Fund, and Redfern Day Nursery. The War Emergency Board report showed a total of £2,642 donated to the Comforts Fund.

The attendance of prominent men at Council's AGM was a tribute to Dr Fanny's leadership and her contribution to the war effort. They included Challis Professor of Law at Sydney University, Professor Julius Stone; the President of the Great Synagogue, Saul Symonds; President of the Zionist State Council, Max Freilich; and JNF President, Horace Newman.[179]

Sydney's Lord Mayor, Alderman Bartley recognised CJW's service to the war effort at a special reception – attended by 200 Council volunteers – to mark the completion of four years' work at the Kiosk in Martin Place. He thanked NCJW and all workers for proceeds from the Kiosk and for assistance in building the Anzac Buffet. The Kiosk had become 'an institution in this city' and he and his colleagues visited it frequently. He received letters of protest when it closed for Jewish holidays, 'thus proving its popularity'. He paid tribute to the 300 volunteers, to whom the Mayoress presented certificates of appreciation signed by the Lord Mayor.[180] At this reception, Dr Fanny reported,

> ... the grand total of £8,441/11/10 had been sent to the Lord Mayor's Patriotic and War Fund to supply comforts and necessities for the men and women of the fighting forces. This magnificent result was due entirely to the continuous and loyal service given by the 300 voluntary workers and supporters who had made such unselfish efforts during four years for this wonderful cause.[181]

Roma Lang: Dr Fanny's leadership style

In 1944, Dr Fanny's receptionist, Roma Lang, entered CJW's annual Queen Competition with high hopes. This was as much a win for Dr Fanny as it was for Roma. This was not a beauty competition but a serious fundraiser for JNF in Palestine. It was a major social event in Sydney's Jewish calendar attracting a large number of participants and even larger number of supporters. With Dr Fanny's enthusiastic support for her special candidate, Roma won the competition outright; and was crowned at a glittering event attended by 700 members of the community. The *Hebrew Standard* wrote that 'Sydney Jewry reaffirmed how wide awake it is to the problems and needs of the day and every Jew feels it to be his duty to respond to the call of the upbuilding of Eretz Israel' and complimented Dr Fanny on her leadership,

> The energetic chairmanship of Dr. Fanny Reading and her appeal to her innumerable friends and supporters resulted in the record amount of £2,643/8/8 being collected on behalf of Miss Roma Lang. Dr. Reading and the NCJW are to be congratulated ...[182]

Dr Fanny was immensely fond of Roma, whom she first engaged in 1940 as her secretary when Lang was 16 years old. She remained with Dr

Fanny for 17 years, 'followed by four years as a companion to the ageing matriarch'.[183] By that time, Dr Fanny suffered from Parkinson's disease and relied on Roma to accompany her to conferences interstate. At the time of Roma's entry in the JNF Queen Competition, she had been Dr Fanny's secretary for four years. She acted as secretary/receptionist at both the Kings Cross surgery and the Bondi Junction surgery. She cooked many of the Friday night Sabbath dinners as 'Dr Fanny couldn't manage it, because she had patients'.[184] In 1998, she commented on Dr Fanny's work-load – and her own – saying there were no set hours of employment and that Dr Fanny would 'cajole' her into staying,

> Would you be able to stay and work with me for a little while tonight? Well, you couldn't say no. She'd say 'Call your mum. You mightn't get home tonight.' We'd finish about four in the morning. I'd sleep there and be up at five to meet the refugees at Circular Quay.[185]

When Dr Fanny expected Roma to accompany her to the docks after she had worked day and night, and slept for only one hour – did this constitute abuse of an employee? Was this an extreme example of an imbalance in the power structure between employer and employee? Roma was sleep deprived and in a state of exhaustion, yet she still complied with Dr Fanny's demands and the inference is clear that this was not an exception but a routine expectation. Were Dr Fanny's expectations of others similarly unrealistic when she delegated challenging tasks? Did she take advantage of their good nature and desire to help? By today's standards, such actions would be deemed, at best, inconsiderate and, at worst, abusive. By any measure, Dr Fanny exerted undue pressure on her followers to maintain her own high ideal of service above self, and to do all that was humanly possible to enact Council's humanitarian and social justice agenda. According to her *modus vivendi*, the wellbeing of the wider community was more important than the individual needs of members and employees.

Lynne Reading, Dr Fanny's niece by marriage to Leigh Reading, her brother Hyman's son, knew Dr Fanny well. Both Lynne's grandmother, Sarah Shaw, and her mother, Ailsa Shaw, were active members of the NCJW in Sydney. Lynne observed, 'Aunt Fanny was hideously demanding. After the Second World War, she would phone my grandmother and demand a pot of soup or blankets for a newly arrived family'.[186] Ailsa Shaw was treasurer of the NCJW in Sydney in the 1950s; and Lynne recalls accompanying her mother to meetings at Dr Fanny's apartment in Kings Cross. 'Aunt Fanny was softly spoken but very determined. It was a case of "Be reasonable, do things my way". When she made up her mind about something, that was that. I felt like Fanny's slave.' Lynne balances these memories with her appreciation of Dr Fanny's generosity to others, 'She really had nothing. Her apartment was basic, her teapot had a broken spout and she threw nothing away. She was always extremely busy, we all were. She held all these meetings and was always surrounded by lovely women seated in a circle in her apartment, with their big handbags on their laps.'

Many of those who recorded memories of Dr Fanny – including family, friends and Council members – spoke of her in superlatives, describing her as gentle, softly spoken, polite and persuasive. Her drive for perfection, undoubtedly a strength in pursuing Council programs and goals, often imposed unrealistic burdens on those with whom she worked. In their recollections, there was often a sub-text that conveyed their acknowledgement of Dr Fanny's subliminal ruthlessness in her dealings with others in order to achieve her goals. Sometimes the pressure she exerted on others was deemed heavy-handed, and at other times it was more subtle. Dr Ian Burman, Dr Fanny's nephew (her sister Rachael's son), who admired his aunt and spoke of her affectionately, nonetheless alluded to her insistence on subjugating your own requirements selflessly to the needs of others, always working towards the greater good of the community. He remembered attending functions at her Kings Cross apartment that were advertised as 'free'. 'You entered without charge, but you never left without paying, in one way or another. That was characteristic of Aunt Fanny,' he said.[187] Former President of NCJWA NSW (1976–1979), Zara Young was a shy fifteen-year-old when she attended a meeting of Council Juniors in Dr Fanny's Kings Cross apartment and met her for the first time. On that occasion, in the absence of any volunteers, Dr Fanny pointed at Zara, handed her a pen and said, 'you are the secretary'. 'I found this very intimidating,' Young said.

Were Dr Fanny's aspirations for others unrealistic at times; and was the 'gentle' persuasiveness praised by some the undoing of others? There is no record of anyone refusing to contribute their efforts when she asked, no matter the personal cost. They did what she requested of them, pushing themselves, as Roma Lang had done on so many occasions, to their human limits. Softly spoken and gentle in manner, for many she was nonetheless an iron hand in a velvet glove. Those who worked with Dr Fanny understood and accepted her leadership style. Everyone knew there was nothing she asked of others that she was not prepared to do herself – she worked side-by-side with Roma at the wharves. She ruled by example and set benchmarks of excellence for all, herself included. Her followers saw a woman at the helm who personified the values she upheld and the mission for which she advocated. When Dr Fanny died on 19 December 1974, the *Council Bulletin* noted in a memorial issue, 'Her devotion was of such character and nature that no one could refuse her request, or having come into contact with her, exclude her influence or sense of commitment'.[188]

Nahlat Dr Fanny Reading and Neve Zippora

In November 1944, Dr Fanny received an honour that moved her deeply, one that forged a meaningful connection between her mission in life and the ancestral homeland she revered. In 1943, NCJW's Melbourne Section raised £4,171 for the JNF and redeemed a portion, *Nahlah*, of land in Palestine in recognition of Dr Fanny's work for Australian Jewry.[189] JNF President in Australia, Dr Leon Jona, made the presentation, the first of its kind to a woman and only the second Nahlah established by Australian JNF. Mrs Archibald Silverman said the honour conferred on Dr Fanny 'will link her name with the redemption of the soil of Eretz Israel'.[190]

Three years later, JNF Head Office in Jerusalem sent to Australia 'a beautiful testimonial', written on parchment and bound in a wooden cover carved by Jewish craftsmen in Palestine, giving a history of 'Nahlat Dr Fanny Reading'. With it came a photograph of the land, and a certificate signed by Dr Abraham Granovsky, testifying to the establishment of the land in Dr Fanny's name. At NCJW's annual meeting in 1947 in Melbourne, Federal President of JNF of Australia and New Zealand, Alec Breckler, presented these artefacts to Dr Fanny,

> ... and quoted instances of Dr. Reading's self-sacrificing efforts in all States of Australia for the good of the Jewish people and the community in general. The General Secretary of the Federal JNF (Dr. K. Fraenkel) then spoke on the significance of a Nahlah which consisted of a part of the most precious possession of the Jewish people, namely its soil in Eretz Israel and was therefore a most outstanding national honor ... the President (Mrs. R. Simons) solemnly handed the testimonial to Dr. Reading, who was deeply moved by the occasion.[191]

The JNF-KKL acknowledged the achievements of Dr Fanny, 'In the course of all these years she has instilled in thousands of Jewish women and girls a high sense of service for the Jewish people of Palestine and for the task of national land redemption'. The certificate stated that Nahlat Dr Fanny Reading comprised 300 dunams (equivalent to 75 acres) in the Negev, in the sub-district of Gaza, about 45 kilometres south of Tel Aviv. It formed part of lands leased for cultivation to the communal settlement Negba. Dr Fanny said she hoped to visit *Eretz Israel* soon 'to spend many happy days with the settlers of the village of Negba established on the land of 'Nahlat Dr Fanny Reading', in the south of Palestine'.[192]

Dr Fanny, who always sought the empowerment of others, acknowledging their efforts and achievements, could not have foreseen an honour of this magnitude. She deflected attention from herself, focusing the spotlight on her organisation. When Rabbi Schenk of Temple Emanuel praised her, she replied,

> ... the Rabbi had paid a magnificent but well-merited tribute to the great band of loyal Council workers, but when he referred to her own influence, he was unduly generous. She felt that her greatest success lay in the fact that the Council provided common ground in which Jewish women of Orthodox, Liberal and even non-religious background could meet and work for the common cause.[193]

The homage 'Nahlat Dr Fanny Reading' conveyed and its significance touched her. For a Zionist who witnessed the emergence of a viable Jewish homeland after her people's exile of 2000 years, there could be no greater honour than having her name associated with that biblical landscape. This honour came at the height of the Nazi Holocaust when Jewish communities were being transported to death camps. Dr Fanny dedicated herself and NCJW to Youth Aliyah's integration of Jewish children in Palestine. As Vice-President of Youth Aliyah in Australia, she focused on giving life, where and when possible, to children whose situation she found heartbreaking. She felt compelled to do all in her power to give these children opportunities for new and better lives. Youth Aliyah ensured their future and thereby the continuity of the Jewish people. These were the times and the context within which she received her honour. It was a gift that wove her name into the fabric of Zionist history and endeavours.

One day after the State of Israel was proclaimed on 14 May 1948, the Arab States of Lebanon, Syria, Jordan, Egypt and Iraq crossed the border with their regular armies. On 21 May 1948, the Negba kibbutz suffered an aerial bombardment; followed by attacks on 2 June 1948 and 12 July 1948 from the Egyptian army. Despite these battles, the kibbutz survived in Israeli hands and became a symbol of an independent Israel.[194]

Dr Fanny never visited Nahlat Dr Fanny Reading. She did, however, visit another settlement named in her honour in Israel. In 1953, the NCJW in New South Wales sent £36,000 to inaugurate a town called Neve Zipporah, in honour of Dr Fanny, whose Hebrew name was Zipporah (a bird). Situated 20 miles from Tel Aviv, Dr Fanny visited Neve Zipporah on 7 April 1957 for the official dedication ceremony, attended by almost all the 400 inhabitants, who resided in 120 houses, many with their own farms. 'It's one of Israel's refugee settlements, and when it is finished there will be 1,500 people living there. Most of them are Jews from North Africa, with quite low standards of living and it'll take a couple of generations for them to be integrated,' Dr Fanny said on her return to Sydney a month later.[195] At the same ceremony in Neve Zipporah, the NCJWA National President Vera Cohen laid the foundation stone of a £6,000 community centre named in her own honour, which incorporated the Gladys Slutzkin Library.

Death of Henrietta Szold

Dr Fanny's great friend and colleague, Henrietta Szold, died on 13 February 1945 aged 85. Known as the 'Mother in Israel', she was buried on Jerusalem's Mount of Olives, and flags flew at half-mast throughout the country. In 1912 Henrietta founded Hadassah, the Women's Zionist Organisation of America. However, it was her work as Director of Youth Aliyah that won her international recognition. From 1934 to the end of the Second World War, Youth Aliyah brought 16,179 Jewish children to Palestine (5,012 before the war, and 11,167 during the war). From July 1945 to October 1948, Youth Aliyah brought a further 14,805 to Israel. Henrietta and Dr Fanny had enjoyed a close professional association and personal friendship over two decades. A month later, on 14 March 1945,

Dr Fanny spoke at a memorial service for Szold in Sydney. She recalled meeting Szold in 1925 in New York, describing 'the insight she was able to gain into the life and character of this great woman and of the inspiration the meeting gave to her'.[196]

Their lives were similar in many ways. Although Dr Fanny was 24 years younger than Szold, there were commonalities that united them. Dr Fanny's escape as a five-year-old child from tsarist Russia in the 1880s could resonate with Henrietta whose parents moved from Hungary to Baltimore in the USA the year prior to her birth, in 1860. Both women were teachers in their youth – Dr Fanny taught music, Hebrew and Jewish studies in Melbourne; and Henrietta established America's first night schools for immigrants, teaching English to refugees of all backgrounds and creeds to aid their integration and employment. She met Russian migrants arriving in the 1880s in America; and, in the 1930s and 1940s, Dr Fanny pioneered similar educational programs in Australia to assist refugees fleeing Nazi persecution.

Henrietta and her mother visited Palestine for the first time in 1909, at that time a 'backwater of the Ottoman Empire'.[197] They were appalled by the 'misery, poverty, filth, [and] disease' among the Jewish communities.[198] In 1913, at Henrietta's instigation, Hadassah sent nurses to Palestine to improve living conditions for women, children and families in the *Yishuv*. In line with Hadassah's principles, their clinical facilities and educational services were available to the Arab and Turkish community. Hadassah's projects reflected American progressive maternalism, a form of social welfare established in New York and Chicago by Lillian Wald and Jane Addams, the latter visiting the Hadassah clinic in Jerusalem.

Dr Fanny and her mother visited Palestine for the first time in December 1925. While there, Dr Fanny reunited with Henrietta whom she had met earlier that year in the United States, and again at the 14th Zionist Congress held in August 1925 in Vienna. Both women were committed Zionists, who believed in the viability of the Jewish homeland and the return of the Jewish people to their ancestral land. Both were especially passionate about child welfare and the work of Youth Aliyah to which Henrietta devoted the latter part of her life. Dr Fanny served as Senior Vice-President of Youth Aliyah in Australia, which brought the women closer together in terms of their common goals and aspirations.

Before the Youth Aliyah fundraising held in July 1945, Dr Fanny requested members and friends to support the organisation,

> The National Council of Jewish Women whole-heartedly endorses the 1945 Youth Aliyah Appeal and pledges its utmost support. No greater privilege or Mitzvah [a good deed] could any Jew or Jewess have than the rescue and future rehabilitation of our orphaned children in Europe. This has an overwhelming claim to our sympathy and support on humanitarian and Zionist grounds alike, and is the proper solution for the thousands and thousands of homeless children wanting a 'home'. The name of Henrietta Szold should be for ever immortalised for her vision and practical work in saving 13,000 children from Nazi brutality and absorbing them in the productive life of the Yishuv. Therefore, it is our solemn privilege in gratitude for the security of our own children, to see that the means are forthcoming through this 1945 Campaign, to give sanctuary and new life for the wandering children of Europe.[199]

NCJW's fundraising for Youth Aliyah was dictated by their needs in Palestine. Labor politician and barrister, Clive Evatt MLA, representing the State Government, was the main speaker at the Youth Aliyah dinner in 1945 in Sydney. That year, the CJW's Bankstown and Illawarra committees handed over £200 towards Youth Aliyah funds, as did the Bondi, Centennial Park, Elizabeth Bay and Rose Bay committees, 'each committee has the proud satisfaction of knowing it has saved one child each from the European tragedy';[200] as did the Bankstown-Canterbury committee, which raised £200 and 'saved one child for Youth Aliyah'.[201] On 24 March 1946, Dr Fanny presented a cheque for £500 to the

President of Youth Aliyah in Australia, Rabbi Schenk, who said 'Palestine was the only hope of the surviving Jews of Europe'.[202]

Dr Fanny and NCJW also raised £1,383 for the United Jewish Overseas Relief Fund (UJORF), which acknowledged their contribution, 'This is one of the finest organisational efforts, and the President of the National Council of Jewish Women, Dr Fanny Reading, and her team of collectors are to be highly congratulated'.[203] Fundraising for Youth Aliyah and the UJORF indicated NCJW's changing focus. While NCJW continued efforts throughout 1945 for local charities and those associated with the war – for example, endowing a bed and presenting a mobile library to the Lady Wakehurst Soldiers' Hospital – the emphasis shifted towards the plight of Jewish refugees in Australia and in Palestine.

War ends 2 September 1945

At a time when irrational hatred was rampant, Dr Fanny stood consistently for tolerance, peace and a more harmonious society. Racist ideology had led to the destruction and death of her people and, wherever she could, she spread her message of goodwill. On 8 March 1945 at Newcastle's International Women's Day celebrations, she spoke on 'Racial prejudice', sharing the platform with Indian feminist Shakuntala Paranjpye, and Australian author Katharine Susannah Pritchard.[204]

On 7 May 1945, the German High Command authorised the signing of an unconditional surrender on all fronts, so war ended in Europe on 8 May 1945. Japan's surrender on 14 August 1945 brought the Second World War to a close. When war ended officially on 2 September 1945, victory crowds erupted; but Jews had little to celebrate. The liberation of the concentration camps revealed the full horror of Hitler's genocide of the Jewish people.

Days after the Second World War ended, Dr Fanny welcomed representatives of 64 organisations – Jewish and gentile – to a NCJW luncheon held in September 1945 in Sydney. After the unremitting pace of her contributions to Australia's war effort, a respite was in order, but this was not her way. She focused on the challenges ahead for herself and NCJW, hoping to engage collaboratively with others committed to the same agenda. She articulated her priorities and that of her organisation, 'the NCJW looked to women's organisations which stood for liberty, justice and freedom, to help Jewish women in the big work they had to do in fighting for a lasting peace and a better world. The NCJW was the platform on which women's organisations could hear and study world affairs …'[205] NCJW immediately turned their efforts to post-war immigration, the rehabilitation of Holocaust survivors and social welfare measures at home and abroad.

When Dr Fanny arrived in Brisbane for the 8th National Council of Jewish Women of Australia (NCJWA) Conference (15–23 June 1946), she foreshadowed NCJW's post-war priorities, 'Peace, post-war relief, migration, rehabilitation of service men and women, and the formation of an International Council of Jewish Women'. She highlighted education and migration, and the challenge of 'getting 600, 000 Jewish people out of Europe, preferably to Palestine'.[206] NCJW's program would include the relief and rehabilitation of European Jewry, Zionism and social and welfare services.[207] NCJW also focused on fundraising for UJORF, which assisted migrants to Australia.[208] As peace dawned, her relief work was only beginning.

Chapter 6
An era of peace

To bring Jewish women to a loftier consciousness of the meaning of public spiritedness.

– Dr Fanny

Dr Fanny's leadership of the NCJW during the Second World War and their contribution to Australia's war effort were recognised by Government and military citations. Her achievements nationally in the area of social welfare for all Australians were widely acknowledged in the 1930s – on 15 May 1935, she received the King George V Jubilee Medal; and on 15 May 1937, the King George VI Coronation Medal.[1] The end of her war-time leadership of her organisation coincided with the closure of the Sir John Monash Recreation Hut and the Anzac Buffet in Hyde Park on Sunday night 3 March 1946. This marked the end of NCJW's efforts in Sydney to establish and maintain the precinct for the Australian Imperial Force. Together with other Jewish organisations, Dr Fanny and NCJW had committed to paying the costs of restructuring and refurbishing the old First World War Anzac Building, so that it could serve as a community centre for troops in Sydney. Operated by the Australian Comforts Fund, in its six years of existence, the voluntary staff served four million meals to servicemen.[2]

Dr Fanny had a proud record on Australia's home front. She initiated and guided NCJW's unremitting efforts for Australia's war requirements.

They raised £300,000 for the Commonwealth War Loans, £18,000 for the Australian Comforts Fund, and made a quarter-million garments for the soldiers.³ In the last year of war alone, NCJW assisted with Button Days, donated to the Red Cross, UNRRA, the Food for Britain Appeal, packed 12 cases of warm clothing and shoes for UJORF, and raised nearly £5,000 for Palestine (supporting JNF, Keren Hayesod, the Hebrew University, Youth Aliyah, MDA. and Ezra).⁴

Did these war years constitute the peak of Dr Fanny's community leadership at home and abroad, with achievements unsurpassed in future years? Dr Fanny's post-war contributions as National President of her organisation continued to improve the quality of life in significant ways for many at home and overseas. Through contributions to Youth Aliyah, NCJW supported the education, training and welfare of child Holocaust survivors in Palestine, and contributed to humanitarian initiatives in the Jewish homeland. In Australia, she remained a player on the national stage, focusing her energies on programs to help newcomers, many of whom were Holocaust survivors.

From 1933 to 1939, 'Australia absorbed between 7,000–8,000 Jewish refugees from Nazism, many from Germany, Austria and Czechoslovakia. Over 5,000 arrived in 1939 – they became known as 'the thirty-niners'.⁵ In 1940, the British Government sent 1780 Jewish internees to Australia on board the *Dunera*. After the war, approximately 27,000 Holocaust survivors came to Australia.

In 1945, Arthur Calwell was appointed Australia's first Minister of Immigration. According to his daughter Mary Calwell, that year her father 'invited close relatives of Holocaust survivors to apply to come to Australia and for Jewish Welfare Societies to process these applications'.⁶ On 2 August 1945, he stated in Parliament,

> We have been too prone in the past to ostracise those of alien birth and then blame them for segregating themselves and forming foreign communities … if we really want more people,

we must change our attitude towards immigrants from foreign countries … Unfortunately, campaigns are fostered in this country from time to time on racial and religious grounds by persons who have ulterior motives to serve. The activities of such people cannot be too strongly condemned. They are anti-Australian and anti-Christian.[7]

There was some disparity between these generous sentiments and the challenging reality for Jews hoping to enter Australia,

Calwell's fear of the negative effect of Jewish migration on his overall migration policy was most clearly evidenced in regard to the International Refugee Organisation (IRO). Under the IRO agreement of July 1947, he agreed to admit workers on a two-year work contract from the Displaced Persons (DP) camps in Europe … Jews were virtually excluded from the program … They had to sign an extra clause agreeing only to work in 'remote areas of Australia'.[8]

Many overcame the hurdles and Holocaust survivors came from the Displaced Person Camps in Germany, Austria and Italy, 'Altogether more than 31,000 Holocaust survivors rebuilt their shattered lives in Australia. In proportional terms, Australia welcomed one of the largest numbers of Holocaust victims'.[9]

NCJW's special committees in every State met and welcomed migrants, and assisted them with services.[10] In 1946, for example, Newcastle CJW hosted a luncheon for 37 refugees from Shanghai, who arrived on board the *Javanese Prince*.[11] Sydney's Council met the *Fochow* and welcomed 27 migrants from Shanghai and Hongkong. The visitors 'were highly gratified with the hospitality'.[12] Dr Fanny thanked those who made 'their arrival so happy by taking the visitors into their homes'.[13] NCJW guest speaker, Jessie Street presented a positive picture of migration to Australia with benefits for the nation, 'It was the intention of the Labor Government to allow 70,000 immigrants into the country. With everybody employed ... the wealth of the country would be assured.'[14]

NCJW's Reception and Transport Committees were busy constantly. In transit in Sydney, a new arrival 'thanked Dr Fanny Reading ... and all the voluntary workers for ... the wholehearted and Jewish way in which all the new arrivals had been made to feel that they were among friends'.[15] When the *Hwa Lien* docked in Sydney, Dr Fanny welcomed 'many beautiful children' and hoped 'that all those weary travellers still in Shanghai and Europe would join their relatives here and make a new and happy life for themselves'.[16] Overwhelmed by the kindness shown to them, the newcomers 'hoped to be able to show their appreciation by helping those who were still to arrive here'.[17]

With every good intention, Council wanted 'to help them to forget the past and to meet and mix with their new countrymen'.[18] This injunction to 'forget the past' – interpreted by many survivors as a blanket ban on talking about their nightmarish experiences – touches on an issue now acknowledged by Jewish communities worldwide, their reluctance after the war to listen to the experiences of newcomers, who were never given the opportunity to debrief, to unburden themselves of their torturous past. Instead, they were expected to get on with their lives by burying the past irrevocably and immersing themselves in the present, which most attempted to do. Psychological wounds and scars, however, bore testimony to hidden sorrows. Melbourne psychologist Dr Paul Valent, worked with survivors to open 'cocoons' of suffering. He identified problems with repressing trauma, 'you keep living it and you can't put the events in a proper historical perspective'.[19] Himself a child survivor of the Holocaust, he noted,

> ... children are highly vulnerable to events and absorb them deeply into their beings ... Sooner or later children need to know the meaning of what happened, why, and who was to blame. Children tend not to question their parents and adults, and often assume guilt. Thus they become morally traumatised

as well. Without retrieving meaning and a sense of goodness, they become alienated from themselves and the world.[20]

Council gatherings were *ad hoc* attempts to assist newcomers, but there was no overall policy framework. Dr Fanny wanted structured protocols for welcoming and integrating newcomers. Before she could further this aim, however, she suffered a bereavement that affected her profoundly. It was some time before she could recommence work and enact the tasks she had in mind.

Death of Esther Rose Reading

Dr Fanny's mother died on 26 September 1946, aged 84. Dr Fanny spent the first five years of her life in the sole care of her mother, who nurtured and supported her in the absence of Dr Fanny's father, who migrated to Australia at the time of her birth. This period together established and consolidated the lifelong bond between mother and daughter.

Esther's sons – Abraham, Hyman and Lewis – while appreciative of their mother's efforts, nonetheless led independent lives; and her younger daughter Rachael was married and raising three sons. There was an unspoken but real family expectation that Dr Fanny would support her mother emotionally and look after her in old age. Esther's grandson, Dr Ian Burman, described the personal sacrifice of a dutiful daughter, who dedicated herself to the wellbeing of her mother, to the exclusion of romance and marriage,

> You should have seen her [Fanny] in her younger years, she was a beautiful woman, in the meaning of beauty at that time. There was talk of an engagement to an American but Fanny felt she had to look after her mother and so that was that. My mother said she gave it up to be with my maternal grandmother. I never heard of any other romance. Never saw a sign in Fanny of regret. She was a gentle soul and saintly.[21]

This was, however, not the only time Fanny rejected a proposal of marriage because of family pressures. Esther's nephew (her sister's child), Abraham Jacob Mecoles (originally Mikuliski), also proposed to Fanny but both families discouraged the couple because they were first cousins. Abraham's granddaughter, Roslyn Marshall, who lives in Melbourne, remembers him well. She said he came from Minsk in Russia to Melbourne, establishing himself in retail in Chapel Street. He visited the Reading family in Ballarat and stayed with them for a while. After Fanny rejected his proposal, Abraham married Sara Malinski and they had five children.

In 1925, Dr Fanny and her mother spent a year together overseas, travelling to the United States, England, Ireland, Europe, Egypt and Palestine, which strengthened their bond. When Nathan died in 1934, Esther moved to Sydney and lived with Dr Fanny for the last 12 years of her life. While she was well and active, she accompanied her daughter to conferences and meetings.

In interviews I conducted in Sydney with Esther Rose's three surviving grandchildren – Jennifer Burman, Dr Ian Burman and Leigh Reading – their memories of their grandmother were of a distant and remote figure, who never inspired real affection. They said she was not demonstrative and they could not recall being hugged or fussed over by her. Their connection with her was devoid of warmth and kindness associated with doting grandparents. It is possible that Esther Rose's temperament, old age and illness – she was bedridden for the latter part of her life – alienated them. Although Esther spoke English, she never did so with the fluency with which she spoke Yiddish. This language barrier would have distanced her further from her grandchildren.

The public perception of Esther was of a devoted wife and mother, whose family values and orthodox lifestyle were respected in the Jewish communities in Ballarat and Melbourne. Esther ran her home according to Jewish laws and worked hard to provide her children with a secure and traditional environment, and educational opportunities, such as home tutoring in Hebrew. She struggled alongside Nathan through financial crises and periods of litigation when he attempted to secure payments due to him. Undeniably, Esther was the stable mainstay of the family throughout the years when their children were dependent on their parents. When the family moved from Ballarat to Melbourne in the first decade of the 20th century, she acquired a reputation for hospitality and acts of charity, assisting Jews in need at home and abroad. Esteemed as the mother of Dr Fanny, she achieved recognition in her own right for her charitable deeds,

> Her teaching and her example were the inspiration of the life and work of her daughter, Dr. Fanny Reading, who founded the NCJW in order to teach other Jewish women the lessons of piety and Jewish practice that her mother had taught her.[22]

Esther Rose Reading, whose Hebrew name was Esther Raizel bat Aharon Moshe (Esther Raizel daughter of Aaron Moses), was buried on 27 September 1946 in Rookwood Cemetery, Sydney. Her epitaph reads, 'In loving memory of Esther Rose, Beloved wife of Nathan Jacob Reading. Devoted mother of Fanny, Abe, Ray, Hyman and Lewis. Passed away 26th September 1946. 1st Tishri 5707. Forever with us.' Her children revered and respected her, yet none was buried alongside her. Her husband Nathan was buried in Melbourne and four of their five children were buried in Rookwood Cemetery – Hyman died on 2 August 1956; Dr Abraham Reading died on 2 September 1958; and Dr Fanny died on 19 November 1974 (and was buried 132 graves away from her mother). The youngest brother, Lewis John Reading, who died in 1972, broke with family tradition and was buried in Matraville Cemetery, Botany. When the sole surviving Reading sibling, Ray Burman, died on 25 September 1981, she was buried in the grave alongside Fanny's. Were these burial arrangements arbitrary or were they indicative of an emotional barrier between children and parent? The married siblings possibly sought grave sites where they could reserve additional plots for their immediate family.

It is possible Dr Fanny intended reserving a grave site close to her mother's but, distracted by Council affairs or shortage of funds, postponed doing so. The most significant of the burial arrangements was the decision taken by Ray Burman to purchase a plot alongside Dr Fanny. Her son, Dr Ian Burman, told me that the sisters' relationship, at times, was fractious, and he attributed the cause to his mother whom he described as 'a difficult woman'. Consciously choosing to rest eternally next to her sister speaks to Ray's profound affection for Dr Fanny, despite any difference they might have had. As the last remaining sibling, she had time to reflect on family relationships and, consequently, made her considered and telling decision.

New procedures for arrivals

In the new year, Dr Fanny resumed her portfolios. On 20 January 1947, together with representatives from 13 community organisations, she attended the first of three conferences 'concerning welcome procedures for new arrivals' at the wharves. Her goal to streamline integration procedures for migrants was now within reach. Welcoming and processing new arrivals was placed on an official footing and documented in a report by Jewish community leader Sydney Einfeld and Walter Brand, Executive Officer of the Australian Jewish Welfare Society, who conferred with the Customs Department concerning the arrival of ships. Passengers should be met early on the day of arrival, so they could travel immediately to destinations interstate. They proposed establishing an office on the wharf for issuing rail tickets. They suggested forming a House Committee, under the auspices of the Jewish Welfare Society, to handle immigrants arriving too late for transportation elsewhere. No matter how well intentioned, unauthorised persons would not be permitted access to the wharves; and those on the wharf had to abide by instructions. They recommended printing a leaflet in English, German, Polish, Dutch, French and Yiddish, setting out passengers' obligations. In particular, they addressed the work of NCJW,

> While the wonderful work of reception and feeding by the NCJW is fully appreciated, it is recommended that in future when a ship arrives carrying a large number of people, and they have to remain on the wharf until four or five o' clock, that canteen be made available on the wharf, staffed voluntarily, to provide light refreshments for the passengers and milk for the children.
>
> It is recommended that ... the Council of Jewish Women might still continue their very good work in entertaining the new arrivals in their rooms, at lunch or dinner, after interstate passengers have been cleared through the Customs.[23]

Dr Fanny submitted eight names, including her own, of NCJW' members able to serve at the Port and Dock. For Dr Fanny, it was always a case of leading by example.

NSW Jewish Board of Deputies' tribute

Personal compliments made Dr Fanny uneasy; she preferred tributes to her organisation. Nonetheless, at a NSW Jewish Board of Deputies meeting in 1947, Saul Symonds congratulated NCJW on its work in welcoming migrants, but shifted the focus fairly and squarely onto Dr Fanny's qualities of leadership,

> It goes without saying that all of this tremendous volume of work calls for the whole-hearted support of a large number of tireless workers, but it must be equally clear that, both as inspiration and coordinating force, it calls for leadership of the highest order. Such leadership it has, in the person of 'Dr. Fanny'. It is an open secret that, high up on the list of those recommended for Empire Honors ... stands the name of Dr. Fanny Reading ... What can be said here and now is that, in the minds and in the hearts of the hundreds, Jews and Christians, who know her and love her, Dr. Fanny Reading holds and will ever hold one of the greatest of all honors, the title of 'Proud and worthy Jewess'.[24]

Symonds' reference in 1947 to a community expectation of 'Empire Honours' for Dr Fanny implied that such an imperial honour for her was probably in the pipeline. If so, they were disappointed. The previous year three women in South Australia – Florence Mack, Mary Showell, Annie Whittle – received the British Empire Medal for services to the Forces in South Australia.[25] Given these precedents, Dr Fanny's supporters clearly thought her worthy of such recognition. In 1948, Dr Fanny commented, 'We do not work for honours. During the war we worked because we, with others, had to right the great injustices that existed in the world, and to make humanity safe for the future'.[26]

Symonds stated that ever since the first small parties of migrants arrived from the East, Council had thrown its resources 'unstintingly into the task of assisting the Welfare Society in the many "personal" directions possible only for a women's organisation'.[27] The aged, nursing mothers and babies received free medical care, and Council found homes and hospitality for 'transients' in Sydney.

Later that year, 100 migrants, mostly Polish Jews, who arrived in Sydney on the *Saggitaire*, expressed their gratitude to Dr Fanny,

> The hand of friendship which was extended to them by Council was more than they had even hoped for, and they expressed the hope that the welcome given to them by Council was a foretaste of the happy days in store for them.[28]

When displaced persons from the camps in Europe came to Australia, they spoke of Dr Fanny's reputation among the 'bewildered and unhappy' at the reception centre in Vienna, where they comforted one another, 'Don't worry. There's a woman in Sydney … her name's Dr Fanny Reading. She'll help you'.[29] Rabbi Benjamin Gottshall recalled meeting Dr Fanny as he left the ship *Surriento*,

> I will always cherish the very first meeting with her … she had a kind word for everyone, shaking hands, making notes, speaking that sweet Yiddish of hers (as we did not speak English),

assuring everyone that one is wanted and welcome here, making a somebody out of you, when one felt so small, unwanted and unimportant.[30]

In Dr Fanny's efforts to help others, she networked across the nation. Internationally, she relied on the sisterhood of Jewish women, their shared values and solutions to mutual problems. To this end, she nurtured helpful connections, such as hosting Enid Alexander, a Sydney girl married to South African parliamentarian Morris Alexander.[31]

Silver Jubilee celebrations

NCJW's Silver Jubilee celebrations began with a dinner on 9 November 1947, a date that marked the 9th anniversary of Kristallnacht (the Night of Broken Glass). Clearly, it was a conscious choice to memorialise the suffering endured by Jews during the pogroms on 9–10 November 1938, throughout Germany, Austria and the Sudetenland in Czechoslovakia. Synagogues were burned, Jewish shops smashed and looted, Jews assaulted and murdered, and 30,000 Jewish men sent to concentration camps. It presaged the horrors the Nazi Reich had in store for Jews and marked the beginning of a murderous trajectory that escalated rapidly into the unimaginable evil of the Holocaust. Almost five years later, delegates to the Sixth NCJWA Conference, held in August 1943 in Sydney, expressed dismay at the negligible results of the Bermuda Conference,

> since delay involves annihilation and asked 'in the name of justice and mercy' that immediate measures of rescue and asylum be taken: namely the 'unrestricted Jewish migration to Palestine' and an 'increase of immigration to Australia'.[32]

The 1943 conference had propelled the issue to the forefront of debate in delegates' homes, potentially helping to unite the Jewish community in their approach to the Australian Government to secure a more liberal immigration policy; and to renounce the MacDonald White

Paper that limited Jewish migration to Palestine. The President of the Zionist Federation of Australia, Alec Masel, delivered their resolution to Prime Minister John Curtin on 18 November 1943. Historian Konrad Kwiet notes, 'not a single concession was granted … only a handful of Jews were granted a landing permit after the outbreak of war',[33]

> Only after the Holocaust, after the extinction of the centres of Jewish life, was Australia prepared to support the creation of a Jewish state as well as to offer … a refuge to survivors of the Holocaust.[34]

Sydney feminist Ruby Rich, guest speaker at the silver jubilee dinner, referred to the genocide of the war, 'We have a special responsibility … towards the pitiful remnants of our people who remain in the Displaced Persons Camps'; and expressed the hope 'that a haven would be found for them in this wonderful country of ours'.[35] Federal parliamentarian, Leslie Haylen had visited DP camps abroad and, horrified at what he saw, expressed sympathy for newcomers and 'hoped that with the aid of Council they would … find peace and happiness here'.[36]

Dr Fanny, Sydney members and friends visited Newcastle for Silver Jubilee festivities there on 23 November 1947. She was proud of their record on migration. Newcastle was the first Council to welcome war arrivals from Shanghai, assisting them in every way they could. She also focused on her cherished project, the future Council House, which would serve 'as a clearing house for new arrivals' and appealed for assistance in realising her goal.[37]

UN General Assembly in favour of Resolution 181

On 29 November 1947, the United Nations General Assembly voted in favour of Resolution 181 that called for the partition of Palestine into a Jewish and an Arab state. The plan called for an economic union between the proposed states and for the protection of religious and minority rights. It was approved with 33 votes in favour, 13 against, 10 abstentions and one absent. The resolution was accepted by the Jews in Palestine but rejected by the Arabs in Palestine and by the Arab states. Britain, the mandatory power for Palestine, declared it planned to complete its evacuation of Palestine by 1 August 1948. Australia's Minister for External Affairs, Dr Herbert Vere Evatt, Australia's representative at the UNO and Chairman of a senior UNO Committee, played a vital role in discussions leading to the decisive vote,

> The devastation caused to world Jewry by the Holocaust offended his sense of justice and democracy and convinced him that the Jews had a right to a sanctuary in Palestine, and his background as a criminal lawyer and judge indicated that he always showed profound sympathy with the underdog and usually sided with those he saw as victims of oppression. He was also seen as the champion of the rights of small nations, and for this reason he became a strong advocate of the importance of the United Nations. His policy in regard to Palestine was influenced by his belief that Australian foreign policy must be formulated independently of Britain.[38]

As Australia's Minister of External Affairs and Attorney-General in John Curtin's Labor Government, Dr Evatt believed that participation in the debate on Palestine's future furthered Australia's interests. 'He felt the Middle East was important for Australian foreign policy, especially as the region was a bridge between Africa and Asia.'[39] He received a deputation led by the President of the NSW Jewish Advisory Board, Saul Symonds, who put forward the Zionist case and the tragedy of European Jewry. In 1944, Dr Evatt met Max Freilich, President of the Zionist State Council in New South Wales, with whom he forged a personal friendship. Several members of the Zionist Executive, possibly envious of Freilich's connection with Dr Evatt, were openly hostile, 'because they considered me a Zionist fanatic and irresponsible … hence they tried to stop me'.[40] In April 1945, Dr Evatt led the Australian delegation to the San Francisco Conference convened to draft a charter for the United Nations. The Australian-Palestine Committee presented a petition to Prime Minister John Curtin and Dr Evatt, 'urging the support of the Australian Government for the establishment of a Jewish Commonwealth in Palestine'.[41] Dr Evatt promised his Government's full support.

Although Dr Evatt was not elected President of the General Assembly, he was elected unanimously to the chairmanship of its *Ad hoc* Committee on Palestine, comprising representatives of all member nations of the United Nations. The partition plan came up for the historic vote by the *Ad hoc* Committee on 25 November 1947, with Dr Evatt voting 'yes' from the chair.[42] On 29 November 1947 at Lake Success, the second General Assembly of the United Nations voted for the partition of Palestine into Jewish and Arab States. Freilich wrote, 'A cable conveying our congratulations and grateful thanks was dispatched to Dr Evatt'.[43] The Zionist Federation in Melbourne decided to plant a JNF forest in Palestine in honour of Dr Evatt for the 'skilful way in which he had conducted the meetings of the *Ad hoc* committee on Palestine so that it was made possible for the United Nations Assembly to arrive at the decision for the partitioning of Palestine into Jewish and Arab States'.[44] Dr Evatt stated, 'what I did to bring about the decision for setting up a Jewish State in a part of Palestine was not an act of favour to the Jews but because I firmly believe in the justice of the Jewish case'.[45]

After 2000 years, the 'Children of Israel' could envisage the rebirth of a Jewish State in their ancestral homeland. For Dr Fanny and NCJW this day in history changed their lives and those of Jewish people everywhere. Hope was reborn after the destruction and death of the Shoah. Conscious of this new chapter in the history of the Jews, Dr Fanny proclaimed, 'Our martyrdom is at an end'.[46]

Resolution 181 was the realisation of a dream for Dr Fanny and NCJW. She had seen the homelessness of the Jewish people during the Second World War and the prohibition on entry into Palestine as a tragedy; and had committed herself to ameliorating circumstances, as best she could. Suddenly, there was the real prospect of a homecoming for survivors in Europe's DP camps. Moved by this change in the circumstances of the Jewish nation, she wrote,

> The conscience of the United Nations of the world has been awakened to the call of Theodor Herzl that we are a nation, not a nation only for persecution, but a nation whose demand for nationhood and the restoration of its national Home has been right and just. We Jewish women of Australia, who 25 years ago took up the banner of Zionism for the redemption, of Palestine, see our prayers, our hopes and longings answered, and we go forward with renewed courage, faith and inspiration, to meet the bigger tasks that await us in the building of our National Home.
>
> We present-day Jews are deeply conscious that we have had the sacred privilege, to witness this epoch-making event in Jewish history. At this time our hearts and minds are filled with intense gratitude for the supreme sacrifices made by our early Chalutzim [male pioneers] and chalutzot for the establishment of a Home for Israel. We also remember that Britain was the first in modern times to undertake the restoration of Palestine for the Jewish people. All the members of the National Council of Jewish Women throughout Australia rejoice with heart and soul with the Yishuv [the Jews in Palestine] and send a message of loyalty and devotion and greetings and good wishes for the complete fulfilment of all our hopes and aspirations. We pledge our fullest support for the further upbuilding of Eretz Israel which will become a home of security for our people in Palestine and abroad. Shalom.[47]

Dr Fanny's message ended with the word 'Shalom', 'Peace', which conveyed the crux of the matter for her. After excesses of hatred, inhumanity and genocide experienced by Jews, suddenly there was peace, the watchword of Chaim Weizmann. Destined to be the first President of the State of Israel, in December 1947 he declared that the most important task ahead was to seek peace with the Arabs.[48] He added that Jews were prepared to assume governmental function, while Palestine Jewry was ready to meet any possible attacks.

Joy erupted wherever Jewish communities existed. Those in European DP camps felt relief. Thirty thousand Jewish refugees in Vienna celebrated and 'Depression among the DPs gave way to joy and confidence'.[49] In the camps, there were services and concerts, an expression of their sense of renewal. At long last, they knew they were going to Palestine. Jewish Agency officials planned a systematic immigration to Palestine; and camp inmates applied for certificates and urged the establishment of training courses.[50]

Playgrounds for children memorialise Jewish pilot

The day after the historic vote at the United Nations, on Sunday 30 November 1947, NCJW dedicated the first of three Philip Myerson Playgrounds in Sydney to the memory of the 20-year-old Jewish pilot killed in action. The playground memorialised a Jewish soldier who 'laid down his life for King and Empire at the very early age of 20'.[51] Philip was the youngest son of Mrs Emanuel Myerson, official organiser for 14 years of NCJW's Charities Committee. Rabbi Falk, who knew Philip from childhood, said 'no better tribute could be paid to his memory than something which made for a happy and healthy childhood'. The plaque read: 'This playground was equipped by the National Council of Jewish Women, Local Charities Committee, in memory of Pilot-Officer Philip Myerson, who was killed in action on January 29, 1945'.[52] For Dr Fanny, the playgrounds also represented Council's commitment to the wellbeing and happiness of children.

Dr Fanny welcomed young migrants brought to Sydney in early 1948 by the Welfare Guardianship scheme and Save the Children Fund, 'ideal types that this country is looking for. Their enthusiasm and curiosity about everything appertaining to the new land of their adoption augurs well for their future'.[53] They expressed their determination 'to be a credit to their guardians and to the Jewish community in general'. NCJW had prepared accommodation for them at the Isabella Lazarus Home; and they were delighted 'with the spaciousness of their new home and the brightness of their surroundings'.[54] Dr Fanny's interest in the wellbeing of children was non-denominational and non-discriminatory, a principle she enshrined in NCJW's practice and policies. As Youth Aliyah was represented on the Australian National Committee for the United Nations and, as Vice-President of Youth Aliyah, she threw her weight behind the 1948 United Nations Appeal for Children.[55]

State of Israel established 14 May 1948

While Dr Fanny conferred with NCJW's members in Newcastle, Brisbane and Adelaide about the Silver Jubilee Conference to be held in July 1948 in Sydney, a new page was written in the history of the Jewish people. In calling for the establishment of a Jewish State, the United Nations General Assembly required the inhabitants of the Jewish homeland to take necessary steps for the implementation of resolution 181. Dr Fanny's dream of a Jewish State – for which she worked all her adult life – became a reality on 14 May 1948, when David Ben-Gurion, head of the Jewish People's Council, proclaimed the establishment of the State of Israel. That night, the United States was the first to recognise the State of Israel *de facto*, followed three days later by Russia, the first to give *de jure* recognition to the Jewish State.

The Declaration of the Jewish People's Council stated that the land of Israel was the birthplace of the Jewish people where their spiritual, religious and political identity was shaped. There they first attained statehood, created cultural values of national and universal significance and gave the Hebrew Bible to the world. After being forcibly exiled from their land, the people kept faith with it throughout their dispersion and never ceased to pray and hope for their return to it and for the restoration in it of their political freedom. The Declaration stated,

> Impelled by this historic and traditional attachment, Jews strove in every successive generation to re-establish themselves in their ancient homeland. In recent decades they returned in their masses ... they made deserts bloom, revived the Hebrew language, built villages and towns, and created a thriving community controlling its own economy and culture, loving peace but knowing how to defend itself, bringing the blessings of progress to all the country's inhabitants, and aspiring towards independent nationhood.
>
> In the year 5657 (1897) ... the First Zionist Congress convened and proclaimed the right of the Jewish people to national rebirth in its own country. This right was recognized in the Balfour Declaration of the 2nd November, 1917, and re-affirmed in the Mandate of the League of Nations which, in particular, gave international sanction to the historic connection between the Jewish people and Eretz-Israel and to the right of the Jewish people to rebuild its National Home ... On the 29th November, 1947, the United Nations General Assembly passed a resolution calling for the establishment of a Jewish State in Eretz-Israel ... This recognition by the United Nations of the right of the Jewish people to establish their State is irrevocable. This right is the natural right of the Jewish people to be masters of their own fate, like all other nations, in their own sovereign State ... The State of Israel ... will guarantee freedom of religion, conscience, language, education and culture; it will safeguard the Holy Places of all religions; and it will be faithful to the principles of the Charter of the United Nations.

> We appeal – in the very midst of the onslaught launched against us now for months – to the Arab inhabitants of the State of Israel to preserve peace and participate in the upbuilding of the State on the basis of full and equal citizenship and due representation in all its provisional and permanent institutions. We extend our hand to all neighbouring states and their peoples in an offer of peace and good neighbourliness, and appeal to them to establish bonds of cooperation and mutual help with the sovereign Jewish people settled in its own land. The State of Israel is prepared to do its share in a common effort for the advancement of the entire Middle East.[56]

When Dr Fanny created the first CJW in 1923, she promised Pevsner 'to make the restoration of Palestine one of the Council's foremost aims'.[57] Openly supporting Zionism in the 1920s was a brave position, as Dr Fanny 'was one of a tiny group of communal activists who believed in the acquisition of the Jewish homeland as a political state'.[58] From the 1920s, NCJW committed to supporting the Jewish homeland. In 1923, Dr Fanny and her Council, 'sent the first monies ever raised by Australian Jewish women to [for] Palestine – £100 – to found a district nursing service in Tel Aviv'.[59] Dr Fanny's humanitarian response to the needs of Palestine's people shaped NCJW policies. In 1926, she appealed to members,

> They are human, as we are human; they have feelings as we have. By what right are we entitled to benefits more than they? The innocent babes – those little beings created in the divine image – why shouldn't they be given the same chance to begin life under the best possible conditions as our own babes.[60]

Dr Fanny never relaxed her efforts to aid the reconstruction of the Jewish homeland and to alleviate hardships endured by all its people. NCJW assisted in Palestine's reconstruction – in areas of social welfare for mothers and babies, Youth Aliyah and JNF tree-planting programs.

In 1948, Dr Fanny was elected to the NSW State Zionist Council, and her main concern was Israel's responsibilities in feeding, clothing and housing new immigrants, who streamed in now the doors were open. NCJW redoubled its efforts,

> With the State of Israel reborn, Dr Fanny, a Zionist of long standing, directed all sections to intensify their commitment to Israel. She taught us that we have a moral obligation to care for the baby we helped to bring into this world. We must help it to crawl, to walk, to reach maturity and economic independence.[61]

In 1948, Dr Fanny travelled widely to promote the Silver Jubilee Conference in Sydney. Brisbane Councils, for example, held several functions for her, including a party in the Botanic Gardens.[62] On her return to Sydney, she celebrated the annual Council Sabbath, attending an evening service at Temple Emanuel and a morning service at the Great Synagogue. By attending both temple and synagogue, she demonstrated that NCJW welcomed Jewish women from all religious streams, a tradition NCJW has upheld. After the synagogue service, she recalled with pride that Council's first meetings in 1923 took place in the Great Synagogue's lounge.[63] She stayed in Sydney briefly before flying to Adelaide to discuss the Silver Jubilee Conference. In press interviews, she outlined NCJW's main tasks, in particular, helping Jewish migrants 'to become good Australian citizens'.[64]

Ninth NCJWA Conference in Sydney

A poignant moment for Dr Fanny and 500 attendees was the opening of the 9th National Council of Jewish Women of Australia Conference, on 25 June 1948 in Sydney. 'We never thought 25 years ago, we would live to see this day,' she said. 'Over the years a bond of sisterhood has united us.'[65] The Premier of New South Wales, James McGirr, paid tribute to Dr Fanny,

> It is most fitting to hear this gathering pay tribute to Dr. Fanny Reading ... Her name is a household word for good work in the State of New South Wales. Wherever I go in Australia, I meet people who ask me about her. Work done by people like her, without great publicity, are the greatest deeds of all.[66]

Member of the NSW Legislative Assembly, Abram Landa, endorsed this view, 'This great personality has engraved her name in the hearts and minds of the Jewish people'. Dr Fanny's response was consistent with her attitude throughout her Presidency – she focused on challenges ahead. She never rested on her laurels and, under her stewardship, neither did NCJW. She could have reminisced about past achievements, of which there were many. Instead, she spoke of their future agenda,

> We will do what we can, in future, to prove ourselves truly worthy of the great honours you have showered upon us ... Council has never appealed for funds to meet its own needs ... but now we feel we must do so ... It is our aim to establish a Council headquarters in Australia, which can be used as a hostel, as a rallying point from which Jewish women can go about their charitable work. To do this ... we are appealing to the Jewish community.[67]

In highlighting the contributions of co-founders and workers, Dr Fanny spoke in an uncharacteristic way, saying that for 25 years they had 'slaved' together. Now, they asked for financial help to carry on their valuable services to the community.[68] On a visit to Newcastle, she expressed appreciation of her fellow citizens' moral support,

> When we Jewish women think of the great tragedy of six million of our people who were slaughtered in cold blood, we feel we have a great debt to our people. We appreciate your outlook and feel our tragedy has been very considerably lessened by people who are as broadminded as you.[69]

At that reception, Rev. Isack Morris described Dr Fanny as 'a woman of great culture who has given her life to work for the welfare of every branch of humanity'.[70]

A Jewish Hospital for Sydney

In 1947, Dr Fanny and NCJW collaborated with stakeholders to establish a Jewish hospital in Sydney. Dr Abraham Reading recalled that NCJW was 'the first body to advocate the establishment of a Jewish hospital'.[71] This project was close to her heart. A Jewish hospital's kosher kitchen would cater for dietary requirements of the orthodox Jewish community. She had worked in many hospitals across Sydney, so her skills and knowledge were crucial to this project. She brought in Sam Karpin, President of the Young Men's Hebrew Association (YMHA) and held discussions with Jewish doctors in Sydney who supported the scheme – including her brother, Dr Abraham Reading, Dr Joseph Steigrad, Dr H. Landecker and Dr A. Owen. They planned a hospital in Wentworth Street, Point Piper.[72]

In addition to Dr Fanny's multiple portfolios in medicine, her general practice in Kings Cross and Bondi Junction, her National Presidency of NCJW, and participation in numerous civic bodies, she also took on the role of honorary secretary of the new Hospital Board tasked with creating and financing the Jewish Hospital in Sydney. NCJW supported the scheme and commenced active fundraising for the hospital. NCJW was the first body in the community 'to organise a public function for the N.S.W. Jewish Hospital, from which effort the sum of £1000 was raised to endow a bed in the hospital in the name of Dr. Fanny Reading'.[73] A hospital spokesman commented,

> We are not surprised at the active role being taken by the N.C.J.W. ... Dr. Fanny Reading was one of the first to support the idea of a Jewish hospital, and was always expected to carry a major share of the burden ... Dr. Fanny and her ladies redemonstrated their unequivocal support of this lofty cause.[74]

Despite Dr Fanny's best efforts and those of NCJW, the project failed, the property was sold and the funds kept in trust. Concurrently, another healthcare initiative took shape, resulting from a bequest to NCJW. Council member Gertrude Stone appreciated the kindness of CJW's Hospital Visiting Committee and, in April 1949, bequeathed her house in Coogee to NCJW. She suggested it be used as a convalescent home and that it be called the Aaron and Gertie Wolper Convalescent Home or Hospital, memorialising the name of her first husband. The house proved unsuitable and NCJW sold it. With the proceeds, they bought a property at 8 Trelawney St, Woollahra, where the Wolper Convalescent Home opened in 1953. Dr Fanny and 120 members of the Jewish community attended the opening by NSW Prices Minister, Abram Landa, and the dedication by Rabbi Leib Falk. The home had 18 beds, including a free one for needy cases, and one endowed by NCJW in the name of Becky Lake, who canvassed support for the project.[75] Stone 'decreed in her will that the convalescent hospital be non-denominational'.[76]

This enterprise also ran into financial difficulties and, in 1959, Wolper amalgamated with the defunct NSW Jewish Hospital. Wolper's executive comprised three trustees from NCJW's Hospital Visiting Committee – Dr Fanny, Becky Lake and Ethel Zion – as well as Sam Karpin of the YMHA and Maurice Allen, the latter two representing the old NSW Jewish Hospital. With the merger complete, the Wolper could use the Jewish Hospital's funds to extend and improve its amenities. On 20 August 1961, the NSW Minister for Health, William Francis Sheahen, opened the renovated Wolper Jewish Hospital. On 14 May 1982, almost eight years after Dr Fanny's death, NCJW's three trustees serving on the executive handed over the title of the land to the Wolper Jewish Hospital.[77] Today, the building has a NCJW lounge in which hangs a portrait of Dr Fanny with a memorial plaque that outlines her role in the establishment of this Eastern Suburbs institution.

Maccabi affiliates with NCJW

Dr Fanny was committed to promoting social interaction between Jewish boys and girls. Concerned about the increasing rate of intermarriage, she devised social programs that brought young people together. On 28 August 1948, she welcomed Maccabi's announcement that this Jewish sports organisation wished to join NCJW. The President of Maccabi, Ron Newman, confirmed that Maccabi 'had joined the ranks of the National Council of Jewish Women'.[78] Dr Fanny responded that NCJW was 'delighted to welcome Maccabi, who would fill the position of a youth section to the National Council of Jewish Women'.[79]

This development was consistent with Dr Fanny's lifelong policy of combatting intermarriage. As early as 1923 in Sydney, she stated, 'the foremost need was to educate young Jewish women in their tradition as assimilation and intermarriage were the most vexing problems of the day'.[80] A quarter-century later, she articulated the same belief, adding that much could be done to address a deteriorating situation,

> ... one of the main objects in embracing the Maccabi to the N.C.J.W. was to afford opportunities to young Jews and Jewesses to meet and eventually marry. One of the most heartbreaking experiences for parents today ... was to see their children marry out of the Faith.[81]

Services to migrants acknowledged

In January 1949, the NSW Jewish Board of Deputies expressed gratitude to Dr Fanny and NCJW for their services in welcoming arrivals at the wharf in Sydney and for providing food and accommodation for passengers bound for Melbourne. The warmth of their welcome mattered, as there was considerable hostility in the general community towards migrants. Sydney Einfeld, commended the large number of women and men who spent a whole day, on 12 January 1949, with arrivals on the

SS Partizanka. He singled out Dr Fanny, 'One couple, with two children, missed the train and Dr. Fanny Reading was kind enough to offer them accommodation for the night in her home'.[82] He stated that the Committee would operate again the following week when the *SS Eridan* was due 'with more than 200 of our people'.[83]

This promising start to 1949 would unravel and Dr Fanny would face challenges ahead that she could not have imagined. In 1949, she was the plaintiff in a defamation case that taxed her strength, concentration and endurance. It affected her health, her practice and her income. Immediately after the trial, despite her exhaustion, she was elected to the Sydney committee of *Oeuvre de Secours aux Enfants (OSE)*, a philanthropic venture based in Switzerland, and operating in Israel, various European countries and North Africa. It directed its efforts 'towards the rehabilitation and the protection of health of the Jewish population in those countries'.[84] Three doctors, who brought groups of Jewish children to Australia, attended the inaugural OSE meeting on 9 May 1949 in Council rooms in Sydney.

Aside from Dr Fanny, the committee included, among others, Ruby Rich, Dr Henry Frant, Dr I.M. Friedman and Dr Frieda Laserson. They planned a social welfare program for babies, young children and their mothers, and resolved to provide domestic help for sick mothers; to establish day nurseries for babies of working mothers, and kindergartens in various districts of Sydney; and to assist Jewish doctors from overseas and to 'help them in adapting themselves to the new conditions'.[85] These activities would be carried out 'in harmonious co-operation with the UJORF and with other Jewish organisations in Sydney doing welfare work';[86] which reflected Dr Fanny's lifelong advocacy of organisations working collaboratively to achieve the best results.

As the tide of Jewish history turned, Dr Fanny's optimism revived. She had nurtured the Newcastle branch since its inauguration in 1929, so she celebrated their 20th anniversary with them. At the AGM, she used the word 'wonderful' repetitively, speaking of 'the wonderful spirit of the

Jewish people during the struggle for the new State'; and stating 'we had passed through the most wonderful period of Jewish history – the declaration of the Jewish State, and Israel's admittance to the United Nations'.[87] She appealed to members 'to support our people who have suffered, and to help those still in need in Europe to be rehabilitated and cured both in mind and body'.[88] She added, 'For 20 years ... you have stuck to the original ideals formed during the inauguration'.[89] Newcastle's President, Mrs Goldring, who presented Dr Fanny with 'a tribute of six trees' planted in her name in Israel, said, 'The efforts of our kin in Israel should act as an incentive to members here'.[90] Five years later, Dr Fanny also marked their 25th anniversary. At a luncheon attended by 100 representatives of charitable organisations in the city, she highlighted CJW's aid to immigrants. 'As so many of our people have been forced to leave the land of their birth, it is our duty to do all we can to help them,' she said.[91]

International Council of Jewish Women

The newly formed International Council of Jewish Women, at their conference in 1949 in Paris, elected Dr Fanny one of five Vice-Presidents of the organisation. This honour was widely reported in the Australian press,

> Dr. Reading is president and founder of the National Council of Jewish Women of Australia, and this most recent honour ... is richly deserved both by herself and the many thousands of women she has represented for the past 25 years.[92]

It is not clear whether her elevation to the Vice-Presidency influenced her decision to retire from active management of Sydney Council's affairs. The appointment certainly brought added responsibilities. She had been a conscientious participant in Council's Sydney section, while monitoring and encouraging the work of Council sections nationally. Her exhaustion following the *Smith's Weekly* court case in 1949 surely played a role. On 19 September 1949, she announced her departure from Council's Sydney section, saying she and her co-executors felt, 'they ought to give the younger women a chance to let them try their hand at managing the various activities of the Council'.[93] She and her associates would be in the background to guide and advise. Dr Fanny thanked members for their work, especially welcoming and looking after new arrivals,

> Their only reward was a smile of thanks on the faces of these migrants. This was considered as the richest reward a Jewish woman could wish for. But ... although we have done good work in the past, we have many responsibilities for the future. Israel and our community will require all we can give them in many ways.[94]

News of her retirement spread quickly, and families gathered 'to pay tribute to a great woman who has done much for Jewry'.[95] Dr Fanny's major contributions to Jewish and gentile charities, organisations and causes at home and abroad were acknowledged,

> With that broad-mindedness and human understanding which characterises all truly great social workers, she has been, and still is, very active in all fields of social welfare in Australia. Thus, she is an executive member of the National Council of Women (N.S.W.), past member of the Honorary Medical Staff of the Rachel Forster Hospital, St. George's District Hospital, and the Community Hospital. She is also a Life Governor of the Crown Street Women's Hospital, the Dalwood Health Homes, the Benevolent Society of N.S.W., and the NCJW Jewish Hospital ... our community may well be proud and thankful to Dr Fanny Reading – truly a leader and lover of mankind.[96]

Dr Fanny's role transformed into that of NCJW's elder stateswoman. She remained active in Council affairs but the intensity of her participation diminished. Her main focus was the State of Israel. In what must have seemed to her a magical occasion symbolic of the new reality for the Jewish people, she attended a reception in May 1951 given by the Minister for Israel, Joseph Linton, to mark Israel's third Independence Day. Flowers in blue and white, Israel's colours, decorated the Minister's Point Piper home, where 150 guests gathered, including the Premier of New South Wales, James McGirr; the Italian Minister, Dr Giulio del Balzo; the American Consul-General, Donald Smith; and Dr Fanny.[97] Also present was Dr Herbert Vere Evatt, Labor MP for Barton, who had facilitated the partition of Palestine.

'The courage of the women ... leading the way'

The courage of women and their unceasing efforts to ameliorate harsh conditions, to alleviate poverty and suffering, and to care for the needy at home and abroad was a theme to which Dr Fanny returned consistently throughout her lengthy tenure of office in the NCJW and in her many roles within the public realm. This belief powered her philosophy, her organisation and, indeed, the way she conducted her life in the service of others. She personified this in her medical career and her presidency of the NCJW. In particular, when it came to the wellbeing of children, no issue was too minor and no challenge too great. As Vice-President of Youth Aliyah, Dr Fanny was aware that many thousands of children still suffered the consequences of war years. In November 1951, she pledged NCJW's support to Jewish Child's Day. Several organisations co-operated to rescue thousands of children in unfortunate circumstances, including the UJORF, the NSW Board of Jewish Education, Youth Aliyah and local women's organisations.[98] At the Silver Jubilee of the Brisbane Council of Jewish Women in 1952, she spoke on the topic 'Women lead the way'.[99] While rejoicing that 'The gates of Israel are now open. It does not matter how many hundred thousand desire to enter'; [100] she understood that immense resources were needed by migrants requiring food, clothes and accommodation. She commended the bravery of Israel's women,

> The State of Israel ... had proved the great compensation for the

Jewish race after the persecutions suffered through Hitler. It was the courage of the women that had enabled them to carry on and which was leading the way despite economic depression.[101]

WIZO emissary, Malcah Weinberg, reinforced this theme when she spoke at Sydney Council's 30th anniversary luncheon,

> … women were playing a major part in the development of social and child welfare and were active in education and politics in Israel. One woman is Minister for Labour, another was our Minister to Russia, and a third a consul in Brazil.[102]

Four years later, in April 1957 in Jerusalem, Dr Fanny and NCJWA National President Vera Cohen heard 'our Minister to Russia', Golda Meir – appointed Israel's Minister of Foreign Affairs on 1 January 1956 – deliver a keynote address. On Dr Fanny's return to Sydney in May, she spoke of Golda Meir,

> She's a very plain woman, but she gave a most stirring speech on the dignity of Israel. She reminded me of a prophetess – Deborah, perhaps – rallying her people for battle. It's [Israel] a land of opportunity for women.[103]

After decades in public life, Dr Fanny deplored an emerging apathy and indifference to 'new ventures and big endeavours'. She still had big dreams, but many ventures were never realised. She prepared an ambitious three-year plan for about 80 farms on land 50 miles from Tel Aviv; and 'expressed the hope that streets and houses would be named after each section of Council'.[104]

A home of their own

Dr Fanny cherished her dream of a Council House in Sydney but it proved elusive. She urged Councils to achieve this in their respective cities. In September 1949, Sydney's CJW announced it acquired a property at 263

Elizabeth Street in the city.¹⁰⁵ They envisaged this three-storey building, facing Hyde Park, would serve as Council's headquarters. One year later, at Council's 25th anniversary dinner, it transpired there had been little or no progress at all, either in reconstructing or refurbishing the building. When Dr Fanny spoke, there was a note of exasperation in the manner in which she admonished her listeners, 'during the 27 years of the Council's existence it had always raised money for others, now … it had the right to expect some practical recognition by the community. This Anniversary Celebration was being held in the hope that such a House would soon become a reality'.¹⁰⁶ She said the upper floor would house Council offices, and the Israel Legation would possibly take one floor. ¹⁰⁷

At this stage in Dr Fanny's National Presidency, some believed she was taken for granted by her organisation, possibly a consequence of relinquishing leadership of the Sydney section, as well as the passage of time. President of the Feminist Club in Sydney, Mrs Crawford Vaughan, certainly thought so. At a dinner in August 1952 to mark Sydney Council's 29th anniversary, she 'stressed the value of a woman like Dr. Fanny Reading in the community and believed that she was taken too much for granted by Jews and non-Jews alike'.¹⁰⁸ Crawford Vaughan spoke about Dr Fanny's vision of a Council House, 'after all these years the Council should have a home of its own'.¹⁰⁹ At this stage, the project revived and the community united to bring her dream to fruition. In 1953, NCJW launched the Fanny Reading Council House Appeal, with 100 guests donating a total of more than £1000, but they were far from their goal,

> It is the duty of everyone in this community … to see that this progressive communal plan shall succeed and thus strengthen and enrich our Jewish life here. Every member of this community should and must be 100 percent behind this drive.¹¹⁰

Dr Fanny told Newcastle's section she hoped they would endow a room in Council House.¹¹¹ The issue, as a tribute to her leadership, took on urgency when she relinquished the National Presidency in March

1955, commending Vera Cohen as the new National President,

> I pray that in eighteen years' time we shall celebrate the golden jubilee of our beloved organisation, the organisation which has meant so much to me personally and which is founded upon the permanent foundations of service and devotion.[112]

The NCJW War Memorial Fanny Reading Council House in Queen Street, Woollahra, opened its doors in December 1963. Dr Fanny, then 79 years of age, saw her dream realised. It was dedicated 'to the servicemen and women of Australia as well as to Dr Fanny Reading MBE',[113] and was 'a building funded by women for women'. It marked a turning point in the fortunes of NCJW in Sydney. Dr Fanny always expressed the hope NCJW's golden jubilee would be celebrated in their own home. In 1973, a frail Dr Fanny, aged 89, attended the Golden Jubilee Morning Tea held in Council House. She received a standing ovation from 400 guests; and said simply, 'I made it'.[114]

On 12 December 1971, three years before Dr Fanny died, Prime Minister McMahon opened the National Jewish Memorial Centre in Canberra, which included 'The Fanny Reading Auditorium', an honour that commemorated NCJW support for this project.[115] Mrs McMahon unveiled the plaque in the Fanny Reading Auditorium.[116] Dr Fanny – suffering from Parkinson's Disease – was too unwell to attend.

The question arises as to whether NCJW has perpetuated Dr Fanny's legacy, her beliefs and her teachings in their 21st-century agenda. Hilary Rubinstein points out that Dr Fanny attempted to fuse the traditional feminine ideal of the 'ministering angel' with increased representation of women in public life; but 'Whether her National Council of Jewish Women satisfactorily achieved this goal, indeed whether this goal was a legitimate one, is to some contemporary feminists debateable'.[117] Before arriving at a conclusion, however, the next chapter describes Dr Fanny's role in the 1949 defamation case that thrust her into media headlines around Australia.

Chapter 7

Background issues to Dr Reading's defamation trial

Nothing had prepared me for that trauma.
– Dr Fanny, commenting on the court case

Background issues

In May 1947, newspaper posters outside newsagencies throughout Australia carried the banner headline, 'Australian Jews financing terrorists in Palestine – killing British soldiers'. This poster referred to a libellous story featured on the front page of *Smith's Weekly*, alleging that Jews at a Youth Aliyah meeting in Sydney raised funds to fight the British in Mandatory Palestine.

In 1947 Dr Fanny was Senior Vice-President of the Australian branch of Youth Aliyah, an international humanitarian organisation dedicated to bringing Jewish children from Nazi Europe and further afield to safety in Palestine, which was administered by the British Mandatory Authority. The Youth Aliyah fundraising event held on 6 May 1947 in Sydney was addressed by visiting speaker Major Michael Comay. Three weeks later, on 31 May 1947, the national newspaper *Smith's Weekly* published their front-page article headlined, 'Jews raise huge sums to fight British – Heavy levies on Jews in Australia'. Appalled and aggrieved, Dr Fanny maintained she had been defamed by this libellous article that alleged the funds she and others had collected to save and nurture Jewish children were being used instead to support terrorism in Palestine. She sued National Press for libel and claimed £10,000 in damages to her reputation.

The Executive Council of Australian Jewry approved the action on behalf of the Jewish community and, in Melbourne, the Jewish Council to Combat Fascism and Anti-Semitism backed the action financially and guaranteed the cost.[1] The NSW Jewish Board of Deputies and the Victorian Jewish Board of Deputies also supported litigation.[2] Sam Wynn, a leading Zionist, philanthropist and pioneer vintner, offered to meet the costs of the Victorian action. With support thus assured, the quest began to find a plaintiff in Victoria and in New South Wales. In the first week of September 1947, Ida Wynn in Melbourne and Dr Fanny in New South Wales gave their permission to appear as plaintiffs in the court proceedings in their respective states. Almost a year later, in August 1948, Ida Wynn died before the case came to court and no suitable substitute could be found in Victoria. In Sydney they decided to go ahead without a Victorian plaintiff and notice was served on *Smith's Weekly*. Rabbi Max Schenk, the President of Youth Aliyah in Australia, confided to Michael Comay that the paper's response was 'extremely dangerous to our work and must be fought',

> I have never for a moment hesitated in regard to the urgent necessity of taking such action as would prevent similar journals from continuing their usual broadcasts against us. We have the finest legal talent in the country pressing our case, and from all indications we should have a very strong one.[3]

Two years later, the case *Dr Fanny Reading v. National Press Pty. Ltd.* was heard before Justice Leslie James Herron over three days, from Tuesday 26 April 1949 to Thursday 28 April 1949, with judgement delivered on the third day of the trial; and a discussion of costs heard on 29 June 1949. The trial was held in the Supreme Court of New South Wales, in Sydney. Solicitors Messrs Abram Landa, Barton & Co. and barrister Jack Evelyn Cassidy KC represented Dr Fanny; and solicitors Keith W. Gunn & Co. and barrister John Wentworth (Jack) Shand KC represented the defendant, *Smith's Weekly* (National Press Pty. Ltd.).

On the first morning of the trial, Dr Fanny stepped into the witness box, prepared for the ordeal she would endure as the plaintiff in this widely publicised defamation trial, which rocked the Australian Jewish community at that time and propelled this 65-year-old medical practitioner into the glare of public scrutiny. Examined by Cassidy, she immediately established her professional credentials and her reputation for humanitarian service:

> My full name is Fanny Reading. I am a highly qualified medical practitioner carrying on my practice at 38 Darlinghurst Rd, Darlinghurst, in partnership with my brother. I am a British subject, having come to Australia when I was two years of age, and having lived here ever since, except for a period when I visited England when I was about a year away from Australia. During that time I visited America, England, Europe, Palestine and Egypt. I spent about six weeks in Palestine and that is the only occasion that I have been there, and other than that period of a year I have been here all my life. I am still in active practice. I have been an honorary physician at various hospitals. For some years I was in the St. George District before I went to Darlinghurst.[4]

In that courtroom – subjected to questions from her barrister, Jack Evelyn Cassidy KC, as well as undergoing a cross-examination by John Wentworth Shand KC, the defendant's barrister – a multifaceted portrait emerges of Dr Fanny and her worldview framed by political ideologies prevailing at that time. The trial revealed the strength of her commitment to the children saved by Youth Aliyah and highlighted her efforts to raise funds for their reception, accommodation, education and training in Palestine. It also showed the strength of her commitment to Zionism and her belief in the rebirth of her people in their ancient homeland, where they might live not on sufferance but as an historic right, in accordance with the promise enshrined in the Balfour Declaration of 2 November 1917 that stated, 'His Majesty's Government view with favour the establishment in Palestine of a national home for the Jewish people, and will use their best endeavours to facilitate the achievement of this object'.[5]

According to Sydney lawyer Peter Wertheim, co-Chief Executive Officer of the Executive Council of Australian Jewry:

> More than 90% of the people in Australia at that time were of Anglo-Celtic heritage, and many of them were staunchly pro-British. *Smith's Weekly* was an extreme right wing, xenophobic, jingoistic Anglophile newspaper which railed against Jewish refugees from Europe who were then arriving in Australia ... and against Jewish boat people arriving in Palestine ... Fanny Reading's case against *Smith's Weekly* resonated with many of the kinds of issues that provoke debate in contemporary Australia – refugee children, terrorism, conflicts in the Middle East. Yet Fanny Reading was steadfast throughout. She said ... 'Those who contributed did so out of sympathy and love for Jewish children, many of them orphans, homeless and unwell'.[6]

The Sydney courtroom became the place and provocation for an in-depth portrait of Dr Fanny, which amplifies our understanding of who she was at that time, what she stood for, what she believed in, and what character traits prompted her to act when her integrity and that of the Jewish supporters of Youth Aliyah were impugned. Despite her reluctance to take centre stage in a defamation drama of national interest, she stood her ground and expressed her firm convictions, her belief in the justice of her cause and the humanitarian mission of Youth Aliyah, and in the right of Jewish people to migrate to Palestine,

She quoted, as examples of the many promises of the Almighty in that regard, in Genesis and elsewhere, that the 'Promised Land' was to be the eternal possession of the Jewish people ... 'And I will plant thee ... in this, my sacred soil, and none shall pluck thee out.'[7]

The trial was firmly anchored within an historic context shaped by the emergence of Youth Aliyah in 1933, and by Dr Fanny's first personal encounters with Zionist leaders in 1925 when she travelled abroad. Both barristers in the trial interrogated these background influences, thus shifting them from the margins to the ideological foreground of the trial. Consequently, Youth Aliyah and Zionism became central issues in the trial.

Youth Aliyah's archives of tragedy and hope

Youth Aliyah, which featured prominently in newspaper coverage of the trial throughout Australia in 1949, had its genesis in Germany in 1933 when Recha Freier witnessed storm-troopers in Berlin celebrating Hitler's electoral victory. The wife of a Berlin rabbi, she was concerned by the escalation of antisemitism and the exclusion of Jewish children and youth from educational institutions and employment. Norman Bentwich, the Attorney-General of Mandatory Palestine, described her as a woman with 'a prophetic vision ... an enthusiastic worker for Palestine, a friend of the young, and an invincible fighter for any cause which she espoused'.[8] In 1932 and 1933 in Germany, she met with a small group of Zionist youth leaders to discuss sending Jewish teenagers to kibbutzim (communal farms) in Palestine, where they could complete their education, work on the land and help in the upbuilding of the Jewish homeland. Initially, she met with resistance from Henrietta Szold, an American working in Palestine, the founder in 1912 of Hadassah Women's Zionist Organization of America, whom Freier approached for help in realising her project. At that time, Szold was hampered by inadequate funds and resources to meet the basic needs of children in Palestine.

Freier hoped to leverage Szold's track record of successful ventures addressing primitive conditions in the *Yishuv*. Undeterred by Szold's initial rejection, Freier persevered. Szold relented and accepted the proposal of the World Zionist Congress that, based in Jerusalem, she should direct the initiative aimed at integrating Jewish children brought from Europe to Palestine, overseeing their social welfare, medical, educational and training needs. The first group of 34 boys and girls from Hitler's Germany arrived on 19 February 1934 in Haifa, where Szold met them, accompanied by Aharon Zisling, a member of Kibbutz Ein Harod, which was to be their new home.[9] Thus began the saga of Youth Aliyah:

> The story of the march … in war and in peace, of ten thousand boys and girls from the lands of Nazi oppression to Palestine, the land of promise, to be apprenticed there for agricultural and industrial life in collective and co-operative villages, and then themselves to form fresh collective and co-operative groups, planting the soil.[10]

When Germany invaded Poland on 1 September 1939, Great Britain and France declared war on Germany on 3 September 1939. Thousands of Jewish youngsters, finding themselves in a life-and-death situation, turned to Youth Aliyah, hoping to reach Palestine. The head of Youth Aliyah's London office, Eva Michaelis-Stern, suggested to her Board that they should adopt a flexible rescue policy to deal with the new situation: 'Let us not forget, she pointed out, that no other organization in the Jewish world is as well equipped to contribute to the rescue of Jewish young people'.[11] Szold, who appealed to the High Commissioner in Palestine for 1000 immigration certificates over and above the usual quota for children and had been turned down, was in a difficult position. While accepting that Youth Aliyah was a rescue operation, she insisted that children be processed according to pre-war criteria, including a medical examination and bureaucratic requirements that were difficult to fulfil: 'We have to consider besides the individual also the country for the building of which we are responsible'.[12] This rigidity, which meant delays and might have cost lives, provoked enduring controversy. In mitigation, Youth Aliyah leaders feared 'that any activity which did not follow clear, accepted policy might lead to chaos and endanger the whole program'.[13]

The archives of Youth Aliyah have been described as 'archives of tragedy and hope'.[14] Those words – tragedy and hope – encapsulate the polarities of Youth Aliyah's struggles throughout the war years,

> ... fraught with the unrelenting political and administrative processes necessary to secure the release of Jewish children from detention, death and displaced person camps throughout Europe. The obstacles were not only related to the impact of the War in Europe but also to the British Mandate Government's limitation on immigration to Palestine.[15]

While Hadassah in America supported Youth Aliyah, fundraising also involved communal leaders in Australia, such as Dr Fanny. The Treasurer of the Jewish Agency's Youth Aliyah Department, Dr Georg Landauer, worked closely with Szold in Palestine, overseeing Youth Aliyah processes.[16] With intimate knowledge of Youth Aliyah's personalities and processes, Dr Landauer flew to Sydney in 1949 to testify at the trial.

Youth Aliyah faced innumerable challenges, including the arrival of the 'Tehran' and 'Trans-Dniestria' children, who reached Palestine in 1942 and 1943 after enduring extreme hardships. They were Polish and German Jewish children, who fled with their parents to the Russian-occupied zone when the Nazis overran Poland and, 'As relations between Russia and Poland took a turn for the worse, these families were deported to Siberia ... [where they] wandered, starving, without means of subsistence, from the Siberian North to Southern Russia'.[17] Hundreds died and surviving orphans found refuge with families, orphanages and hospitals.

Some continued in their own groups. Great numbers of children travelled to Tehran with the Polish army mobilised by General Anders. Randy Grigsby, who documented the journey of a thousand Jewish children originally from Poland and Germany, stated 'The story of the Tehran Children is one of those remarkable tales of the human struggle to survive'.[18]

The Jewish Agency and Szold negotiated with the British High Commissioner for Palestine, who provided entry visas for the children and, on their arrival in Palestine, Youth Aliyah assumed responsibility for them,

> About a year later, two convoys of children were collected in Trans-Dniestria, orphans from all parts of Rumania whose parents had met their end in death camps. These children had spent some time in German slave-labour camps before the International Red Cross and the Joint Distribution Committee arranged for their transport to a special camp, from where they were to be taken to Palestine. Here again visas were secured only after difficult negotiations with the British Mandatory authorities.[19]

It was not easy to rehabilitate thousands of orphaned Jewish children, 'whose development and growth had been disturbed, twisted and delayed'. They needed clothing, sound nutrition and social and spiritual guidance to ensure their integration.[20]

Dr Fanny meets Henrietta Szold

Dr Fanny and Henrietta Szold met three times in 1925, firstly in New York, and then in Vienna, where Dr Fanny represented Australia as an official member of the press corps accredited to the 14th Zionist Congress, which Szold also attended. They met again in Jerusalem when Dr Fanny and her mother visited Palestine later that year. These meetings cemented a friendship that only ended with Szold's death in 1945.[21]

Andgel notes: 'The year 1925 was a highlight in her [Dr Fanny's] life as she strengthened her ideas and personal ties on the international scene'.[22]

When Dr Fanny and Szold first met, they were acknowledged founders of significant women's organisations. In Australia, Dr Fanny formalised the Council of Jewish Women of New South Wales on 30 July 1923, at the third of a series of preliminary meetings held to discuss the proposed organisation. She dedicated the Council to 'Service to our religion, to our people and to the country in which we live'.[23] Eleven years earlier, Szold had established Hadassah, the American Women's Zionist Organization, which contributed to pioneering and medical services in Palestine. When she met Dr Fanny, she was serving a second term as Hadassah's National President (from 1923 to 1926).

Both women broke the mould of the Jewish woman's traditional role and challenged their society's conservative expectations of Jewish women. Both were passionate Zionists, who believed in the viability of a national Jewish home in Palestine. In the 1930s and 1940s, Szold submitted to British Mandatory officials requests for additional entry permits for Jewish migrants to Palestine. Dr Fanny wrote to Australian ministers in the hope of securing entry permits for those wishing to come to Australia. In concert with Australian women's organisations, she also made representations to leaders abroad to open the gates of Palestine to Jews fleeing Nazi persecution. These two leaders shared values and principles that shaped their lives and those of countless others.

Szold's humanitarian agenda mirrored the concerns that engaged Dr Fanny throughout her life. Szold focused on social welfare measures, 'in the fields of health, social work and education, she gave expression to her abiding interest in children, in those deprived of a home or of physical and mental health, in those in need of a helping hand'.[24] Before Szold settled in Jerusalem in 1921, she confided to a friend: 'At the bottom of my heart I have always held that I should have had children, many children'.[25] Neither Szold nor Dr Fanny married, yet their work – professional and honorary – focused substantially on children.

Dr Fanny attended the 14th Zionist Congress, from 18 to 31 August 1925 in Vienna, where she renewed her connection with Szold. On her return to Australia, she commented,

> The outstanding woman was Miss Henrietta Szold of New York, a Vice-President of the Zionist organisation [sic], President and founder of the American Women's Zionist Organisation, the Hadassah. She was the only one of her sex who had a seat on the platform – [and] is a woman of tremendous achievements, personality, influence, and intellect.[26]

Szold was not a Vice-President on the Executive of the World Zionist Organisation (WZO) in 1925 and it is likely that the reporter who wrote the story made this error, which has misled scholars in the past to make that assumption. Two years later, however, in 1927, she was appointed WZO's Education Director in Palestine. It is likely that her position as founder and President of Hadassah, the Women's Zionist Organisation of America, accounted for her seat on the platform, alongside the WZO Executive at the 1925 Zionist Congress. Dr Fanny's admiration for Szold endured through the decades. Their liaison strengthened during the Second World War, when the rescue of Jewish children in Nazi Europe was one of Dr Fanny's priorities. In 1945 – two years before the defamatory allegations about Youth Aliyah were published by National Press in *Smith's Weekly* – Dr Fanny stated:

> The NCJW whole-heartedly endorses the 1945 Youth Aliyah Appeal and pledges its utmost support. No greater privilege or Mitzvah [good deed] could any Jew or Jewess have than the rescue and future rehabilitation of our orphaned children in Europe. This has an overwhelming claim to our sympathy and support on humanitarian and Zionist grounds alike, and is the proper solution for the thousands and thousands of homeless children wanting a 'home'. The name of Henrietta Szold should be for ever immortalised for her vision and practical work in

saving 13,000 children from Nazi brutality and absorbing them in the productive life of the Yishuv. Therefore, it is our solemn privilege in gratitude for the security of our own children, to see that the means are forthcoming through this 1945 Campaign, to give sanctuary and new life for the wandering children of Europe.[27]

Dr Fanny's first meeting with Szold was a seminal event in her life that fuelled her dedication to Youth Aliyah. When Szold died, Dr Fanny spoke at a memorial meeting, on 14 March 1945 in Sydney, acknowledging the impact their first meeting had on her own life and work,

> Dr. Fanny Reading, President of the NCJW, told of her meeting with Miss Szold in 1925 in New York and the insight she was able to gain then into the life and character of this great woman and of the inspiration the meeting gave to her.[28]

Zionist Congress in 1925 in Vienna

As Dr Fanny's defamation action in 1949 in Sydney revealed, she was a Zionist dedicated to the return of the Jewish people to the biblical land of their ancestors after an exile of 2000 years. It was her attendance at the 14th Zionist Congress, in 1925 in Vienna, that strengthened her commitment to Zionism. Australian Zionists had appointed her their representative, but accreditation failed to come through in time, so she obtained a press pass and sat with the press corps on the platform, where she had an excellent view of proceedings.

The 14th Zionist Congress was an island of hope in a sea of antisemitism that raged through Vienna before and during the Congress. Dr Fanny witnessed these antisemitic demonstrations. In Australia, newspapers throughout the country covered the riots with headlines focusing on the violence erupting in the city. On 19 August 1925, Melbourne's paper the *Argus* stated that 6,000 police 'mustered for the occasion'.[29] The *Daily Examiner* in Grafton headlined their story, 'Zionist Congress serious riots in Vienna August 18'.[30] The *Advertiser* in Adelaide had a banner headline, 'Fight in Vienna'.[31] In Hobart, the *Mercury* reported that police were injured and 106 demonstrators arrested for rioting, 'Many of the men arrested were found to be armed with revolvers, knives, and other weapons'.[32] The *New York Times*, on 19 August 1925, under a banner headline 'Antisemitic and anti-government demonstrations against holding of 14th international Zionist congress in Vienna', stated that the majority of those arrested were intellectuals and State officials.[33] It is likely that articles such as these alarmed Dr Fanny's family and friends, who knew she had travelled from Venice to Vienna for the Congress.

Dr Fanny recorded her observations of Congress. She noticed detectives and police guarding all entrances, and police cordons surrounding streets leading to the Congress venue. She wrote that the Zionist flag, together with the Austrian flag, 'flew boldly in front of the hall in defiance of all political demonstrations'.[34] When she entered the hall on the first day, 'it seemed to me as if our people had joined together in solemn celebration of some holy festival of our liturgy so imbued were they with the gravity of the situation and of the tremendous task ahead'. She noted, 'The crucial moment was the entrance of the President Dr Chaim Weizmann and Mr Nahum Sokolov to the two seats of honour. A tremendous ovation greeted them, the outburst lasting ten minutes and was joined by all present'.[35]

Chaim Weizmann outlines principles of Zionism

Weizmann stated in his opening address, 'Many leading personalities of the political world who, three years ago, treated our work in Palestine as a romantic dream, now reckon with it as a real fact'.[36] In evaluating relations between Jews and Arabs – a theme pursued by the barrister for the defendant in Dr Fanny's defamation action in Sydney's Supreme Court in 1949 – Weizmann emphasised,

> Two things are necessary in order to establish normal relations between the two peoples: our Arab neighbours must be convinced that we are in earnest about the establishment of our Home, that no boat shall arrive in Palestine without putting down immigrants. On the other hand, they must be equally convinced that the spirit in which we build our Home is that of freedom, tolerance and fraternity towards all elements of the population in Palestine.[37]

Weizmann stated that the fundamental principles of Zionist work in Palestine were national soil, national work, national language and culture. He concluded, 'It is our duty to make the best use of our energy for the work of reconstruction'. Dr Fanny was impressed by his command of languages, as he spoke perfect English, German and Hebrew. She commented that his Hebrew 'became a language so eloquent, emphatic, expressive, so full of charm and poetry', and marvelled at how he showed, 'that the rebuilding of Palestine is an accomplished fact and a progressive process. Through this process will come the revival and renewal of the Jewish Nation – the spirit of Israel will live again ... He ended with the blessing of peace for all'.[38]

Delegates applauded Weizmann's efforts to create a Hebrew University on Mount Scopus in Jerusalem, which opened earlier that year. It was tangible evidence of a Zionist program in action. Lord Arthur Balfour, who attended the opening, said,

> This occasion marks a great epoch in the history of a people who have made this little land of Palestine a seed-ground of great religion, and whose intellectual and moral destiny is again, from a national point of view, reviving.[39]

Weizmann hoped the University would foster a cultural and scientific renaissance in the Middle East: 'Our University would not be true to itself or to Jewish traditions if it were not a house of study for all peoples and more especially for all the peoples of Palestine'.[40]

Revisionist leader Ze'ev Jabotinsky

On the third day of Congress, Dr Fanny heard Ze'ev (Vladimir) Jabotinsky, founder of the Revisionist Movement, to whom the barrister Shand would refer 24 years later in the Sydney defamation trial. Only four years younger than Dr Fanny, Jabotinsky was born in Odessa, where he organised a Jewish self-defence corps to counter the pogroms. He was a political Zionist, who advocated for a 'Herzlian political struggle for a state'.[41] This was not his first congress but his first as leader of the new Union of Zionist Revisionists, and he called for an activist policy for the Zionist movement, writing earlier that same year, 'It is time to proclaim loud and clear that the aim of Zionism is the establishment of a Jewish State'.[42] Mehlman states in his pamphlet on Jabotinsky:

> To appreciate the dimensions of this 'heresy,' it must be borne in mind that even Jabotinsky's closest collaborators in 1925 ... shrank from the term 'Jewish State'. It was treated like a high explosive that might go off at the slightest jolt, gutting the Zionist relationship with the British Mandatory power in Palestine, inciting the Arabs to riot and murder and as one contemporary Revisionist put it, 'frightening away even our friends'.[43]

Jabotinsky stated unequivocally:

> The aim of Zionism is the gradual transformation of Palestine (Trans Jordan included) into a Jewish Commonwealth, that is into a self-governing Commonwealth under the auspices of an established Jewish majority. Any other interpretation of Zionism, especially the White Paper of 1922, must be considered invalid.[44]

Jabotinsky had served on the Zionist Executive in 1921 but had clashed ideologically with Weizmann, as their methodologies for fulfilling the Zionist aim of a Jewish homeland differed radically:

Jabotinsky believed in rapid mass immigration to Palestine and in mobilizing Jewish military and police units. Weizmann called for careful colonization and trusted the British. Within two years Jabotinsky resigned, charging that his colleagues' policies would result in the loss of Palestine.[45]

In 1923, Jabotinsky published his political manifesto, 'On the Iron Wall', outlining his thoughts on the Arab question in Palestine. It highlighted, 'his belief that force and military power should be at the core of the Zionist movement's policies, and it revealed his aversion to any sort of ideological or political compromise'.[46] Jabotinsky stated that Zionism was 'moral and just' and predicted that there would always be two nations in Palestine – Jews and Arabs – with the Jews in the majority,

> We will never attempt to expel or oppress the Arabs ... it is absolutely another matter if it will be possible to achieve our peaceful aims through peaceful means. This depends, not on our relationship with the Arabs, but exclusively on the Arabs' relationship to Zionism.[47]

Jabotinsky concluded: 'A living people yields in such enormous, fatal issues only when no single loophole is visible in the iron wall. It is only then that the radical groups ... lose their charm and influence passes over to moderate groups'.[48]

According to Jabotinsky's close associate Joseph Schechtman, Jabotinsky was reluctant to go to the 1925 Zionist Congress, as it meant rejoining the Zionist Organization, which would constrain his independence: 'Should our Union develop well, I would be able to do things which a member of the Zionist Organization ... has no right to do.[49] Thus, Jabotinsky came to the Congress in 1925 not only with a history of conflict between himself and Weizmann but also with an increasingly hard and unyielding ideological position. At Congress, they again engaged in a bitterly fought contest of ideas, with Jabotinsky demanding a more activist policy for the Zionist movement. In particular, he was opposed to Weizmann's negotiations with wealthy and influential non-Zionists to secure their participation in the Jewish Agency in order to fund the nascent building industry in Palestine,

> To him it was tantamount to giving up the sovereignty of the democratically elected Zionist Congress, making its decision in all matters of Zionist policy and work dependent on the approval of a self-appointed group of non-Zionist financial potentates. He deemed it the elementary duty of every Zionist patriot not to let such a scheme pass.[50]

Although it was with some reluctance that Jabotinsky attended the Zionist Congress, he knew it was the only forum where he could effectively combat the scheme. His speech to delegates caused a stir, which Dr Fanny noted. Firstly, he defined and developed his program; then he attacked. The President of the Zionist Organization of America, Louis Lipsky, noted: 'When he … launched into a grand criticism of Zionist policy – satiric, courteous, denunciatory – he was like the Angry Conscience of the movement. He poured acid on open wounds. He reminded us of the goal and made us ashamed of the results.'[51] The ovation Jabotinsky received demonstrated the dissatisfaction of Congress with England, 'perhaps with the Weizmann policies which lately brought about some appreciable setbacks'. Jabotinsky challenged Weizmann directly: 'If not my program, what have you to offer?'.[52] Jabotinsky urged the Zionist Executive and Congress to prepare world public opinion:

> The world can be convinced if we demand logical things from it … We need demonstrations, we need what we call a political offensive in order to instill our demands, until they are accepted … Either it is possible to convince the world to accept the truth, or it is not. If not, then we are finished, because we want something impossible. But if it is possible, then let's make the effort to convince it.[53]

This generated a heated response from Weizmann, to whom it seemed incomprehensible that Jabotinsky was insisting on a confrontation between the Zionist movement and the British Government:

> The starting point of our diplomatic work in the future must be ... maintaining our friendly relations with the Mandatory authority and with its emissaries in Palestine. This is a truth that should not be refuted ... We must not allow any part of the [Zionist] Organization, or any individual Zionist, to place obstacles in our way by means of irresponsible demonstrations in Jerusalem, in London, or anywhere else.[54]

This acrimony came to a head when chairman Leo Motzkin called on Jabotinsky to state the Revisionist Union's attitude toward the new Zionist Executive:

> The statement read by Jabotinsky ... sharply criticized the political passivity of the Zionist Executive and its lack of program in the economic field coupled with the neglect of the security of Palestinian Jewry; it maintained that the Executive's tactics were 'gravely endangering the sovereignty of the Zionist Organization'. Therefore, the Revisionist delegates 'will vote against the motion of confidence for the Executive'.[55]

Dr Fanny was impressed with Jabotinsky's reputation as an orator and soldier, and noted: 'He outspokenly and freely condemned the administration of the Zionist organisation'; and when Weizmann replied to these charges, 'He was listened to by an enraptured audience who didn't miss a word – every argument was met in so clever and scientific a manner'.[56]

When Dr Fanny witnessed their verbal duelling, it was clear this was a battle for the minds and hearts of the Zionist delegates. Jabotinsky was not without his critics, who were vocal in response to his address. Dr Shmaryahu Levin, whom Dr Fanny had met in the United States, accused him of sending 'soldiers to Palestine before we have Jews there'.[57]

Weizmann stated that Jabotinsky's demand for a Jewish Legion was 'not only useless but even harmful' at present; 'The key to the situation is to be found on a different level: we have to open up the Near East to Jewish initiative, in genuine friendship and cooperation with the Arabs'.[58]

The relationship between Jabotinsky and Weizmann had not always been this fractious and unyielding. There had been periods of cooperation. In 1916, with the help of Weizmann and the consent of the British Government, Jabotinsky had realised his aim of creating an official Jewish fighting force – the Jewish Legion under the command of British Colonel John H. Patterson, comprising three battalions of British, American, Canadian and Palestinian Jews – the first in 1300 years. Known as the Judeans, they saw active service. The first of these battalions, the 38th Fusiliers, fought with General Edmund Allenby in the 1918 Palestinian campaign, thus participating in the liberation of Palestine from Turkish forces. Benzion Netanyahu, Jabotinsky's executive assistant, stated that the Jewish Legion was a great achievement because it was established by Jabotinsky 'as a private person without any support from the Jewish leadership'.[59] In 1919, those still serving in the battalions were given a regimental cap badge depicting a Menorah (a seven-branched candelabrum) engraved with the word Kadima (forward and/or eastward). The battalions – the 38th, 39th and 40th – were disbanded between 1919 and 1921. In 1920, during the Arab riots in Palestine, Jabotinsky organised a self-defence corps in Jerusalem.

Four months after the conclusion of the 14th Zionist Congress in August 1925, with Jabotinsky's words still fresh on her mind, Dr Fanny and her mother attended a special service at Jerusalem's oldest synagogue. In a letter to family, she described the unique ceremony that took place there on the 6th day of Chanukah (17 December 1925), a ceremony recalling a signal triumph of Jabotinsky's militarism:

> It was the occasion of depositing the colours of the 40th Palestine Battalion Royal Fusiliers ... It was brought by a special

messenger from London and is given a home in this shool [synagogue]. Police band soldiers and servicemen met the flag at the station, then marched through the streets with music and singing, through the old city to the shool. Lord Plumer, consuls and high officials attended and the ceremony was solemnly conducted, Rabbi Kook delivering a fine address in Hebrew.[60]

When Dr Fanny and her mother heard Rabbi Abraham Isaac Kook, the first Chief Rabbi of British Mandatory Palestine, deliver that 'fine address', he was 60 and a revered figure, with a reputation for supporting Zionism despite the secularism of many of its leaders. There were strong connections between Rabbi Kook and Jabotinsky, which made it appropriate that he delivered the sermon at the service Dr Fanny attended. In 1920, Jabotinsky and selected members of the Jewish Legion had defended the Jewish population of Jerusalem against Arab attacks and, shortly thereafter, the British Mandatory Authority imprisoned them in Acre, where they commenced a life-threatening hunger strike. It was Rabbi Kook who prevailed on Jabotinsky and his followers to end their hunger strike. 'Stay strong dear brothers and wait for salvation to come,' he wrote.[61]

It is likely that Dr Fanny's views on Rabbi Kook were somewhat conflicted. As a feminist with progressive ideas, she would have opposed his view, expressed in the 1920s, that women should not be given the vote. Despite his conservative views on women's suffrage, Dr Fanny respected him as the father of religious Zionism and admired his moral stature as an orthodox mystic. He held advanced political views and, while in London, participated in behind-the-scenes activities leading to the Balfour Declaration. Only two months prior to Herzl's death on 3 July 1904, when Rabbi Kook arrived in Jaffa, he scandalised many rabbis by eulogising Herzl as 'the suffering harbinger of the Davidic redeemer'.[62]

Jabotinsky revived his quest for a Jewish army during the Second World War, hoping to reinstate the Legion. When war broke out, he had hoped that the Jewish people would be recognised and treated as one of the allied peoples, and he offered Jewish troops and other forms of collaboration. All was rejected, he said; the Jewish ally was not wanted and his problems were rigorously excluded from the list of war aims.

'If you will it, it is no dream' – Herzl

The late Dr Theodor Herzl's legacy still had power to bring delegates together to fulfil a common aim, as he attempted to do in his lifetime, uniting 'in the ranks of the Zionist Organisation all forces in Jewry without any regard to their religious, social and other differences'.[63] With Herzl's portrait above the delegates' heads, his 'presence' was inescapable, as was his mantra: 'If you will it, it is no dream'. Dr Fanny would have known of his attempt to rescue Russian Jewry, after the brutal 1903 Kishinev pogrom, when he requested assistance from the Russian Government to facilitate the exodus of Russian Jews to Palestine. When he convened the first Zionist Congress, held 29–31 August 1897 in Basle, Switzerland,

> the delegates adopted the Basle Programme, the programme of the Zionist movement, and declared, 'Zionism seeks to establish a home for the Jewish people in Palestine secured under public law'. At the Congress the World Zionist Organisation was established as the political arm of the Jewish people, and Herzl was elected its first president.[64]

Retrospectively, Weizmann accused Herzl of emphasising political rather than practical Zionism: 'For them it was always political Zionism first and practical work nowhere',[65] and this political-versus-practical controversy echoed in the courtroom during Dr Fanny's defamation case in 1949. However, Herzl and his colleagues were, indeed, aware of the necessity for practical work as demonstrated by Article iii of the Basle Programme, which recommended, 'the organisation and binding together of the whole of Jewry by means of appropriate institutions, local and international, in accordance with the laws of each country'.⁶⁶ It was Herzl who founded the Jewish National Fund (JNF) in 1901 for the purpose of acquiring land in Palestine. Although Herzl died in 1904 aged 44, he left an enduring manifesto in his writings.

At the Zionist Congress in 1925, Dr Fanny seized the opportunity to meet delegates from all over the world, among whom were a number of influential German delegates, for whom 'Zionism was a means for them to achieve Jewish self-respect and foster ties to their people'.⁶⁷ Delegates expressed divergent views, from the secular to the religious, all cogently argued. Exposed to this range of opinions, Dr Fanny wrote:

> At this conference criticisms were freely made on various important matters and appeared wholly sound – then in Dr Weizmann's reply to these, he answered each critic sanely, clearly, and most satisfactorily, that one wondered who then could be right … All the speakers had put forth sound arguments for their respective parties.⁶⁸

Dr Fanny immersed herself in Congress proceedings and broadened her understanding of the movement and its personalities. She renewed her friendship with Pevsner, Australia's official representative, who two years earlier in Sydney had encouraged Dr Fanny to start the Council of Jewish Women. Together in Vienna, they attended meetings of separate Commissions. Dr Fanny was impressed by the brilliance of Congress participants, who in their urgency to complete two years' work in 10 days ignored meals and sleep, walking back to their hotels in the early hours of the morning, as she did.

The Congress was punctuated by historic moments that electrified Dr Fanny, who documented the voting process that led to Weizmann's resignation as President:

> The vote of confidence was the most dramatic thrill of all … The voting resulted in 136 for and 17 against. Considering the number of delegates was more than 300, this spoke tragedy

– a large number would not vote against Dr Weizmann and his Executive, and [yet] would not cast a vote of confidence in his leadership and policy. Then Dr Weizmann very pale ascended the speaker's place, said he had observed the vote and understood its significance.[69]

This event was widely reported in Australian papers, such as the *Newcastle Morning Herald and Miners' Advocate*, which stated: 'A telegram from Vienna reports that … 156 Socialists abstained from voting, and therefore Dr. Weizmann resigned the presidency'.[70] On the second last night of Congress, a vote of confidence was taken again, resulting in 217 for and 15 against, which was greeted by a storm of cheers. 'I trudged home to our hotel at 2 am,' Dr Fanny wrote. But that late hour paled beside the session of the final night. With her knowledge of Yiddish, the '*mamaloshen*' that was her 'mother tongue' and that of the Eastern European Jewish communities, she praised the farewell address in Yiddish by Congress Chairman, Leo Motzkin, whose speech was 'full of humour, chastising the various factions for their petulance and transgressions of law and order. He hoped that the future would be one of unceasing prosperity for Eretz Yisroel.' Then came Nahum Sokolov's address: 'We followed every word he uttered, priceless pearls, and left enthused and full of admiration for the man and the cause'. Dr Fanny only left at 6 am the next day, 'somewhat weary but still appreciative of the spirit and sincerity of the masses of our people who had come from the four corners of the earth to forward this grand project'.[71]

Dr Fanny was concerned for the safety of the Jewish community in Vienna once the police force withdrew. She hoped common sense would prevail and derived comfort from an incident she witnessed:

> … scores of delegates and friends assembled in a large café nearby and enjoyed lovely Viennese coffee to well-known Jewish strains by the café orchestra which happened to be under Jewish leadership. On their playing the *Hatikvah* [the unofficial

national anthem of the Jewish people] at which all of us stood, the non-Jewish habitués made no visible comment, showing that the general Viennese public were not hostile to the Congress being held there.[72]

Dr Fanny left Vienna conscious of responsibilities to be faced 'with heart and soul'. She recorded impressions of the delegates: 'The wildly enthusiastic, the ordinary curious, the intellectual (both men and women), the extremely orthodox, the idealistic, the politic, the socialist, the materialistic, the scientific – but all united by one common cause of kinship'.[73] She mentioned several American delegates whom she had met in New York, including Judge Bernard Rosenblatt, Rabbi Stephen S. Wise, Rabbi A. Hillel Silver, the poet Re'uven Brainin, and Schmaryahu Levin, a writer living in Palestine.

While Congress was a hotbed of dissent, delegates were determined to translate theory into reality. Dr Fanny stated: 'There were great varieties and shades of opinions, and conflicts between parties, but in the end one saw that above all this was the big ideal, the unity of the cause pervaded the factions'.[74] She returned to Australia with faith in the future of a Jewish National Home:

> The Fourteenth Congress was to my mind a most important milestone in the history of the Jews of the Diaspora ... We have now before us the transit of the ideal to the practical, a dream becomes a reality, in which we Jews must shoulder the burden to carry out this reality. Now we have to face facts, complications and difficulties – the rebirth of a nation brings with it social, economic and national problems which must be adjusted. [75]

Dr Fanny's participation in the 1925 Congress ensured that Zionism became a foundational value of the Council of Jewish Women's (CJW) agenda (as the organisation was known in 1925). With the years, her knowledge of Zionism deepened and she acquired a nuanced understanding and knowledge of the ideological, political and pragmatic

Zionistic issues that proved crucial to her role as plaintiff in the 1949 court case. As National President of NCJW, she was well placed to interact with Zionist leaders in Australia and those visiting from abroad, thereby gaining insight into the impact of political and historic events on the Zionist enterprise. The views she expressed in 1925 when exposed for the first time to the ideological platforms of Weizmann, Jabotinsky and Sokolov, all of whom she found equally appealing, were light years away from the insightful, analytical and measured responses on Jewish and Zionist history she gave during the Trial in 1949. Whereas in 1925 she had vacillated in equal admiration between Weizmann and Jabotinsky, in the courtroom she displayed a political maturity and decisiveness that enabled her to be categoric and clear in her exposition of events and appraisal of Zionist leaders. Seminal historical events, such as the rise of Nazism and the industrialised genocide of the Jews had compelled her to recalibrate her position and strategies. In 1949, she was at a diametrically different stage in her life to that of the younger Dr Fanny, who 24 years earlier was exposed for the first time to the charismatic Zionist leaders of the day and their competing ideologies. As the world changed so radically around her, so did she; and the tragic events of the intervening decades accelerated her process of political maturation. The woman who entered the courtroom in 1949 was composed, calm and in possession of knowledge that would enable her to respond effectively to the interrogation to which she was subjected by one of the most brutal barristers of the day, Jack Shand KC.

Chapter 8

The trial: *Dr Fanny Reading v. National Press Pty. Ltd.*

These children were hunted and driven to concentration camps, and we were endeavouring to get them out before Hitler got them.
– Dr Fanny Reading

The eyes of the nation were on proceedings in a courtroom in the Supreme Court of New South Wales in Sydney, on Tuesday 26 April 1949, where a dignified and elderly woman alleged she and the organisation she represented had been grossly defamed. The trial, *Dr Fanny Reading v. National Press Pty. Ltd.*, began before Justice Herron and a jury of four and played out over three gruelling days. Aside from the plaintiff in this case, Dr Fanny, the cast of characters included two of the best barristers in the country, who pitted their wits and brains and legal strategies against each other. The substance of the trial as reported extensively in the press inflamed heated discussions in pubs and homes, where newspaper readers applauded or condemned the central figure in this legal drama.

The defamation case concerned allegations trumpeted on *Smith's Weekly* front page that funds collected in Sydney by the humanitarian organisation Youth Aliyah, were used to support terrorism against the British in Palestine. As Vice President of Youth Aliyah Australia, this report besmirched Dr Fanny's reputation and that of the organisation that rescued child survivors of the Holocaust, bringing them to safety in Palestine. By 1949, Dr Fanny was a prominent public figure nationally with a reputation for good deeds. For the past 20 years, she had served as National President of her organisation, the NCJW, a body esteemed for philanthropy and social welfare programs at home and abroad.

Dr Fanny's barrister, Jack Evelyn Cassidy KC, an eloquent and charismatic figure, questioned her throughout the morning of the first day, crafting a portrait of a selfless caring doctor, a humanitarian well known in the Jewish and gentile communities throughout Australia. He established her national reputation and prestige as President of NCJW:

> Cassidy: And in capacity as President of the NCJW, did you meet Committees and Presidents and Vice-Presidents of other charitable organizations from time to time?
>
> Dr Fanny: Yes.
>
> Cassidy: And did you become well known as the President over that long period of years?
>
> Dr Fanny: Yes. We [NCJW] were the representative of the Jewish Women of Australia, and I, as National President of the whole of Australia, must be known.[1]

Cassidy documented her service as honorary physician for five years at St George Hospital; the NSW Community Hospital and the Rachel Forster Hospital. He traced her impressive fundraising for the Jewish and general communities, her commitment to social welfare projects at home and abroad, and the community initiatives she launched through NCJW. He focused on her service to the nation during the war years, noting projects she launched and directed in Australia from 1939 to 1945, her answers painting a picture of the role of women manning the home-front during the critical war years:

> Cassidy: What class of work has it [NCJW] been engaged in?
>
> Dr Fanny: Every class of work: humanitarian, philanthropic,

social welfare, and for our people wherever they are – Jewish and non-Jewish work.

Cassidy: You might tell me what are some of the works you have done, say, within recent years: say, during the war?

Dr Fanny: Well, we played our part and I was one of the principals, in the war efforts ... We enlisted the women straight away at the outbreak of war in September, 1939, and from that time until the finish of the war we did all we could to help the war effort in every way possible: Soldiers' Comfort Fund, Red Cross, and in other fields they helped ... Before the war we did philanthropic work. We assisted all the hospitals, practically, in the city with large sums of money. We visited the hospitals. We did a very wide Australian-wide work, making migrants Australian citizens and we were commended by high officials from the Government for that, and I was instrumental in doing that work with our organisation.[2]

As President of NCJW, she and her volunteers raised £300,000 for the Commonwealth War Loan, Council made a quarter-million garments for the Lord Mayor's Appeal, they financed three mobile canteens; and for five-and-a-half years, their volunteers ran the Martin Place Kiosk, providing meals and refreshments. It was difficult for Dr Fanny to convey the magnitude of their efforts and achievements in a few words. Her short phrase, 'making migrants Australian citizens', speaks to NCJW's nation-wide provision of services, including meeting new arrivals, language classes, accommodation, employment guidance, household goods, transport and hospitality. Cassidy asked her what other class of work she did:

In this city I think we were very well known for that kiosk [for] ... at the top of Martin Place. We carried on there with three hundred volunteer workers a month, and we raised £11,500 for the Australian Soldiers' Comforts Fund and the Lord Mayor's

Comforts Fund. We carried that on for five and a half years. We gave mobile canteens, one in the city of Sydney, which you see running around the city, one for the bombed areas of London, and one for Palestine.

I was on all ... the Voluntary Women's Organisations which enlisted the women of N.S.W. to give voluntary service, and I was on the Lord Mayor's Comforts Fund Committee. I was on practically every war committee.[3]

Cassidy also focused on her position as Vice-President of Youth Aliyah in Australia, the organisation at the centre of the defamation action. Cassidy's questions revealed her commitment to saving Jewish children threatened with murder:

Dr Fanny: We were raising funds to rescue the children from Nazi Germany, and other satellite countries – Nazi satellite countries – and bringing them to safety in Palestine where they could live a normal life. These children were hunted and driven to concentration camps, and we were endeavouring to get them out before Hitler got them. That started in 1933 and went on.

Cassidy: And by 1938 and 1939 what had become the position in Germany as regards getting children out of there? Do you know?

Dr Fanny: It became more difficult, but still funds were needed to help these children when we got them away.[4]

Youth Aliyah meeting in Sydney

Cassidy focused on the Youth Aliyah fundraiser in Sydney on 6 May 1947, which Dr Fanny attended as Senior Vice-President of Youth Aliyah in Australia. Major Michael Comay was the principal speaker. Official envoy of the Jewish Agency for Palestine and the executive of the World Zionist Organisation, he was sent to meet the Prime Minister of New Zealand, Peter Fraser, and the Prime Minister of Australia, Ben Chifley.[5] He was asked to address the Youth Aliyah meeting, deputising for Ilse Radday of Haifa, whose arrival in Sydney was delayed.[6] As Dr Fanny remarked, 'he [Comay] was just a stop-gap but he was not there to launch the appeal';[7] that role was Ida Wynn's, President of WIZO in Australia. It was Comay's address that triggered the defamatory article published by *Smith's Weekly* on 31 May 1947.

Dr Fanny emphasised that at the meeting, 'Nobody is forced to give anything', and all funds were transmitted directly to Youth Aliyah.[8] Recalling precisely financial details from 1946 to 1948, she denied anything was said about Jews raising funds to fight the British, stating that nobody suggested levies on Hebrews in Australia.[9] She added there were 54,000 Jewish children waiting in Europe [for immigration certificates to Palestine].

Dr Fanny remained calm when Cassidy's question about the controversial phrase 'Zionist Commando Group' – reported in the article in *Smith's Weekly* – provoked a flurry of questions by Shand and an interjection by Judge Herron:

> Cassidy: Did a Zionist Commando Group go into action to boost the appeal, that you know of?
>
> Dr Fanny: There was no such group. It was just a figure of speech by the correspondent who wrote that report.
>
> Shand: I did not catch that.
>
> His Honor: She means the reporter.
>
> Shand: But which reporter?
>
> Dr Fanny: Her name is appended to the report in the *Hebrew Standard*, and she coined that phrase.
>
> Shand: You do not mean the defendant? The reporter?
>
> Dr Fanny: Did I remember the name of the reporter?

Shand: No, do you mean the reporter from the *Jewish Standard* – the *Hebrew Standard*?

Dr Fanny: *Hebrew Standard*, but this was given by a specific person, this report. Her name is appended to the report.

Cassidy: Was there any Zionist Commando Group that you know of?

Dr Fanny: No, she just meant an enthusiastic body of the committee were prepared to launch this movement.

Cassidy: Was that the committee of which you were [a member]?

Dr Fanny: Yes. I do not think I was a commando.[10]

Dr Fanny's explicit answers defused suspicion that the phrase 'Zionist commando group' had any military meaning. It was important that she clarified the reporter's use of these words as a figure of speech.

Zionist history, British legislation and Comay's talk

Standing in the witness box and interrogated by Cassidy, Dr Fanny spoke with impressive mastery of the evolution of Zionism, its achievements and setbacks, including the stringent immigration controls in the 1922 White Paper, which led to Winston Churchill's demand that the Jewish immigration quota to Palestine be relaxed. She revealed detailed knowledge of the provisions of the 1939 White Paper, which limited immigration into Palestine, with tragic consequences for Jews trapped in countries under Nazi domination. Nonetheless, the British Government co-operated with all Youth Aliyah's appeals. 'They promised us certificates for children to go to Palestine,' she said.[11]

Dr Fanny stressed Comay did not appeal for funds for Youth Aliyah and that he gave a personal review of the situation in Palestine. Cassidy asked her to recall what Comay said at the fundraising event:

Well, he told us among other things, that the Jews in Palestine were carrying on their work in spite of the trouble there, and he compared them with the London people who had the same courage during the Blitz ... He also said that because of the British Administration so much was disastrous to our people ... I take it at present to mean in Europe. As we know, we had lost 6 million dead in Europe, and now there were about a million and a half people waiting to come to some place in the world, and the only gates that were open to them were Palestine's, and these were closed to them ... He also spoke of there being a clique in Whitehall who controlled the affairs of Palestine, but ... I did not know of a clique, but I do know that members of the House of Commons and even Churchill, Winston Churchill, asked for a relaxation of the British Administration laws as far as immigration went. He also said – I remember this distinctly, that the British people ... probably did not understand the policy of the Administration in Palestine, and, if they did, things might have been better – the position of the British in Palestine might have been better.

I do remember that he said that the Jewish Agency and the people of Palestine were totally against the acts of terrorism that had taken place.[12]

Cassidy asked Dr Fanny about the Jewish community's response to news of 'terrorist' activities in Palestine and her personal views:

Cassidy: Have you ever taken part in any anti-British movement in the whole of your career?

Dr Fanny: No.

Cassidy: And have you ever been associated, at all in the last war, of this war, with disloyalists?

Dr Fanny: No.[13]

Cassidy focused on the public response to the article in *Smith's Weekly* and asked whether people mentioned it to her. She replied that many people had seen the article and spoken to her about it. Justice Herron intervened on a point of law:

> I can imagine a case happening that some person, a candidate for Parliament, was being introduced at a meeting and somebody got up in the audience and used defamatory words and everybody walked out … But, to merely ask her whether or not, in general terms, a lot of people took less notice of her, or mentioned the article to her, is merely to make an allegation that you are quite capable of making from the floor of the Court, Mr Cassidy. In other words, this is a presumption that it does harm but that is no more than a general allegation of it.[14]

Shand's harsh interrogations

Dr Fanny endured 'sleepless nights' and 'anguish' when subjected to harsh interrogations in court by Jack Shand KC, barrister for the defendant. There was also 'the angst of long consultations with … legal advisers'.[15]

Shand's bullying and intimidating strategies were well known. Dr Fanny needed intellectual and emotional resources to withstand his aggression. Familiar with Zionist history, she responded with clarity and logic to his cross-examination conducted on the first afternoon of the trial. He dealt in detail with a letter sent on 1 September 1947 – three months after the publication of the article – by her solicitor to the editor of *Smith's Weekly*; and the editor's reply sent two days after that, on 3 September 1947. He focused on the proceedings of the Youth Aliyah meeting on 6 May 1947 in Sydney, her response and that of the audience to Comay's address, hammering on details that taxed her concentration and mental acuity:

> Shand: It is correct that his speech received great applause, did it not, at that meeting.

Dr Fanny: I cannot remember whether it received great applause.

Shand: Well, you yourself, I suppose, clapped, did you not?

Dr Fanny: I do not remember.

Shand: Well, you agreed with it, did you not?

Dr Fanny: I was interested to hear what he had to say, but I did not say I agreed with the speech.

Shand: Well, did you disagree with it?

Dr Fanny: In some parts.

Shand: What parts did you disagree with?

Dr Fanny: Well, about the clique he talked about at Whitehall. I know nothing about that.

Shand: The clique at Whitehall?

Dr Fanny: Yes.

Shand: You know nothing about it, but did you disagree with it?

Dr Fanny: Well, I listened, I could hear it.

Shand: You did not know anything about it, and you did not disagree, or agree, with that part?

Dr Fanny: I would not worry about it very much.

Shand: Is that the position – you either agreed or did not agree?

Dr Fanny: As far as I knew, I did not know anything about the clique.

Shand: I suppose you were not in a position to do either?

Dr Fanny: So I would not agree with that statement.

Shand: But you will not deny that you personally clapped his speech, would you?

Dr Fanny: I do not know what I did. I am generally busy at those appeal meetings.

> Shand: But you were up on the platform?
>
> Dr Fanny: There was no platform. It was a dinner.
>
> Shand: In that part where the official party was?
>
> Dr Fanny: I might have clapped out of courtesy to a visiting speaker.[16]

Shand's structured cross-examination established and advanced his hypothesis and argument that the Jewish community in Palestine felt betrayed by the British, resented their anti-immigration policies in Palestine, and therefore used funds to support 'terrorist' activities against the British. He posed his questions within parameters that offered no tolerance for nuanced replies, constraining Dr Fanny to monosyllabic responses:

> Shand: Do you remember him [Comay] saying this? 'British policy in Palestine is a disastrous one, and the Jewish community there feels bitter about it.' This is correct, is it not?
>
> Dr Fanny: Yes, but there was an interpretation that I could give you.
>
> Shand. Never mind about the interpretation.[17]

Shand questioned Dr Fanny at length on Comay's address, quoting topics from his speech, including the Colonial Office's anxiety about immigration: '[The Colonial office] had taken to pleading with European governments, with governments bordering the Mediterranean to cooperate in preventing and forbidding the movement of Jewish masses towards the coast'.[18]

Shand's attempts to elicit from Dr Fanny a condemnation of the British Mandatory government in Palestine were doubly barbed. Knowing how passionate she was about the fate of Jewish children in Europe, he aimed for an emotional and unguarded response to bolster his contention that the Jews supported sabotaging the British Administration in Palestine, as alleged in *Smith's Weekly's* article. Dr Fanny, however, responded in measured tones and words, giving due weight to her conviction that the British had not lived up to their promise in the Balfour Declaration. She avoided Shand's trap, his attempt to provoke her condemnation of the British. She responded by differentiating between the British generally and the particular British Mandatory Authority in Palestine:

> Shand: I want to ask you this – is it your view that the British through the years ... have they in your opinion spared no pains whatever to try and solve the problem that exists between the Arabs and Jews with regard to Palestine?
>
> Dr Fanny: Well, I would not say they have spared no pains. They probably tried, but I say ...
>
> Shand: And in your opinion have done their very utmost?
>
> Dr Fanny: I would not say they have done their very utmost, otherwise things would have probably been done in Palestine.
>
> Shand: You would not think that?
>
> Dr Fanny: No, I would think they could have done more.
>
> Shand: We will deal with that presently?
>
> Dr Fanny: Because I mean by their promise in the Balfour Declaration – I was in Palestine in 1925 and they had not fulfilled their promises then, and they did not after.
>
> Shand: You put a good deal of the trouble down to that?
>
> Dr Fanny: But that is the Administration in Palestine that I am criticizing.
>
> Shand: Broken promises by the British?
>
> Dr Fanny: By the British Administration and the Mandatory power.[19]

Shand covered aspects of Zionist history, questioning Dr Fanny on the Balfour Declaration, the 1922 White Paper, and the 1939 White Paper, the latter viewed by Zionists as a threat to, if not a negation of, the Balfour Declaration. Dr Fanny remained steadfast in her convictions concerning the Balfour Declaration, 'I think we should have the country in face of all we have gone through, and Great Britain offered it to us in 1917'.[20] Later, she commented, '[The Balfour Declaration] said it would give them their national home. It said it would give them a national home in Palestine ... after the first war'.[21]

'I can still be a Jew and still be an Australian citizen'

Throughout Shand's cross-examination, Dr Fanny maintained her composure and stated unambiguously her opinions, despite his barrage of questions designed to confuse her. At great length, Shand pursued the bogey of dual loyalties, quoting 90-year-old Sir Isaac Isaacs, former Governor General of Australia and Chief Justice of the Commonwealth, who alleged that Zionism fostered allegiances to two countries, Australia and the Jewish National Home, an accusation supported by an elite of assimilated and well-established Jews. Shand quoted Isaacs: 'To demand at the same time two homelands for the same person is as if a demand were for two religions or two wives,' to which Dr Fanny responded succinctly, 'I can still be a Jew and still be an Australian citizen'.[22] Their exchange alluded to the controversy that the conservative Sir Isaac unleashed in the Jewish community:

> Shand: I only want your views?
>
> Dr Fanny: My views? I said he was rather old when he wrote that. I think he was 90 when he wrote those views.
>
> Shand: You think he was failing?
>
> Dr Fanny: He had never visited Palestine, otherwise he would

have known the state of affairs there.

Shand: And you had visited there for six weeks?

Dr Fanny: I was there, but I knew a great deal about it.

Shand: He was a very learned man?

Dr Fanny: I know he was, but I just want to say that he looked at it purely from a theoretical legal mind ... and we looked at it from the humanitarian point of view. There were so many million Jews murdered – as I said, six million – and we needed a home for them, and I said before that the country shut its doors. We only had the home, and that was Palestine, and you know the result of the Lake Success meeting of the U.N.O of November 1947, which gave us Palestine. So, I say, Sir Isaac Isaacs, had he lived to hear that, might have changed his views.

Shand: It partitioned the country, did it not?

Dr Fanny: Partitioned it.

Shand: It gave you Palestine?

Dr Fanny: Well, gave us only Palestine?

Shand: It gave you part?

Dr Fanny: But we would like the whole.[23]

Stone's rebuttal of Isaacs' views

Shand had referenced a controversy, Isaac's opposition to Zionism, that provoked bitterness and divisive debate in the Jewish community. Professor Julius Stone, Challis Professor of Jurisprudence and International Law at the University of Sydney, wrote in his book *Stand Up and Be Counted!*:

> There have been two distinct objects of Sir Isaac's attacks ... One of these objects is the exercise by his fellow-Jews of their right as citizens to criticise, as unjust, unwise and, amidst the present

sufferings of European Jewry even inhumane, the prohibition of immigration of Jews into Palestine under the Chamberlain White Paper of 1939 … The other is the propriety of Australian Jews participating in the Zionist movement. I am satisfied, with respect, that Sir Isaac is in grave error as to both.[24]

The central and the desperately urgent issue is immigration, both from the viewpoint of Palestinian Jews, condemned by the White Paper of 1939 to permanent minority status, and from that of the survivors of Hitler's Europe, disinherited by that same White Paper. Whether they refer to a Jewish commonwealth or not, the gist of all Zionist proposals is immigration. They insist that immigration shall proceed on the objective tests of human needs in Europe, and the demonstrable welfare of all inhabitants of Palestine. They insist, in short, upon a dynamic test of economic absorptive capacity and the abolition of the 'political' tests applied by the 1939 White Paper.[25]

Stone highlighted the contradiction between the refuge Australia offered Isaacs' parents when they fled antisemitic persecution and Isaacs' denial of that right to others suffering under Nazi tyranny:

For us to deny the right of European Jews to flee persecution as Sir Isaac's father and my own dear parents fled it, because he and I are more than content with our lot, is neither noble, nor patriotic, nor heroic. If they are justified in seeking a new home, then we have a duty to help them, and to see that their suffering hands do not beat in vain on doors illegally and immorally locked against them. No Zionist proposes that Sir Isaac and I and other happy Jews should change our present allegiance. But we must not deny our persecuted brethren their solution to their problems, merely because we may not share those problems.[26]

Does Sir Isaac regard Czechs or Poles who are citizens of the United States as bad Americans because they feel a special bond with their fellows in Europe and a duty to aid them in their struggle for liberty and justice? Or did he so regard Irish Americans or Irish Australians who felt up to a generation ago a special interest in the fate of the Irish people of Ireland?[27]

Dr Fanny stands her ground

Subjected to Shand's bombardment of historic facts, figures and theories, Dr Fanny never yielded ground on the facts she knew or compromised her stand ideologically. She responded now and then with a retort that betrayed her impatience with the questioning. She even echoed satirically his repetitive phrase, 'is it not?':

> Shand: We have not come to Lord Balfour yet, he was in 1917, was he not?
>
> Dr Fanny: Yes. What dates are you talking about?
>
> Shand: I am talking about a little earlier, about 1914/1915. You remember, or you read, did you not …
>
> Dr Fanny: 35 years ago?
>
> Shand: Yes? You can still read things?
>
> Dr Fanny: But do I remember?
>
> Shand: Do you remember having read?
>
> Dr Fanny: I do not think I do.
>
> Shand: Have you read the literature on the subject?
>
> Dr Fanny: I have read a good bit of this literature.
>
> Shand: You have read, have you not, that at the time of the first war the security of the Arabs in Palestine was promised by His Majesty's Government?
>
> Dr Fanny: I date my knowledge from the Balfour Declaration and the Mandate given to Great Britain, is that before that?

Shand: We will come to the Balfour Declaration, if you like, that was in 1917, was it not?

Dr Fanny: Yes. In 1918 the Mandate was given, was it not?

Shand: Go slowly. Do not rush ahead. The effect of the Balfour Declaration was that the Jews in Palestine – it was promised that they could establish in Palestine a national home?

Dr Fanny: Yes.

Shand: There was no promise to give them the whole of Palestine. You understand that?

Dr Fanny: That was understood to be the whole of Palestine.

Shand: But they were not the words of the Declaration, were they?

Dr Fanny: I think you ought to have an expert to explain that to you.[28]

In articulating her views, Dr Fanny denied any subordination of Arabs in a future Jewish national homeland, as that would contradict the tenets of Zionism as expounded by its leaders. She demonstrated a grasp of realpolitik and revealed her knowledge of history, her familiarity with the Biltmore Program that called for unlimited immigration into Palestine, the Peel Report, the Woodhead Report and a number of other Commissions. She never faltered when responding to Shand's questions on Zionist history or his repeated attempts to trap her into condemning the British Mandatory administration in Palestine or sympathising with those engaged in sabotaging British interests. In an earlier exchange, she contended there had been, 'Great restraint, yes, on the part of the British and on the part of the Jews there'.[29] On several occasions in her testimony, she deplored any acts of terror:

> I deprecate the loss of life of any one individual, but in considering all this, there was great restraint in Palestine during the

last few years ... it would be worse in India. It was worse in India. Look at the massacres there. Hell was let loose.[30]

Dr Fanny maintained that the British in Palestine could have done much more to foster the emergence and consolidation of a Jewish homeland by relaxing the stringent immigration quota imposed in 1939 at a critical time for European Jewry. She showed her concern for Holocaust victims denied entry to Palestine: 'I remember that they restricted immigration to 1500 per month for five years, which was a terrible blow to me at that time'.[31]

Consistently demonstrating loyalty to the British Crown, she defended her right to criticise the Mandatory administration in Palestine for not doing more; and was forthright in her criticism:

> Shand: I suppose you do appreciate, or do you remember, that it was pointed out that if the British allowed unlimited immigration it would mean a rule of force, because the Arabs would fight?
>
> Dr Fanny: Might I say something here?
>
> Shand: Yes?
>
> Dr Fanny: The same thing happened last year, or the year before. There was going to be a big uprising of Arabs if we were given the country. If there was a great uprising, the whole Moslem world would have come in. We were not afraid, and the British should not have been scared of an uprising of Arabs, if they had given us the right of unlimited immigration. History proves it.[32]

When Shand asked whether she agreed that British policy in Palestine had been a disastrous one, she replied: 'Disastrous ... to our people in Europe who could not come to Palestine ... We think the Administration could have relaxed its immigration laws. That was the basis of it all.'[33] Dr Fanny revealed an understanding of global interests in the Middle East: 'The British Administration had interests with Arabs outside'.[34]

Whether due to the tension of the proceedings or the effort in concentrating on details, each of which could have legal implications, her patience wore thin at times:

> Shand: Do you know anything about the history of Palestine?
>
> Dr Fanny: Yes, but I need not know all these details.
>
> Shand: But you have read a copy have you not?
>
> Dr Fanny: I cannot remember.
>
> Shand: Have not you debated it? Have you not debated the Mandate with other leading Jews here?
>
> Dr Fanny: There was no need to debate something which took place in 1922. We have more modern things to debate about the Jewish movement.
>
> Shand: What about at the time?
>
> Dr Fanny: I was not in debating classes at the time.
>
> Shand. I was not asking you about debating classes?
>
> Dr Fanny: I was not debating those problems in 1922, I was a Doctor of Medicine; doing Medicine.[35]

Dr Fanny refused to allow Shand to diminish her standing as a competent witness:

> Shand: Perhaps you do not know very much about the history, do you?
>
> Dr Fanny: Well, I know a good bit, but I might not remember every detail.[36]

Dr Fanny's responses revealed her determination to stand up to Shand's badgering:

> Shand: I suppose you appreciate that in 1942, during this war, things looked very bad, did they not?

> Dr Fanny: In 1942, thousands of our Jews ...
>
> Shand: I am leaving Palestine now?
>
> Dr Fanny: I thought you wanted to know about Palestine.[37]

Shand returned repeatedly to the topic of immigration, suggesting that unlimited immigration of Jews into Palestine might have resulted in 'considerable loss of life'. Dr Fanny attempted to reply, 'I was there in 1925 ...', only to be cut off abruptly by Shand, who commanded her peremptorily to 'Just answer my question?' Displaying presence of mind, she continued calmly:

> I want to tell you that if there is authority, yes, the Arabs would not have resorted to violence. I was in Palestine in 1925 when such an uprising could have happened. If stern measures were not taken, as it was taken then by Lord Plumer, the High Commissioner, the Arabs could not do anything, or very little.[38]

Dr Fanny's ordeal in the witness box during her cross-examination by Shand prompted Justice Herron to intervene shortly after the above exchange: 'It would not be any injustice to you if you said you had a general or vague notion it was true, without knowing the details'; to which she replied gratefully, 'Yes'.[39]

Although Cassidy had warned Dr Fanny that Shand would not permit her to ask questions, he also advised her, 'If you do not know, say so'.[40] By all accounts, Dr Fanny projected an image of dignity and quiet reserve throughout the proceedings, but she was never passive or meek in the witness box. She showed no hesitation in asserting her right to clarification before answering and conveyed her ideological and practical commitment to saving as many surviving children as she could. It was apparent that the facts of annihilation weighed heavily on her. When Shand asked her whether boys of all ages were eligible for entry through Youth Aliyah, she replied, 'No, from about eight years to sixteen, whatever children could be found,' adding a moment later, 'but there were not many children left of younger ages. Hitler had destroyed them all you know'.[41]

The issues of legal and illegal immigration

The subject of immigration, both legal and illegal, was a dominant and recurring theme of the trial, with Shand approaching it from diverse perspectives, homing in always on diverging views on immigration policy held by Jews and the British Mandatory Authority respectively:

> Shand: I think you have already indicated … that you thought that unrestricted immigration into Palestine of Jews was proper in your view. That is all I want to know.
>
> Dr Fanny: If it were legal, it would have been proper.
>
> Shand: Did you think it was legal? That was your own view?
>
> Dr Fanny: Legal immigration of great numbers would have been proper because we had not so many in Europe.
>
> Shand: You know the British Government took the opposite view do you not?
>
> Dr Fanny: Yes.
>
> Shand: You thought there should be unrestricted immigration?
>
> Dr Fanny: Yes.
>
> Shand: I am not saying that is right or wrong. You know that they took that view?
>
> Dr Fanny: Yes.
>
> Shand: You took the view that there should be room, they should be accommodated there, as many as you could get across and settle?
>
> Dr Fanny: Yes, they would have been absorbed.
>
> Shand: That is your view of it? I think you did say that you have

always been in favour of unlimited immigration because you could absorb them there. That is your view of that?

Dr Fanny: Because we have had professional advice on that, that they should be absorbed.

Shand: And in fact that is what you set out in this pamphlet, that was the aim, was it not, of this Youth Aliyah? That was the aim of it?

Dr Fanny: To bring as many children as possible, to save as many.

Shand: To bring all children into Palestine?

Dr Fanny: Yes, over time, over a period of years ... You could not leave them in camps in Europe.[42]

Despite being in the witness box almost the whole day and immersed in the vortex of Shand's questions that whirled around the same subjects, Dr Fanny gave due consideration to her responses, emphasising the legality of Youth Aliyah policies:

Shand: I want to know whether you agree that the British policy in Palestine has been a disastrous one?

Dr Fanny: Disastrous to the Jews who are in Europe, disastrous to our people in Europe who could not come to Palestine.

Shand: And disastrous even for, generally speaking, the Jews as to their right in Palestine?

Dr Fanny: Yes.

Shand: And is it correct that there is, in your view, a bitter feeling in that connection?

Dr Fanny: I think there is a great deal of restraint about that feeling.

Shand: There may be, but underneath is there some bitter feeling?

Dr Fanny: That the promises were not kept.

Shand: That may be the reason, but there may be some bitter feeling?

Dr Fanny: Yes. We think the Administration could have relaxed its immigration laws. That was the basis of it all.

Shand: And is it correct that you yourself put that down to the fact that the Government administration has favoured the Arabs?

Dr Fanny: I would say that it did not favour the Jews as far as the immigration was concerned. If we could have got more people there ...[43]

When Shand asked Dr Fanny about 'The Terror' in Palestine, she said it was carried out by 'A small body of lawless people', groups with 'relatives in Europe wanting to come to join them, and they were forbidden'.[44] Shand then conflated these groups with the Haganah, which he termed an 'underground' army that 'organised immigration', the implication being that the Haganah contravened British Mandatory laws. Dr Fanny pointed out that the British Government recognised Haganah as a 'self-defence army', 'as the army which was defending the colonies',[45] a few of whose members 'went to Europe to rescue probably relatives from concentration camps'.[46] When Shand questioned her on Comay's view that the 1939 White Paper's restriction of immigration was illegal under the Mandate, Dr Fanny concurred: 'If the international authorities say it is illegal I would agree with them ... Yes, under the Mandate it is illegal. Under the Mandate it did not restrict'.[47]

As the afternoon wore on, the court transcript reflects Dr Fanny's increasing fatigue. There was a note of exasperation in her responses, and occasional lapses in concentration:

Shand: I am asking you – is it your view that it is illegal [the 1939 White Paper's restriction of immigration]?

Dr Fanny: Does my view matter?

Shand: Well, it does in this Court.

Dr Fanny: What was the question again?[48]

Towards the end of the first day of the trial, Shand concluded his cross-examination of Dr Fanny by focusing on the structure and program of Youth Aliyah in Australia. She displayed detailed knowledge of the Australian Jewish community, noting in her evidence that there were between 5,000 and 6,000 subscribers to Youth Aliyah in Australia – correcting Shand's suggestion of 20,000 – out of a total Jewish population of 40,000 in Australia at that time. Once again, Shand interrogated her on Comay's criticism of the British administration in Palestine. She qualified Shand's statement, exploring alternative meanings:

> Shand: You will agree that a man who suggested that England was being unjust would be deserving of criticism from Australians?
>
> Dr Fanny: It depends on how he said it.
>
> Shand: If he said it publicly?
>
> Dr Fanny: He might have prefixed it or affixed it with some other sentiments.
>
> Shand: If he had just said that he would have been deserving of censure?
>
> Dr Fanny: If he only said that.[49]

Shand probed the reasons Dr Fanny took on the role of plaintiff in this case, to which she replied comprehensively, referring to her national prestige, her personal response to the issue, her position as an office bearer of Youth Aliyah, and her sense of personal injury: 'As I was the best known probably, I offered to … It affected me personally too … I was the Vice President … it affected me too'.[50] It had been a gruelling day for Dr Fanny, but her ordeal was not over, as she would be recalled twice on the following two days.

The second day of the trial

A group of leaders of the Zionist Movement in Sydney and Melbourne, the Council to Combat Fascism and Anti-Semitism, the NSW Jewish Board of Deputies, the Victorian Jewish Board of Deputies and the Executive Council of Australian Jewry ... made a commitment to support the suggested litigation ... The costs of the action were to be borne from their own pockets.[52]

In court, Dr Fanny also mentioned support from specific members of her own organisation, whose names she gave reluctantly – Sasha Freilich and Mrs Whitefield – clearly wishing to spare them embarrassment at being identified in court proceedings:

> My own members are helping me, should I need them ... There are so many ... They would stand behind me ... they know I was taking this action ... we discussed it at an informal meeting ... I had a few friends in my own home one evening, and we just discussed it, and they said they would stand behind me ... I would say about eight ... they promised if I needed them ... but I could probably meet it myself if I had to.[53]

Dr Fanny's mental acuity was evident when she corrected Shand's error in the exchange that followed. He said a cable about a quota of 4,000 children was received in 1949. She pointed out the correct date was 1947, prompting an unexpected apology from Shand. He appeared even further confused – or perhaps biased – conflating foreign names and identities, which contrasted with Dr Fanny's precise and accurate answers:

> Shand: The members of the executive, Miss D Abramovitch [Dora Abramovitch, a member of the Youth Aliyah executive]. Do you say that she is not a relation of yours?
>
> Dr Fanny: No relation.

Shand: That was your name?

Dr Fanny: Never.

Shand. Abramovitch?

Dr Fanny: My name, my father's name, was Rubinovitch [sic].

His Honor: She is a lady doctor, Dr Abramovitch?

Dr Fanny: She is a doctor.

Shand: I think you, at some stage, changed your name to your present name, did you not, at some stage?

Dr Fanny: In 1918. Could I correct that? I did not change my name, my father did.[54]

Shand's questions on Ernest Bevin

Dr Fanny's response to shifting political currents in Palestine and her grasp of contemporary events and policies in the Middle East came into sharp focus again when Shand questioned her concerning Ernest Bevin. Dr Fanny referenced a time when Ernest Bevin was a member of the British War Cabinet during the Second World War, serving as foreign secretary in the post-war Labour government, from 1945 to 1951, when Palestine was transferred from the control of the Colonial Office to the Foreign Office. While some commentators concluded: 'In spite of his controversial handling of the Palestine situation, he is generally regarded as a great foreign secretary',[55] others believed Bevin applied severely repressive measures against the *Yishuv*, the Jewish community in Palestine. This latter perspective reflected Dr Fanny's view, which she expressed forthrightly in an exchange with Shand:

Shand: I take it that while Mr Bevin was in charge of affairs he was doing his best, did you think, in the situation?

Dr Fanny: I thought they had a very difficult job in Palestine.

Shand: And that he was doing his best?

Dr Fanny: To his way of thinking.

Shand: But, to your way of thinking?

Dr Fanny: Well, I think he had a difficult problem, because …

Shand: I do not want to stop you?

Dr Fanny: He had a difficult problem in Palestine.

Shand: I am still asking you the question – to your mind was he doing his best with the difficult problem?

Dr Fanny: He did not do his best in this way, that promises of the Labour Government to the Jewry had not been carried out. They said, after the Anglo-American Commission, whatever it decided, that they would carry it out, and one hundred thousand Jews were to be taken from Europe to Palestine. That was under the Bevin Government. Had that happened there probably would not have been the difficulties in Palestine.

Shand: That is your criticism of the position?

Dr Fanny: Yes.

Shand: So in your opinion the British authorities … following the Balfour Declaration right up to the present time, when I say the present time I do not mean when the United Nations took over, it continued to break promises?

Dr Fanny: Not continued. They gave a promise in the Balfour Declaration.[56]

Taxed with questions relating to personalities, policies and events in Zionist, British and world history, Dr Fanny was under mounting pressure. She made an effort to answer Shand accurately and advantageously. When Shand suggested she had implied earlier that trouble ceased after Palestine was partitioned, her plea for a moment's respite to review and order her thoughts revealed her desperation, and even confusion, under his belligerent cross-examination. Her words betrayed her state of mind: 'Just let me think a minute, what did I say? I am trying to think what I did say'.[57] Regaining her composure and marshalling her thoughts with clarity once more, she told Shand that partition was the best solution under the circumstances: 'That we should have something in Palestine ... We were satisfied to have that'.[59]

Cassidy's re-examination of Dr Fanny

Cassidy's courteous and respectful tone was a welcome change after a morning of Shand's cross-examination. He established that Dr Fanny contributed substantially to non-Jewish enterprises; and that immediately the war began she issued a bulletin in which she stated:

> The War Emergency Board of the National Council of Jewish Women notifies members that all activities other than war work should be temporarily suspended ... It is our duty to help the British and the Allied Armies who are fighting desperately with sublime courage and heroic fortitude with every sacrifice in our power.[59]

Strategically, Cassidy documented Dr Fanny's loyalty and commitment to the British Empire and the war effort, highlighting her dedication, philosophy and initiatives that he reinforced with her published words: 'We have not done all we ought till we have done all we can'.[60] 'Yes, during the war our main work was war work, throughout Australia that was,' she told Cassidy. Through questioning, Cassidy portrayed Dr Fanny as a woman of distinction in the wider community, who personally received acknowledgment from authoritative sources of her philanthropy and efforts for beneficiaries in Australia. In her responses, she confirmed she was awarded the King George V1 Coronation Medal in 1937 and the King George V Jubilee Medal in 1935, and that she received many citations for war work and contributions to the War Loans, and acknowledgments of donations to Australian charities, including the H.M.A.S. Sydney Fund, Great Britain's Civilians War Relief Victims Fund, the Lord Mayor's Patriotic and War Fund, the Australian Red Cross and the Catholic organisation Boys Town. 'Our work made no discrimination of race or creed, we work for everything,' she explained.[61]

Cassidy questioned Dr Fanny about the former President of Youth Aliyah in Australia, Rabbi Max Schenk. He came to Australia in 1939 to serve as minister of Temple Emanuel in Sydney; and returned 10 years later to the United States.[62] His wife, Faye, had served as president of Hadassah, the Women's Zionist Organisation of America, which supported Youth Aliyah in Palestine. 'He [Schenk] always stressed the humanitarian part of Youth Aliyah and said it was a non-political work,' Dr Fanny told Cassidy.[63]

Cassidy addressed the negative implications of questions posed by Shand, who had quoted at length from Comay's speech delivered at the Youth Aliyah fundraiser in Sydney. Cassidy asked Dr Fanny to whom Comay referred when he said that members of the Army 'are organizing the underground exodus of Jews from Europe to Palestine, and the story of these Jewish Scarlet Pimpernels, when it is told, will be spectacular'. She responded:

> It refers, I think to some individuals of the Haganah probably who went to Europe to endeavour to get people … out of concentration camps and organise them to several ports, Genoa or Trieste, where they waited to get certificates for permission [to enter Palestine].[64]

Her brief response shone a light on conditions in Europe for persecuted Jews and the courage of those risking their own lives to rescue children from concentration camps, labour camps and ghettoes.

In relation to the payment of legal fees associated with the case, Cassidy questioned Dr Fanny at some length about financial support offered to her, and whether it was binding. 'All that we discussed was that they would help me if it was necessary,' she stated.⁶⁵ It is not improbable that Cassidy provided his services pro bono, given that he posed this question: 'You might have got a barrister for nothing, I suppose?' Dr Fanny replied somewhat mysteriously, 'I may have'.⁶⁶

Nothing more was said about this intriguing exchange, as at this juncture Shand questioned Dr Fanny again about the frequency of Youth Aliyah meetings: 'We met when there were appeals, very often, but when there were no appeals just spasmodically,' she replied.⁶⁷ Her choice of the word 'spasmodically' hints at her mental state. It was her second lengthy day in the witness box, resulting in considerable inner tension, despite her efforts to remain calm and focused. Most people would use the word 'infrequently', 'now and again', 'seldom' or 'only occasionally'. The word 'spasmodically' conveys an impression of extreme nervosity.

Landauer testifies on behalf of Youth Aliyah

At this point, Dr Fanny retired and Cassidy began his examination of Georg Landauer. Director and Treasurer of the Jewish Agency's Youth Aliyah Department from 1933 to 1948, he came from Palestine to Sydney to give evidence as a witness in the case. He spoke with authority on matters pertaining to Youth Aliyah, as he was on personal terms with Youth Aliyah personnel, their field workers and British administrators in the Department of Migration:

> I had to contact the various governmental agencies in connection with my work, sometimes the Department of Migration, sometimes the Chief Secretary of the Government, and sometimes other officials ...⁶⁸

He testified that Youth Aliyah had no political policies but was exclusively dedicated to saving Jewish children trapped in Nazi Europe and further afield.

Importantly, Landauer established his credentials, which gave him a degree of moral authority, 'I am a Doctor of Laws and I live in Jerusalem',[69] and then vouched for the integrity of Youth Aliyah. He stated that General Jan Christiaan Smuts of South Africa – former Prime Minister, statesman, soldier and scholar – was Youth Aliyah's patron. This carried weight, as General Smuts served in the Imperial War Cabinet during World War I, and in 1941 was Field Marshal of the British Army. He played an important role in drafting the constitution of the League of Nations, forerunner of the United Nations.[70] His name guaranteed the probity and transparency of Youth Aliyah. Landauer confirmed to Cassidy that he himself had close contact with the British Administration and British officials in connection with Youth Aliyah. He was, therefore, an authoritative source for establishing that Youth Aliyah was not anti-British in any way and never supported illegal immigration. He confirmed the object of Youth Aliyah was 'to rescue as many children from Germany as possible who were threatened by the Nazi persecutions … We followed the path of Hitler, first through Germany, and then through Austria and then through Czechoslovakia and slowly through other countries'.[71]

In response to Cassidy's questions concerning Youth Aliyah's financial responsibilities, Landauer said:

> The practice was to have regular payments made to educational institutions or settlements, payment for the maintenance and education of the children … sometimes for accommodation, for housing, or clothing and medical and social care of the children according to fixed rates … Fifty per cent of the absorption places were settlements and fifty per cent were educational institutions. … We took only either orphans or children who had been sent by their parents and their parents stayed behind.[72]

Landauer, who negotiated with the British Administration's Migration Department for children's certificates to enter Palestine, stated their immigration was restricted by the economic absorptive capacity of the country. 'That is the difference,' he said, explaining that this rule was fixed by the British White Paper of 1922 and he thought it unjust.[73] A discussion ensued regarding the British implementation of the Balfour Declaration, Arab uprisings and their attempts to forestall further Jewish immigration.

In reply to Shand's questions, Landauer emphasised that there was never any question of illegal immigration:

> We applied to the Mandatory Government and asked for the immigration certificates. Abroad in the countries of origin our affiliated offices assisted the children, and according to the number of certificates allocated to us it was applied to the British Passport Control Office to get the entry permits, and then they were sent to Palestine.[74]

He explained that after the war in 1945, the Jewish Agency subdivided the total monthly allocation of 1,500 certificates, giving a share of that to Youth Aliyah, a process followed in 1946. In this way, children from France, Holland and Belgium entered Palestine. In 1947, with a large number of Jewish children detained in Cyprus, he asked for an additional 3,000 certificates, which were granted. Youth Aliyah obtained immigration certificates for all the children arriving before, during and after the war under the Youth Aliyah scheme: 5,012 before the war; 11,167 during the war; and 14,805 from July 1945 to October 1948.[75] He confirmed that Youth Aliyah funds were never spent in support of 'terrorists', or the Irgun Zvai Leumi; and stated he thought the terrorists were 'dirty murderers'.[76]

Shand's attempts to discredit Landauer

In Landauer's testimony, he denied the existence of any anti-British hostility that could serve Shand's aim of validating defamatory statements published in *Smith's Weekly*. In Shand's cross-examination of Landauer, he attempted to create a picture of a German citizen who fought against the British in the First World War. Landauer pointed out he had no choice in the matter, military service was compulsory and he was conscripted. Shand then attempted to obtain an admission that there had been attempts at illegal immigration, which Landauer described as 'very inconsiderable. Very small numbers perhaps arrived at the country, not any sizeable number'.[77] He tried to discredit Landauer's evidence, accusing him of making a 'gross mistake within five minutes', to which Landauer responded 'surely not. I would not make deliberate mistakes'.[78] Shand endeavoured to elicit an admission that Youth Aliyah viewed the British policy in Palestine as a disastrous one, to which Landauer responded adamantly, 'Youth Aliyah has no political views on policy, neither British or other policies'.[79] When he failed to obtain from Landauer any denunciation of the British and their policies, Shand re-framed the question: 'Will you agree then that in Palestine, in your view, the British have done all that could be expected of them in their treatment of the Jews?' Landauer stated he would not say 'all that could be expected', but much.[80]

Shand, continuing with his harsh phraseology and bullying tone (e.g. 'Just answer my question, will you') asked Landauer whether he thought that under the mandate the British had the right to restrict immigration to 1,500 per month for a period of 5 years. Landauer's response moved the issue beyond narrow legalities, as he positioned British action within an ethical context, drawing a distinction between a legal right and the broader concept of justice:

> Shand: They had the right, that is your view?
>
> Landauer: They had a right. I would not acknowledge that this is just, but they had a right. A government has the right, any government has a right to restrict.
>
> Shand: But you think it was unjust, do you?
>
> Landauer: I think it was unjust.[81]

Shand interrogated Landauer concerning subjects he had covered in cross-examining Dr Fanny, attempting to paint a picture of their extreme dissatisfaction with the British that, he implied, might veer into supporting 'terrorists'. Landauer's responses were carefully calibrated, highlighting subtle distinctions in language. He never allowed Shand to rush him into ill-considered replies but gave due weight to every word and their implications. His testimony confirmed Dr Fanny's in many instances, for example, their shared view of the British Mandatory Authority's interpretation of the Balfour Declaration and implementation of the Mandate:

Shand: And I suppose you know Article 6 of the Mandate, do you?

Landauer: Yes, I know that.

Shand: And this is it, is it not, I will just read it. I will just ask you if this is it – 'The administration of Palestine, while ensuring that the rights and positions of other sections of the population are not prejudiced, shall facilitate Jewish immigration under suitable conditions and shall encourage in co-operation with the Jewish Agency referred to in Article 4, closer settlement of the Jews on the land'. So that is what you understand. That is your understanding of Article 6 of the Mandate?

Landauer; Yes.

Shand: And you understand, do you, it is your understanding, that under that, of course, other peoples, including Arabs, had to be considered, the claims of other people, including the Arabs had to be considered?

Landauer: Had to be considered.

Shand:. Of course, you are aware of the wording of the Balfour Declaration?

Landauer: I am.

Shand: And do you agree that the British followed, in their

conduct of Palestinian affairs, what was laid down in that Declaration?

Landauer; That may be debatable.

Shand: Well, I am asking you your opinion?

Landauer: It is debatable, I say.

Shand: Will you agree with me that in your opinion the British followed the terms of the Balfour Declaration?

Landauer: Not always, not always.

Shand: Your view is that they did not?

Landauer: No, I said 'not always'. Sometimes they did, sometimes they did not.

Shand: And I suppose your claim is that when they did not do it they were unjust to the Jews?

Landauer: It depends on the occasion. They may have been forced by circumstances, which should be acknowledged.

Shand: On any occasion, do you think they were unjust to the Jews?

Landauer: Not on any occasion.

Shand: Not on any occasion?

Landauer: Not on any occasion, on certain occasion[s] sometimes.[82]

Re-examined by Cassidy, Landauer stated that Comay was not connected with Youth Aliyah. He answered questions concerning the source of funds for transporting children to Palestine, which Shand wrongly presumed was provided by Youth Aliyah. Landauer said funds arose from recommendations made by the Inter-Governmental Committee of Refugees, an initiative of the League of Nations. It was succeeded by the International Refugee Organisation, which disbursed

£1 million solely for this purpose. He added that Youth Aliyah needed £3 million 'this year alone' for the maintenance of the children, representing a monthly expenditure of £250,000. He said he was a member of a committee that encouraged volunteering among Palestinian Jews and about 2,000 graduates of Youth Aliyah's training courses had volunteered for the [British] army. He had contact with various government agencies in connection with his work, including the Department of Migration, the Chief Secretary of the Government and other officials. 'I maintained, I must say, very cordial relations,' he said.[83]

Dr Fanny recalled to the witness box

At this stage, Dr Fanny was recalled and, once again, submitted to Shand's questioning aimed at establishing a connection between Youth Aliyah and payment for transporting the children to Palestine. Familiar with Shand's badgering, she was steadfast in countering his allegations:

> Shand: But you will not deny, will you, that your association was paying for the transport of the children?
>
> Dr Fanny: No, we knew we did not pay the transport.[84]

Shand questioned her about the late Ida Wynn's reference to the high cost of 'transporting and tending' the children in the first few years of their life in Palestine, which he asked Dr Fanny to confirm. 'I cannot remember that she said that,' she replied.[85] When she stepped out of the witness box, her relief was short-lived, as she was recalled a short while later that same morning. This time, Cassidy questioned her about Ida Wynn, whom Dr Fanny confirmed had been Youth Aliyah campaign director in Victoria, and that Wynn had issued a writ against the paper. In a pivotal moment of the trial, Cassidy asked Dr Fanny about the letter Wynn wrote to *Smith's Weekly*. Dr Fanny announced that a copy of Wynn's letter sent to the editor of *Smith's Weekly* was available in court, the letter Shand alleged *Smith's Weekly* had never received:

Cassidy: Have you got the copy with the solicitors here?

Dr Fanny: Yes I have it.

Cassidy: Is it in your bag?

Dr Fanny: No, it is in that black bag (indicating bag handed to witness).[86]

Judge comments on Cassidy's revelation

After Dr Fanny retired from the witness stand, a scene of acrimony and disputation erupted between the two barristers. Cassidy announced he would call for the letter to be produced, to which Shand angrily retorted: 'I have given an answer. I do not want to repeat it. We have no such letter and never had such a letter'.[87] Cassidy applied for an adjournment, which Justice Herron granted, in order that a Melbourne witness with knowledge of the letter could travel to Sydney to testify to its existence and that it had been received by the defendant. Justice Herron, who dismissed the jury, was critical of these developments:

> I will tell you now that I propose to grant this adjournment ... the interests of justice are to be served here, and although we are faced with procedural upsets such as this is, if it is in the interest of justice that the plaintiff should have time to procure evidence about this matter, then it is my duty to see that she has reasonable time to do so. Mr Cassidy has shown me his brief, which contains a statement by a now deceased person ... where that person says ... that that letter, after it was sent to *Smith's Weekly*, later was discussed with the then managing director of the company, and reference was made to it ... I propose to allow him an adjournment until 10 o' clock in the morning.[88]

Recalling the jury, Justice Herron told them:

> At some earlier stage in this case a reference was made to a letter said to have been sent to the defendant company, and at the

present time there is no evidence that that letter was in fact sent, and there is no admission by the defendant that it was received ... Now it appears that Mr Cassidy has requested me to adjourn the case in order for him to bring a witness from Melbourne, so that he may prove something in connection with the letter ... he has satisfied me that the request is not unreasonable and I feel that the interruption in the case, whilst it is a nuisance to us all, is a matter of justice prevailing over our personal inconvenience, and therefore I propose to grant it.[89]

Ida Wynn's honest error in dating her letter

The court adjourned and reconvened the following morning at 10 am, the third day of the trial, Thursday 28 April 1949, to hear the testimony of Samuel Wynn of Melbourne, whose late wife, Ida was President of Youth Aliyah in Victoria. Questioned by Cassidy, Wynn said his wife issued a writ in respect of the article in *Smith's Weekly* and that she had attended the fundraising meeting in Sydney. He confirmed that the letter shown to him by Cassidy was typed on their typewriter on 29 May 1947 at their home and that it was addressed to the Editor of *Smith's Weekly*, Sydney NSW, and that he had posted it at the Toorak Post Office. He stated that, after posting the letter, he had a conversation with Mr W.J. Smith [William John Smith, the paper's owner].[90] He and his wife came to Sydney and saw Smith on a Saturday morning and left Sydney the following Tuesday.

In the official transcript of the trial, the date of the letter is recorded as 29 May 1947, which in my opinion reflects an honest mistake made by Ida Wynn when she dated the letter '1947' instead of '1948'. However, if the copy of the letter produced in court was not the original carbon copy, the error could be attributed to whomever re-typed the copy. The letter could not have been penned on 29 May 1947 as that date precedes publication of the article in *Smith's Weekly* on 31 May 1947. From the transcript, it is apparent Shand was aware of the discrepancy in the date and had begun to interrogate Wynn on the subject, when the judge intervened and curtailed his cross-examination:

> Shand: When you participated in the construction of this document did you have the paper in front of you, the paper that you are complaining about?
>
> Wynn: Yes.
>
> Shand: And I suppose you were not in doubt as to what date you wrote, when you wrote the letter?
>
> Wynn: No, I did not have any doubts about that.
>
> Shand: Approaching witness: I want to show you first of all the date.
>
> His Honour: it would be just as convenient if this question of law was dealt with in the meantime. If there is any occasion for you to re-open the cross examination (Witness retired).[91]

The barristers concluding summations

The opposing barristers then addressed the court: Shand restated Smith's argument that Major Comay had come to Australia to raise money for buying armaments to harass the British in Palestine; that the Major and the Jewish Agency had a reputation for anti-British activity ... that reference to the 'alleged missions of mercy of Youth Aliyah were merely a cover for the sinister, undercover intrigues of the murderous Zionist underground'; that 'the Jews were ungrateful to the British who had undertaken the thankless task of policing the land and protecting it at a time of unrest'.[92]

Cassidy followed with a brilliant summation, in which he referred to Hitler's plans to exterminate the Jewish people; how Hitler had written about it in *Mein Kampf*, and had implemented those plans when he achieved power in 1933, and how the horrors and cruelties became worse after war started in 1939,

> ... how babies and little infants were torn from their mothers' arms and children were separated from their families, never to see them again; how youngsters were improperly fed and denied necessary medical attention and some were put to arduous work in factories; how millions went to their death, including over a million children, in circumstances of great cruelty.[93]

Cassidy explained that Youth Aliyah was founded in Germany in the year the Nazi Party took office, to rescue children, taking them to Palestine, housing, settling and educating them in an atmosphere of loving-kindness, surrounded by Jewish carers and foster parents. He referred to the activity of young Jewish men and women who penetrated Germany and embattled Europe, seeking Jewish children and rescuing them. Their efforts were not always successful, and many lost their lives. He stated: 'The British Mandatory Authority impeded these rescue attempts as well, and children were turned back from Palestine into lands in which they had no hope of surviving'.[94] He explained that the work of Youth Aliyah was ongoing, as many Jewish children were now homeless in Europe living in displaced persons camps, or unsatisfactorily accommodated. *Smith's Weekly* had done a grave disservice to the cause of justice, 'for it had blatantly condemned this fine organisation on the basis of circumstantial evidence'.[95] He outlined the grievances of the Jewish community in Palestine that believed the administration was tainted by British self-interest, a lack of altruism and that British officials favoured the Arabs. In particular, 'great ill-will resulted when boatloads of "illegal" immigrants were turned back from the beaches, preventing reunions of family members who had been cruelly separated by the events of World War II'.[96] He asked:

> How would any of you react ... if you were in their position? If you could see your mother and your son had disembarked on a beach, but they were being forced back onto the flimsy boats on which they had arrived, and that British naval cutters were towing them

back out to sea! And you were prevented from going to them by British Tommys with fixed bayonets! History has recorded that there was great ill-will, due to these and other heartless policies … Now I ask you, how could *Smith's* equate the compassionate rescue of those children by Youth Aliyah with the efforts of a minority to end what they regarded as an unjust administration? … And that violence is completely irrelevant to the rescue of the children, those most innocent and helpless victims of war. We of the Christian persuasion will recall that one of the most touching and compelling of our Saviour's requests was 'Suffer (allow) the little children to come unto me' (Matthew 19:14). Shall we concur with that goodly injunction when it concerns ourselves but deny it to those of the Jewish Faith?[97]

Cassidy concluded with a plea that focused particularly on Dr Fanny:

We are told that Dr Reading was not libelled because she was not specifically named. I say she was libelled just as clearly as she would have been, had her name been shouted from the roof-tops! Not only was she libelled but the entire Jewish Community was libelled! A generation of Jewish folk was libelled! The brave pioneers in the Holy Land were libelled! The victims of the Holocaust were libelled! The Youth Aliyah – that kindly body of goodly men and women, with its programme of compassion for, and rescue of Jewish children was libelled! The alleged inadequacy of the law of Libel must not be allowed to stand in the way of Justice. Not only was Dr Reading chosen as the plaintiff because she is the leader of Australian Youth Aliyah; she was chosen because she stands high in the ranks of the goodly leaders of Australian Jewry; she is the fearless lady who volunteered to bring this injustice before the court; she is a foremost contributor to all charities both within and beyond her community. If not Dr Reading, then WHO, pray tell me, was libelled? Blatant naked libel has been committed! Will you allow it to go unpunished?[98]

When Cassidy referred to 'the genocide of the infants', his voice was choked with emotion and many in the court, including officials, were visibly affected. Justice Herron adjourned the court until 2 pm that afternoon, 'to enable us to regain our composure'.[99] It is worth noting that Cassidy had visited Germany at the end of the Second World War to observe the International Military Tribunal's prosecution of Nazi war criminals held in Nuremberg.[100]

Justice Herron delivers his judgement

Justice Herron delivered his judgement on Thursday 28 April 1949, the afternoon of the third day of the trial. In preliminary comments, he stated that the libel in question arose out of the publication by *Smith's Weekly* of an article that contained defamatory statements, in that it criticised in no uncertain way the activities connected with certain Jewish organisations, with relation to their loyalty to Britain.[101]

Justice Herron outlined the major considerations of the case:

> 1. Can the article, having regard to the language, and read in light of relevant circumstances, be regarded as capable of referring to the plaintiff? And 2. If it can be regarded in law as capable of referring to the plaintiff, does the article in fact lead reasonable people who know the plaintiff to the conclusion that it does refer to her? That is a question of fact ... It is essential in law that the words be published of the plaintiff.[102]

Justice Herron presented his perspective on the legal task before him, as well as the central issue of the case, whether it was an attack of a personal or general nature:

> It is my duty, sitting as a Judge, to decide the law of the case to read this article ... I assume that my task is to read it as an ordinary reader would read it, as a member of the jury would be expected to read it, read it straight through as an item in a

newspaper, in order to see what it means ... In the first place, in my opinion, quite clearly and contrary to Mr Cassidy's view of it, it is an attack of a general character on the policy of Jews in this country subscribing to Palestine troubles. The paper apparently took the view ... quite wrongly in the case of the Youth Aliyah movement, that it was a matter of condemnation that Jews in Australia should subscribe any money which would go to the maintenance or continuance of the troubles that were being experienced in Palestine at that particular time, between the Arabs and the Jews and the British Administration there.[103]

After outlining various cases pertinent to these legal issues, Justice Herron commented:

In short, where the plaintiff is not actually named, there must be something in the defamatory matter, or in the circumstances in which it is published, which indicates and enables a jury to find that the plaintiff is defamed, although she is not named.[104]

Justice Herron stated that the article was a most clear – the clearest possible – libel on the work of the Youth Aliyah movement; and that it clearly criticised and condemned that Youth Aliyah movement:

Any fair-minded reading of this article will, I think, show that no mention is made of the plaintiff. She is not referred to in any way. There is no reference to her ... It might have described her as a prominent woman in the Jewish community, as a Doctor of Medicine, as a Vice President of the Youth Aliyah movement in this State ... The article, however, attacks all Jews who support this illegal purpose. It possibly embraces the members generally of Youth Aliyah, but no mention of the plaintiff is made in particular in it ... Mr Cassidy contends that this defames all at the meeting. I cannot agree with that ... I cannot agree ... that this article is capable of referring to the plaintiff.[105]

Finally, Justice Herron declared:

The result is that in my view the plaintiff has no right of action in law for libel against the defendant newspaper. I have given this decision after what little time I had at my disposal to consider the matter, and I may also say that I give it with some regret. The plaintiff appears on the evidence to be a woman of distinction in the Jewish community and a woman who has contributed much in time and money towards the social and patriotic causes of Australia. The article ... casts an unwarranted aspersion on this Youth Aliyah movement, an organization of which the plaintiff was a supporter. I believe that the article must have wounded her feelings and filled her with a sense of injustice, not only against the Jews, but also against those who supported this Youth Aliyah movement. However it is, I suppose, cold comfort for her to know that as the law stands no such attack on a class or sect or congregation of people, however unwarranted, can be the subject of a libel action in this court, and this court cannot assist the plaintiff to condemn the paper. It is for Parliament to re-shape the law if any redress is thought to be necessary in such a case as this, but hard cases make bad law, and I have to give to the law the effect as I see it, although, as I say, it brings about a regrettable decision so far as the plaintiff is concerned.[106]

In Justice Herron's judgement, he commented on Dr Fanny's character, compassion, philanthropy, social activism and humanitarian agenda, characterising her as 'a woman of distinction'. Although the judgement was not in her favour, he expressed regret at having to administer the law as it then stood, stating that 'hard cases make bad law'. This led the Jewish community to affirm that Dr Fanny as the plaintiff had won a moral victory. She was a respected figure in the Jewish and general communities, and her role in this case added to her stature as a leader, a view confirmed by Max Freilich:

The statutes of Australia did not provide for group libel and an individual had to be found on whose behalf Court action could be taken. The courageous and gracious woman leader Dr. Fanny Reading, in her capacity of Youth Aliyah Vice-President, volunteered to be the plaintiff and proceedings were instituted against the publishers and editor of *Smith's Weekly*'.[107]

Dr Fanny, who stated she had 'no skills in the parry and thrust of legal debate',[108] had entered this legal arena reluctantly. She was determined, however, to redress the defamatory lies *Smith's Weekly* published nationwide. In this, she succeeded. Justice Herron's references to Dr Fanny's character, standing and achievements were widely reported throughout Australia, as were her responses during the three days of the trial. She compelled admiration for her rebuttal of the lies published by *Smith's Weekly*. Despite the inadequacy of libel laws preventing Justice Herron from delivering a judgement in her favour, many of her goals were accomplished, in particular, telling her truth and those of Youth Aliyah and Zionism to the wider Australian world.

For Dr Fanny, it was an ordeal. Reflecting on the process, she commented: 'I was questioned by Mr Shand KC for three days, he was so aggressive, but the judge was a very kind person …'.[109] Dr Fanny was determined to stand up and be counted in things big and small; and in that way she wrote her own history. She was insistent on her right to her untarnished reputation. As a high-profile individual who represented Jewish values and principles, she had much to lose from mudslingers, of whom there were many. She was firm in her resolve to restore her good name and that of Youth Aliyah and the Jewish community in Australia. As plaintiff, she was the central protagonist in a highly politicised case that became a national *cause celebre*, one that aroused strong responses in several constituencies throughout Australia. She hoped the broader narrative and themes of the court proceedings would serve a valuable public information purpose. She aimed to ventilate the issues and to convey her position to a broader audience and thereby negate the toxic effects of the paper's defamatory claims against Youth Aliyah, Zionism, and the Jewish people.

When Justice Herron directed his verdict for the defendant on the ground that the libellous article sued upon was not capable of referring to the plaintiff, he pointedly referred to the issue of costs:

> Under Section 265 of the Common Law Procedure Act, it is quite clear that the costs of the finding or judgment for the defendant must follow the event and therefore I enter a formal verdict and judgment for the defendant with costs according to Section 265.[110]

In response to Cassidy's request that Justice Herron refuse costs in this case, Justice Herron took the unusual step of deferring the question of costs. He replied: 'I will reserve the question of costs. There may be some law on the subject, I do not know'.[111]

On 29 June 1949, Justice Herron heard the action for costs and raised significant issues in relation to the costs:

> There was a plea of truth and public benefit filed by the defendant upon which the plaintiff joined issue and indeed the plaintiff called certain evidence in her own case dealing with that particular subject. I think it is a matter entirely for the Taxing Officer to say what the effect of the judgment for costs which I have just pronounced.[112]

One of the long-term consequences of this landmark case concerned Justice Herron's observation that Australian defamation law at that time made no provision for group libel. He said, 'It is for Parliament to re-shape the law if any redress is thought to be necessary in such a case as this'.[113] His comments paved the way for future parliamentary discussion and reform of the laws of libel.

According to Peter Wertheim, Co-CEO of the Executive Council of Australian Jewry,

Those who would dismiss Australia's laws prohibiting racial vilification as a mere concession to latter-day political correctness and the 'culture of complaint' should remember that such laws were called for by a distinguished Supreme Court judge as far back as 1949.[114]

Australia's first laws against racial vilification were only introduced in 1989 in New South Wales. The Australian Human Rights Commission states:

> In 1989, New South Wales became the first state [in Australia] to make it unlawful for a person, by a public act, to incite hatred towards, serious contempt for, or severe ridicule of a person or groups on the grounds of race. The 1989 amendment to the Anti-Discrimination Act 1977 also created a criminal offence for inciting hatred, contempt or severe ridicule towards a person or group on the grounds of race by threatening physical harm (towards people or their property) or inciting others to threaten such harm.[115]

Six years later, in 1995, the Australian Parliament enacted such laws for the whole country. In tracing the link between Justice Herron's judgement and the multiple iterations of group libel laws in Australia, there remains the question why it took 40 years, until 1989, for these laws to be enacted in Australia. In an interview conducted in 2020, Wertheim said:

> Justice Herron's statement that 'It is for Parliament to re-shape the law if any redress is thought to be necessary in such a case as this' was probably about as far as a Judge in the process of delivering a judgment could go at that time in suggesting possible law reform. Justice Herron was not necessarily suggesting that any reform should take the form of a law prohibiting 'group libel'. I would argue that by using the word 're-shape' Justice Herron envisaged the possibility that any new law might not necessarily fit within the 'libel' paradigm.[116]

Focusing specifically on why it took 40 years to effect these legal changes, Wertheim suggests that ordinarily the law in Australia has followed, not created, social changes and changes in attitudes. By the end of World War II, the White Australia Policy had been in force for more than 40 years. About 95 per cent of the Australian population was of British or Irish ancestry, and English was the language spoken at home, and everywhere else, for virtually the entire population. After the War, the Australian Government commenced a large-scale immigration program in order to meet labour shortages, protect Australia from external threats and stimulate economic growth. From 1945 to 1975 about three million migrants and refugees arrived in Australia, including many from Italy, Germany, the Netherlands and Greece. After 1975, following the dismantling of the White Australia policy, new groups of migrants arrived in Australia increasing the diversity of Australia's population. In 1988, permanent settler arrivals in Australia numbered about 150,000. Approximately 45 per cent of them were from Asia, Africa or the Middle East.[117] Wertheim concludes:

> It took, in effect, two generations of large-scale migration to Australia and broad social acceptance of the benefits it brought, for social attitudes to change, and to break down the cultural expectation of migrants to assimilate and downplay their cultural differences from the Anglo-Celtic majority. Australia began to pride itself on its diversity. Racial *discrimination* was widely seen as a barrier against migrants becoming equal citizens, and as offending against Australia's egalitarian ethos. The law followed this change in public attitudes, and racial discrimination was legally prohibited by the Racial Discrimination Act in 1975. Racial *vilification*, although widely seen as bad form, seemed to many people at first not to warrant legal prohibition, because freedom of expression is considered sacrosanct in Australia, and rightly so. As Australia's population continued to diversify, it became more widely understood that racial vilification

causes real and measurable harm to people and communities, and therefore exceeds the proper limits of individual freedom. Once again, the law followed changes in public attitudes, and the first legal prohibitions against racial vilification began to be introduced from 1989 onwards.[118]

In late 2014 the NSW Jewish Board of Deputies came into possession of a 'Youtube' video of a speech delivered on the streets of Sydney by an extremist religious leader, inciting violence against Jews. The Board lodged a complaint with the NSW Anti-Discrimination Board in early 2015, which agreed that there had been a breach of the NSW Anti-Discrimination Act. Under the law as it stood, there was a 6-month window in which legal action could be taken. The 6-month window closed with no action being taken. The NSW Jewish Board of Deputies reached two conclusions: that if it was possible to publicly threaten violence against any group of Australians, with the law taking no action, it placed everyone at risk; and that this was a whole-of-society issue. The NSW Jewish Board of Deputies CEO at the time, Vic Alhadeff, told the author:

> We formed an alliance of 34 community organisations under the banner Keep NSW Safe and launched the Keep NSW Safe campaign (www.keepnswsafe.com). Our objective was to lobby the NSW Government to introduce a law which outlawed incitement to violence on the basis of race, religion, gender, sexual preference and a number of other categories. In late 2017, NSW Attorney-General Mark Speakman took the proposed law to the government; it was thrown out, with free-speech champions speaking against it. I recalibrated the campaign and narrowed the focus ... specifically on incitement to violence in the categories mentioned above. Six months later, the identical bill was passed unanimously – by the NSW Government, NSW Legislative Assembly and NSW Legislative Council. It became law on June 27, 2018.[119]

Chapter 9

Conclusion

The day after our arrival, an angel appeared to us. That angel was Dr. Fanny Reading, and the minute we met her, everything changed for us for the better ... We could not believe that such a person existed.
— *Jana Gottshall, 2003*

The threat of anti-Jewish pogroms hung over Fanny Rubinowich's childhood in Russia and shattered the world into which she was born. The experiences of fear, displacement and migration shaped her lifelong concern with victims of persecution and her dedication to helping them through their physical and emotional pain and the challenges of building a new life in a new land. For the first five years of Fanny's life, she was in the care of her mother Esther Rose, who was effectively a single mother with sole responsibility for Fanny's welfare until Nathan established himself in country Victoria in Australia and they could reunite. Esther's lifelong mentoring role and her example inspired her daughter to follow an orthodox-Jewish lifestyle governed by Jewish ethics.

In Fanny's school years, her love of classical music and her musicality presaged a career as music teacher and performer. She changed her mind, however, when the first world war broke out in 1914, which impacted her family and community. With three brothers serving in the Second Australian Imperial Force, she wanted to contribute to the welfare of her country in troubling times; and thus began medical studies at the

University of Melbourne. Hers was an altruistic medical career, working in Sydney's seedy and unfashionable Kings Cross where she looked after disadvantaged women and children. She also held positions as honorary medical officer in several Sydney hospitals and joined her brother's practice in Bondi Junction.

In her mature years, Dr Fanny shared her personal creed, 'the Law of Lovingkindness',[1] with thousands of her followers, members of the Council of Jewish Women she founded in 1923, which evolved in 1929 into the National Council of Jewish Women of Australia. She established a sisterhood powered by the Judaic precept 'Tikun Olam', repairing the world. The NCJW improved thousands of lives in Australia, while also addressing the ill effects of persecution, poverty and disease in several countries abroad. With the outbreak of the second world war in 1939, Dr Fanny rallied her members and resources for NCJW's major contribution to Australia's war effort. She emerged as a national leader on Australia's home-front. She focused on the needs of the armed forces, the population at home and communities abroad, championing a broad range of humanitarian and social justice issues. The support given to refugees fleeing the Nazi genocide of Jews during the Second World War ranks as one of NCJW's greatest achievements. Dr Fanny and NCJW members provided guidance, transport, food, accommodation, medical services, language tuition and employment options for men, women and children who found sanctuary in Australia.

A definitive portrait of Dr Fanny emerges as a skilled leader and community activist, who understood the socio-political structures within Australian society, civic institutions and government. Through her organisation, she enacted a feminist agenda that changed the mindset of thousands of women throughout the country, many of whom came from conservative families with patriarchal values. Through educational programs and her own example, she showed them how to participate constructively in civic life. She gave them confidence to take their place on public platforms and shaped generations of women for leadership positions in humanitarian and civic organisations nationwide.

Dr Fanny believed education was an engine of enlightenment, enabling women to transform their lives and the lives of others. Her sisterhood of Jewish women, her 'beloved organisation'[2] spoke with an authoritative voice on local and global issues, engaging in social welfare, philanthropic, religious and educational enterprises nationally and internationally. She coaxed her members along an upward trajectory that took them from domesticity into wider worlds, introducing them to national and global issues. As a social activist, she envisaged goals for women they had never considered before, and she mapped pathways they never knew they were capable of traversing. She expanded their intellectual horizons, deepened their knowledge and observance of Judaism, and created an ethos of service-above-self that strengthened their understanding of their duties as Australian citizens.

A child refugee herself who fled persecution and pogroms, Dr Fanny was profoundly moved by the tragic situation of Jewish children and youth threatened with death in Nazi-dominated Europe and countries further afield. She was Vice-President in New South Wales of Youth Aliyah, which brought Jewish children to safety in Palestine and post-1948 Israel. The organisation was attacked in a scurrilous article published by *Smith's Weekly*, which alleged that funds collected in Sydney supported terrorism against the British in Mandatory Palestine. Dr Fanny sued the paper for defamation and the case was publicised throughout Australia. According to contemporary reports – and the testimony of surviving relatives, friends and colleagues interviewed for this biography – Dr Fanny had a gentle and kindly disposition. However, she transformed into a warrior for justice, showing courage and tenacity throughout this legal battle that taxed her mental and physical strength. She believed in standing up and speaking up wherever and whenever she perceived injustice, whether to a reputation, a person or a people. An examination of the trial transcript, which forms a core chapter in this biography, reveals her grasp of history and contemporary events. We see Dr Fanny's heritage, identity and mission within global, historical and political contexts. Justice Leslie Herron, in his judgement, praised her contribution to society and to Australia, including her efforts for the nation during the Second World War. His judgement called for Parliament to address the absence of group libel laws in Australia, which planted the seeds for the plethora of Federal and State anti-vilification and anti-discriminatory legislation enacted in succeeding decades that have gone a long way to safeguarding the security and wellbeing of Australians of different faiths and ethnicities.

The larger narrative of Dr Fanny's life addressed universal themes, such as loneliness, racism, antisemitism, women's rights, justice, social disadvantage and marginalisation, education, displacement and rehabilitation. As a doctor, social activist, feminist, community leader, educator and humanitarian, she dedicated herself to creating a more tolerant and harmonious society.

Dr Fanny was revolutionary for her time, a changemaker bringing about socio-cultural and organisational reform of women's lives in spheres within and beyond the Jewish community. She was undaunted by obstacles that included the conservative nature of the Australian Jewish community and the narrow aspirations of Jewish women whose homes and families constituted their entire world. As founding 'mother' of an organisation advocating for the agency and creativity of women, she mentored members for societal roles she envisioned for them.

Dr Fanny cared about her patients, her people and humanity. She forged connections with the greater community, addressing their prejudices about Jewish people. Throughout her life, she advocated for her people in particular and for humanity in general. She was generous in helping others, whether friends or total strangers. She stated,

> The Council has set before its members the brightest and noblest of Jewish ideals and has proved quite practically that all these ideals can be carried out and used for the benefits of humanity.

> Only knowledge can break down the ignorance and prejudices of the ages, and Jewish women are equipping themselves with that knowledge of their own people, which alone can make possible a right pride of race and stem the tide of religious intolerance.[3]

She dedicated herself and her organisation to counteracting apathy and indifference among Jewish women in the community. As a woman of faith, she derived strength from an identity rooted in Judaism. Judaism's ethical principles governed her actions and organisational programs. She reached out to the wider community among whom she promoted her values of caring and sharing, ensuring an equitable society for all. She changed attitudes incrementally by creating an ethos of communal service and goals, inspired by her mantra of 'service above self'. In so doing, she changed the role of women in Australian society. By communal service, she meant more than charitable work and monetary donations, although she never disparaged measures that helped others. She broadened the base of women's societal obligations that comprised 'a fuller sense of the greater responsibility that should rest on the shoulders of the Jewish women, viz., in the study of educational, domestic, personal, charitable and national movements both at home and abroad'.[4]

In creating an ideological framework for NCJW, Dr Fanny incorporated the values by which she lived and the ideals towards which she aspired. She stated that Council's ideal was 'a linking together of all Jewish women for the betterment of themselves'. She decried superficial and trivial issues that potentially caused division, 'No one is so perfect they cannot be better … We want to educate you to get rid of all pettiness …'[5] She set benchmarks of excellence, and embraced the disadvantaged and marginalised, 'This is not a charity organisation. There are organisations here to do that work, and we will help them. But our work is bigger – to make Jewish women bigger in mind, heart, and outlook'.[6]

Dr Fanny succeeded in her mission. With her leadership and initiatives, she welded together women from different social strata, rich and poor, gifted and uneducated, leaders and followers, the religiously orthodox and the secular – and embraced them all. She harnessed their diverse talents and created an organisation that earned a reputation for good works and responsible citizenship. In 1933, she urged members to begin NCJW's second decade with 'renewed courage, perseverance and understanding'.[7] Without her passion, sustained over decades, for the expansion and development of NCJW, it would not have flourished as it did. She was the driving force, giving speeches, presiding at countless meetings, travelling endlessly around the country, energising members to support Council's many spheres of interest at home and abroad.

Dr Fanny was a pragmatist seeking viable solutions to problems. With a childhood embedded in traumatic memories, she was alert to the dangers of antisemitism threatening Jewish communities abroad. She channelled her disquiet and empathy into programs to help the unemployed, the marginalised and the persecuted. In her they found an articulate advocate. During the Second World War, she did all in her power to assist refugees fleeing countries where they were delegitimised and faced annihilation only because they were Jews. As a medical doctor who specialised in maternal and child health, she was concerned about the welfare of children and profoundly saddened by the genocide that engulfed Jewish children in Europe. When child migrants arrived in Australia, she expressed gratitude for 'beautiful and sturdy children'.[8] She saw in them the remnants – and the hope – of her people.

Dr Fanny stepped onto the national stage during the Second World War. She embarked on major projects aimed at the welfare and support of Australian Imperial Forces and the country's war effort. She suspended all regular NCJW activities and dedicated herself and her organisation to war work. This was her finest hour, rising to the challenges of war, both material and spiritual. She taught members that they should give service 'to the country in which we live'[9] and they responded with hard work and united efforts. She and NCJW earned the respect and gratitude of Australian authorities and military personnel for their support, including her leadership in the reconstruction of the Sir John Monash Recreation Hut and the Anzac Buffet in Hyde Park, substantial fundraising, the endowment of hospital beds, a quarter-million garments made by members for the military, and three mobile canteens that operated in Sydney, London and Palestine. She launched initiatives such as the construction and running of the Kiosk in Sydney's Martin Place – staffed by 300 NCJW volunteers – that became a popular venue for tea and meals, where military personnel obtained information about services and home hospitality. Proceeds from the Kiosk and NCJW's two gift shops in Sydney were donated to the Australian Comforts Fund. These undertakings benefited the country as a whole, as official citations testified. NCJW conducted comparable programs in every state in Australia, and it was acknowledged generally that no other women's organisation rivalled the magnitude of NCJW's contributions to the country's war effort. Dr Fanny deflected personal tributes from herself to her organisation. She never courted the limelight unless it focused on the achievements of her organisation. Her leadership during the war years, her name and good works were known and acknowledged throughout the country. On 25 June 1948, at the opening of the 9th NCJWA Conference, the Premier of New South Wales, James McGirr, stated,

> It is most fitting to hear this gathering pay tribute to Dr. Fanny Reading ... Her name is a household word for good work in the State of New South Wales. Wherever I go in Australia, I meet people who ask me about her. Work done by people like her, without great publicity, are the greatest deeds of all.[10]

Dr Fanny connected with women leaders in the general community, and NCJW contributed to their work among the disadvantaged and those with disabilities. She launched initiatives to assist institutions and organisations in the wider community. In Sydney, she extended the concept of 'sisterhood' to bodies such as the National Council of Women, the Racial Hygiene Society, the Dalwood Children's Home, the Rachel Forster Hospital, and the Isabella Lazerus Home. Enacting her program in towns throughout Australia, she achieved a multiplying effect, with constructive outcomes for the health and wellbeing of thousands of all faiths and ethnicities. This was a major part of her non-denominational outreach program that fostered goodwill among people from different backgrounds.

In all Dr Fanny's connections with non-Jewish groups, she never hesitated to speak with conviction about her own faith, its values, ethics, biblical messages, and importance to her and her members. She derived comfort from her Judaic heritage and had a strong sense of Jewish identity. With the rise of antisemitism in Australia and overseas, she courageously proclaimed her Judaism. From the very beginning she insisted that the new body be called the National Council of Jewish Women, despite the fears of some who thought it might provoke antisemitism. This confidence in her heritage and faith never diminished. A spokeswoman for her people, she encouraged members to take pride in their traditions and history, inspiring them with confidence, 'The Catholics, the Protestants and the French hold meetings in our midst and are not ashamed of the fact. Why should we be? Can we not have racial pride and yet be sound citizens of the country we live in?'[11]

In 1926, on Dr Fanny's return to Sydney from travels abroad, she said that the Council of Jewish Women was her 'first born', but that she had acquired 'a second child' and that was Palestine, the National Home,

> The hills attracted her, and she felt that they were issuing a call to the Nation to come back to the soil. The schools and the University and the revival of Hebrew were a wonder and surprise to her. It was a country in which the Jew is free – freer than anywhere else in the world and where no apology is needed for being a Jew or excuse for the practice of his religious rites and traditional customs.[12]

Dr Fanny was moved by the return of a dispersed people to their ancestral homeland after an exile of 2000 years. She supported people and institutions in Palestine and, after 1948, in the State of Israel. She was concerned with maternal and child welfare and improved facilities there for mothers, babies and children. She supported healthcare amenities that were always open to all sections of the population, whether Jewish, Christian or Muslim. This was her 'undenominational' humanitarian agenda in action.

When Dr Fanny created the CJW in 1923, she promised Bella Pevsner 'to make the restoration of Palestine one of the Council's foremost aims'.[13] Openly supporting Zionism in the 1920s was a brave stance, as she 'was one of a tiny group of communal activists who believed in the acquisition of the Jewish homeland as a political state'.[14] In Australia, from the 1920s onwards, her organisation supported the Jewish homeland. Dr Fanny and CJW in 1923 'sent the first monies ever raised by Australian Jewish women for Palestine – £100 – to found a district nursing service in Tel Aviv'.[15]

From 1923, Dr Fanny's humanitarian response to the needs of people in Palestine foreshadowed the policies of her organisation. In 1926, she wrote,

> Here in this prosperous sunny land [Australia], the poorest mother can obtain the best treatment throughout Public Hospitals; but in Palestine ... the people cannot have the necessities they should have, then WE must come forward and help them to have what they have a right to have. They are human, as we are human; they have feelings as we have. By what right are we entitled to benefits more than they?[16]

Dr Fanny was an astute observer of global politics and was familiar with the provisions of the United Nations General Assembly's resolution passed on 29 November 1947. In calling for the establishment of a Jewish State, the General Assembly required the Jewish homeland to take necessary steps to implement that resolution. Dr Fanny's dream of a Jewish State – for which she worked most of her adult life – became a reality on 14 May 1948, when David Ben-Gurion, head of the Jewish People's Council, declared the establishment of the State of Israel. On that day, a new page was written in the history of the Jewish people.

The Declaration of the Jewish People's Council (JPC) referred to pivotal events in recent Jewish history, which also featured in Dr Fanny's defamation trial – the First Zionist Congress in 1897; the Balfour Declaration of 2 November 1917; and its reaffirmation in the Mandate of the League of Nations. The JPC Declaration stated that the State of Israel would 'guarantee freedom of religion, conscience, language, education and culture'. It ended with an appeal to Arab inhabitants of Israel,

> ... to preserve peace and participate in the upbuilding of the State on the basis of full and equal citizenship and due representation in all its provisional and permanent institutions. We extend our hand to all neighbouring states and their peoples in an offer of peace and good neighbourliness, and appeal to them to establish bonds of cooperation and mutual help with the sovereign Jewish people settled in its own land. The State of Israel is prepared to do its share in a common effort for the advancement of the entire Middle East.[17]

Dr Fanny conceptualised NCJW's relationship with Israel in nurturing and maternal terms. It was an infant in need of protection and care. Mina Fink, former national president of NCJW, stated,

> With the State of Israel reborn, Dr Fanny, a Zionist of long standing, directed all sections to intensify their commitment to Israel. She taught us that we have a moral obligation to care for the baby we helped to bring into this world. We must help it to crawl, to walk, to reach maturity and economic independence.[18]

In 1923, Dr Fanny started a conversation about Zionism among her members. NCJW alleviated hardships endured by the people in Palestine, whether Turk, Jew, Muslim or Christian. In Israel, NCJW supported social welfare programs, healthcare initiatives for mothers and babies, Youth Aliyah and the Jewish National Fund. In 1948, she was elected to the NSW State Zionist Council, where her efforts complemented NCJW's priority – feeding, clothing and housing new immigrants, who streamed through Israel's open doors.

In 1955, aged 71, Dr Fanny resigned as National President of NCJW, having held the position for 26 years. Overnight, she transformed from NCJW's aspirational visionary into its elder stateswoman. No longer centre stage, she was still available to guide and encourage. At the 11th NCJWA Conference, in Sydney, she said, 'I pray that in 18 years' time we shall celebrate the Golden Jubilee of our beloved organisation ... which is founded upon the permanent foundations of service and devotion'.[19] In 1973, when NCJW celebrated its 50th anniversary, Gertie Bartak wrote,

> We all had a sense of joy and thanksgiving that our 'living legend' Dr Fanny Reading ... should see its [NCJW] 50th Anniversary. Dr Fan's personal delight and satisfaction in attending both functions were expertly expressed in her own words – 'I made it'. She received a standing ovation from 400 guests when she arrived.[20]

Dr Fanny travelled a long road from 1923 to 1973, with many landmark milestones. What emerges from an overview of her life is her ideological consistency and loyalty to the agenda she envisioned at the formation of CJW in 1923 in Sydney. These were initiatives for the religious education of Jewish women and girls; communal service 'on behalf of her people and the Empire'[21]; philanthropy and social welfare at home and abroad; Zionism 'aimed at the restoration of Palestine';[22] charitable work throughout Australia; and promoting women's involvement in the wider world of public policy and politics.

Throughout Dr Fanny's life, she was a teacher in a pedagogic sense, instructing her members, and as a role model embodying values to which members aspired. She led by example, enabling her followers to model her conduct and uphold her standards. Her actions were aligned with her values. She articulated her vision for her organisation, defining goals for their collaborative mission. She introduced 'lecturettes' that educated members. She refined their taste with cultural evenings that also brought people together socially. She held that all members were equal, irrespective of their social status, education, income, or religious affiliations. She said, 'We all have the same problems and interests at heart, and it is our duty to meet freely and promote open discussion of them'.[23] She taught members how to speak in public, how to conduct meetings and debate amicably. NCJW's ideals and agenda reflected her core values. Through Dr Fanny's moral teachings, she embedded NCJW's programs within Jewish ethics, traditions and observance, celebrating festivals and encouraging members to transmit knowledge of their heritage to their families and children. In pragmatic ways, she closed the gap between ideals and social realities.

By speaking openly about her Jewish identity and the ideals of her organisation, Dr Fanny taught the wider community about the complexity of Jewish history and the values of Judaism. Media articles testified to her role as unofficial ambassador for the Jewish people in Australia. She created connections between faiths that contributed to harmony and tolerance in Australian society. Speaking of those who inspire others to explore new directions, Lord Jonathan Sacks stated, 'those who teach people to see, feel, and act differently, who enlarge the moral horizons of humankind, are rare indeed'.[24] This is precisely what Dr Fanny achieved, thereby transforming the lives of fellow travellers who accompanied her on her life's journey.

Dr Fanny's story enables us to understand her times, her challenges and how she met them. Despite a childhood fractured by pogroms, she remained positive throughout her life and engaged in programs to improve the quality of life for thousands at home and abroad. She never lost hope for a new dawn and she imagined a different future for Jewish women and girls and for the Jewish people. Her humanitarian agenda was non-sectarian. As a child of refugee parents fleeing violent antisemitism in Russia, she could speak with compassion and empathy for the voiceless in society, the orphan, the refugee, the marginalised in Kings Cross where she lived and worked as a medical doctor, and for the isolated and lonely women in country towns throughout Australia, with whom she identified. They were all her constituency and they were the beneficiaries of her medical skills, organisational ability and social welfare agenda. She emphasised leading a purposeful life, being part of a meaningful whole and contributing to society.

After the genocide of the Jewish people in the Second World War, she was part of 'a generation haunted by ghosts'.[25] As Elie Wiesel noted,

> The challenge of our generation of survivors was, what would we do with our memories? Would we allow them to drown us in despair, or would they somehow give us the strength to respond to other people's suffering?[26]

Dr Fanny's view of suffering was redemptive. Devastated by the Holocaust, she found strength to move forward towards socio-cultural and political goals. She had hope. She created new and complex organisational structures in society – the multi-layered NCJW that hosted sections for Seniors, Young Marrieds, Juniors and Sub-Juniors – enabling thousands of her followers to work towards a safer, healthier and more harmonious world.

NCJW is Dr Fanny's bequest to Jewish women in Australia, who continue to channel energies into programs for the benefit of all Australians, the Jewish community and the people of Israel. Through NCJW, her transformative impact on others continues. NCJW, now called the National Council of Jewish Women of Australia (NCJWA) has continued to evolve, while still honouring Dr Fanny's original mission. According to former Co-National President Sylvia Deutsch, 'this organisation can be a thought leader and an activist organisation for Jewish women in Australia'.[27] Former President of NCJWA's NSW division, Victoria Nadel joined in 2007. She said she wanted to be involved in volunteer communal work within an organisation that 'encompassed many fields of endeavour',

> This incredible organisation allows me to be involved in social justice issues in the Jewish community and the wider Australian community. It is an organisation that – because of its outreach and approach to the transcultural community – is building a harmonious multicultural society and also supporting Israel. NCJWA does it all and that's why I joined. When I look at what Dr Fanny did, I think she found a balance between responsibilities to our own Jewish community and our responsibilities to the wider Australian community in which we live.[28]

Today NCJWA re-invents itself according to contemporary challenges. Current initiatives reflect Dr Fanny's values, especially her commitment to the wellbeing of mothers, babies and children. NCJWA's activities in Sydney alone include packing and sending transcultural birthing kits to Africa; the 'Mum for Mum' program to counteract loneliness and depression among young mothers; 'Cuddle Bundles' providing baby gifts to mums with limited means; the 'Gene Circle' supporting women carrying the BRCA gene fault; and the NCJWA Cancer Support Network assisting cancer survivors and female carers. In the advocacy area, NCJWA has links with the International Council of Jewish Women and, through them, subscribes to the United Nations' sustainable development goals. NCJWA has a portfolio dedicated to interfaith and multicultural connections. Projects in Israel include the ILan Foundation, providing wheelchairs and computers to disabled children; university scholarships for Ethiopian Jewish women; the establishment and support of the Haifa Rape Crisis Centre; and JNF projects, such as a children's playground in Shlomit.[29]

At their 96th AGM in 2019 in Sydney, in the Dr Fanny Reading Council House, Co-President Miri Orden told those present, 'we think of our wonderful founder Dr Fanny Reading MBE and we often wonder how she would have approached a problem. She is my hero, a woman ahead of her time.' As in Dr Fanny's day, cheques were presented to both Jewish and gentile charities. The 'Dr Fanny Reading MBE Honour Award' was presented to a young member – reflecting the need to engage a younger demographic – for her contributions to National Council in the past year. Their manifesto still mirrors Dr Fanny's values: responding to community needs, empowering women, working for Israel, promoting social justice and strengthening transcultural interaction. Their words could have been written by Dr Fanny,

> Our commitment to *tikkun olam* [repairing the world] remains ever strong. Our core belief in the importance of community service and advocacy for the dignity of women and girls continues to drive us.[30]

The collective good accomplished by NCJWA has grown exponentially. Former National President, Negba Weiss-Dolev, stated, 'NCJWA continues to be an inspiring avenue for Jewish women to make a difference'.[31] The organisation Dr Fanny established in 1923 to heal a fractured world still enacts the values for which she stood, and remains a force within the Jewish and wider communities in Australia and abroad. Dr Fanny's NCJW has expanded through the years, as she would have wished. Its viability validates 'The quiet revolutionary of her time' and her life of service to others.[32]

Dr Fanny moved well beyond her initial aim of counteracting the Jewish community's rate of intermarriage and assimilation. She ensured far more than a line of leadership succession. At a time when female figures were mostly silent, she taught generations of women to be social activists and to cultivate a deeper connection to life. She gave Jewish women a collective voice and focused their energies on humanitarian programs that changed lives and destinies. Through her actions, she showed others how to live a meaningful life. She reinforced the agency of the individual, while empowering the community. She equipped women and girls with the skills needed to play a constructive role in society. She encouraged her followers to find solutions to seemingly intractable problems. She and her members worked co-operatively, laying the foundation for future generations. She dared to dream and transformed that dream into reality.

Dr Fanny was a trailblazer who believed in human rights and civil liberties for all and who never wavered from the standards she upheld. She was a witness to the perturbations of history, including the resurgence of antisemitism and the Holocaust of the Second World War, yet she never despaired and she continued to inspire hope in others. She demonstrated conclusively that, with effort and dedication, one can change the trajectory of one's own life, improve the lives of others, and heal schisms in society. Above all, she cared – for family, friends and total strangers. Her generosity was legendary. As a leader she healed the wounds of war and laid foundations for peace at home and abroad.

On 19 November 1974, Dr Fanny died at the Wolper Hospital in Sydney and was interred two days later in Rookwood Cemetery. Ninety years of age, she was acknowledged for her lifelong adherence to her own 'law of loving-kindness' and her belief in the transformative power of *tikkun olam*, healing the world. She faced tragedy and loss with fortitude, resilience and hope. She was never captive to the past. She crafted the person she became and lived constructively in the present. A pioneer in socio-cultural and political fields, she was aspirational for herself and for others, encouraging her members to fulfil their potential and to use their abilities in the service of their own and the wider community. She bequeathed NCJW – her sisterhood with a humanitarian philosophy – to the Jewish community. To the nation, she left a legacy of service and dedication to all, irrespective of race, colour or creed. With her open mind, open heart and open hand, she conducted a lifelong dialogue with her community and the wider world at home and abroad. The Hebrew Bible commands that we remember, an imperative that has resounded with enduring effect among Jews since biblical times.[33] Remembering Dr Fanny can foreground for future generations the core values by which she lived, so that they might transform lives as she did and make the world better, more tolerant and more harmonious.

Time has effaced many of Dr Fanny's achievements and she has receded into the shadows of the past. Hers, however, is a life worth examining, so that her place in Australian and Jewish history can be re-evaluated and acknowledged, which this biography attempts to do. Professor Emerita Rosemary Johnston suggests that, ideally, biography is written,

> … to encourage a looking again at the past from the ever-changing context and knowledge of the present, to stimulate new knowledge and bring it into the intellectual thought arena of the present so that others can engage with it, celebrate it and challenge it … to inspire and propagate new ways of thinking, a deeper appreciation for what has been done as well as an enhanced hope for what can be done.[34]

Hopefully, with that accomplished, Dr Fanny can move from the footnotes of history into the prominence she merits.

Appendix: Hyman Reading in court

In 2017, I interviewed Leigh Reading and his wife Lynne in their Woollahra apartment in Sydney, within walking distance of the headquarters of the National Council of Jewish Women in New South Wales, known as the Dr Fanny Reading War Memorial Council House. Leigh is Dr Fanny's nephew, the son of her brother, Hyman 'Red' Reading, and his second wife Enid Esther (née Herman).

During the interview, Leigh shared the story of his father Hyman's marriage to his first wife, Elma May (also called Mary) Dickinson of Newcastle. At the time of their marriage in 1920, Hyman was 25 and Elma May 21 years of age. Their daughter, June Reading, was born on 25 July 1921. In 1922, the parents separated and Hyman moved to Dr Fanny's residence at 19 Belgrave Street, Kogarah. In 1925, June's mother died, aged 26, allegedly from an abortion. Together with Dr James Kingpatrick and Nurse Esma Dihms, Hyman was charged with conspiring to procure 'an illegal operation' for Elma. The coroner found there was insufficient evidence and all three were discharged.

Two years later, in April 1927, Hyman sought custody of his six-year-old daughter, who had been living with her maternal grandmother Alice and bachelor uncle George Dickinson. Lionel Dare represented Hyman in court and the case was heard by Justice Davidson. George Dickinson contested Hyman's application for custody of June.

Leigh Reading stated that this court case was a challenging chapter in his father's personal life. Both Dr Fanny and her brother, Dr Abe

Reading, supported Hyman through this crisis. Dr Fanny was involved briefly in the proceedings, as she offered to bring up her niece or to support her brother in doing so, a position that revealed her sense of family solidarity and her love of children. However, Justice Davidson awarded custody of June to Elma's brother, George Dickinson, who stated she would live with their married relatives.[1]

The case was sensationalised, with lurid details published in newspapers of the day. Photographs of Dr Fanny and her brother appeared in papers throughout the country. It was with a degree of reluctance that Leigh and Lynne spoke of these events. It was clear that the family had buried this episode.

On 16 January 1936, Hyman married for the second time, to Enid Esther Herman. Leigh was their only child. According to Leigh, Hyman, established contact with his daughter June and visited her as often as he could. He died on 2 August 1956. In succeeding years, Leigh befriended June's two sons, his nephews, of whom he is most fond; and the circle finally closed.

Notes

Chapter 1: Introduction

1. Ochert, S. 1996, 'Dr Fanny Reading v. Smith's Weekly', *Australian Jewish Historical Society Journal*, Vol xiii, part 2, p. 310.
2. Newton, M. 2000, *Making a Difference: A history of the National Council of Jewish Women of Australia*, Hybrid Publishers, Melbourne, p. 6.
3. Rubinstein, H. 1991, *The Jews in Australia: A Thematic History*, volume I, 1788–1945, William Heinemann Australia, p. 11.
4. Rubinstein, W.D. 1991, *The Jews in Australia: A Thematic History*, Vol II 1945 to the Present, William Heinemann Australia, p. 262.
5. Rutland, S. 1988, *Edge of the Diaspora: Two centuries of Jewish settlement in Australia*, Collins Australia, p. 158.
6. Blakeney, M. 1985, *Australia and the Jewish Refugees 1933–1948*, Croom Helm Australia, p. 107.
7. Rutland, S. 1987, 'The changing role of women in Australian Jewry's communal structure', *Jews in the Sixth Continent*, ed. Rubinstein, W.D., Allen & Unwin, Sydney, p. 105.
8. Troy, G. 2018, *The Zionist Ideas: Visions for the Jewish Homeland – Then, Now, Tomorrow*, The Jewish Publication Society Philadelphia, p. xliii.
9. Cohen, L. 1987, *Beginning with Esther: Jewish women in New South Wales from 1788*, Ayres and James Heritage Books, Sydney, p. 74.
10. The town is also spelt Karelichy (Belarussian), Karelicy (Russian), Korolieicai (Lithuanian), Korolicze (Polish) and Korelitz (Yiddish), although the Rubinowich family used the spelling 'Karelitz' in all documentation.
11. Antin, M. 2012, *The Promised Land*, Penguin Books New York, p. 26.
12. Rubinstein, H.L. 1986, *The Jews in Victoria*, George Allen & Unwin Sydney, p. 87.

13. Ricoeur, P. 2024, *Memory, history, forgetting*, trans. K.P. Blamey, The University of Chicago Press, Chicago, London, p. 449.

14. Andgel, A. 1998, 'The law of loving kindness', *Australian Jewish Historical Society Journal*, vol. XIV, no. Part 2, p. 201.

15. Newton, M.L. 2000, p. 9.

16. Andgel, A., p. 206.

17. Rutland, S. 1988, p. 169.

18. Ibid., p. 169.

19. Inglis, K., Spark, S. and Winter, J. 2018, *Dunera Lives: A visual history*, Monash University Publishing, Melbourne, p. 109.

20. Kwiet, K. 1985, 'Be patient and reasonable', The internment of German-Jewish refugees in Australia', *The Australian Journal of Politics and History*, vol. 31, no 1, p. 63.

21. Blakeney, M., p. 107.

22. Newton, M., p. 21.

23. Rubinstein, H. 1991, p. 400.

24. Rutland, S. 1988, p. 301.

25. Ibid., p. 302.

26. Rubinstein, H. 1991, p. 401.

27. Herron, J. 1949, 'Reading v. National Press Pty. Ltd.' Supreme Court of NSW. Sydney transcript, p. 10.

28. Rutland, S. 1988, p. 40.

Chapter 2: Childhood and the voyage to a new land

1. Polonsky, A. 2013, *The Jews in Poland and Russia: A Short History*, The Littman Library of Jewish Civilization, Portland Oregon, p. 96.

2. Aronson, M. 1990, *Troubled Waters: The Origins of the 1881 Anti-Jewish Pogroms in Russia*, University of Pittsburgh Press, Pittsburgh Pa, pp. 31–2.

3. Anne Sarzin's interview with Dr Ian Burman, 2018 Sydney.

4. Polonsky, A., p. 98.

5. Klier, J. 2011, *Russians, Jews, and the Pogroms of 1881–1882*, Cambridge University Press, Cambridge, pp. 11–12.

6. Turtel-Oberzhanski, H. 1973, *A History of the Jews of Korelitz*, <http://www.

jewishgen.org/yizkor/Korelicze/kor018.html>.

7. Ibid.
8. Rosenthal, N. 1979, *Formula for survival: the saga of the Ballarat Hebrew Congregation*, The Hawthorn Press, Melbourne, p. 7.
9. Ibid., p. 17.
10. Ibid., p. 49.
11. Ibid., pp. 26–8.
12. Ibid., p. 58.
13. Newton, M.L. 2000, Making a difference: *A history of the National Council of Jewish Women of Australia*, Hybrid Publishers, Melbourne, p. 7.
14. Rosenthal, N., p. 58.
15. Baffsky, W. 2018, 'My memories of Dr Fanny', interviewed by Anne Sarzin.
16. Ibid.
17. Balkelis, T. 2010, 'Opening Gates to the West: Lithuanian and Jewish Migrations from the Lithuanian Provinces, 1867–1914', *Ethnicity*, vol. 1, p. 2.
18. O'Day, R. n.d. 'The Jews of London: From Diaspora to Whitechapel', <fathom.lse.ac.uk/Features/122537>.
19. Radi, H. 1989, *200 Autralian women: a Redress anthology*, Women's Redress Press Inc, Broadway, Sydney.
20. Antin, M. 2012, *The promised land*, Penguin Group, New York, p. 133.
21. Zangwill, I. 2017, *Children of the Ghetto*, Lavergne Tennessee, p. 104.
22. Valman, N. 2015, 'Walking Victorian Spitalfields with Israel Zangwill', *Interdisciplinary Studies in the Long Nineteenth Century*, vol. 2015, no. 21.
23. Ibid.
24. Russell, C. & Lewis, H.S. 1900, *The Jew in London: A study of racial character and present-day conditions, being two essays prepared for the Toynbee trustees*, Thomas Y Crowell & Co., New York, pp. 170–171.
25. Ibid.
26. O'Day, R.
27. Mendelsohn, R. & Shain, M. 2008, *The Jews in South Africa: An illustrated history*, Jonathan Ball Publishers Johannesburg & Cape Town, p. 33.
28. Valent, P. 2002, *Child survivors of the Holocaust*, Taylor & Francis, p. 284.
29. 'To organise Jewish women: Arrival of Dr. Fanny Reading', *The Register*

News-Pictorial, 28 September 1929, p. 28.
30. SS *Nurnberg*, Fiche 252, page 4, port F.
31. Russell, R. 2016, *High seas & high teas :Voyages to Australia*, NLA Publishing, Canberra, ACT, p. 167.
32. Longway, M. 1889, *London to Melbourne*, Remington & Co. Publishers, London, Covent Garden, pp. 189–190.

Chapter 3: Music and Medicine
1. 'Dr Fanny Reading in Brisbane', *Courier-Mail*, 13 May 1939, p. 3.
2. Stevens, R.S. 2003, 'Why teach music in schools', paper presented to the *XXIVth Annual Conference of AARME, Ninth Annual Assembly of the Music Council of Australia.*
3. *Music* 1898, Royal South Street Society, Ballarat, <https://results.royal-southstreet.com.au/results/1898-09-05-music>.
4. Debney-Joyce, J. 2019, *Dr Fanny Reading: 'A clever little bird'*, PhD thesis, Federation University, Ballarat, p. 168.
5. Taft, M., Markus, A., 2018, *A second chance: The making of Yiddish Melbourne*, Monash Univ ersity Publishing, Melbourne, Victoria, p. 46.
6. Ibid., p. 46.
7. Barrett, J. 1935, Address delivered by Sir James Barrett, Deputy Chancellor, on the occasion of the opening of the Marshall-Hall Wing, University Conservatorium of Music, 21st March 1935, University of Melbourne, Melbourne, p. 2.
8. Radic, T. 1994, Australian Music biography and the Skew of Cultural Context: Changing viewpoints to assess significance, The Percy Grainger Lecture edn, University of Melbourne, Melbourne, p. 5.
9. 'Victoria', *The Hebrew Standard of Australasia*, 4 January 1907, p. 6.
10. *University of Melbourne: Faculty of Fine Arts and Music* 2019, University of Melbourne, <https://finearts-music.unimelb.edu.au/about-us/mcm>.
11. Barrett, J., p. 3.
12. Hatchia, J. 1913, 'Victorian Zionist League', *Jewish Herald*, 4 July 1913, p. 6.
13. Barrett, J. 1935, p. 3.
14. Ibid., p. 5.

15. Newton, M.L. 2000, *Making a difference: A history of the National Council of Jewish Women of Australia*, Hybrid Publishers, Melbourne, p. 8.
16. Brentnall, T. 1938, *My Memories: Being the Reminiscences of a Nonagenarian*, Robertson & Mullens Limited, Melbourne, p. 116.
17. The Royal Melbourne Philharmonic Choir is Australia's oldest surviving cultural organisation. The RMP performed Handel's Messiah every year. The conductors included Alberto Zelman. 'The Messiah: Philharmonic Society. A memorable occasion', 1905.
18. Newton, M.L. 2000, p. 10.
19. Burman, Ian, 2018, 'Burman email' to Anne Sarzin.
20. Maltese, J.A. 2010, *Jascha Heifitz: God's Fiddler,* https://www.pbs.org/wnet/americanmasters/jascha-heifetz-biography-and-timeline/3731/
21. Shavit, A. 2014, *My promised land: The triumph and tragedy of Israel*, Scribe, Melbourne, London, pp. 44–46.
22. Singer, C. 2017, 'Carole Singer interview', by Anne Sarzin.
23. Ibid.
24. *The Sun*, 19 November 1933, p. 35.
25. Singer, C. 2017.
26. Women's Page: Council of Jewish Women', *Hebrew Standard*, 8 February 1929, p. 8.
27. 'Council of Jewish Women: General meeting', *Hebrew Standard*, 6 May 1932, p. 6.
28. 'Council of Jewish Women', *Sydney Morning Herald*, 21 July 1932, p. 4.
29. 'Council of Jewish Women', *Hebrew Standard*, 6 November 1931, p. 6.
30. 'Council of Jewish Women', *Sydney Morning Herald*, 26 April 1933, p. 4.
31. 'NCJW Sydney Section: Melech Ravitsch evening', *Hebrew Standard*, 1 September 1933, p. 6.
32. Taft, M., Markus, A., 2018, p. 26.
33. *Jewish Herald*, Victoria, 13 July 1917, p. 13.
34. Department of External Affairs, M. 1897, *Nathan Jacob Rubinowich Naturalization*, 36625 barcode, National Archives of Australia, Canberra.
35. Department of External Affairs, M. 1904, *E.R. Rubinowich Naturalization*, National Archives of Australia, Canberra.

36. National Archives of Australia 1916, *Rubinowich, Abraham Solomon; age 25; born 1890; address – St Kilda*, Canberra.
37. Australian Imperial Force, 1914–1920b, *Rubinowich, Lewis Judah : Service Number – 18729* (8073054), B2455, National Archives of Australia, Canberra.
38. Australian Imperial Force, 1914–1920, *Rubinowich, Hyman Samuel : Service Number – 2128*, 1914–1920, National Archives of Australia, Canberra.
39. Ibid., *Rubinowich, Hyman Samuel.*
40. Dr Ian Burman interviewed by Anne Sarzin, 2019.
41. Newton, M.L., 2000, p. 8.
42. 'To form Council of Jewish Women', *The Observer*, 5 October 1929, p. 52.
43. 'The Woman of the Day: Dr Fanny Reading', *The Daily Telegraph (Social Gossip)*, 21 August 1928, p. 20.
44. Pensabene, T.S. 1980, The rise of the medical practitioner in Victoria: Research Monograph 2, The Australian National University, Canberra, p. 70.
45. University of Melbourne, 1916–1922, *Reading, Dr Fanny-Papers*, Mitchell Library, Sydney.
46. *Strength of Mind: 125 years of women in medicine* 2013, Medical History Museum, University of Melbourne, p. 5.
47. Newton, M.L., 2000, p. 11.
48. Cohen, L. 1987, *Beginning with Esther: Jewish women in New South Wales from 1788*, Ayers & James Heritage Books, pp. 72–3.
49. *Strength of Mind,* 2013, p. 32.
50. Burman, Ian, interviewed by Anne Sarzin, 2018.
51. 'For women. Dr Fanny Reading. Child Welfare Abroad', *Sydney Morning Herald,* 5 March 1926, p. 5.
52. Pensabene, T.S., 1980.
53. Ibid., p. 68.
54. McCarthy, L. 2001, *Uncommon Practices: Medical women in NSW 1885–1939,* University of New South Wales, p. 42.
55. Ibid., p. 309.
56. Pensabene, T.S., p. 49.
57. Dalton, R. *Aunts up the Cross*, 1996, Text Publishing Melbourne, p. 28.
58. Burman, Ian, interviewed by Anne Sarzin 2018.

59. Ochert, M. 1996, 'Dr Fanny Reading v. Smith's Weekly', *Australian Jewish Historical Society Journal*, vol. XIII part 2, June 1996, p. 310.
60. Andgel, A. 1998, 'The law of lovingkindness', *Australian Jewish Historical Society Journal*, vol. XIV, part 2, p. 251.
61. Reading, Leigh, interviewed by Anne Sarzin, 2019.
62. Andgel, A., p. 251.
63. Ibid., p. 247.
64. Cohen, L. 1984, *Rachel Forster Hospital, The first fifty years* Rachel Forster Hospital, Sydney, p. 21.
65. Street, J. 1990, *Documents and essays*, Women's Redress Press Inc., Sydney, p. 113.
66. Ibid., p. 149.
67. Cohen, L. 1987, *Beginning with Esther: Jewish women in New South Wales from 1788*, Ayers & James Heritage Books, p. 222.
68. Memorandum and Articles of Association of the Racial Hygiene Association of New South Wales (nla.gov.au) p. 5.
69. Puckey, M.C. 1950, 'Rachel Forster Hospital for Women and Children', *Journal of the American Medical Women's Association*, Schaumburg, Illinois, p. 294.
70. Cohen, L. 1987, p. 222.
71. Grimshaw, P., Lake, M., McGrath, A. and Quartly, M. 2006, *Creating a nation*, Penguin Books, Ringwood, Victoria, pp. 262–263.
72. Memorandum and Articles of Association of the Racial Hygiene Association of New South Wales (nla.gov.au) p. 13, item 15.
73. Foley, M. n.d. 'Goodison, Lillie Elizabeth (1860–1947)', *Australian Dictionary of Biography*, National Centre of Biography, ANU, first published in hard copy 1983.
74. 'Racial Hygiene: Canon Hammond urges sterilisation', *Lithgow Mercury*, 23 November 1933, p. 2.
75. 'Racial problems sterilisation of low types', *Irwin Index*, 16 November 1929, p. 10.
76. Rees, Anne 2012, 'The quality and not only the quantity of Australia's people', *Australian Feminist Studies*, 27 (71), 71–92.
77. Ibid., Rees, A., 2012.

78. Ibid., 2012.
79. Wyndham, D.H., 1996, 'Striving for national fitness: Eugenics in Australia 1910s to 1930s', University of Sydney.
80. Ibid., p. 178.
81. Rees, Anne, 2012.
82. Lemieux, Nina, 2012, Honours thesis, 'Australian eugenics from 1900 to 1961', University of Texas, Austin, 2017.
83. *Jessie Street: Documents and Essays*, 1990, p. 150.
84. Grimshaw, P., p. 263.
85. Street, J., p. 39.

Chapter 4: NCJW, 1920s and 1930s

1. 'Hospital benefit ball', *Daily Telegraph* 3 August 1922, p. 3.
2. 'New ambulance: St George acquisition', *Evening News Monday*, 4 February 1924, p. 9.
3. 'Social and General: Weekly news', *Hebrew Standard of Australasia (Social and General)*, 16 December 1927, p. 8.
4. Newton, M.L. 2000, *Making a difference: A history of the National Council of Jewish Women of Australia*, Hybrid Publishers, Melbourne, p. 4.
5. 'Council of Jewish Women of N.S.W. First Annual Meeting and Report', *Hebrew Standard*, 8 August 1924, p. 8.
6. Cohen, L. 1987, *Beginning with Esther: Jewish women in New South Wales from 1788*, Ayers & James Heritage Books, p. 74.
7. Newton, M.L. 2000, p. 5.
8. 'NSW Jewish War Memorial official opening', *Hebrew Standard*, 21 September 1923, p. 13.
9. 'Council of Jewish Women of N.S.W. First Annual Meeting and Report', *Hebrew Standard*, 8 August 1924, p. 8.
10. Ibid., p. 8.
11. Taft, M., and Markus, A., 2018, *A second chance: The making of Yiddish Melbourne*, Monash University, Melbourne, p. 85.
12. Rubinstein, W.D. 1987, *Jews in the Sixth Continent*, Rutland, S. 'The changing role of women in Australian Jewry's communal structure', p. 101,

Allen & Unwin, Sydney.
13. Rutland, S. 1988, *Edge of the Diaspora*, pp. 158–9, Collins Australia.
14. Ibid., pp. 158–9.
15. 'Council of Jewish Women of N.S.W. First Annual Meeting and Report', *Hebrew Standard*, 8 August 1924, p. 8.
16. Ibid., p. 8.
17. Ibid., p. 8.
18. Ibid., p. 8.
19. Ibid., p. 8.
20. Rubinstein, H.L. 1991, *The Jews in Australia: A thematic History*, vol. 1, p. 295, William Heinemann Australia, Melbourne.
21. 'Council of Jewish Women of N.S.W. First Annual Meeting and Report', *Hebrew Standard*, 8 August 1924, p. 8.
22. Ibid., p. 8.
23. Rubinstein, H.L. 1991, *The Jews in Australia: A thematic History*, vol. 1, p. 12, William Heinemann Australia, Melbourne.
24. 'Council of Jewish Women of N.S.W.: Pageant of Fairyland', p. 8, *Hebrew Standard*, 29 August 1924.
25. Ibid., p. 8.
26. 'Women's column', *Sydney Morning Herald*, 19 March 1925, p. 5.
27. Ibid., p. 5.
28. 'ICW: Quinquennial Conference: Lady Forster writes from Federal Government House, Melbourne', *West Australian*, 26 February 1925, p. 9.
29. 'Council of Jewish Women of N.S.W,: The June general meeting', *Hebrew Standard*, p. 12, 11 June 1926.
30. 'ICW: Quinquennial Conference, *West Australian*, p. 9, 26 February 1925.
31. 'Council of Jewish Women of N.S.W.: Reception of visiting artistes presentation to Dr. Fanny Reading', *Hebrew Standard*, p. 5, 6 March 1925.
32. 'Council of Jewish Women of N.S.W. Attendance at AGM', *Hebrew Standard*, 7 August 1925, p. 5.
33. Ibid., p. 5.
34. 'Dr. Fanny Reading', *Hebrew Standard*, 22 January 1926, p. 12.
35. 'Palestine: Under British rule woman doctor's views', *Daily News*, 12

February 1926, p. 5.

36. Ibid., p. 5.
37. 'Dr Fanny Reading arrived this morning, enthusiastic welcome', p. 15, *Sun*, 4 March 1926.
38. 'For Women. Dr. Fanny Reading. Child Welfare Abroad', 5 March 1926, *Sydney Morning Herald,* p. 5.
39. 'Council of Jewish Women: 250 at Maccabean Hall', *Hebrew Standard,* p. 6, 12 March 1926.
40. Ibid., p. 6.
41. Family letter 13 December 1925, Jerusalem.
42. Family letter, 28 December 1925, Jerusalem.
43. Family letter, 10 January 1926, Tel Aviv.
44. Mandate for Palestine – League of Nations 12th session – Minutes of the Permanent Mandates Commission – Question of Palestine (un.org).
45. Family letters, 28 December 1925.
46. Ibid., 1925.
47. Ibid., January 1926.
48. Ibid., 13 October 1925.
49. Ibid., 1925 (State Library of NSW, Series 03:Fanny Reading realia).
50. Ibid., 16 July 1925.
51. Ibid., 13 August 1925.
52. Ibid.
53. Ibid., 18 September 1925, p. 3.
54. Ibid., 23 November 1925.
55. Ibid., 28 December 1925.
56. Ibid., n.d.
57. 'Council of Jewish Women', *Hebrew Standard,* p. 7, 19 March 1926.
58. Ibid., 'A welcome home party', p. 7.
59. Ibid., p. 7.
60. 'Council of Jewish Women of NSW: The 12 April 1926 general meeting', *Hebrew Standard,* p. 4.
61. Ibid., p. 4.

62. 'Council of Jewish Women: The Girls' Committee', *Hebrew Standard*, 28 May 1926, p. 5.
63. 'Council of Jewish Women of N.S.W,: The June general meeting', *Hebrew Standard*, 11 June 1926, p. 12.
64. *Hebrew Standard*, 'The May General Meeting', 7 May 1926, p. 13.
65. 'National Council of Women', *Sydney Morning Herald*, 19 April 1929, p. 5.
66. 'Council of Jewish Women: AGM [6 August]', *Hebrew Standard*, p. 11, 10 August 1928.
67. Ibid., p. 11.
68. Ibid., p. 11.
69. 'Social gossip: The woman of the day Dr Fanny Reading', 21 August 1928, *Daily Telegraph*, p. 20.
70. 'Council of Jewish Women: An enjoyable and interesting evening', 20 April 1929, *Brisbane Courier*, p. 29.
71. Council of Jewish Women [Brisbane report], *Hebrew Standard*, 10 May 1929, p. 2.
72. Ibid., p. 2.
73. 'Junior session: Jewish women's meeting', *Sun*, 23 May 1929, p. 15.
74. 'National Council of Women', *Sydney Morning Herald*, 19 April 1929, p. 6.
75. 'Jewish women: Proposed Council', *Daily News*, Perth, Tuesday 17 September 1929, p. 6.
76. 'Jewish Women Council to be formed: Aims explained', *West Australian*, 17 September 1929, p. 16.
77. Ibid., p. 16.
78. 'Council of Jewish Women: Visit of Dr Fanny Reading. Welcome in Kalgoorlie', *Kalgoorlie Miner*, 26 September 1929, p. 2.
79. Leigh, E. 1929, 'To form council of Jewish women: Dr Reading on Personal Service', *Register News-Pictorial (Elizabeth Leigh's pages for women)*, 30 September 1929, p. 24.
80. Ibid., p. 24.
81. Rutland, S.D., *Edge of the Diaspora*, Collins Australia, 1988, p. 141.
82. 'Tragedy in Europe', 1929, *Register News-Pictorial*, 3 October 1929, p. 23.
83. 'Daughters of Israel: Jewish girls organise', *Register News-Pictorial*, 3

October 1929, p. 23.

84. 'For Women: Jewish Women, Formation of National Council', *Sydney Morning Herald*, 1 March 1930, p. 12.

85. 'Daughters of Israel: Jewish girls organise', *Register News-Pictorial*, 3 October 1929, p. 23.

86. 'Formation of Council of Jewish Women in Newcastle', *Hebrew Standard*, 20 December 1929, p. 10.

87. 'Council of Jewish Women (contributed)', *Hebrew Standard*, 29 November 1929, p. 9.

88. 'Visit of Dr Fanny Reading', *Newcastle Morning Herald and Miners' Advocate*, 5 December 1929, p. 2.

89. 'For Women: Jewish Women, Formation of National Council', *Sydney Morning Herald*, 1 March 1930, p. 12.

90. 'Council of Jewish Women of NSW: Eighth annual meeting', *Hebrew Standard*, 14 August 1931, p. 5.

91. 'For Women: Jewish Women, Formation of National Council', *Sydney Morning Herald*, 1 March 1930, p. 12.

92. *Defining Moments: Great Depression*, National Museum Australia, viewed 1 July 2019, <https://www.nma.gov.au/defining-moments/resources/great-depression>.

93. 'Council of Jewish Women of N.S.W. New club rooms opened', 9 October 1931, *Hebrew Standard*, p. 7.

94. 'Council of Jewish Women of NSW: Eighth annual meeting', *Hebrew Standard*, 14 August 1931, p. 5.

95. Rubinstein, H.L. 1991, *The Jews in Australia: A thematic History*, vol. 1 William Heinemann Australia, Melbourne, p. 163.

96. Ibid., p. 165.

97. 'Council of Jewish Women of NSW: Eighth annual meeting', *Hebrew Standard*, 14 August 1931, p. 5.

98. 'Presentation to Dr. Fanny Reading', *Hebrew Standard*, 9 October 1931, p. 7.

99. 'Council of Jewish Women of N.S.W. New club rooms opened', 9 October 1931, *Hebrew Standard*, p. 7.

100. A plea for Judaism: Address to Jewish Women', *The Age*, 5 January 1932, p. 7.

101. 'Chanucah Entertainment', *Hebrew Standard*, 10 January 1930, p. 4.
102. 'For Women: Jewish Women, Formation of National Council', *Sydney Morning Herald*, 1 March 1930, p. 12.
103. A plea for Judaism: Address to Jewish Women', *The Age*, 5 January 1932, p. 7.
104. 'Jewish Women's Council: Reception to Dr Reading', *The Argus*, 5 January 1932, p. 9.
105. Rubinstein, H.L. 1991, *The Jews in Australia: A thematic History*, vol. 1 William Heinemann Australia, Melbourne, p. 165.
106. 'Crowd Clamored For Admission', *Daily Telegraph*, 9 March 1932, p. 4.
107. 'For Women: Jewish Women Opening of Conference', *Sydney Morning Herald*, 9 March 1932, p. 6.
108. 'Crowd Clamored For Admission', *Daily Telegraph* 9 March 1932, p. 4.
109. 'Jewish women: annual conference', *Sydney Morning Herald*, 10 March 1932, p. 4.
110. 'Jewish women down to business ', *Daily Telegraph*, 10 March 1932, p. 4.
111. 'For women: Jewish women conference activities', *Sydney Morning Herald*, 11 March 1932, p. 4.
112. Ibid., 9 March 1932, p. 4.
113. 'For women: Jewish women conference activities', *Sydney Morning Herald*, 11 March 1932, p. 4.
114. 'Council of Jewish Women's Big Conference', *The Sun*, 13 March 1932, p. 24.
115. *The Mercury*, 'Working for peace', 6 June 1931, p. 11.
116. WILPF Australia – Women's International League for Peace and Freedom.
117. 'Council of Jewish Women: General meeting', *Hebrew Standard*, 3 June 1932, p. 6.
118. 'Council of Jewish Women [Benno Moseiwcitch reception]', *Sydney Morning Herald*, 21 July 1932, p. 4.
119. 'Council of Jewish women: Council Seniors annual meeting', 5 August 1932, *Hebrew Standard*, p. 6.
120. Rubinstein, H.L. 1991, *The Jews in Australia: A thematic History*, vol. 1 William Heinemann Australia, Melbourne, p. 160.

121. 'Council of Jewish women: Council Seniors annual meeting', 5 February 1932, *Hebrew Standard*, p. 6.
122. 'Council of Jewish Women: Council Seniors New Year Communal Goodwill Social', *Hebrew Standard*, 23 September 1932, p. 9.
123. 'Jewish Council: An important movement', *Mercury*, 5 November 1932, p. 6.
124. 'Council Seniors general meeting;' *Hebrew Standard*, 9 December 1932, p. 6.
125. '100 Women: List of Feminist Club Guests', *The Sun*, 15 March 1933, p. 12.
126. Newton, M.L. 2000, *Making a difference: A history of the National Council of Jewish Women of Australia*, Hybrid Publishers, Melbourne, p. 11.
127. 'Council of Jewish Women of NSW: Council Sabbath', *Hebrew Standard*, 24 March 1933, p. 6.
128. Ibid., p. 6.
129. Ibid., p. 6.
130. 'Tenth birthday celebration', *Hebrew Standard*, 8 September 1933, p. 7.
131. Ibid., p. 7.
132. Ibid., p. 7.
133. Ibid., p. 7.
134. Ibid., p. 7.
135. 'Council of Jewish Women: Building Acquired', *Argus*, 16 February 1934, p. 10.
136. 'Congratulations: 10th Birthday Dinner Jewish Council', 1933, *The Sun*, 31 August 1933, p. 39.
137. Ibid., p. 39.
138. 'Tenth birthday celebration' 1933, *Hebrew Standard*, p. 7.
139. 'British Empire Pageant', *Hebrew Sandard*, 6 October 1933, p. 7.
140. Ibid., p. 7.
141. Ibid., p. 7.
142. Wedgwood, Camilla Hildegarde – Woman – *The Australian Women's Register* (womenaustralia.info)
143. Wetherell, D, 'Wedgwood, Camilla Hildegarde (1901–1955)', *Australian Dictionary of Biography*, National Centre of Biography, Australian National University.

144. Stein, Joshua B. 'Josiah Wedgwood and the Seventh Dominion Scheme' *Studies in Zionism*, vol. 11, no. 2, Taylor & Francis Group, Sept. 1990, pp. 141–55.
145. Ibid., p. 142–143.
146. Ibid., p. 143.
147. Ibid., p. 146.
148. Ibid., p. 148.
149. Ibid., p. 151.
150. Ibid., p. 153.
151. Ibid., p. 153.
152. 'Jews look to Britain', *Newcastle Morning Herald and Miners' Advocate*, 8 May 1941, p. 2.
153. NCJW Sydney Section: *Hebrew Standard*, 'Lady Wakehurst's Reception', 2 November 1939, p. 7.
154. 'Big Zionist gathering', *Hebrew Standard*, 10 November 1933, p. 6.
155. 'Jewish Leader', *The Sun* 19 November 1933, p. 35.
156. 'NCJW Sydney Section: Council Seniors Card Party 9th June', *Hebrew Standard*, 11 May 1934, p. 6.
157. 'National Council of Jewish Women: Sydney Section, Seniors', *Hebrew Standard*, 18 May 1934, p. 6.
158. 'Eleventh annual dinner', *Hebrew Standard*, 24 August 1934, p. 7.
159. 'Jewish Women's Conference', *Daily Telegraph*, 26 October 1934, p. 13.
160. 'Jewish Women's Conference: Tribute to British Empire', 8 November 1934, *Age*, p. 6.
161. 'Woman's realm and social news: Lady Huntingfield attends congress', *Argus*, 23 November 1934, p. 5.
162. 'Jewish women welcome Lady Isaacs', *Sydney Morning Herald*, 18 March 1935, p. 4.
163. 'Jewish Women: Council dinner', *Sydney Morning Herald*, 27 May 1935, p. 4.
164. 'Jewish Council's Banquet', *Daily Telegraph*, 27 May 1935, p. 10.
165. Ibid., p. 10.
166. 'NCJW Sydney Section: Special unity meeting', *Hebrew Standard*, 22 November 1935, p. 7.

167. NCJW: 'Sub-Juniors', *Hebrew Standard*, 6 March 1936, p. 7.

168. NCJW: Sub-Seniors', *Hebrew Standard*, 6 March 1936, p. 6.

169. Rubinstein, H.L. 1991, *The Jews in Australia: A thematic History*, vol. 1 William Heinemann Australia, Melbourne, p. 165.

170. 'Council of Jewish Women: Sydney section', *Hebrew Standard*, 11 June 1936, p. 7.

171. Ibid., p. 7.

172. 'NCJW Sydney Section: General Meeting', *Hebrew Standard*, 16 July 1936, p. 2.

173. *The Advertiser*, 'Papers by distinguished women at Jewish Congress', 14 November 1936, p. 14.

174. Ibid., p. 14.

175. *The Advertiser*, 'Goering as Hitler's crown prince', 12 November 1936, p. 18.

176. 'Reception to Jewish Women Lord Mayor Welcome', *The News*, 10 November, 1936, p. 3.

177. 'Religious air at conference: Jewish women meet' *The News*, 11 November 1936, p. 10.

178. 'Conference Proceedings', *The Advertiser*, 11 November 1936, p. 11.

179. Ibid., p. 11.

180. Ibid., p. 11.

181. 'Jewish Women Entertained', *The Mail*, 14 November 1936, p. 19.

182. 'Address by Jewish Women's President', *The News* 13 November 1936, p. 8.

183. 'Jewish Women's President Outlines Benefits from Conference', *The News*, 14 November 1936, p. 5.

184. 'Jewish Women's Work for Social Welfare', *The Advertiser*, 17 November 1936, p. 8.

185. 'Broadcast by Dr. Fanny Reading', *Hebrew Standard*, 25 Feb 1937, p. 2.

186. 'Afternoon Party', *Sydney Morning Herald*, 16 July 1937, p. 5.

187. 'Causes of declining birthrate: Existing economic environment blamed', *Labor Daily*, 26 July 1937, p. 6.

188. Cohen, 1987, p. 73.

189. Ibid, p. 73.

190. 'Work of Jewish Women: Story of modern Palestine', *Newcastle Sun*, 2

August 1937, p. 5.
191. 'Jewish women: Reception for Lady Wakehurst', *Sydney Morning Herald*, 23 November 1937, p. 4.
192. 'NCJW Change of Council Rooms' 1937, *Hebrew Standard*, p. 7.
193. Ibid., p. 7.
194. 'National Council of Jewish Women', *Hebrew Standard*, 11 February 1937, p. 6.
195. Newton, M., 2000, p. 254.
196. 'At Jewish Women's garden party', *Sydney Morning Herald* 10 March 1938, p. 22.
197. 'NCJW Sydney Section: Fifth Jewish Women's Conference', *Hebrew Standard*, 24 February 1938, p. 7.
198. Ibid., p. 1.
199. Ibid., p. 1.
200. Ibid., p. 1.
201. 'For Women: Children's need: "world fit to live in"', *Sydney Morning Herald*, 16 March 1938, p. 9.
202 Ibid., p. 9.
203. 'A large gathering of members attended the 15th annual meeting of the Sydney Section. Dr Fanny Reading presided', *Hebrew Standard*, 19 May 1938, p. 7.
204. Rubinstein, H.L. 1991, *The Jews in Australia: A thematic History*, vol. 1 William Heinemann Australia, Melbourne, p. 489.
205. Rubinstein, H. 1991, pp. 489–490.
206. Ibid,, p. 490.
207. 'NCJW Sydney Section: 15th anniversary dinner brilliant celebration', *Hebrew Standard*, 8 December 1938, p. 7.
208. 'NCJW Sydney section: card party, Polish relief', *Hebrew Standard*, 15 September 1938, p. 7.
209. 'Sherry Party and High Tea in aid of General Refugees' Fund', *Hebrew Standard*, 13 October 1938, p. 7.
210. 'NCJW Sydney section: card party, Polish relief', *Hebrew Standard*, 15 September 1938, p. 7.

211. 'NCJW Sydney Section: 15th anniversary dinner brilliant celebration', 1938, *Hebrew Standard*, 8 December 1938, p. 7.

Chapter 5: The war years 1939–1945

1. Radi, H. 1989, *200 Autralian women: a Redress anthology*, Women's Redress Press Inc, Broadway, Sydney, p. 155.
2. Rubinstein, H.L. 1991, *The Jews in Australia: A thematic History*, vol. 1 William Heinemann Australia, Melbourne, p. 491.
3. Ibid., p. 494.
4. Rutland, S.D. 1988, *Edge of the Diaspora: Two centuries of Jewish settlement in Australia*, William Collins, Sydney, Australia, p. 202.
5. 'NCJW Sydney Section: 16th Annual Meeting', *Hebrew Standard*, 25 May 1939, p. 7.
6. 'Dr Fanny Reading's Council Tour', *Hebrew Standard*, 27 July 1939, p. 7.
7. 'Jewish Women's President', *Advertiser*, 21 June 1939, p. 8.
8. Ibid., p. 8.
9. 'Dr Fanny Reading's Council Tour', *Hebrew Standard*, 27 July 1939, p. 7.
10. Ibid., p. 7.
11. Ibid., p. 7.
12. 'Woman 's Realm Helping Refugees. Work of Jewish Women', *West Australian*, 4 July 1939, p. 5.
13. 'Jewish Girls Coming as Domestics', *Daily News* 27 June 1939, p. 4.
14. Ibid., p. 3.
15. 'Woman 's Realm Helping Refugees. Work of Jewish Women', *West Australian*, 4 July 1939, p. 5.
16. 'Jewish Women's Council', *West Australian*, 26 June 1939, p. 11.
17. 'Jewish Girls Coming as Domestics', *Daily News*, 27 June 1939, p. 3.
18. 'Dr Fanny Reading's Council Tour', *Hebrew Standard*, 27 July 1939, p. 7.
19. Ibid., p. 7.
20. Newton, M. Making a Difference, 2000, p. 255.
21. 'Dr Fanny Reading's Council Tour' 1939, p. 7.
22. Ibid., p. 7.

23. Ibid., p. 7.
24. Ibid., p. 7.
25. Blakeney, Michael. 'Proposals for a Jewish Colony in Australia: 1938–1948', *Jewish Social Studies*, vol. 46, no. 3/4, 1984, pp. 277–292.
26. Ibid., p. 279.
27. Rubinstein, H.L. 1991, *The Jews in Australia: A thematic History*, vol. 1 William Heinemann Australia, Melbourne, p. 507.
28. Steinberg, I.N., Australia The Unpromised Land: In Search of a Home, 1948, Victor Gollancz Ltd., London, p. 161.
29. Ibid., p. 13.
30. Ibid., p. 102.
31. Ibid., p. 14.
32. Ibid., p. 110.
33. Ibid., p. 140.
34. Suzanne D. Rutland, 'Falk, Leib Aisack (1889–1957)', *Australian Dictionary of Biography*, National Centre of Biography, Australian National University.
35. Ibid., 1981.
36. Horowitz, B., Studia Judaica 20 (2017), nr 1 (39), s. 105–124.
37. 'NCJW Sydney Section: Palestine Fete', *Hebrew Standard*, 7 March 1940, p. 7.
38. Steinberg, I.N., Plain Words to Australian Jews: Translated from Yiddish by I. Ripps, Jewish Publishing Company 'Freeland', 1943, Melbourne, p. 19.
39. Ibid., p. 26.
40. Ibid., pp. 9–10.
41. Weizmann C., 'Settlement of Refugees', *Manchester Guardian*, May 1936.
42. Crown, Alan D. 'The Initiatives and Influences in the Development of Australian Zionism, 1850–1948', *Jewish Social Studies*, vol. 39, no. 4, 1977, pp. 299–322.
43. Ibid., p. 307.
44. Ibid., p. 314.
45. Ibid., p. 314.
46. Gettler, L., An Unpromised Land, Fremantle Press, WA, 1993, p. 46.

47. Ibid., p. 46.
48. Wimborne, B., 'A Land of Milk and Honey? A Jewish Settlement Proposal in the Kimberley', *Australian Dictionary of Biography*, National Centre of Biography, Australian National University, 2014.
49. Steinberg, I.N., *Plain Words to Australian Jews*: Translated from Yiddish by I. Ripps, Jewish Publishing Company 'Freeland', 1943, Melbourne, p. 17.
50. Gettler, L., *An Unpromised Land, Fremantle Press*, WA, 1993, p. 46.
51. Steinberg, I.N., *Australia The Unpromised Land: In Search of a Home*, 1948, Victor Gollancz Ltd., London, p. 153.
52. Ibid., p. 154.
53. Steinberg, I.N., *Plain Words to Australian Jews*: Translated from Yiddish by I. Ripps, Jewish Publishing Company 'Freeland', 1943, Melbourne, p. 3.
54. Ibid., p. 5.
55. Ibid., p. 5.
56. Ibid., p. 7.
57. Ibid., p. 12.
58. Murdoch, W., 'Our Opportunity: A Home for Refugees', Australians and Jewish settlement in the Kimberleys: a collection of articles from the Australian press, Western Australia, 1939, Unpromised land | Australian Jewish community and culture | Stories | State Library of NSW, p. 5.
59. Melville, G.F., 'The Undeveloped North', The West Australian, Melbourne, 22 July 1939, p. 7.
60. Boote, H.E., 'Commendable Jewish Settlement Scheme', The Australian Worker, March 1940, Australians and Jewish settlement in the Kimberleys : a collection of articles from the Australian press. (nsw.gov.au), p. 15.
61. Ibid., p. 16.
62. Wimborne, B., 'A Land of Milk and Honey? A Jewish Settlement Proposal in the Kimberley', *Australian Dictionary of Biography*, National Centre of Biography, Australian National University, originally published 22 May 2014.
63. Stedman, S., A Jewish Settlement in Australia, 1940, Sydney, p. 3.
64. Ibid., p. 5.
65. Ibid., p. 8.

66. Ibid., p. 9.
67. Ibid., pp. 9–10.
68. Ibid., p. 12.
69. 'Council Defence Work', *Hebrew Standard*, 21 September 1939, p. 7.
70. 'NCJW Sydney Section: Lady Wakehurst's Reception', *Hebrew Standard*, 2 November 1939, p. 7.
71. Ibid., p. 7.
72. 'NCJW Sydney Section: Save a Child Fund Cabaret', *Hebrew Standard*, 7 December 1939, p. 3.
73. 'NCJW Sydney Section: Save a child appeal', *Hebrew Standard*, 11 January 1940, p. 6.
74. Ibid., p. 6.
75. 'National Council of Jewish Women: Sydney Section General Meeting', *Hebrew Standard*, 16 May 1940, p. 8.
76. 'NCJW Sydney Section: War Emergency Board', *Hebrew Standard*, 6 June 1940, p. 7.
77. 'NCJW Sydney Section: Cultural Groups', *Hebrew Standard*, 20 June 1940, p. 6.
78. 'NCJW Sydney Section: War Emergency Board', *Hebrew Standard*, 6 June 1940, p. 7.
79. 'NCJW Sydney Section: Cultural Groups', *Hebrew Standard*, 20 June 1940, p. 6.
80. Ibid., p. 6.
81. 'NCJW Sydney Section: WIZO, Youth Aliyah Bazaar', *Hebrew Standard*, 5 September 1940, p. 7.
82. Bell, R., 1977, Censorship and War: Australia's Curious Experience 1939–1945 (sagepub.com) Melbourne.
83. *Newcastle Morning Herald and Miners' Advocate*, 26 June 1942, 'Polish Jews slaughtered: Nazis exposed in smuggled report', p. 3.
84. Stedman, S., 'The Jewish press in Australia', *Jewish Historical Society Journal*, vol. 6, pt. 1, 1943, Sydney.
85. *Hebrew Standard*, 21 September 1944, 'Dutch Help', p. 8.
86. *Hebrew Standard*, 26 October 1944, 'Dutch Refugees Tales', p. 2.

87. 'NCJW Sydney Section: War Emergency Board', *Hebrew Standard*, 6 June 1940, p. 7.
88. 'NCJW Sydney Section: WIZO, Youth Aliyah Bazaar', *Hebrew Standard*, 5 September 1940, p. 7.
89. Ibid., p. 7.
90. 'Jewish women to confer', *The Age*, 24 June 1940, p. 12.
91. 'NSW Jewish Citizens' War Effort: War activities to be co-ordinated', *Hebrew Standard*, 18 July 1940, p. 4.
92. *Sydney Morning Herald*, 20 September 1940, p. 1.
93. 'NCJW Sydney Section: Community, War Chest Shop Appeal', *Hebrew Standard*, 19 September 1940, p. 7.
94. 'Splendid War Effort of Jewish Women', *The Sun*, 25 July 1940, p. 23.
95. 'NCJW Sydney Section: Opening New Shop – Martin Place', *Hebrew Standard*, 3 October 1940, p. 14.
96. 'NCJW Sydney Section: Community, War Chest Shop Appeal', *Hebrew Standard*, 19 September 1940, p. 6.
97. 'NCJW Sydney Section: WIZO, Youth Aliyah Bazaar', *Hebrew Standard*, 5 September 1940, p. 7.
98. 'National Council of Jewish Women: Sydney Section General Meeting', *Hebrew Standard*, 16 May 1940, p. 2.
99. 'Women Honor Feminist Leaders', *The Sun*, 7 March 1941, p. 8.
100. 'Jewish women's work: Cheque for hospital ward', *Sydney Morning Herald* 20 March 1941, p. 14.
101. 'NCJW New war effort launched for a mobile canteen. 18th annual meeting', *Hebrew Standard*, 8 May 1941, p. 7.
102. 'Jews look to Britain', *Newcastle Morning Herald and Miners' Advocate*, 8 May 1941, p. 2.
103. Ibid., p. 2.
104. 'Diana's Notes: By the way', *Newcastle Morning Herald and Miners' Advocate* 10 May 1941, p. 4.
105. 'War work by Jewish women' 1941, *Argus*, p. 6.
106. 'National Council of Jewish Women: Special Reception', *Hebrew Standard*, 28 August 1941, p. 7.

107. Ibid., p7.
108. Dunera Lives, 2018, p. 43.
109. Ibid., p. 71.
110. McFadzean, M. (2008) Internment during World War II Australia in Museums Victoria Collections https://collections.museumsvictoria.com.au/articles/1618.
111. Singapore Internees – The Dunera Association.
112. Mockridge, M., 2014, *Art behind the Wire: The Duldig Studio*, Art-Behind-the-Wire-Education-Kit.pdf (duldig.org.au).
113. Ibid., p. 4.
114. 'NCJW: Council W.I.Z.O.', 1941, *Hebrew Standard*, 2 October 1941, p. 8.
115. Ibid., p. 8.
116. Eva Duldig's email to Anne Sarzin 16 February 2021.
117. Duldig, E., *Driftwood: Escape and survival through art*, Australian Scholarly Publishing Ltd., Melbourne, 2017, p. 172.
118. Koehne, S. 2006, 'Disturbance in D Compound: The question of control in Australian internment camps during World War ll. *Melbourne Historical Journal* 34, pp. 71–86.
119. Ibid., pp. 71–86.
120. Eva Duldig's email to Anne Sarzin, 14 February 2021.
121. Rubinstein, H.L. 1991, *The Jews in Australia: A thematic History*, vol. 1 William Heinemann Australia, Melbourne, p. 200.
122. Ibid., p. 201.
123. 'NCJW: An appeal', *Hebrew Standard*, 2 July 1942, p. 6.
124. 'NCJW: First Aid Classes', 1942, *Hebrew Standard*, 5 February 1942, p. 7.
125. Newton, M.L. 2000, *Making a difference: A history of the National Council of Jewish Women of Australia*, Hybrid Publishers, Melbourne, p. 4.
126. 'NCJW: General Meeting', *Hebrew Standard*, 23 October 1941, p. 8.
127. 'National Council of Jewish Women: Jack's Day – N.S.W. Appeal', *Hebrew Standard*, 22 January 1942, p. 6.
128. 'NCJW Martin Place Kiosk', *Hebrew Standard*, 19 March 1942, p. 7.
129. 'NCJW: First Aid Classes', *Hebrew Standard*, 5 February 1942, p. 7.
130. Ibid., p. 7.

131. Ibid., p. 7.
132. Ibid., p. 7.
133. 'NCJW: Younger set', 2 July 1942, *Hebrew Standard*, p. 6.
134. *Who are we* 2019, Keren Hayesod, Jerusalem.
135. 'Farewell to Dr. Michael Traub', *Hebrew Standard*, 9 April 1942, p. 2.
136. 'NCJW: An appeal', 23 July 1942, *Hebrew Standard*, p. 6.
137. 'Women's News: Aid for Loan on Birthday', *Daily Telegraph*, 6 April 1943, p. 12.
138. Ibid., p. 12.
139. Andgel, A. 1998 'The Law of Loving Kindness', *Australian Jewish Historical Society Journal*, vol X1V, Part 2, p. 211, Sydney.
140. Rutland, S.D. 1988, *Edge of the Diaspora: Two centuries of Jewish settlement in Australia*, William Collins, Sydney, p. 169.
141. *Council Bulletin*, November 1928.
142. 'Concern for Jewish Refugees', *Sydney Morning Herald*, 7 July 1943, p. 5.
143. 'Plight of Jews in Europe', 1943, *Barrier Miner* 22 November 1943, p. 2.
144. *Sydney Morning Herald*, 'Plea for aid to Jews: Woman suggests Allied Action', 22 November 1943, p. 7.
145. *Jessie Street: A revised autobiography* 2004, Federation Press, Sydney, p. 172.
146. Ibid., p. 173.
147. *A war to win a world to gain. Australian Woman's Charter, 1943: which comprises the resolutions adopted by the Australian Women's Conference for victory in war and victory in peace, November 19–22, 1943, Sydney, New South Wales, Australia*. 1943, p. 20.
148. Street, J. 1990, *Jessie Street Documents and Essays*, Women's Redress Press Inc., Sydney, p. 156.
149. 'Message from Dr Fanny Reading, President National Council of Jewish Women of Australia', *Hebrew Standard*, 21 January 1943, p. 6.
150. Newton, M.L. 2000, *Making a difference: A history of the National Council of Jewish Women of Australia*, Hybrid Publishers, Melbourne, p. 255.
151. 'NCJW 20th birthday celebration – 6th NCJW conference', *Hebrew Standard*, 22 July 1943, p. 7.
152. Ibid., p. 7.

153. Ibid, p. 7.
154. Ibid., p. 7.
155. Ibid., p. 7.
156. Ibid., p. 7.
157. Ibid., p. 7.
158. 'National Council of Jewish Women: Council Luncheon', *Hebrew Standard*, 5 August 1943, p. 7.
159. Ibid., p. 7.
160. Ibid., p. 7.
161. 'National Women's Conference Sydney', *Newcastle Sun*, 9 November 1943, p. 3.
162. Rutland, S., Caplan, S., *With one voice: A history of the New South Wales Jewish Board of Deputies*, Australian Jewish Historical Society, Sydney, p. 20.
163. Freilich, M. 1967, *Zion in our time: Memoirs of an Australian Zionist*, Morgan Publications, Sydney, p. 102.
164. Rutland, S.D.C., Sophie 1998, *With one voice*, Australian Jewish Historical Society, Sydney, p. 17.
165. Ibid., p. 23.
166. 'Proposed Board Jewish Deputies: Provisional committees hold first meeting', *Hebrew Standard*, 12 August 1943, p. 2.
167. 'Public Relations Committee replies', *Hebrew Standard*, 25 November 1943, p. 6.
168. 'To speak today in Sydney', *Daily Telegraph*, 7 September 1943, p. 4.
169. 'Jewish women's war work', *Argus*, 28 October 1943, p. 6.
170. 'NSW Jewish War Services Committee: Chairman's report', *Hebrew Standard*, 23 December 1943, p. 1.
171. 'National Council of Jewish Women – To purchase comforts', *Hebrew Standard*, 23 November 1944, p. 8.
172. 'National Council of Jewish Women: Council Sabbath', *Hebrew Standard*, 2 March 1944, p. 8.
173. 'National Council of Jewish Women – To purchase comforts', 1944, *Hebrew Standard*, 23 November 1944, p. 8.
174. 'National Council of Jewish Women: 1st Victory Loan Objective

£100,000', *Hebrew Standard*, 17 February 1944, p. 8.

175. Museum, R.B.o.A. 2019, *Make your money fight: Filling the Loans*, <https://museum.rba.gov.au/exhibitions/make-your-money-fight/filling-the-loans/>.

176. 'NCJW: Future functions', 1945, *Hebrew Standard*, 12 April 1945, p. 8.

177. Splendid Year of Service-Annual Meeting of the N.C.J.W.', *Hebrew Standard*, 31 August 1944, p. 8.

178. *The Sun*, 'Jewish Aid For Charities', 7 August 1944, p. 7.

179. Splendid Year of Service-Annual Meeting of the N.C.J.W.', *Hebrew Standard*, 31 August 1944, p. 8.

180. 'NCJW – Red Cross Stall', *Hebrew Standard*, 9 November 1944, p. 8.

181. Ibid., p. 8.

182. 'Jewish National Fund – Sydney JNF's great success', *Hebrew Standard*, 6 April 1944, p. 7.

183. Newton, M.L. 2000, *Making a difference: A history of the National Council of Jewish Women of Australia*, Hybrid Publishers, Melbourne, p. 9.

184. Ibid., p. 10.

185. Ibid., p. 10.

186. Reading, Lynne, interview with Anne Sarzin 27 November 2020, Sydney.

187. Burman, I. 2020. Second interview with Anne Sarzin, Sydney.

188. Newton, M.L., 2000, p. 10.

189. 'National Council of Jewish Women – To purchase comforts', *Hebrew Standard*, 23 November 1944, p. 8.

190. Ibid., p. 8.

191. 'Unique honour for Dr. Fanny Reading', *Hebrew Standard*, 8 May 1947, p. 4.

192. Ibid., p. 4.

193. 'Temple Emanuel Weekly Bulletin: Council Sabbath', *Hebrew Standard*, 21 March 1946, p. 8.

194. Negba (zionism-israel.com) Isseroff 2008.

195. *Sun-Herald*, 5 May 1957, p. 99.

196. 'Children and Youth Aliyah: Henrietta Szold Memorial Meeting', *Hebrew Standard*, 22 March 1945, p. 2.

197. Simmons, E. 2006, *Hadassah and the Zionist Project*, Rowman & Littlefield Publishers Inc, Lanham, Maryland, p. 4.
198. Ibid., p. 13.
199. *Hebrew Standard*, 'The call to Australia to save 1000 children', 3 May 1945, p. 6.
200. 'NCJW Council luncheon: TB Director guest speaker', *Hebrew Standard*, 8 November 1945, p. 8.
201. Ibid., p. 8.
202. 'NCJW: [£500 for Youth Aliyah]', *Hebrew Standard of Australasia*, 4 April 1946, p. 10.
203. 'United Jewish Overseas Relief Fund in N.S.W.', 1945, *Hebrew Standard*, 23 August 1945, p. 3.
204. 'International Women's Day, *The Newcastle Sun*, 14 December 1944, p. 5.
205. *Hebrew Standard*, 27 September 1945, 'NCJW: Representative gathering hears Mrs Lindheim', p. 8.
206. 'Jewish Women's Plans for Peace, Migration', *Telegraph*, 11 June 1946, p. 3.
207. 'Jewish Women Meeting here this morning', *Telegraph*, 15 June 1946, p. 3.
208. 'Jewish Women's Conference', *Telegraph*, 8 June 1946, p. 4.

Chapter 6: An era of peace

1. "Truly a leader and lover of mankind': Dr. Fanny Reading', *Hebrew Standard of Australasia*, 13 February 1953, p. 2.
2. 'Anzac Buffet Closing', *Sydney Morning Herald*, 2 March 1946, p. 4.
3. 'National Council of Jewish Women Celebrates Silver Jubilee: Official Opening of Ninth Conference', *Hebrew Standard*, 1 July 1948, p. 4.
4. 'NCJW Record achievements of NCJW committees', *Hebrew Standard*, 19 September 1946, p. 11.
5. Rutland, S. n.d. Post-War Jewish Migration – Israel & Judaism Studies (IJS).
6. Calwell, M.E., 'Arthur Calwell and the gift of immigration', MOAD, 2017, Museum of Australian Democracy at Old Parliament House (moadoph.gov.au).
7. *Hebrew Standard*, 'Realism in immigration', 16 August 1945, p. 9.

8. Rutland, S. n.d. Post-War Jewish Migration – Israel & Judaism Studies (IJS)
9. Kwiet, K., 17 December 2020, International Migrants Day: Waves of Jewish migration to Australia – Sydney Jewish Museum.
10. 'NCJW: Service to new arrivals committee', *Hebrew Standard* 25 April 1946, p. 8.
11. 'Jewish Women Members of Newcastle Section', *Newcastle Morning Herald and Miners' Advocate*, 11 April 1946, p. 8.
12. 'National Council of Jewish Women: Council luncheon', *Hebrew Standard*, 26 September 1946, p. 8.
13. Ibid., p. 8.
14. Ibid., p. 8.
15. Ibid., p. 8.
16. 'National Council of Jewish Women: Reception to new arrivals', *Hebrew Standard*, 6 February 1947, p. 6.
17. Ibid., p. 6.
18. Ibid., p. 10.
19. Szego, J. *The Age*, 'Sentimental journey from war's scars', 3 August 2002, Melbourne.
20. Valent, P. 2002, *Child Survivors of the Holocaust*, p. 287, Taylor & Francis, Milton Park, United Kingdom.
21. Burman, Dr Ian, interviewed by Anne Sarzin, Sydney 2018.
22. 'In Memoriam', *Hebrew Standard*, 3 October 1946, p. 8.
23. Einfeld, S.B., Walter, 'Report and recommendations for the handling of new arrivals', paper presented to the *Migrants Reception Committee Conference*, Sydney, 20 February 1947.
24. 'Proud Jewesses, outstanding record of Council of Jewish Women', *Hebrew Standard*, 27 March 1947, p. 10.
25. Gazette, T.L. 1946, *Fifth Supplement to The London Gazette*, Authority, London, p. 167.
26. 'Jewish Women Visit Newcastle', *Newcastle Morning Herald and Miners' Advocate*, 8 July 1948, p. 4.
27. 'Proud Jewesses, outstanding record of Council of Jewish Women', *Hebrew Standard*, 27 March 1947, p. 10.

28. 'NCJW New section formed at Wollongong: Welcome to new arrivals', *Hebrew Standard*, 9 October 1947, p. 8.
29. Cohen, L. 1987, *Beginning with Esther: Jewish women in New South Wales from 1788*, Ayers & James Heritage Books, p. 75.
30. Newton, M.L. 2000, *Making a difference: A history of the National Council of Jewish Women of Australia*, Hybrid Publishers, Melbourne, p. 82.
31. 'Jewish women: High tea and card party', *Hebrew Standard*, 5 June 1947, p. 8.
32. Kwiet, K. 'Responses of Australian Jewry's leadership to the Holocaust', p. 211, *Jews in the Sixth Continent*, ed. Rubinstein, W.D., Allen & Unwin, 1987, Sydney.
33. Ibid., p. 212.
34. Ibid., p. 213.
35. 'NCJW: Silver Jubilee inauguration celebration', *Hebrew Standard*, 13 November 1947, p. 10.
36. Ibid., p. 10.
37. 'NCJW: Philip Myerson Memorial handed over, Visit to Newcastle', *Hebrew Standard*, 11 December 1947, p. 10.
38. Rutland, S., *Edge of the Diaspora*, Collins Australia, 1988, p. 311.
39. Ibid., p. 311.
40. Freilich, M., *Zion in our Time*, Morgan Publications, Sydney, 1967, p. 115.
41. Ibid., p. 124.
42. Ibid., p. 195.
43. Ibid., p. 198.
44. Ibid., p. 199.
45. Ibid., p. 199.
46. 'Dr. Fanny Reading: President, National Council of Jewish Women of Australia', *Hebrew Standard*, 4 December 1947, p. 2.
47. Ibid., p. 2.
48. 'Palestine Jewry ready to meet any attack', *Hebrew Standard*, 4 December 1947, p. 1.
49. 'Joy among DP's: illegal immigration to stop', *Hebrew Standard*, Thursday 4 December 1947, p. 1.
50. Ibid., p. 1.

51. 'NCJW: Philip Myerson Memorial handed over, Visit to Newcastle', *Hebrew Standard*, 11 December 1947, p. 10.
52. Ibid., p. 10.
53. 'NCJW: Young member to leave for study in Palestine', *Hebrew Standard*, 12 February 1948, p. 10.
54. Ibid., p. 10.
55. 'United Nations appeal for children', 1948, *Hebrew Standard*, 8 July 1948, p. 8.
56. Ben-Gurion, D. 1948, *Declaration of Establishment of the State of Israel*, Israel Ministry of Foreign Affairs, Israel.
57. Rubinstein, W.D. 1987, *Jews in the sixth continent*, Allen & Unwin, Sydney, p. 107.
58. Newton, 2000, p. 95.
59. Ibid., p. 96.
60. Reading, F. 1926, 'The President's Message', *The Council Bulletin*, vol. 1, no. 4, December 1926.
61. Fink, M. 1974, 'In Memoriam Dr Fanny Reading', *The Council Bulletin*, 1974.
62. 'National Council of Jewish Women: Future April Functions', *Hebrew Standard*, 1 April 1948, p. 9.
63. Ibid., p. 9.
64. 'To Discuss Jewish Jubilee Conference', *News*, 14 April 1948, p. 11.
65. 'National Council of Jewish Women Celebrates Silver Jubilee: Official Opening of Ninth Conference', *Hebrew Standard*, 1 July 1948, p. 4.
66. Ibid., p. 4.
67. Ibid., p. 4.
68. Ibid., p. 4.
69. 'Jewish Women Visit Newcastle', *Newcastle Morning Herald and Miners' Advocate*, 8 July 1948, p. 4.
70. Ibid., p. 4.
71. 'Council Celebrates 27th Anniversary', *Hebrew Standard*, 10 August 1950, p. 3.
72. Newton, p. 217.
73. 'New drive planned for Jewish Hospital', *Hebrew Standard*, 5 August 1948, p. 5.

74. 'Hospital dinner plans', *Hebrew Standard*, 26 August 1948, p. 5.
75. 'Wolper Home Opened', *Hebrew Standard*, 22 May 1953, p. 6.
76. '120 Jews at ceremony: Wolper Home Opened', *Sydney Morning Herald*, 18 May 1953, p. 2.
77. Hospital, W.J. 2018, *Wolper Jewish Hospital: Our History*, Wolper Jewish Hospital, Sydney, <https://wolper.com.au/about-us/our-history/>.
78. 'Maccabi affiliates with N.C.J.W.', *Hebrew Standard*, 9 September 1948, p. 3.
79. Ibid., p. 3.
80. Andgel, A. 1998, 'The law of lovingkindness', *Australian Jewish Historical Society Journal*, vol. XIV, no. Part 2, p. 206.
81. Maccabi affiliates with NCJW, *Hebrew Standard*, 9 September 1948, p. 3.
82. Einfeld, S. 1949, *Migrants Reception Committee of the NSW Jewish Board of Deputies Report*, New South Wales Jewish Board of Deputies, Sydney.
83. Ibid., 1949.
84. 'O.S.E. Committee in Sydney', *Hebrew Standard*, 19 May 1949, p. 11.
85. Ibid., p. 11.
86. Ibid., p. 11.
87. 'NCJW Newcastle section: Twentieth annual meeting', *Hebrew Standard*, 2 June 1949, p. 12.
88. Ibid., p. 12.
89. Ibid., p. 12.
90. Ibid., p. 12.
91. 'Helping migrants major aim of Jewish women', *Newcastle Morning Herald and Miners' Advocate* 13 May 1954, p. 5.
92. 'Dr. Reading Elected to International Post', *Hebrew Standard*, 9 June 1949, p. 3.
93. 'Dr Fanny Reading to retire', *Hebrew Standard*, 22 September 1949, p. 3.
94. Ibid., p. 3.
95. Ibid., p. 3.
96. "Truly a leader and lover of mankind': Dr. Fanny Reading', *Hebrew Standard*, 13 February 1953, p. 2.
97. 'Israel's Independence Day celebrated at reception ', *Daily Telegraph*, 11 May 1951, p. 10.

98. 'Jewish Child's Day', *Hebrew Standard*, 30 November 1951, p. 2.
99. 'Women never cease to work', *Brisbane Telegraph*, 5 June 1952, p. 14.
100. Ibid., p. 19.
101. 'Jewish women entertained', *Brisbane Telegraph*, 3 June 1952, p. 19.
102. 'Anniversary of Jewish Women's Group', *Sydney Morning Herald*, 27 August 1953, p. 11.
103. *Sun-Herald*, 'Women's Section', 5 May 1957, p. 99.
104. 'NCJW in Newcastle', *Hebrew Standard*, 5 June 1953, p. 7.
105. *Hebrew Standard*, 'NCJW Council House', 15 September 1949, p. 12.
106. 'Council Celebrates 27th Anniversary', *Hebrew Standard*, 10 August 1950, p. 3.
107. Ibid., p. 3.
108. 'National Council of Jewish Women: The official dinner', *Hebrew Standard*, 15 August 1952, p. 7.
109. Ibid., p. 7.
110. 'Fanny Reading Council House Appeal Launched', *Hebrew Standard*, 20 February 1953, p. 3.
111. 'NCJW in Newcastle', *Hebrew Standard*, 5 June 1953, p. 7.
112. Andgel, 1998, p. 236.
113. Newton, 2000, p. 219.
114. Andgel, p. 237.
115. 'A national centre for Jews', *Canberra Times*, 4 December 1971, p. 14.
116. 'Jewish centre opened', *Canberra Times*, 13 December 1971, p. 3.
117. Rubinstein, H.L. 1991, *The Jews in Australia: A thematic History*, vol. 1 William Heinemann Australia, Melbourne, p. 294.

Chapter 7: Background to the Trial

1. Schenk, M., 'Rabbi Schenk to Major Comay', personal letter, 9 September 1947, sent from Sydney to Jerusalem. Rabbi Max Schenk was a member of the Executive Committee of the Zionist Federation of Australia and New Zealand. NCJW archives.
2. Ochert, M. 1996, 'Dr Fanny Reading v. Smith's Weekly', *Australian Jewish Historical Society Journal*, vol. X111, Part 2, p. 331.

3. Schenk, M. 1947, letter to Comay.
4. Herron, J. 1949, 'Reading v. National Press Pty. Ltd.', in S.C.o. NSW (ed.) Court transcript, p. 1.
5. Schneer, J. 2010, *Balfour Declaration: The origins of the Arab-Israeli conflict*, Random House, New York, p. 341.
6. Wertheim, P. Law against racial vilification steeped in Australian history – On Line Opinion – 20/12/2013.
7. Ochert, M. 1996, p. 317.
8. Bentwich, N. 1944, *Jewish Youth Comes Home: the story of the Youth Aliyah*, 1933–1943, Victor Gollanz Ltd. London, p. 35.
9. Pincus, C. 1970, *Come from the four winds: the story of Youth Aliyah*, second edn, Herzl Press, New York, p. 17.
10. Bentwich, N. 1944, p. 9.
11. Ofer, D.W., Hannah 1996, *Dead-End Journey: The tragic story of the Kladovo-Sabac Group*, trans. B. Anna, University Press of America, Inc., Lanham Maryland, p. 122.
12. Ibid., p. 122.
13. Ibid., p. 123.
14. Glowinski, P. 2015, *Youth Aliyah Records in the Hadassah Archives* Hadassah, the Women's Zionist Organization of America Dates: 1928–2009 Dates: bulk 1935–98.
15. Ibid., 2015.
16. Bentwich, N., 1944.
17. Kahanoff, J. 1960, *Ramat-Hadassah-Szold, Youth Aliyyah Screening and Classification Centre*, Publishing Department of the Jewish Agency, Jerusualem, p. 19.
18. Grigsby, R., *A train to Palestine: The Tehran Children, Anders' Army and their escape from Stalin's Siberia, 1939–1943*, Valentine Mitchell, London, 2020, p. 243.
19. Kahanoff, J. 1960, p. 20.
20. *Group care: An Israeli approach, the educational path of Youth Aliyah* 1971, Gordon and Breach, New York and London, p. 32.
21. 'Our living legend: a woman of vision' 1964, *The Council Bulletin*, p. 7.

22. Andgel, A. 1998, 'The law of lovingkindness', *Australian Jewish Historical Society Journal*, vol. XIV, no. Part 2, p. 210.
23. Newton, M.L. 2000, *Making a difference: A history of the National Council of Jewish Women of Australia*, Hybrid Publishers, Melbourne, p. 6.
24. Kahanoff, J. 1960, pp. 7–8.
25. Bentwich, N. 1944, p. 45.
26. Reading, F. 1925, 'Impressions of the Fourteenth Zionist Congress ', *Hebrew Standard*, 20 November 1925, p. 3.
27. 'Youth Aliyah Campaign: Appeal opens next Tuesday night', *Hebrew Standard*, 12 July 1945, p. 1.
28. 'Children and Youth Aliyah: Henrietta Szold Memorial Meeting', *Hebrew Standard*, 22 March 1945, p. 2.
29. *The Argus*, Melbourne, 'Anti-Jewish riots. Armed mobs in Vienna. Police precautions fail', 20 August 1925, p. 9.
30. 'Serious riots in Vienna', *The Daily Examiner*, Grafton, 19 August 1925, p. 5.
31. *The Advertiser*, 19 August 1925, Adelaide, p. 14.
32. *The Mercury*, Hobart, 20 August 1925, 'Zionist Congress. The Disturbances in Vienna', p. 7.
33. 'Antisemitic and anti-government demonstrations against holding of 14th international zionist congress in Vienna', New York Times, 19 August 1925.
34. Reading, F., Impresssions of the Fourteenth Zionist Congress, *Hebrew Standard*, Sydney, 20 November 1925, p. 3.
35. Ibid., p. 3.
36. *Chaim Weizmann: A tribute on his seventieth birthday* 1945, Victor Gollancz Ltd., London, p. 183.
37. Ibid., p. 185.
38. Reading, F, 1925, p. 3.
39. *Speeches on Zionism by the Right Hon. The Earl of Balfour* 1928, Arrowsmith, London, p. 75.
40. Chaim Weizmann, 1945, p. 89.
41. Troy, G. *The Zionist Ideas: Visions for the Jewish Homeland – Then, Now, Tomorrow*, The Jewish Publication Society, Philadelphia, 2018, p. 67.
42. Mehlman, W. 2010, *Jabotinsky ... The man and the vision*, Americans for a

safe Israel, Jerusalem.

43. Ibid., pp. 7–8.
44. Schechtman, J., 1961, *The Vladimir Jabotinsky Story*, Thomas Yoseloff, New York, p. 38.
45. Troy, G. 2018, p. 68.
46. Sorkin, David. *The Origins of Israel, 1882–1948 : A Documentary History*, edited by Eran Kaplan, and Derek J. Penslar, University of Wisconsin Press, 2011, p. 257.
47. Troy, G., 2018, p. 73.
48. Sorkin, D., 2011, p. 263.
49. Schechtman, J. 1961, p. 39.
50. Ibid., p. 39.
51. Ibid., p. 41.
52. Ibid, p. 41.
53. Netanyahu, B., *The Founding Fathers of Zionism*, Gefen, Jerusalem, 2012, p. 217.
54. Ibid., p. 217.
55. Schechtman, J. 1961, p. 43.
56. Reading, F., 1925, p. 3.
57. Schechtman, J., 1961, p. 42.
58. Ibid., p. 43.
59. Netanyahu, B. 2012, p. 192.
60. Reading, F., Family letters, 1925.
61. Melamed, E. *Besheva*, DUS IZ NIES !! Rare View …: Who was Ze'ev Jabotinsky?, 2019.
62. Schoffman, S. *Jewish Review of Books*, 'Shabtai at Seventy', Spring 2018, p. 47.
63. Rabinowicz, O. 1950, *Fifty years of Zionism: A historical analysis of Dr. Weizmann's 'Trial and Error'*, Robert Anscombe & C. Ltd., London, p. 24.
64. *Jewish Virtual Library* 2018, AICE, <https://www.jewishvirtuallibrary.org/ernest-bevin>.
65. Rabinowicz, O. 1950, p. 23.
66. Ibid., p. 30.

67. Berkowitz, M. 2004, *Nationalism, Zionism and Ethnic Mobilization of the Jews in 1900 and beyond* Brill, Leiden, Boston, p. 195.
68. Reading, F. 1925, p. 3.
69. Ibid, p. 3.
70. *Newcastle Morning Herald and Miners' Advocate*, 28 August 1925, 'Zionist Congress', p. 5.
71. Reading, F. 1925, p. 3.
72. Ibid., p. 3.
73. Ibid., p. 3.
74. Ibid., p. 3.
75. Ibid., p. 3.

Chapter 8: The Trial

1. Herron, J. 1949, 'Reading v. National Press Pty. Ltd.', in S.C.o. NSW (ed.) Court transcript, pp. 2–3.
2. Ibid. transcript pp. 2–3.
3. Ibid. transcript p. 3.
4. Ibid. transcript p. 4.
5. Freilich, M. 1967, *Zion in our time: Memoirs of an Australian Zionist*, Morgan Publications, Sydney, p. 169.
6. 'Jewish women: Council Reception', *Hebrew Standard of Australasia*, 5 June 1947, p. 8.
7. Herron transcript, p. 8.
8. Ibid. transcript, p. 5.
9. Ibid. transcript, p. 7.
10. Ibid. transcript, p. 8.
11. Ibid. transcript, p. 9.
12. Ibid. transcript, p. 10.
13. Ibid. transcript, p. 11.
14. Ibid. transcript, p. 11.
15. Ochert, M. 1996, 'Dr Fanny Reading v. Smith's Weekly', *Australian Jewish Historical Society Journal*, vol. xiii, no. Part 2, p. 332.

16. Herron, transcript, pp. 14–15.
17. Ibid., transcript, p. 15.
18. Ibid., transcript, p. 16.
19. Ibid., transcript, p. 18.
20. Ibid., transcript, p. 20.
21. Ibid., transcript, p. 21.
22. Ibid. transcript, p. 20.
23. Ibid., transcript, p. 22.
24. Stone, J. 1944, *'Stand up and be counted!': An open letter to the Rt.Hon.Sir Isaac Isaacs, P.C., G.C.M.G., on the twenty-sixth anniversary of the Jewish National Home* Second edn, Ponsford, Newman & Benson Sydney, p. 5.
25. Ibid., p. 6.
26. Ibid., p. 16.
27. Ibid., p. 17.
28. Herron, transcript., p. 23.
29. Ibid, transcript, p. 28.
30. Ibid., p. 28.
31. Ibid., p. 27.
32. Ibid., p. 27.
33. Ibid., p. 32.
34. Ibid., p. 33.
35. Ibid., pp. 24–5.
36. Ibid., p. 26.
37. Ibid., p. 28.
38. Ibid., p. 28.
39. Ibid., p. 29.
40. Ibid., p. 29.
41. Ibid., p. 31.
42. Ibid., pp. 30–1.
43. Ibid., p. 32.
44. Ibid., p. 33.

45. Ibid., p. 34.
46. Ibid., pp. 35–6.
47. Ibid., pp. 35–6.
48. Ibid., p. 36.
49. Ibid., pp. 38–9.
50. Ibid., p. 39.
51. Schenk, M. 1947, 'Rabbi Schenk to Major Comay', personal communication, 9 September 1947, Sydney.
52. Ochert, M. 1996, 'Dr Fanny Reading v. Smith's Weekly', *Australian Jewish Historical Society Journal*, vol. xiii, no. Part 2, p. 331.
53. Herron, transcript, p. 43–4.
54. Ibid, p. 45.
55. *Jewish Virtual Library* 2018, AICE, <https://www.jewishvirtuallibrary.org/ernest-bevin>.
56. Herron, transcript, p. 47.
57. Ibid., p. 48.
58. Ibid., p. 48.
59. Ibid., pp. 48–9.
60. Ibid., p. 49.
61. Ibid., p. 50.
62. 'Max Schenk dies led Rabbis Board', *New York Times*, 26 May 1974, p. 45.
63. Herron, transcript, p. 50.
64. Ibid., p. 50.
65. Ibid., p. 51.
66. Ibid., p. 51.
67. Ibid., p. 51.
68. Ibid., p. 69.
69. Ibid., p. 51.
70. *General Jan Christiaan Smuts* 2018, biography, South African History Online, 2018, <https://sahistory.org.za/people/general-jan-christiaan-smuts>.
71. Herron, transcript, p. 53.

72. Ibid., pp. 56–7.
73. Ibid., p. 65.
74. Ibid., p. 57.
75. Ibid., p. 58.
76. Ibid., p. 59.
77. Ibid., p. 60.
78. Ibid., p. 62.
79. Ibid., p. 64.
80. Ibid., p. 65.
81. Ibid., p. 65.
82. Ibid., pp. 65–6.
83. Ibid., p. 69.
84. Ibid., pp. 69–70.
85. Ibid., p. 70.
86. Ibid., p. 72.
87. Ibid., p. 73.
88. Ibid., p. 74.
89. Ibid., p. 75.
90. Rimmer, G. 1988, *Smith, William John (Bill) (1882–1972)*, MUP, Melbourne, <http://adb.anu.edu.au/biography/smith-william-john-bill-8492>.
91. Herron, transcript, p. 76.
92. Ochert, M. 1996, 'Dr Fanny Reading v. Smith's Weekly', *Australian Jewish Historical Society Journal*, vol. xiii, no. Part 2, p. 318.
93. Ibid., p. 319.
94. Ibid., p. 319.
95. Ibid., p. 320.
96. Ibid., p. 320.
97. Ibid., pp 320–321.
98. Ibid., p. 321.
99. Ibid., p. 321.
100. John Kennedy McLaughlin, 'Cassidy, Sir Jack Evelyn (1893–1975)',

Australian Dictionary of Biography, National Centre of Biography, Australian National University.

101. Herron, J. 1949, *Judgement*, 28 April 1949 edn, Sydney, pp. 1–2.
102. Ibid., p. 2.
103. Ibid., p. 7.
104. Ibid., pp. 3–4.
105. Ibid., pp. 8–9.
106. Ibid., pp. 10–11.
107. Freilich, M. 1967, *Zion in our time: Memoirs of an Australian Zionist*, Morgan Publications, Sydney, p. 170.
108. Ochert, M. 1996, 'Dr Fanny Reading v. Smith's Weekly', *Australian Jewish Historical Society Journal*, vol. xiii, no. Part 2, p. 331.
109. Symon, E. 1973, *Australian Jewish Times* 21 June 1973.
110. Herron, J. 29 June 1949, 'Costs', no 1 Supreme Court of NSW, Sydney, p. 1.
111. Herron, J., *Judgement*, 28 April 1949 edn, Sydney, p. 1.
112. Herron, J., 'Costs', 29 June 1949, pp. 1–2.
113. Herron, J., *Judgement*, 28 April 1949, Sydney, pp. 10–11.
114. Wertheim, P., *Law against racial vilification steeped in Australian history*, 19 December 2013, ECAJ.
115. Racial Vilification Law in Australia | Australian Human Rights Commission 2002.
116. Wertheim, P. 24 December 2020, Interview with Anne Sarzin, Sydney.
117. Australian Bureau of Statistics 1989.
118. Wertheim, P. 24 December 2021, Interviewed by Anne Sarzin, Sydney.
119. Alhadeff, V. 29 December 2020, Sydney, interviewed by Anne Sarzin.

Chapter 9: Conclusion

1. Andgel, A. 1998, 'The Law of Loving Kindness', *Australian Jewish Historical Society Journal*, vol. xiv, no. 2.
2. Ibid., p. 236.
3. 'Council of Jewish Women: Visit of Dr. Fanny Reading. Welcome in Kalgoorlie', *Kalgoorlie Miner*, 26 September 1929, p. 2.

4. Andgel, A. 1998, p. 205.
5. 'Council of Jewish Women: Dr Reading urges broad outlook', *Observer* 5 October 1929, p. 54.
6. Ibid., p. 54.
7. Tenth birthday celebration, 1933, *Hebrew Standard of Australasia*, 8 September 1933, p. 7.
8. 'NCJW New section formed at Wollongong: Welcome to new arrivals', *Hebrew Standard*, 9 October 1947, p. 8.
9. Tenth birthday celebration, *Hebrew Standard*, 8 September 1933, p. 7.
10. 'National Council of Jewish Women Celebrates Silver Jubilee', *Hebrew Standard*, 1 July 1948., p. 4.
11. Tenth birthday celebration, 1933, *Hebrew Standard*, 8 September 1933, p. 7.
12. 'Council of Jewish Women', *Hebrew Standard*, 12 March 1926, p. 6.
13. Rubinstein, W.D. 1987, *Jews in the sixth continent*, Allen & Unwin, Sydney, p. 107.
14. Newton, M.L. 2000, *Making a difference: A history of the National Council of Jewish Women of Australia*, Hybrid Publishers, Melbourne, p. 95.
15. Ibid., p. 96.
16. Reading, F., 'The President's Message', *The Council Bulletin*, vol. 1, no. 4, December 1926.
17. Ben-Gurion, D. 1948, *Declaration of Establishment of the State of Israel*, Israel Ministry of Foreign Affairs, Israel.
18. Fink, M. 1974, 'In Memoriam Dr Fanny Reading', *The Council Bulletin*, 1974.
19. Andgel, A. 1998, p. 236.
20. Ibid., p. 237.
21. 'Proposed new Jewish women's movement: Council of Jewish Women of New South Wales', *Hebrew Standard*, 13 July 1923, p. 8.
22. Ibid., p. 8.
23. 'Dr Reading's Broadcast Address', 1933, *Hebrew Standard*, 8 September 1933, p. 7.
24. Sacks, J. 2019, The Teacher as hero: Devarim 5779, Office of Rabbi Sacks, London, http://rabbisacks.org/the-teacher-as-hero-devarim-5779/
25. Burger, A. 2018, *Witness: Lessons from Elie Wiesel's classroom*, Houghton

Mifflin Harcourt, Boston, New York, p. 20.

26. Ibid., p. 20.
27. Brender, Y. 2017, 'Changing of the NCJWA guard', Melbourne, *Australian Jewish News*, 2 July 2017.
28. Nadel, V., 'Interview Victoria Nadel', conducted 26 August 2019 by Anne Sarzin.
29. *NCJWA NSW Past, Present and Future* 2019, NCJWA NSW, Sydney, <https://ncjwansw.org.au/programs/israel-projects/>.
30. National Council of Jewish Women, *Annual General Meeting 26 August 2019, 96th Annual Report*, NCJWA NSW Div., Sydney, p. 7.
31. Ibid., p. 40.
32. Gelman, S. 1974, 'In Memoriam, NCJW NSW, *The Council Bulletin*, 1974.
33. Yerushalmi, Y.H., 1989, *Zakhor: Jewish History and Jewish Memory*, 1996, University of Washington Press, Seattle and London, p. 5.
34. Professor Emerita Rosemary Johnston, correspondence with A.Sarzin, 16 March 2021.

Appendix

1. *Truth*, 10 April 1927, p. 15.

Bibliography

This biography relies largely on the following primary sources: contemporary newspaper reports, editorials and opinion pieces; Dr Reading's radio broadcasts, her published speeches and articles; archival NCJW records, including original documents (letters, citations, certificates and awards) and publications; the researcher's personal interviews with Dr Reading's family members and friends, current NCJW members and office-bearers; family photograph albums; Dr Reading's music scores and sheet music; government documents, including naturalisation certificates, military records and letters; the original court transcript of the landmark defamation trial in 1949; and the Mitchell Library's collection titled 'Dr Fanny Reading papers, photographs and realia, ca. 1890–1974', which comprises graphic materials, textual records and objects.

Secondary sources include journal articles; dissertations; websites; and books and articles by authoritative scholars in the disciplines of culture, sociology, religion, history, philosophy, politics, psychology, biography, and feminist studies.

Primary sources

'A war to win a world to gain. Australian woman's charter, 1943: which comprises the resolutions adopted by the Australian Women's Conference for victory in war and victory in peace, November 19–22', 1943, <https://trove.nla.gov.au/version/21399361>.

Alhadeff, Vic. 2020, interview with Anne Sarzin, Sydney

Australian Imperial Force, 1914–1920, *RUBINOWICH Hyman Samuel: Service Number – 2128*, National Archives of Australia, Canberra.

Australian Imperial Force, 1916, *Rubinowich/Abraham Solomon*, National Archives of Australia, Canberra.

Australian Imperial Force, 1914–1920, *RUBINOWICH Lewis Judah: Service Number – 18729* (8073054), B2455, National Archives of Australia, Canberra.

'Australian woman's charter, 1943: which comprises the resolutions adopted by the Australian Women's Conference for victory in war and victory in peace, November 19–22, 1943, Sydney, New South Wales, Australia', 1943, *Australian Women's Conference for Victory in War and Victory in Peace*, Sydney, p. 22.

Australian Women's Register 1943, *The Australian Women's Conference for Victory in War and Victory in Peace (1943)*.

Baffsky, W. 2018, 'My memories of Dr Fanny', interview with Anne Sarzin.

Balfour, Arthur, 1928, Speeches on Zionism by the Right Hon. The Earl of Balfour, Arrowsmith, London.

Barrett, J. 1935, Address delivered by Sir James Barrett, Deputy Chancellor, on the occasion of the opening of the Marshall-Hall Wing, University Conservatorium of Music, 21st March 1935, University of Melbourne, Melbourne.

Ben-Gurion, D. 1948, *Declaration of Establishment of the State of Israel*, Israel Ministry of Foreign Affairs, Israel.

Bentwich, N. 1944, Jewish Youth Comes Home: The Story of the Youth Aliyah, 1933–1943, Victor Gollancz Ltd., London.

Burman, I. 2018, interview with Anne Sarzin, Sydney.

Burman, J. 2018, interview with Anne Sarzin, Sydney.

Chaim Weizmann: A tribute on his seventieth birthday 1945, Victor Gollancz Ltd., London.

Congress, Z.O. 1925, Resolutions of the 14th Zionist Congress, Vienna, Aug. 18–31, 1925: With a Summary Report of the Proceedings, Central Office of the Zionist Organisation.

Department of External Affairs, M. 1897, *Nathan Jacob Rubinowich Naturalization*, 36625 barcode, National Archives of Australia, Canberra.

Department of External Affairs, M. 1904, *E.R. RUBINOWICH Naturalization*, National Archives of Australia, Canberra.

Duldig, E. 2021, email correspondence with Anne Sarzin, February 2021.

Einfeld, S. 1949, Migrants Reception Committee of the NSW Jewish Board of Deputies Report, New South Wales Jewish Board of Deputies, Sydney.

Einfeld, S., 1947, 'Report and recommendations for the handling of new arrivals', paper presented to the *Migrants Reception Committee Conference*, Sydney, 20 February 1947, viewed 2017.

'For Women: Children's need: 'world fit to live in'', 1938, *Sydney Morning Herald*, 16 March 1938, p. 9.

Gazette, T.L. 1946, *Fifth Supplement to The London Gazette*, Authority, London, <https://www.thegazette.co.uk/London/issue/37411/supplement/167>.

Herron, J. 1949a, *Costs*, Supreme Court of NSW, Sydney.

Herron, J. 1949b, *Judgement*, 28 April 1949 edn, Sydney.

Herron, J. 1949c, 'Reading v. National Press Pty. Ltd.', Supreme Court of NSW, Sydney transcript.

'J.Y.P.A. Section, Sixth annual meeting of the J.Y.P.A.', 1917, *Jewish Herald (Victoria)*, 13 July 1917.

Leigh, E. 1929, 'To form Council of Jewish women: Dr Reading on Personal Service', *Register News-Pictorial (Elizabeth Leigh's pages for women)*, 30 September 1929.

National Archives of Australia 1916, *Rubinowich, Abraham Solomon; age 25; born 1890; address-St Kilda*, Canberra.

Nadel, V. 2018, 'Interview Victoria Nadel', with Anne Sarzin, conducted 26 August 2019.

'Reading, Dr Fanny, 1884–1974 Papers' n.d., Mitchell Library, Sydney,

Reading, Dr Fanny. Photographs and Realia c.1890–1974. Series 02. Mitchell Library, Sydney.

'Reading, Dr Fanny – Papers' 1923, *Council of Jewish Women of NSW*.

Reading, Leigh. 2017, 'Family history', interview Anne Sarzin, Sydney, 16 September 2017.

Reading, Lynne. 2019, 'Buenavista Hospital', personal communication, 28 May 2019.

RUBINOWICH Hyman Samuel: Service Number – 2128 1914–1920, National Archives of Australia, Canberra.

Singer, C. 2017, Carole Singer interview with Anne Sarzin.

Stedman, S., 'The Jewish press in Australia', *Jewish Historical Society Journal*, 1943, Sydney (7.4.2-AJHS-Vol.06-Part.01-The-Jewish-Press-in-Australia-Stedman-1964.pdf).

Steinberg, I.N. 1948, *Australia – The unpromised land: In search of a home*, Victor Gollancz Ltd., London.

'The Messiah: Philharmonic Society. A memorable occasion', 1905.

Wertheim, P., Interview with Anne Sarzin, 24 December 2020.

Young, Z., Zara Young interview with Anne Sarzin, 2018.

Zionist Congress–Serious riots in Vienna <https://trove.nla.gov.au/newspaper/article/195410184>.

Zionist Organization 1925, *Resolutions of the 14th Zionist Congress, Vienna, Aug. 18–31, 1925: With a Summary Report of the Proceedings*, Central Office of the Zionist Organisation.

Primary sources: newspapers

Argus, 1934–1941

Barrier Miner, 1943

Brisbane Courier 1929

Brisbane Telegraph, 1952

Canberra Times, 1971

Courier-Mail, 1939

Daily News (Perth) 1926–1939

Daily Telegraph, 1928–1951

Evening News (Kogarah) 1924

Hebrew Standard of Australasia, 1907–1953

Irwin Index, 16 November 1929

Jewish Herald (Victoria) 1917

Kalgoorlie Miner, 1929–1939

Labor Daily, 1937

Lithgow Mercury, 1933

Mercury (Hobart) 1932

New York Times, 1925–1974

Newcastle Morning Herald and Miners' Advocate, 1925–1954

Newcastle Sun, 1937–1943

News, 1948

Observer, 1929

Propeller, 1926

Register News-Pictorial, 1929

Reuters, 1925

Smith's Weekly, 1949

Sydney Mail, 1933

Sydney Morning Herald, 1889–1974

Telegraph, 1946

The Advertiser, 1925–1936

The Age, 1925–1943

The Argus, 1932–1943

The Council Bulletin, 1926–1974

The Daily Examiner (Grafton), 1925

The Mail, 1936

The Mercury (Hobart), 1925

The News, 1936

The North Western Courier, 1947

The Observer, 5 October 1929

The Register News-Pictorial, 1929

The Sun, 1926–1944

The West Australian, 1938–1939

Truth, 1927–1949

West Australian, 1925–1939

Secondary sources

Adler, N.L. and Leydesdorff, S. 2013, *Tapestry of memory: Evidence and testimony in life-story narratives,* Transaction Publishers, New Brunswick, N.J.

Adorno, T.W. 2003, *Can one live after Auschwitz? A philosophical reader*, Stanford University Press, Stanford, California.

AICE, *Zionist Congresses during British Mandate (1923–1946)* <https://www.jewishvirtuallibrary.org/zionist-congresses-during-british-mandate-1923-1946>.

Almog, S., Reinharz, J. and Shapira, A., 1998. *Zionism and religion*, University Press of New England, Hanover.

Alter, R. 2015, *The poetry of Yehuda Amichai*, trans. L. Wieseltier, first ed., Farrar, Straus and Giroux, New York.

Anderson, H. 1960, The colonial minstrel, F.W. Cheshire, Melbourne.

Antin, M. 2012, *The Promised Land*, Penguin Group, New York USA.

Appignanesi, L. 1999, *Losing the dead*, Chatto & Windus, London.

Archives Hadassah, the Women's Zionist Organization of America, American Jewish Historical Society.

Armstrong, D. 1999, *Mosaic: A chronicle of five generations*, Random House, Australia.

Aronson, M. 1990, *Troubled waters: The origins of the 1881 anti-Jewish pogroms in Russia*, University of Pittsburgh Press, Pittsburgh PA.

Australian Human Rights Commission 2013, *At a glance: Racial vilification under sections 18C and 18D of the Racial Discrimination Act 1975 (Cth)*.

Australian Law Reform Commission, 2010, *Reporting, prosecution and pre-trial processes: Attrition in sexual assault cases*.

Backscheider, P.R. 2001, *Reflections on biography*, Oxford University Press, Oxford.

Baker, M.R. 1997, *A Journey through memory: The fiftieth gate*, Flamingo, Australia.

Balfour, A.J. 1971, *Speeches on Zionism*, Arrowsmith, New York.

Balkelis, T. 2010, 'Opening gates to the west: Lithuanian and Jewish Migrations from the Lithuanian Provinces, 1867–1914', *Ethnicity*, vol. 1, no. 2.

Bell, S. 2009, *DES Daughters: Embodied knowledge and the transformation of Women's health politics*, Temple University Press, Philadelphia.

Bell, Y.L. 2016, *Psalms that speak to you*, trans. Y.L. Bell, first hardback edn, Tehillim Today, Israel.

Berkowitz, M. (ed.) 2004, *Nationalism, Zionism and ethnic mobilization of the Jews in 1900 and beyond*, Brill, Leiden.

Berlin, I.K. 1970, 'Chaim Weizmann as leader: Inaugural lectures of the Israel Goldstein chair of the history of Zionism and the Yishuv at the Institute of Contemporary Jewry', Hebrew University of Jerusalem.

Blakeney, M. 1985, *Australia and the Jewish refugees 1933–1948*, Croom Helm Australia, Sydney.

Blumberg, H.M. 1975, *Weizmann: His life and times*, St. Martin's Press, New York.

Brendon, P. 1979, *Eminent Edwardians*, Andre Deutsch, London.

Brentnall, T. 1938, *My memories: Being the reminiscences of a nonagenarian*, Robertson & Mullens Limited, Melbourne.

Buckrich, J. 2017, *Acland Street: The grand lady of St Kilda*, ATOM, Melbourne.

Butler, T. 1989, *Memory: History, culture and the mind*, Basil Blackwell Ltd., Oxford.

Caine, B. 2010, *Biography and history*, Palgrave Macmillan, New York.

Cesarani, D. 2001, *Remembering for the future: The Holocaust in an age of genocide*, vol. 3, Palgrave.

Cohen, L. 1984, *Rachel Forster Hospital, The first fifty years*, Rachel Forster Hospital, Redfern Sydney.

Cohen, L. 1987, *Beginning with Esther: Jewish women in New South Wales from 1788*, Ayers & James Heritage Books.

Connerton, P. 1989, *How societies remember*, Cambridge University Press.

Court, J.H.C. 1973, *Stand up and be counted*, Lutheran Publishing House, Adelaide.

Crick, S. 1940, *The Lord Mayor of Sydney, Sydney City Council, Sydney*.

Dalton, R. 1996, *Aunts up the Cross*, Text Publishing, Melbourne, Australia.

Draaisma, D. 2004, *Why life speeds up as you get older: How memory shapes our past*, trans. A. Pomerans, Cambridge University Press, Cambridge, UK.

Draaisma, D. 2013, *The Nostalgia factory: Memory, time and ageing*, Yale University Press, New Haven and London.

Duldig, E. 2017, *Driftwood: Escape and survival through art*, Australian Scholarly Publishing Ltd., Melbourne.

Eagar, M. 1906, *Six years at the Russian Court*, Charles L. Bowman & Company, New York.

Egan, B. 1993, *Ways of a hospital: St. Vincent's Melbourne 1890s–1990s*, Allen & Unwin, St. Leonards, NSW.

Epstein, J. 1988, *Woman with two hats: An autobiography*, Hyland House, South Yarra, Vic.

Falk, B. 1988, *No other home: An Anglo-Jewish story 1833–1987*, Penguin Books.

France, P. and St Clair, W. eds., 2004. *Mapping lives: The uses of biography*, Oxford University Press, Oxford.

Frankl, V. 1962, *Man's search for meaning: An introduction to logotherapy*, trans. L. Ilse, Hodder and Stoughton, London.

Gelber, K.M. 2018, 'Why Australia's anti-vilification laws matter', *The Conversation*.

Gettler, L. 1993, *An unpromised land*, Fremantle Press, WA.

Glowinski, P. 2015, *Youth Aliyah records in the Hadassah archives* <https://archives.cjh.org/repositories/3/resources/18295>.

Gold, S., Tsoulos, J. et al, 2003, *Living History Project: Meeting new migrants on the wharves*, Sydney.

Goodman, P. 1945, *Chaim Weizmann: A tribute on his seventieth birthday*, Gollancz, London.

Grigsby, R. 2020, *A train to Palestine: The Tehran Children, Anders' Army and their escape from Stalin's Siberia, 1939–1943*, Valentine Mitchell, London.

Grimshaw, P., Lake, M., McGrath, A. and Quartly, M. 2006, *Creating a nation*, Penguin Books, Ringwood, Victoria.

Hastings, D. 2007, Over the mountains of the sea: Life on the migrant ships 1870–1885, Auckland University Press.

Healy, J.E. 1945, *Strength of mind: 125 years of women in medicine*, University of Melbourne, Melbourne.

Hennessee, J.A. 1999, *Betty Friedan: Her life*, Random House, New York.

Hirst, D. 1983, *The gun and the olive branch*, Faber and Faber, London, Boston.

Hoffman, E. 1989, *Lost in translation: A life in a new language*, Vintage Books, London.

Human Rights and Equal Opportunity Commission, Australia 2002, *Racial vilification law in Australia*.

Hutton Neve, M. 1980, *'This mad folly!': The history of Australia's pioneer women doctors*, Library of Australian History, Sydney.

Hyman, M. 1998, *Who is a Jew? Conversations, not conclusions*, Jewish Lights, Woodstock, Vt.

Inglis, K., Spark, S. and Winter, J. 2018, *Dunera lives: A visual history*, Monash University Publishing, Melbourne.

Jewish Virtual Library n.d., *Zionist congress: Zionist Congresses during British*

Mandate (1923–1946), AICE.

'Jews temporary shelter', London Metropolitan Archives, London, <https://www.cityoflondon.gov.uk/things-to-do/london-metropolitan-archives/the-collections/Pages/jews-temporary-shelter.aspx>.

Judaica 2011, 'Photo exhibit 18 Fanny Reading', University of Sydney, Judaica Library, Sydney.

Kahanoff, J. 1960, *Ramat-Hadassah-Szold, Youth Aliyah Screening and Classification Centre*, Publishing Department of the Jewish Agency, Jerusalem.

Karsh, E. 2010, *Palestine betrayed*, Yale University Press, New Haven

Kassow, S.D., 2007, *Who will write our history? Emanuel Ringelblum, the Warsaw Ghetto, and the Oyneg Shabes Archive*, Indiana University Press, Bloomington, Ind.

Kayyali, A.W. 1981, *Palestine: A modern history*, Third World Centre for Research and Pub, London.

Klier, J.D. 2011, *Russians, Jews, and the Pogroms of 1881–1882*, Cambridge University Press, Cambridge.

Koehne, S. 2006, 'Disturbance in D Compound: The question of control in Australian internment camps during World War ll' *Melbourne Historical Journal*, 34, p. 71–86.

Koven, S. 2010, 'The Jewish question and the social question in late Victorian London: The fictions and investigative journalism of Margaret Harkness', *Imagination and commitment. Representations of the social question, Groningen studies in cultural change*. Peeters, Leuven.

Kremer, S.L. 1999, *Women's Holocaust writing: Memory and imagination*, University of Nebraska Press, Lincoln, London.

Kwiet, K. 1985, '"Be patient and reasonable!" The Internment of German-Jewish refugees in Australia', *The Australian Journal of Politics and History*, vol. 31, no. 1, pp. 61–78.

Kwiet, K. 1987, 'Responses of Australian Jewry's leadership to the Holocaust', pp. 201–213, *Jews in the sixth continent*, ed. W.D. Rubinstein, Allen & Unwin, Sydney.

Laqueur, W. 1976, *A history of Zionism*, Schocken Books, New York.

Lee-Wong, S.M. 2012, *Beyond the bow: Nelson Cooke's life in music*, Estrella Books, North Charleston.

Levy, M. 2001, *Remembering for the future: The Holocaust in an age of genocide, volume 3: Memory*, Palgrave, New York.

Lewis, M. 2017, *The Undoing Project: A friendship that changed our minds*, WW Norton & Company, New York.

Leydesdorff, S., Passerini, L. and Thompson, P.R. eds. 2007. *Gender and memory*. Transaction Publishers, New Brunswick (USA).

Lipsky, L. 1957, *Herzl, Weizmann and the Jewish state*, Yad Chaim Weizmann, Rehovoth.

Litvinoff, B. 1983, *The letters and papers of Chaim Weizmann: August 1898 – July 1931*, Series B, Israel Universities Press, New Brunswick, N.J.

Longway, M. 1889, *London to Melbourne*, Remington & Co. Publishers, London.

Lukens, K.P. 1969, *Thursday's child has far to go*, Prentice-Hall, Englewood Cliffs, N.J.

Macintosh, A., 1988. *Memories of Dr Robert Scot Skirving 1859–1956*. Foreland Press, Darlinghurst, N.S.W.

Mandelstam, N.Y. 1999, *Hope against hope: A memoir*, trans. M. Hayward, The Harvill Press, London.

McCarthy, L. 2001, *Uncommon practices: Medical women in NSW 1885–1939*, University of New South Wales.

McFadzean, M. 2008, *Internment during World War II Australia*, Museums Victoria Collections, <https://collections.museumsvictoria.com.au/articles/1618>.

Mehlman, W. 2010, *Jabotinsky … The man and the vision*, Americans for a safe Israel, Jerusalem, <https://afsi.org/wp-content/uploads/2017/08/JabotinskyPamphlet201007141.pdf>.

Melba, N. 1915, *Melba's gift book of Australian art and literature*, George Robertson, Melbourne.

Mendelsohn, R. & Shain, M. 2008, *The Jews in South Africa: An illustrated history*, Jonathan Ball Publishers Johannesburg & Cape Town.

Miller, A. 2015, *The simplest words: A storyteller's journey*, Allen & Unwin, Sydney.

Mockridge, M., 2014, *Art behind the wire: The Duldig Studio*, <http://www.duldig.org.au/wp-content/uploads/2013/12/Art-Behind-the-Wire-Education-Kit.pdf>.

Moore, D.D. 2009, *Hadassah in the United States, Jewish Women's Archive*, United States, <https://jwa.org/encyclopedia/article/hadassah-in-united-states>.

Morgan, E.S. 1970, *A short history of medical women in Australia*, The Author, Hawthorn, S.A.

National Council of Jewish Women, 2019, *AGM 26 August 2019, 96th Annual Report*, NCJWA NSW Div., Sydney.

Netanyahu, B. 2012, *The founding fathers: Zionism*, Gefen Publishing House, Jerusalem.

Newton, M.L. 2000, *Making a difference: A history of the National Council of Jewish Women of Australia*, Hybrid Publishers, Melbourne.

O'Day, R., 'The Jews of London: From Diaspora to Whitechapel' <fathom.lse.ac.uk/Features/122537>.

Ofer, D. and Weiner, H. 1996, *Dead-end journey: The tragic story of the Kladovo-Šabac group*, University Press of America, Lanham, MD.

Pensabene, T.S. 1980, *The rise of the medical practitioner in Victoria: Research Monograph 2*, The Australian National University, Canberra.

Peterson, F. 1896, *Elements of music*, Augener Ltd., London.

Pincus, C. 1970, *Come from the four winds: The story of Youth Aliyah*, second ed., Herzl Press, New York.

Polonsky, A. 2013, *The Jews in Poland and Russia: A short history*, The Littman Library of Jewish Civilization, Oxford Portland, Oregon.

Prager, D.T. and Telushkin, J. 2003, *Why the Jews? The reason for antisemitism*, Simon & Schuster, New York.

Pringle, R.M. 1998, *Sex and medicine: Gender, power and authority in the medical profession*, Cambridge University Press, Cambridge.

Purbrick, L., Aulich, J. and Dawson, G., 2007. *Contested spaces: Sites, representations and histories of conflict*. Palgrave.

Rabinowicz, O. 1950, *Fifty years of Zionism: A historical analysis of Dr. Weizmann's 'Trial and Error'*, Robert Anscombe & C. Ltd., London.

Radi, H. 1989, *200 Australian women: A Redress anthology*, Women's Redress Press Inc, Broadway, Sydney.

Radic, T. 1994, *Australian music biography and the skew of cultural context: Changing viewpoints to assess significance, The Percy Grainger Lecture*, University of Melbourne, Melbourne.

Ricks, T.E. 2017, *Churchill and Orwell: The fight for freedom*, Penguin Press, New York.

Ricoeur, P. 2004, *Memory, history, forgetting*, trans. K.P. Blamey, The University of Chicago Press, Chicago, London.

Robertson, G. 1999, *Crimes against humanity: The struggle for global justice*, Penguin Press, Allen Lane.

Roe, M. 1984, *Nine Australian progressives: Vitalism in bourgeois social thought, 1890–1960*, University of Queensland Press, St. Lucia.

Rogger, H. 1986, *Jewish policies and right-wing politics in imperial Russia*, University of California Press, Berkeley.

Rosen, M. 2017, *The disappearance of Zola: Love, literature and the Dreyfus case*, Faber & Faber, London.

Rosenthal, N. 2010, *Formula for survival: The saga of the Ballarat Hebrew Congregation*, Hawthorn Press, Melbourne.

Ross, E.E. 2007, *Slum travellers: Ladies and London poverty, 1860–1920*, University of California Press, Berkeley, Los Angeles.

Roth, J. and Maxwell, E. eds., 2017. *Remembering for the future: The Holocaust in an age of genocide*, Springer.

Rubinstein, H.L. 1986, *The Jews in Victoria 1835–1985*, George Allen & Unwin, Sydney.

Rubinstein, H.L. 1991, *The Jews in Australia: A thematic History*, vol. 1 William Heinemann Australia, Melbourne.

Rubinstein, W.D. 1987, Jews in the sixth continent, Allen & Unwin, Sydney.

Russell, C. & Lewis, H.S. 1901, *The Jew in London: A study of racial character and present-day conditions, being two essays prepared for the Toynbee trustees*, Thomas Y Crowell & Co., New York.

Russell, R. 2016, *High seas & high teas: Voyages to Australia*, NLA Publishing, Canberra, ACT.

Rutland, S.D. 1988, *Edge of the Diaspora: Two centuries of Jewish settlement in Australia*, William Collins, Sydney, Australia.

Rutland, S.D. and Caplan, S. 1998, *With one voice: A history of the New South Wales Jewish Board of Deputies*, Australian Jewish Historical Society, Sydney.

Sands, P. 2017, *East West Street: On the origins of 'genocide' and 'crimes against humanity'*, Weidenfeld & Nicolson, London.

Sarzin, L.M. 2017, *Seeking truth and challenging prejudice: Confronting race hatred through the South African Greyshirt case of Levy v. Von Moltke*, PhD thesis, University of Technology Sydney, Sydney.

Schechtman, J., 1961, *Fighter and prophet: The Vladimir Jabotinsky story*, Thomas Yoseloff, New York.

Schneer, J. 2010, *Balfour Declaration: The origins of the Arab-Israeli conflict*, Random House, New York.

Serle, G. 1982, *John Monash: A biography*, Melbourne University Press in association with Monash University, Carlton, Vic.

Shavit, A. 2014, *My promised land: The triumph and tragedy of Israel*, Scribe, Melbourne, London.

Shawcross, W. 2011, *Justice and the enemy: Nuremberg, 9/11, and the trial of Khalid Sheikh Mohammed*, Public Affairs, New York.

Simmons, E. 2006, *Hadassah and the Zionist Project*, Rowman& Littlefield Publishers Inc, Lanham, Maryland.

Speakman, M. 2018, 'New laws to target incitement of violence', Department of Justice, NSW Government.

Stevens, R.S. 2003, 'Why teach music in schools', paper presented to the XXIV Annual Conference of AARME, Ninth Annual Assembly of the Music Council of Australia, 28 September 2013.

Stone, J. 1944, *'Stand up and be counted!': An open letter to the Rt.Hon. Sir Isaac Isaacs, P.C., G.C.M.G., on the twenty-sixth anniversary of the Jewish National Home*, second edn, Ponsford, Newman & Benson, Sydney.

Strachey, L. 1971, *Eminent Victorians*, Penguin Books England.

Street, J. 1990, *Documents and essays*, Women's Redress Press Inc., Sydney.

Street, J. 2004, *A revised autobiography*, The Federation Press, Sydney.

Taft, M. and Markus, A. 2018, *A second chance: The making of Yiddish Melbourne*, Monash University Publishing, Melbourne, Victoria.

Troy, G. 2018, *The Zionist ideas: Visions for the Jewish Homeland – then, now, tomorrow*, University of Nebraska Press, Lincoln.

Turtel-Oberzhanski, H. 1973, *A History of the Jews of Korelitz*, <http://www.jewishgen.org/yizkor/Korelicze/kor018.html>.

United Nations n.d. *The question of Palestine: Minutes of the 15th Session of the League of Nations Permanent Mandates Commission, 24 October to 11 November*

1927, <https://www.un.org/unispal/document/auto-insert-193243/>.

Valent, P. 2002, *Child survivors of the Holocaust*, Taylor & Francis, New York.

Valman, N. 2015, 'Walking Victorian Spitalfields with Israel Zangwill', *Interdisciplinary Studies in the Long Nineteenth Century*, vol. 2015, no. 21.

Walsh, M.R. 1977, *'Doctors wanted, no women need apply': Sexual barriers in the medical profession*, Yale University Press, New Haven, Conn.

Wasserstein, B. 2012, *On the eve: The Jews of Europe before the Second World War*, Simon & Schuster, New York.

'Wedgwood, Camilla Hildegarde (1901–1955)' 2018, The Australian Women's Register.

Wiesel, E. 1967, *The gates of the forest*, Heinemann, London.

Willis, E. 1989, *Medical dominance: The division of labour in Australian health care*, Allen & Unwin, St. Leonards, NSW.

Wistrich, R.S. 1991, *The longest hatred*, Thames Methuen, London.

Wittlin, J.S. and Sands, P. 2016, *City of lions*, Pushkin Press London.

Wolins, M., and Gotesman, M. (eds.) 1971, *Group care: An Israeli approach: The educational path of Youth Aliyah*, Gordon and Breach, New York.

Wright Mills, C. 1973, *The sociological imagination*, Penguin Books, England.

Yerushalmi, Y.H. 1989, *Zakhor: Jewish history and Jewish memory*, 1996 edn, University of Washington Press, Seattle and London.

YIVO Encyclopedia of Jews in Eastern Europe: 'Pale of Settlement'.

York, J.R. 2015, *The Rachel Forster Hospital 1922–2000*, Phillip Mathews Book Publishers, Willoughby NSW.

Zangwill, I. 2017, *Children of the Ghetto*, Lavergne Tennessee.

Index

14th Zionist Congress (Vienna, 1925) 4, 62, 67, 92, 102, 144, 169, 208, 211, 213–15, 218–21, 224, 227

Abramovich, Dora 75, 107, 251–2
Alhadeff, Vic 275
antisemitism 2–4, 6, 9, 12, 56, 58, 78–9, 84, 89, 94, 96, 99, 101, 110, 113–15, 120, 123, 127, 132, 208, 214–15, 241, 279, 281, 283, 288, 291
Anzac Buffet 7, 135–7, 161, 173, 282
Australian Comforts Fund 113, 147, 155, 159, 173–4, 230, 282

Baffsky, Warren 17
Balfour, Lord Arthur James 66–7, 92, 216, 242
Balfour Declaration 66–7, 94–5, 190, 207, 222, 238–9, 242–3, 253, 258, 260–1, 285
Ballarat
    Jewish community 15–16, 178
    Synagogue 15
Bentwich, Norman 68, 208
Bevin, Ernest 252–3
Brand, Walter 180
Breckler, Fanny 117–18

Burman, Dr Ian (nephew) 12, 35, 38, 41, 164, 177–8, 180
Burman, Jennifer (niece) 42–3, 178
Burman, Rachael 'Rae/Ray' (sister) 16, 25, 34, 69–70, 164, 177, 179–80

Calwell, Arthur 174–5
Cassidy, Jack Evelyn KC 206, 229–35, 246, 254–7, 261–9, 272
Cohen, Rabbi Francis Lyon 56, 148
Comay, Major Michael 204–05, 231–3, 235, 237, 249–50, 255, 261, 265
Council of Jewish Women
    Adelaide 152
    Ballarat 152
    Brisbane 152, 200
    Geelong 152
    Kalgoorlie 79, 152
    Melbourne 152
    Newcastle 152
    Perth 78–9, 152
    Sydney 2, 41, 48, 52, 54, 57, 86, 109, 152, 212, 224, 277, 283

Dalwood Children's Homes 26, 37, 105, 199, 283
defamation, *Dr Fanny Reading v National Press Pty Ltd* (1949) 8,

27, 93, 110, 197, 203, 206–07, 213–15, 217, 223, 228, 231–2, 235, 258, 268–9, 271–2, 278, 285
Duldig, Eva 142–3
Duldig, Karl and Slawa 142–3

Einfeld, Sydney 158, 180, 196
Evatt, Dr Herbert Vere 156, 185–6, 200

Falk, Rabbi Leib 54, 121–2, 134, 158, 188, 195
Fanny Reading Council House 84, 202–03, 290
Feminist Society (Sydney) 2, 137
Freeland League 120, 122, 124, 128
Freier, Recha 208–09
Freilich, Max 125, 157–8, 161, 185–6, 270

Great Synagogue (Sydney) 56–7, 82, 122, 124, 148, 158–9, 161, 192

Hadassah (Women's Zionist Organization of America) 64–5, 73, 95, 97, 115, 168–9, 208, 210, 212–13, 255
Herron, Justice Leslie James 9, 205, 228, 232, 235, 246, 263, 268–73, 279
Herzl, Theodor 53, 92, 102, 122, 187, 217, 222–4
Hitler, Adolf 8, 47, 84–5, 103, 109–10, 121, 126, 132, 139, 142, 150, 152, 154, 171, 201, 208–09, 231, 241, 247, 257, 265
Holocaust 2, 9, 22, 46, 49, 85, 123, 167, 172, 174–6, 183–5, 229, 244, 267, 288, 291

hospitals
    Crown Street Women's Hospital (Surry Hills, Sydney) 37, 61, 76, 199
    Great Ormond Street Hospital (London) 39, 63
    Jewish Hospital (Point Piper, Sydney) 194–5, 199
    Melbourne Hospital 36
    Rachel Forster Hospital (Redfern, Sydney) 25, 31, 43, 45, 48, 53, 93, 199, 229, 283
    Rotunda Women's Hospital (Dublin) 39, 63, 70–1
    Royal Hospital for Women (Paddington, Sydney) 26
    St George's District Hospital and Community Hospital (Kogarah, Sydney) 25, 53, 199, 206, 229
    Wolper Hospital (Woollahra, Sydney) 17, 32, 38, 195, 291

immigration 1, 3–4, 6–8, 13–15, 18–20, 22–3, 26–7, 29–30, 39–40, 52, 58, 61, 68, 74–8, 83–5, 90, 94–6, 99, 101, 107, 111, 115–16, 118–21, 123–5, 128–9, 134, 138, 146–50, 154, 156, 169, 172, 174–5, 177, 180–4, 188–9, 192, 196, 198–200, 207, 209–10, 212, 216, 218, 230, 232–4, 237, 241, 243–4, 246–9, 256–60, 262, 266, 274, 276, 281, 286
International Council of Jewish Women 172, 198, 289
International Council of Women 4, 39, 59
internment camps 7, 141
Isaacs, Sir Isaac 9, 99, 239–41

Israel 2, 54, 80, 97, 104, 167–8, 186–92, 197–201, 216, 278, 284–6, 288–90

Jabotinsky, Ze'ev 92, 95, 122, 217–22, 227
Jewish People's Council Declaration 285
Jewish Women's Conference of Australasia
  First 57, 76
  Second 85
  Third 98
  Fourth 102
  Fifth 107
  Sixth 152, 183
  Eighth 172
  Ninth 192, 282
  Eleventh 286
Jewish Young People's Association (JYPA) 34

Karelitz 4, 11, 13, 15, 18–20
King George V Jubilee Medal (1935) 88, 173, 254
King George V1 Coronation Medal (1937) 88, 173, 254
Kings Cross 1–2, 6, 9, 17, 25, 30, 32, 38, 40–3, 45, 53, 146, 163–5, 194, 277, 288
Kook, Rabbi Abraham Isaac 222

Landauer, Dr Georg 210, 256–61
Lang, Roma 17, 41, 162–3, 165
Law of Loving Kindness 53, 86, 277, 291

Marks, Percy 55–6
Mecoles, Abraham Jacob 178
migrants/migration *see* immigration
Monash, Sir John 54, 86, 129
Myerson, Philip 188

Nadel, Victoria 289
National Council of Jewish Women (NCJW/NCJWA) 2–3, 7–8, 10, 30, 37, 51–2, 57, 77, 81–2, 84, 86–90, 96, 98, 101, 105, 109, 111–13, 115–19, 123, 130–2, 134–40, 142–5, 147, 149, 152–3, 155–6, 158–62, 164–8, 170–6, 179–81, 183, 186, 188–9, 191–6, 199–203, 213–14, 227, 229–30, 277, 280–2, 285–91
National Council of Women (NCW) 2, 60, 75, 78, 85–6, 91, 99, 103–04, 109, 118, 158, 199, 282
Nazism/Nazi Party 2, 9, 26, 46–7, 49, 51, 84, 94, 109–10, 113–15, 119, 121, 123, 126, 128, 130, 133–5, 141–3, 146–7, 149–51, 155–6, 167, 169–70, 174, 183, 204, 209–10, 212–14, 227, 231, 233, 241, 256–7, 266, 268, 277–8
New Guard 109–10
NSW Jewish Board of Deputies 58, 100, 156–7, 181, 196, 205, 251, 275

Ochert, Morris 41–2
Orden, Miri 290
OSE: Oeuvre de Secours aux Enfants 197

Palestine 2–4, 8, 14, 30, 53–4, 58–9,

62–4, 66–9, 72–4, 76–8, 80–1, 84, 90–7, 103–07, 111, 115–16, 118, 121–5, 129, 131, 137, 140, 145–8, 150–2, 154–6, 159, 162, 166–72, 174, 178, 183–8, 191, 200, 204–13, 215–24, 226, 228–9, 231–4, 237–50, 252–62, 265–6, 269, 278, 282–6

Pevsner, Bella 53, 144, 191, 224, 284

philanthropy 2, 19, 42, 53–4, 57, 59, 75–6, 81–2, 84, 86, 88, 90, 111, 115–16, 139, 153–4, 197, 205, 229–30, 254, 270, 278, 286

pogroms 4, 9, 11–13, 19, 58, 122, 183, 217, 223, 276, 278, 287

Racial Hygiene Association/Society 43–9, 102, 107, 283

Reading, Abraham Solomon Stanley 'Abe' (brother) 3, 16–17, 25, 34, 36, 38, 53, 63, 69–72, 87, 106, 160, 177, 179, 194

Reading, Dr Fanny
  childhood and arrival in Australia 2, 5, 11–12, 17, 23–4, 276, 281, 287
  defamation case *see* defamation, *Dr Fanny Reading v National Press Pty Ltd* (1949)
  MBE (1961) 37, 88, 203, 290
  study of music 5–6, 25–34, 36, 91, 169, 276

Reading, Esther Rose (mother) 4–5, 13–23, 27, 34, 66, 97, 177–9, 276

Reading, Hyman Samuel (brother) 16, 25, 34–5, 69, 164, 177, 179

Reading, Jennifer (niece) *see* Burman, Jennifer

Reading, Leigh (nephew) 16, 43, 164, 178

Reading, Lewis Judah 'Lew' (brother) 16, 25, 34–6, 69–70, 72, 177, 179

Reading, Lynne (married to Leigh) 16, 164

Reading, Miriam 'Minnie' (sister) 16, 25

Reading, Nathan Jacob (father) 4, 12–18, 21, 27, 34, 69, 97, 178–9, 276

Reading, Rachael (sister) *see* Burman, Rachael

refugees 2–3, 6–8, 16, 19, 26, 51, 84, 94, 107, 111, 116–21, 124, 138–41, 146, 149, 151, 154–6, 163, 168–9, 171, 174–5, 188, 207, 274, 277–8, 281, 288

Rich, Ruby 44, 47, 50, 102, 107, 111, 184, 197

Rubinowich, Wolf and Yetty 15–16

Schenk, Rabbi Max 121–2, 136, 167, 171, 205, 255

Shand, John Wentworth KC 'Jack' 206, 217, 227, 232–3, 235–40, 242–56, 258–65, 271

Singer, Carole 30–2

Sir John Monash Recreation Hut 7, 135–6, 155, 173, 282

Smith's Weekly 8, 198, 204–07, 213, 228, 232, 235, 238, 258, 262–4, 266–8, 271, 278

Smuts, Jan Christiaan 257

Spielvogel, Nathan 15

St Kilda Hebrew Congregation 5, 34

Stedman, Solomon 128–9

Steinberg, Dr Isaac 119–22, 124–9

Stone, Julius 9, 161, 240–1

Street, Jessie 43–4, 50–1, 75, 114, 126, 137, 150–1, 175

Symes, Sir George Stewart 67–8
Symonds, Celia 60–1
Symonds, Saul 136, 158, 161, 181–2, 185
Szold, Henrietta 95, 168–70, 208–14

Traub, Michael 146

University of Melbourne
  Conservatorium of Music 5, 27–9, 32–3
  Medical Faculty 37–8
Ussishkin, Menachem 67, 144

War Emergency Board 131, 137–9, 145, 161, 254
Wedgwood, Camilla Hildegarde 93
Wedgwood, Josiah 93
Weizmann, Chaim 92, 95, 122–3, 188, 215–21, 223–5, 227
Wertheim, Peter 207, 272–4
World War I 2, 5, 25, 34, 67, 173, 257, 259
World War II 2, 7, 45, 49, 112–13, 117, 125, 130, 164, 168, 171, 173, 187, 213, 222, 252, 266, 268, 274, 277, 279, 281, 288, 291
Wynn, Ida 205, 232, 262, 264
Wynn, Samuel 27, 205, 264–5

Young Men's Hebrew Association (YMHA) 3, 87–8, 92, 159, 194–5
Young Women's Hebrew Association (YWHA) 74
Young, Zara 165
Youth Aliyah 2, 8–9, 116, 137, 151–2, 154, 167–8, 170–1, 174, 189, 191, 200, 204–11, 213–14, 228, 231–3, 235, 246, 248, 250–1, 255–9, 261–2, 264–7, 269–72, 278, 286

Zelman, Alberto 29
Zionism 2, 4, 6, 9, 14, 54, 75, 92–3, 96, 121–4, 172, 187, 191, 207–08, 214–15, 217–18, 222–4, 226, 233, 239–40, 243, 271–2, 284–6

Acknowledgements

The publication of this book – the first authoritative biography of Dr Fanny Reading – would not have seen the light of day without the generous support of **Eva Engel, Maurice Linker, Dr Ian Burman** and **Pearl Adams**. I am grateful to them for their belief in the merit of this biography.

Professor Emerita Rosemary Johnston, former Chair of Culture and Education at the University of Technology Sydney, who supervised the doctoral thesis on which this biography is based, provided wise counsel that was foundational to my exploration of Dr Reading's life. **Associate Professor Bhuva Naroyan** of UTS co-supervised my PhD thesis and, importantly, has provided ongoing guidance and friendship.

Chief Justice of New South Wales, The Honourable T F Bathurst AC, very kindly gave me access to the archived transcript of *Dr Fanny Reading v National Press Ltd:* 'to inspect the transcript and the judgment in the Registry of the Court'. His generous permission facilitated my writing the first fully comprehensive analysis and deconstruction of the trial transcript. Retired Sydney barrister **David Cowan** provided explanations of legal terms and procedures; Co-CEO of the Executive Council of Australian Jewry, **Peter Wertheim**, shared his pertinent views; and former CEO of the NSW Jewish Board of Deputies, **Vic Alhadeff**, provided insights into the parliamentary legacy of the trial.

Surviving members of Dr Reading's family gave generously of their time and recollections. I interviewed her nephew **Dr Ian Burman** and his partner **Pearl Adams** several times, and their readiness to share their memories and the friendship that evolved over Pearl's delicious teas were deeply appreciated. **Leigh Reading**, also a nephew, and his wife **Lynne**, recalled memories of 'Aunt Fanny' and welcomed me into their home on several occasions for lengthy discussions, giving me access to their family archive. I first met Dr Reading's niece, **Jennifer Burman**, when we both travelled to Ballarat on a tour organised by the National Council of Jewish Women of NSW. Subsequently, I interviewed her in her Bondi apartment, and she generously brought her Aunt to life for me.

Carole Singer, Dr Reading's schoolgirl piano protégeé, shared her memories of playing the piano for 'Dr Fanny' on several occasions in her Kings Cross apartment, and described their relationship vividly. She gave me access to Dr Fanny's music manuscripts, which proved a great source of information about her artistic life.

Eva de Jong, founder of the Duldig Studio, provided valuable information about the internment of children in the Tatura Internment Camp during the Second World War.

Wendy Bookatz, Office Manager of the NCJW NSW, has been most helpful in facilitating access to Council's archives.

My children encouraged me to pursue my research and writing. Thank you to my daughters Dr Lisa Miranda Sarzin and Zara Inga Perlman, and my son Francois Andre Sarzin, and their respective partners Adam Pozniak, Elliot Perlman and Tanya Sarzin.

This biography is also for my grandchildren Gideon, Gabriel, Micah, Nicholas, Alexander, Dov, Miri, Rafaela, Jonathan, Noa and Daniel.

www.ingramcontent.com/pod-product-compliance
Lightning Source LLC
Chambersburg PA
CBHW032012300426
44117CB00008B/995